P9-COP-024

THE RECREATIONAL SPORTS PROGRAM

THE RECREATIONAL SPORTS PROGRAM:

Schools . . . Colleges . . . Communities

VIOLA K. KLEINDIENST
*Consultant in Recreation
And Recreation Education
Bellingham, Washington*

ARTHUR WESTON
*Chairman
Department of Physical Education
Brooklyn College of the
City University of New York*

PRENTICE-HALL, INC., *Englewood Cliffs, N. J. 07632*

Library of Congress Cataloging in Publication Data

KLEINDIENST, VIOLA K. (date).
    The recreational sports program.

    Bibliography
    Includes index.
    1. Recreation—United States—History 2. Leisure—United States—History 3. Intramural sports.
I. WESTON, ARTHUR (date) joint author.   II. Title.
GV53.K57   790'.0973   77-12636
ISBN   0-13-767905-X

©1978 by Prentice-Hall, Inc., Englewood Cliffs, N.J.   07632

All rights reserved.
No part of this book may be reproduced in any form
or by any means
without permission in writing from the publisher.

Printed in the United States of America

10   9   8   7   6   5   4   3   2   1

PRENTICE-HALL INTERNATIONAL, INC., *London*
PRENTICE-HALL of AUSTRALIA PTY. LIMITED, *Sydney*
PRENTICE-HALL of CANADA, LTD., *Toronto*
PRENTICE-HALL of INDIA PRIVATE LIMITED, *New Delhi*
PRENTICE-HALL of JAPAN, INC., *Tokyo*
PRENTICE-HALL of SOUTHEAST ASIA PTE. LTD., *Singapore*
WHITEHALL BOOKS LIMITED, *Wellington, New Zealand*

Contents

3

The Recreational Sports Program in Education   **59**

II

The Community and the School

4

Community Recreation in Transition   **81**

5

Community Recreation in Education   **105**

III
The Human Dimension

IV
Organization and Administration

10

The Extramural Sports Program   **203**

11

The Recreation Association:
An Organizational Approach   **219**

V

Operational Policies and Procedures

12

Financial Support and Management   **247**

13

Publicity and Public Relations   **259**

19

National Organizations and Sports Information Sources   **383**

20

Sports Tournaments, Meets, and Matches   **405**

21

Special Recreation and Recreational Sports Programs   **461**

Contents

14

Awards, Point Systems and Records

15

Health, Safety, Accidents and Legal Liability

16

Facilities, Equipment and Supplies   **319**

VI
The Functioning Program

17

Units of Competition, Regulations, and Tournament Plans   **341**

18

Planning, Time, and Scheduling   **365**

Preface

This is an analytical and descriptive account of the recreational sports program as this program presently exists and functions in modern American schools, colleges and communities. It focuses on such central subjects as the historical evolution of the recreational sports program and the contemporary features, issues, and trends that distinguish it. But much attention has also been given to the main lines of its organizational and administrative structure and to the social philosophy that pervades, animates and shapes its workings. The term "recreational sports" encompasses the spectrum of physical activities that have been traditionally placed under such titles or headings as intramurals, extramurals, sports clubs, girls' and women's recreation association activities, unstructured or free play recreational sports, and school-college-community recreational sports activities. In short, the sports found in the fields of physical education and recreation comprise the recreational sports. This terminology is in accordance with the major trends of American education, life and society. And it fits a national ethos that views physical activity as one of the important ways of developing a constructive and well-balanced life.

The keen desire to participate in recreational sports—which has long been present in American society—became more intensive and pervasive during the twentieth century. Many reasons for this change can be advanced; but one of them, surely, is the increasingly affluent tone of American life. More money and more hours of leisure have meant for many a share in the sports activities that belonged in earlier periods of history to the privileged few. Another point to be stressed is the leadership displayed by the Federal Government in what have so often been the emergency conditions of the twentieth century. Thus the national concern for physical fitness was nourished by World War II (1939-1945) and the subsequent cold war between the United States and Russia. But also consequential, and not to be overlooked, is the personal factor; that is, the role of those who have given the nation leadership at the highest level. The mind leaps at once to the colorful, dynamic President John F. Kennedy, whose presidency dramatized, perhaps as never before, the fundamental role of sport in the life of the individual and the nation. The combination of these conditions and circumstances produced an atmosphere in which the gates opened wide to new dimensions in the recreational sports program in schools, colleges, and communities.

This book, first published in 1964 under the title *Intramural and Recreation Programs for Schools and Colleges*, is designed for those wishing to acquire a specific and comprehensive knowledge of the recreational sports program and an understanding of its place and value in education and society. It is in six parts, which may be quickly summarized. Part I describes the recreational sports program in education with stress on its historical evolution and philosophical foundations. Special attention is given to Title IX legislation and its far-reaching implications for the program. Part II brings out the manner in which school and community recreation have converged to produce the community school and a community education philosophy. Part III, on the other hand, contains a lengthy description of the "new" participants of recent years in the recreational sports program and also discusses the effect on professional leadership of the social change flowing out of Title IX legislation. Part IV identifies the organizational and administrative pattern for recreational sports that has the most support but also brings out alternative patterns including the one associated with campus recreation. Other aspects of the recreational sports program such as finances, publicity, awards, safety, and the purchase and care of equipment are considered in Part V, while Part VI supplies details about tournaments, meets, and special recreation programs to which the leadership and the participant alike will want to turn.

While it is not possible to list everyone who has given assistance in preparing this book, the authors wish to single out for special mention a number of persons who have facilitated its completion. Acknowledgment should be made of the assistance forthcoming from such state consultants in physical education, recreation and athletics as Don Cox (Iowa); Jim Goddard (Oregon); Fillmore Hendrix (Texas); Barbara Landers (California); and Howie Schaub (Washington). We are also grateful to such professional leaders in the public schools as John E. Suzick, Renton, Washington; J. LaVere Shaffer, Bellingham, Washington; Hulin Smith, Hurst, Texas; Virginia Lohmiller, Davenport, Iowa; and Ray Byrnes, West Des Moines, Iowa. Jerry Thornton of the Washington Center for Community Education in Olympia and Dr. Steven Sherman, Director of the Recreational Sports Program at Brooklyn College, provided valuable advice and counsel.

THE RECREATIONAL SPORTS PROGRAM

I

Historical
and
Philosophical
Foundations

Leisure and Recreation.
Courtesy Whatcom County Parks, Whatcom County, Washington.

1

Leisure and Recreation
in an Affluent Society

The recreational sports program in schools, colleges, and communities is directly influenced and shaped by the complex world of twentieth-century America within which the participants live, work, and pursue their individual goals. That world has been profoundly altered, and continues to be altered, by the Industrial and Scientific Revolutions. The first term is applied to the process by which machines replaced hand labor, factories sprang up, and the country became predominantly urban. The Industrial Revolution, born in the British Isles, spread from its homeland to the United States well before the Civil War (1861–1865), but its tempo speeded up enormously in the wake of that great conflict until the United States by the end of the nineteenth century achieved the industrial primacy among nations that it has never yielded. The Scientific Revolution is, on the other hand, an essentially twentieth-century phenomenon that began early in the century when atomic particles were first used in industry. "I believe," wrote C. P. Snow, the well-known author and physicist, "the industrial society of electronics, atomic energy, automation, is in cardinal respects different in kind from any that has gone before, and will change the world much more." To this transformation Snow applied the term Scientific Revolution.[1]

A POST-INDUSTRIAL SOCIETY

The two revolutions have transformed American society and imparted to the American people a distinctive world view. For the United States, to

[1]*The Two Cultures: And A Second Look* (Cambridge, Cambridge Unversity Press, 1965), p.30.

a degree not true of the other great countries of the world, has attained the status of a post-industrial society. Such a society has an economy where, in the words of Herman Kahn, writing in *The Next 200 Years* (1976), "the task of producing the necessities of life has become trivially easy because of technological advancement and economic development." Kahn and his associates at the prestigious Hudson Institute perceive in such a phase the natural corollary or successor to the Industrial Revolution, one that will occur in other countries as well. Striking symbols of post-industrial United States, dramatizing the high quality of its technological and scientific achievements, were provided for millions when American astronauts—in a series of flights to the moon that began in the late 1960s—walked on the surface of the moon. Their statements and activities there were recorded electronically and transmitted to earthbound spectators glued to television screens all over the world. No less spectacular from the technological point of view was the feat carried out in the summer of 1976 when the Viking space-craft mission penetrated Mars and sent back to the earth a memorable picture of the cold desert surface of the red planet. It also made possible a scientific sampling of the soil of the Martian plain.

To this post-industrial United States other peoples of the world now look for a preview of what they must expect to see in the development of their own countries. They do so with mixed feelings. At times they view the American scene with trepidation as they note signs of endemic violence. And well they might. For the assassination of a president in 1963 was followed by the spectacle of burning cities and civil rights riots and then by the agony of a prolonged war in southeast Asia that divided the American people in a way not seen in recent memory. Everywhere, at the same time, was the pattern of crime, often violent in nature, that has accompanied an accelerating Industrial Revolution and its attendant social dislocations. Not surprisingly the national mood became indigo,[2] and it further darkened with the political abuses at the center of the federal government, which are collectively known as Watergate. The existence of such abuse offended American standards of political morality while raising serious questions about the manner in which Americans customarily viewed themselves and their political institutions. Yet most interested observers agree that these dark clouds form only part of the picture. There is also much that is hopeful in the American experience as the twentieth century approaches its close. On this side of the ledger are to be found the continually rising standard of living for millions of individuals in the United States, the resilience of the famed American economy, the widespread and varied educational system with it continuing promise of social mobility for large numbers of Americans, the heightened sensitivity to the physical environment and the call for clean air and water, the increased awareness of the need to protect the political and social rights of the various minorities such as women, Blacks, Chicanos, etc. And it is widely considered that the era of Watergate

[2]Vermont Royster, "Mood Indigo," *Thinking Things Over, Wall Street Journal,* 31 December, 1975.

finally came to an end in the national elections of 1976 when Jimmy Carter, a political figure in no way connected with the national trauma of the Nixon years, inaugurated a new era of presidential leadership.

A DEMOGRAPHIC REVOLUTION AND THE RISE OF SUBURBIA

In close association with the Industrial and Scientific Revolutions has come what is called a demographic revolution—that is, a striking rise in population. As one modern authority on the Industrial Revolution pointed out, "One of the features that distinguishes the modern industrial (or industrializing) economy from its predecessors in the chain of economic development is that it involves sustained long-term growth in *both* population *and* output."[3] It cannot be doubted that just such a sustained growth in population has taken place in the United States. A country with a population of about 3 million at the time of the American Revolution had attained two hundred years later, by 1976, a population of 215 million, and this is expected to swell to a figure somewhere between 245 and 276 million by the year 2000. Another characteristic of the population, noticeable since the very beginning of the country, is a marked mobility. Americans move, although not necessarily great distances. Two centuries ago 95 percent of the population lived in the country; and Philadelphia, with 30,000 inhabitants, was the largest city. Today, three-quarters of the American people live in the cities and suburbs that make up about 1.5 percent of the country's land mass, and there are thirty-three metropolitan areas with at least a million inhabitants each. New York City, the preeminent city of the United States and perhaps of the world, has a population of 16 million people if the greater metropolitan area is taken into account.

A few comments are called for about the urban situation, which is sometimes described as the urban crisis. With the spread of the railroad and the growing use of the automobile and with the encouragement of such governmental programs as roadbuilding, ready financing for home ownership, etc., there has been a steady flow of middle-class white people from the centers of the metropolitan areas (especially in the Northeast and the Midwest) into the outlying suburbs, thus creating by a reverse process an urbanized countryside where the inhabitants are typically more affluent and better educated than the population now existing in what are frequently referred to as the central cities of the metropolitan areas. The contrast became striking with the arrival in the central cities of new ethnic minorities whose previous experience had little to do with city life. That is, at about the same time much of the middle-class white population began the trek from the cities to the suburbs, a revolution in agriculture in the American South forced from the land large numbers of tenant families, mostly Black, who became new

[3]Phyliss Deane, *The First Industrial Revolution* (Cambridge: Cambridge University Press, 1965, reprinted 1967), p. 20.

inhabitants of the central cities, their presence going far to explain the characteristics of these cities. Ill-equipped by education and past experience to meet the demands of an urban environment, many of them became dependent on governmental help for the necessities of life. In the central cities they were joined by an influx of emigrants from the Caribbean such as Puerto Ricans, whose problems and background resembled those of the Blacks, although the Puerto Rican movement into cities such as New York seems to have been due less to changing agricultural conditions at home than to the rising level of expectations that swept the developing regions of the world after World War II. With reference to the migration of the Blacks to the central cities, a generalization that might have also included the new migrants from the Caribbean, *The New York Times* editorialized as follows:

> Cities have carried the nation's culture and absorbed its shocks. They are reeling now from the impact of the migration of 4 million mostly rural blacks from the South over the three decades beginning in 1940 and from Federal housing, tax and spending policies which encouraged middle-class whites to create homogeneous turbulence-free zones outside the cities.[4]

The editorial also recognized that despite the high levels of urban Black poverty, the middle-class Blacks in Detroit, the prototype of the central cities described above, were displaying signs of a rising political power and a surging optimism that promised future change for cities of this kind.

What then of the future? Some experts on the urban scene believe that while the Blacks, Puerto Ricans, and other ethnic minorities who are relative newcomers to American cities are likely to move to nearby suburbs as they prosper, following the example set earlier for them by the migrating white middle classes, other will remain in the central cities and form increasingly a new urban middle class. But the process, it is agreed, will be slow; and it appears that as late as the year 2000 the central cities will have "a large under-class of jobless residents who pay little in taxes but use many public services."[5] It should be added, moreover, that the pattern just described is not applicable to all American cities to the same degree. It applies on balance to the older cities such as New York, Chicago, Philadelphia, Detroit, and St. Louis, which have social problems of varying degrees of severity, but to a much lesser degree to the growing cities of the Sunbelt such as Dallas, Houston, Miami, Phoenix, San Diego, Tucson, and even Los Angeles.

AN AFFLUENT SOCIETY

Along with the enormous increase in population has come a continued rise in the output of goods and services that has made the United States

---

[4]*New York Times,* 6 August 1976.

[5]"The Future Revised: Cities may Flourish in South and West, Decline in Northeast." *Wall Street Journal,* 6 April 1976.

one of ths great affluent societies of all time. The United States, it cannot be too often stated, is a society with an advanced standard of living virtually unparalleled in the history of the world. This is true, on balance, despite such disquieting areas of poverty as white Appalachia and the economic distress that so often disfigures the present central cities. But if the number of people experiencing economic and social distress in the central cities constitutes a seeming contradiction to this assertion of national abundance, such facts, grim as they are, must be kept in perspective. It must not be overlooked that from the beginning of the twentieth century national income has risen steadily with the exception of the temporary setback administered by the Great Depression that began in 1929. This is quickly seen from the marked increase in the gross national product (the total of goods and services for a given year) as recorded in the pivotal decade from 1965 to 1975. The GNP, as it is called, went straight up, from $688 billion for 1965 to $982 billion for 1970 to $1,499 billion in 1975. It is expected to double between 1975 and the year 2000. Such statistics convey a vivid impression of rising national prosperity, an impressive one by any standard. Not only has national income grown steadily, it has also been broadly distributed because of such factors as almost full employment since World War II (1939–1945) and the impact of progressive income tax policies. It is a trend that is expected to continue.

The rising affluence since World War II has been reflected in the widespread ownership of material goods that were once viewed as luxuries beyond the reach of the ordinary household but now assumed to be necessities. In the 1920s the prosperous American housewife made the acquaintance of electric refrigerators, vacuum cleaners, and washing machines; a generation later these consumer goods were in all types of homes, and such complicated devices as television sets, transistor radios, freezers, dishwashers, and air conditioners were becoming common. It should be remarked in passing that the appearance of color television sets has enormously enhanced the popularity of sports, bringing to them both a national and at times international audience. Meanwhile the almost universal ownership of the automobile, which was at first regarded as the plaything of the rich, has revolutionized society and the countryside. Its very abundance is striking since it is not uncommon for most families in rural and suburban areas to possess a car for personal use, and the two-car family is by no means unusual. Here, however, a sobering note has been introduced by changes that were not foreseen by earlier forecasters of how the American economy would develop by the year 2000. In the year 1966, when a rather different national mood prevailed, gasoline as the energy source for the automobile was relatively inexpensive and available in quantity to the motorist; and although a deepening concern was evident about the effects of pollution, traffic congestion, etc., it was assumed that technological answers could be found to the problems posed by the expanding ownership of automobiles and that the process at work of selling more and more cars would continue to accelerate. New car sales would rise from about 10 million a year (as in 1976) to about 20 million a year by the year 2000, possibly to as much as 25 million. But the coming together of the oil-producing countries of the Middle East in 1974 to form the cartel known as OPEC (the Organization of Petroleum Exporting Countries), which controls the sale of oil to the industrial countries of the world, has introduced far-reaching changes. At the same time that the Arab oil embargo made energy more costly and harder to secure, it became evident that the technological improvements required to meet environmental problems were not forthcoming at the rate that had been anticipated, and the result was that the ownership of automobiles began to lose some of its old magic. At the least, a questioning had set in about the desirability of powerful automobiles at the expense of efficiency in their operation. Formerly treated as the ultimate object of desire, its efficiency subsidiary to styling, power, and speed, the automobile was increasingly discussed in terms of improving efficiency. As a Stanford Research Study has suggested, "changes in the fundamental lifestyles of Americans may affect the way people look upon car ownership and usage."[6] And another observer remarked perceptively, this means "spending less for things and more for experiences."[7] The same kind of expectation that affected the views taken with regard to automobiles in the 1960s also shaped the attitude of Americans toward air travel; and here too, sobering after-thought has entered. The energy crisis has led to higher fares for air travel, and with higher fares has come a reluctance to undertake long journeys for vacation purposes. Environmental considerations have likewise played a part, and in some cases the desire for high-speed travel by air has yielded to a concern to protect people from the noise and polluting of the environment that so often accompanies advances in aviation technology. It was considerations such as these that prompted resistance to allowing the supersonic British-French Concorde to land in the United States.

Despite qualifications, American society is affluent, and this affluence sets its tone. Acquiring wealth today is easier than in the past, and the possession of wealth is more acceptable, perhaps because the ownership of material goods is so widespread. An example may be drawn from politics. In 1958, an article appeared in *The New York Times Magazine* entitled "The Log Cabin Myth Comes to an End." Its author pointed out that great wealth was no longer the political disability that it had been earlier in the nation's history. Then, it was deemed desirable to have a background that centered on life in a log cabin. The notable example was furnished by the "Log Cabin and Hard Cider" campaign of 1840, in which William Henry Harrison, the idol of the frontiersmen, defeated Martin Van Buren, who was portrayed by his political enemies as a privileged aristocrat. In 1958, however, more than a hundred years later, the Democratic and Republican parties of New York nominated

---

[6]"The Future Revised: Transportation in 2000 to Rely on Equipment Much Like Today's," *Wall Street Journal*, 1 April, 1976.
[7]*Ibid.*

for governor Averell Harriman and Nelson Rockefeller respectively, both scions of very wealthy families and in their own right multimillionaires. Why was it possible by this time to nominate men like these for high office? Numerous explanations were offered, and among them was a reminder of how affluent American society has become. It was pointed out that while Harriman and Rockefeller were well able to buy Cadillacs, television sets, and power boats, so too could tens of thousands of voters who set the climate for hundred of thousands of others. The point was that material goods were now within the reach of nearly all. The mass of people had gained access to privileges once reserved for a small elite; and the disparity that had once aroused envy was fast disappearing.

The big change has occurred since 1900. The public image of a man of gentility at the turn of the century was of one owning numerous homes, vacationing in Europe in the summer and Florida in the winter, spending leisure time in sailing and golfing, sending his son to Andover and then to Harvard, etc. What has happened to this image today? For one thing, some 30 million Americans owned their homes by the early 1960s, and possession of a second home, while still a status symbol, is becoming much more commonplace. Moreover, two former citadels of the rich have fallen: the suburbs and the Ivy League universities, whose student bodies have become much more representative of the various segments of society. Travel, which fifty years ago was "an upper-income pleasure, a middle-income prize, and a lower-income dream," has become available to great masses of people. Of the 286,000 passports issued by the State Department in the summer of 1962 for travel in foreign countries, 76,000 were to skilled workers, 64,000 to housewives, 41,000 to students, 23,000 to teachers, and 18,000 to clerks and secretaries. Though some qualifications may be introduced into this picture of continual material progress as the twentieth century runs its course, it was possible, nevertheless, for Dr. Kahn of the Hudson Institute, after examining the relevant data, to draw a highly optimistic scenario for the year 2000. According to his expert opinion, the average income of Americans by that time will be $25,000 a year, the four-day work week will prevail for forty weeks of the year, most families will possess two homes, one in the city or suburb and the other in the country, the environment will have been successfully purified with air, and water supply much improved in quality, etc. Even if this picture is discounted substantially as much too optimistic in its overall conclusions, the contrasts are startling between the material conditions of the American people as the twentieth century began and those as this momentous century is coming to an end.

THE NEW LEISURE

The average man or woman in this affluent society has an unprecedented amount of leisure. In fact, the word "leisure" is used today in a manner that reveals how the concept of leisure as an acceptable facet of life has gained ground in a society that under the influence of a stern Calvinism had once viewed free time as wasted hours and as breeding ground for the devil's work. In a recent study he made for the Twentieth Century Fund, Sebastian de Grazia, a professor of political science at Rutgers University, pointed out that the extensive use of the word "leisure" was in itself evidence of the changed attitude. After noting the prevalence of the word, he wrote: "We now have leisure time, leisure rooms, leisure trips to leisure lakes, leisure clothes, leisure equipment, leisure spending on leisure items."[8]

The word "leisure," rising from the Latin *licere*, has been defined as "freedom from occupation, employment, or engagement," and it is used in this sense in the following pages, unless otherwise stated. This view of leisure was held by the common Greek of antiquity though not, on the whole, by philosophers such as Aristotle and Plato. The former, however, sometimes used the word in this sense. In his study, de Grazia suggests that the philosophers viewed leisure as the opportunity for a man to use his highest abilities in religion and politics for the service of the state; and, according to de Grazia, who writes approvingly of this ideal, "Fun never dominated the picture."[9] This "classical ideal" of leisure should not be confused with the present-day usage, which equates leisure with free time that can be used in an infinite variety of ways.

The new leisure is the outgrowth of the steady reduction of the workweek that has come in the wake of the Industrial and Scientific Revolutions. Thus, in 1800 the workweek was eighty-four hours. It had been reduced to seventy-two by 1850, and fifty years later it was sixty. The same trend is conspicuous in the twentieth century, as the following chart reveals. Not surprisingly, under these circumstances, the *U.S. News and World Report* carried this telling headline. "Is U.S. heading for a 32-hour workweek?"

The decline of the workweek has been accompanied by a greater flexibility in scheduling the timespan when the worker is at his task and even in the amount of vacation time allotted in the course of the year. The timing of the vacation period has also altered as Christmas vacation time, for example, becomes more prevalent. In short, new ways are continually being found to relieve the rigidity traditionally imposed upon workers by technology, and much ingenuity is lavished on the attempt to adapt the demands of productivity to the imperatives of the employees' lifestyle. It is a matter of self-interest for companies as they have increasingly recognized that their employees are more productive if allowed to choose their own time schedules, and the latter have been allowed to do so within limits. This is how the system works. Management may set the limits of the work day, from about 7:00 in the morning, for example, until 7:00 at night. Early risers are in a position to complete their assignments by mid-afternoon and have time thereafter for the

---

[8]*Of Time, Work, and Leisure* (New York: Doubleday and Company, Inc., 1964), p. 142.
[9]*Ibid.*, p. 322. For a fuller analysis, see *Ibid.*, 9-19.

Figure 1–1   The Shrinking American Workweek

needs and desires rising out of their personal life. Other workers, who dislike beginning the work day in the earlier hours, may choose to begin work at mid-morning, etc. At the center of the work is a "core" period when all the employed are at their various tasks. The new system of flexible hours, or "flextime", was first applied to industrial workers, from which it spread to salaried employees; and experience to this point suggests that the system works best for the latter group, who are not involved in shift work or with machines that must operate at certain hours of the day. The new outlook is also reflected in the appearance of winter vacations for employees, notably in the industrial contracts of 1970 by which the United Automobile Workers were given vacations at Christmas. The provision brought much satisfaction. "Where else can you get a job with 10 days off at Christmas?" asked the assembly-line worker at a plant of the Chrysler Corporation's Dodge Division. And he added. "My job just gets better all the time." Also part of the picture is the advance made in lowering the age of retirement. One manpower expert recently predicted that retirement at the age of 55 would be the normal procedure by the end of the twentieth century.

An Abundance of Leisure?

It would be misleading, however, to imply that all the time spent away from work, not devoted to providing food, clothing, and shelter, is leisure. Usually, if an individual has a small or medium income, he has other activities in which he feels compelled to engage. If leisure is viewed as free time, then a true leisure activity should be defined in the manner of George Friedmann, who wrote that "a true leisure activity is one freely chosen and pursued at the moment and in the way desired by the individual concerned, who expects from it satisfaction and even a certain inner growth."[10]

There are other types of obligations outside the regular job that lessen free time. These include possible second jobs held by people seeking to elevate their standard of living; husbands' helping with household chores; do-it-yourself projects that allow families to avoid expensive outside help, etc. A necessary part of family life may be attending church or even taking study courses for the purpose of advancement. It is a leading thesis of de Grazia that obligations outside the regular job are so extensive as to make the decline in work hours as commonly cited more apparent than real. He concludes: "The great and touted gains in free time since the 1850s . . . are largely myth."[11]

Whether this conclusion is valid or not, it is still safe to assume that leisure time is available to many Americans if they choose to use it for leisure purposes and that the amount of it will continue to increase. Whether he chooses to spend his time in do-it-yourself projects or in second jobs taken in order to enlarge his income or in a way of life that enriches his individuality, the average American has the choice to make; and the opportunity exists for him to make it. That he is doing so can be seen in the results of a Gallup Poll (February 1963) in which individuals were asked to indicate their activities during the last year. They were given a card listing eleven pursuits and asked whether they had engaged in any of them. The results revealed that 54 million adults had seen a motion picture, 50 million had read a book, 26 million had bowled, a similar number had attended a football game, and so on. Despite considerable evidence of cultural interests (attendance at a theater production, symphony), more displayed a preference for watching or participating in sporting events such as basketball, football, or bowling.

Startling as the change has been in the workweek since 1850, in the years ahead Americans will undergo even more shattering changes in the pattern of their lives, largely as a result of the Scientific Revolution that began early in the twentieth century but is only now making a deep impression on the public consciousness. Unfortunately, in the rush for scientific exploration, little substantial research has been devoted to the economic and social impact of one aspect of the Scientific Revolution that may conveniently be termed "cybernation."

Cybernation

The term "cybernation" has been coined to denote the systematic design and application of automation and computers. Automation is an

---

[10]*The Anatomy of Work: Labor, Leisure and the Implications of Automation*, trans. Wyatt Rawson (New York: The Free Press of Glencoe, Inc., 1961), p. 108.

[11]*Of Time, Work, and Leisure*, p. 79.

automatic producer of material objects, and computers analyze and interpret complex data. As the defintion just given implies, both may be used in a mixed system. Cybernation has been described in a recent thought-provoking study made by the Center for the Study of Democratic Institutions, entitled *Cybernation: The Silent Conquest* (1962). According to its author, Donald N. Michael, cybernated systems "perform with a precision and a rapidity unmatched in humans."[12] And his account reveals that they can emulate many human characteristics. They can be built to detect and correct the errors in their own performance, even indictating which of their components is the source of the error; they can make judgments; they can profit from past experience; they can receive information; and they are beginning to perceive and recognize. Cybernation is spreading throughout industry.[13] The London transit system, the largest in the world, operates from a program of punched tape. The Bank of America possesses an electronic computer that has replaced almost four hundred clerical workers. It can make 237,000 additions and subtractions per minute. American Airlines is using electronic computers to make plane reservations. In one-tenth of a second the machine will show if a seat is available on any American Airline flight out of New York City. Companies in the steel industry are moving toward the cybernation of steelmaking with computers controlling the furnaces and rolling mills. Some firms are carrying on research with the aim of making the entire steel production process a truly continuous operation. And so it goes.

Cybernation and Leisure

While the leaders of the steel industry are delighted by the progress of cybernation in the nation's mills, presumably the members of the United Steelworkers of American are less so. For the spread of cybernation, if carried as far as some proponents contemplate, is ominous for the future employment of workers. Michael forecasts four types of leisure classes as society changes from a partially to a fully automated economy.

The first of these consists of the unemployed: the poorly educated blue-collar worker in the factory, the displaced service worker, and even, for a time at least, the relatively well-trained, white-collar worker who will have to change his occupation. The main concern of this group as a whole will be to find work and security. One of two things will probably happen to its members. Either they will become unemployed and spend their time lounging around and drawing unemployment checks, or they will take the initiative in acquiring the education necessary to secure a job in an automated industry. Since retraining will encounter numerous obstacles, many will remain unemployed; and the result may be a catastrophic social illness.

[12]P. 6.
[13]*Ibid.*

A contributing factor, to be noted at this point, is the failure of the economy already to provide places in sufficient number for the young people who have failed to complete high school and are not sufficiently skilled to obtain positions in a technological society. According to James B. Conant, former president of Harvard University, commenting in the early 1960s, in an economically depressed section of one of the largest American cities, 70 percent of the boys and girls between the ages of 16 and 21 were out of school and without employment, and in another large city, in a comparable area, 63 percent of the high school drop-outs had found no work.[14] The danger is that young people with time on their hands, lacking the challenging, adventuresome, and socially acceptable recreation skills, will find their satisfaction in challenging but socially unacceptable activities. Reckless driving, a violation rate three times that for adults, vandalism, wanton destruction of public and private property, gang fights, and youth arrests that are, by far, greater than the increase in population of children are indications of misspent leisure. When to this adolescent group is added the class left unemployed by cybernation, social problems will assume new dimensions.

The effect of cybernation on other classes may be described more briefly. A second class is the low-income group that will retain jobs with a shorter work week and reasonable security. This class will have a tendency to take second jobs so as to enlarge its income. "Moonlighting," rather than the constructive use of leisure time, will probably characterize its members. Class three consists of workers with adequate incomes and much leisure. It is possible that they will be the chief beneficiaries of the Scientific Revolution. The majority of this class will be professional, semi-professional, or skilled workers, who will be needed in an automated economy but not for more than forty hours a week. They will command good salaries. If they are informed about leisure-time activities, they will benefit from them. Class four consists of the overworked executive and professional people, whose work will not be lessened to the same degree by the conquest of cybernation. Because their numbers are insufficient, they can be expected to be overburdened in the years ahead. If they can reduce their working time to the forty-hour week, they will use their leisure time constructively.[15]

CREATIVE LEISURE

Such modern philosophers as John Dewey and Bertrand Russell have noticed that leisure potentially has many wholesome and creative uses. The former stressed that "education has no more serious responsibility than making adequate provision for enjoyment of recreative leisure; not

[14]Conant, "Social Dynamite in Our Large Cities," *Vital Speeches*, #18, July 1, 1961, p. 554 ff., cited in Michael, *Cybernation: The Silent Conquest*, p. 22.
[15]Michael, *Cybernation: The Silent Conquest*, 29–33.

only for the sake of immediate health, but still more if possible for the sake of its lasting effect upon habits of the mind."[16] And Russell declared that education "should aim, in part, at providing tastes which would enable a man to use leisure intelligently."[17]

Leisure is essential for creative activity, as Dewey and Russell implied, for it provides time beyond daily personal demands for furthering the intellectual, moral, spiritual, artistic, and physical interests of the individual. Used constructively, leisure time makes way for new activities that enrich the life of the individual and society. Though few, it is true, add to the total of human knowledge and beauty, still they may help to preserve it for future generations, and, in the process, be refreshed themselves. Twentieth-century Americans have a unique opportunity to become acquainted with the best that has been thought and created in the world's history. Equipped with an unprecedented amount of leisure, which may become overwhelming as cybernation spreads, and the heirs of all previous civilizations, the people of the United States, it has been remarked, could become more constructive than the Greeks, more powerful than the Romans, wiser than the Chinese, more responsible than the Victorians, and happier and more scientific than all of these peoples combined.

THE PROBLEMS OF LEISURE

Yet constructive results will not be automatically forthcoming from the expanding leisure; and, if leisure classes develop in the manner postulated by Michael, large and serious problems will face society. Two aspects of these problems will be noted here. First of all, the replacement of human work by cybernation will in itself have potentially very harmful results. Workers, already dissatisfied with work dehumanized by mass-production techniques, will become more restless as the process is extended. One wonders how people who lose their jobs will respond to the changed conditions. What will be the effect, for example, of the loss of jobs on people who equate their work with security and for whom work has been the very center of life? Can leisure, even if used in the most beneficial manner, impart equal benefits? It is permissible to doubt it.

Secondly, it is by no means clear that those with more leisure will use it properly. The values needed for discernment among various recreational activities often seem to be lacking, and lengthy hours spent before the television screen raise questions about the capacity of the population to make the most worthy use of its free time. When various elements go further and indulge in unsocial or antisocial activities, the misuse of time

[16]John Dewey, *Democracy and Education: An Introduction to the Philosophy of Education* (New York, The Macmillan Company, 1916, 29th printing, 1957), p. 241.

[17]"In Praise of Idleness," *Mass Leisure,* edited by Eric Larrabee and Rolf Meyersohn (Glencoe, Ill., The Free Press, 1958), p. 103.

may threaten the foundations of democracy and undermine the way of life that has been shaped by generations of Americans who lived under very different circumstances.

These problems, and many like them, have been little studied; much less have they been the subject of systematic investigation. Even if one doubts that cybernation will spread as quickly and as completely as has been forecast—and some observers strongly doubt it—its very existence and the changes already underway make it clear that its effects will have to be reckoned with in coming years. It follows that in any social engineering or planning undertaken to meet the dislocations created by the Scientific Revolution due attention will have to be given to the role of recreation in a society in which the declining, perhaps vanishing, workweek opens the vista of abundant free time for more and more people.

RECREATION DEFINED

The word "recreation" is derived from the Latin *recreatio*, which means the state of being recreated or refreshed. As initially employed, the word denoted a form of freely chosen human activity from which an individual emerged refreshed and reinvigorated, in a fit state for carrying on his work. But some time around World War II the definition ceased to be satisfying to those professionally concerned with programs of organized leisure, and much more was now said about broader personal goals in recreation and about its social purpose and significance for society as a whole. A more comprehensive meaning was then attached to the word "recreation", as may be seen in the comments of Richard Kraus and Barbara Bates. According to these scholars, recreation is properly regarded "as an activity, an experience, or an emotional condition brought about in an individual as a result of engaging in leisure pursuits within a certain framework of personal motivation and expectation." It might "involve a tremendously broad set of possible interests that range from sports, hobbies, and social cultural interests, to mathematical, scientific, or exploratory involvements." And it might "consist of a superficial, momentary episode, or . . . demand a lifetime of serious commitment."[18] Presumably a recreational experience might vary from cardplaying to dancing, from spectatorship at sports contests to skindiving, from painting Grandma Moses type "primitives" to staging Eugene O'Neill's *Long Day's Journey into Night.*

Generally accepted criteria exist for classifying an activity as recreational in nature. The individual should engage in it for pleasure, gain personal satisfaction from it, and carry it on during leisure. Recreation, then, is a voluntary action taking place during leisure. Even though it is

---

[18]Richard G. Kraus and Barbara J. Bates, *Recreation Leadership and Supervision: Guidelines for Professional Development* (Philadelphia: W. B. Saunders Company, 1975), 6.

an aspect of leisure, recreation may be serious and purposeful; and deep concentration often attends recreational activities.

In general, participation in recreation varies with income, age, and education. Smaller numbers engage in sports and games requiring special skills or equipment. The aging tend to shun the most active sports, and the better educated participate more fully. Consequently, even the spread of education carries implications for recreation.

THE EDUCATIONAL VALUES OF RECREATION

Recreation in schools and colleges, as found in the programs of intramurals and recreation, has inherent educational values which can transform the mental, physical, emotional, and social qualities of an individual to approach more closely the ideal of the educated person. These educational values include an understanding and respect for the human body as a means of expression; the development of the fundamental skills of movement so necessary in all daily activities; essential contributions to the physiological development of the human body; an understanding and knowledge of the care needed by the human body to enable it to function at peak efficiency; the development of interests and playing skills in a variety of wholesome leisure-time activities; and the realization that recreational activities are one of the best avenues of education leading to group understanding and cooperation. These values have provided the ideological framework of the recreational sports program that is described in later chapters of this book.

THE CHANGING VIEW OF RECREATION

In the last quarter of the twentieth century recreation opportunities and skills are coveted by all age groups; and recreation, once eyed skeptically, has attained the status of being described, even by official governmental groups, as a national need. In colonial America an austere Calvinism condemned recreation as idleness and the potential source of evil. The respect of the community was reserved for those who worked twelve or more hours a day. The men cleared the land, the women worked long hours in the kitchen, and children had chores that left little time or energy for play. Furthermore, the traditional philosophical concepts of education, derived from asceticism and scholasticism, provided few opportunities for play in the schools, to which, in any case, few would have had access. But the Industrial Revolution created a new climate of opinion. Leisure formed an integral part of the seven-day week, and the word "recreation" shed its old associations. Cities built playgrounds and parks; professional recreation associations sprang up; and the schools' curricula widened to include physical activity and recreation. A new impetus emanated from the age of automation, and provided an explosive revaluation of the values of and need for recreation in an affluent society. By the time that the impact of the Scientific Revolution was felt, increasing numbers of individuals in all walks of life were awakening to the values of recreational activities.

RECREATION AND PHYSICAL HEALTH

A growing knowledge of how activity may aid in developing and maintaining good health is today arousing popular public interest in recreation. Very important support for carefully regulated programs of sports and games and vigorous exercise has come from the influential American Medical Association. At its annual meeting in Miami, Florida, in June 1960, the House of Delegates approved a series of resolutions supporting programs of recreational sports. Of greatest moment was a resolution placing the American Medical Association on record in support of programs of sports and games because these imparted leisure-time skills that relieve tensions and help to alleviate the effects of a sedentary life. Dr. Paul Dudley White, well-known cardiologist and physician to former President Dwight D. Eisenhower, voiced the position on personal health of the American Medical Association when he stated that the absence of disease was not enough. "What we should aim for in our programs," he stressed, "is positive health."[19] He recommended establishing a regular habit in some form of exercise and maintaining it steadily. "I have thought of it [exercise] as being as important as many other things that we do, such as eating, sleeping, working."[20]

On all sides awareness is increasing that exercise is basic to normal growth and development. The physiological axiom, "that which is used, develops; that which is not used, atrophies," steadily gains ground. Many parents now realize that children require many hours of daily activity and that a definite relationship exists between the physically vigorous child and the physically vigorous adult. Progress will continue for many reasons, not the least of these being the fact that the elementary-school teacher who has to provide physical education and recreation periods for his pupils understands more of their need for physical activity because he himself has studied required professional courses in physical education and recreation. Courses of this type have become standard in the college and university curriculum.

[19]Paul Dudley White, "Health and Sickness in Middle Age, "*Journal of the American Association for Health, Physical Education and Recreation,* (Washington, D.C.: American Association for Health, Physical Education and Recreation, 1960), October, 1960, Part I, p. 21.

[20]"Interview with Dr. Paul Dudley White," *U.S. News and World Report* (August 23, 1957), p. 51.

Moreover, young and old alike, concerned about physical appearance and weight, are turning to greater physical activity. Transportation conveniences and numerous labor-saving devices have eliminated from modern life much of the physical activity that ensures good muscle tone and the proper functioning of the organic system. Yet American men and women still desire and appreciate good health, fit bodies, and trim figures as conditions of a satisfying life and for reasons of personal pride. Knowing that muscles lose their tone through inactivity and become soft and flabby, they are learning to add physical activity to their routine in an effort to counteract the effects of a sedentary life. The success of morning exercise programs on radio and television, courses stressing fitness, "slim gym" courses for men and women, and the sale of books on exercise attest to an awakening interest and realization that fit bodies and abundant health, if not developed by the normal labor of the day, must come through various forms of substitute exercise and recreation. Insurance companies also remind listeners and readers that to be overweight is to shorten the life span; Americans who live the longest weigh twenty pounds less than the average. Generally, the condition of being overweight is attributed to poor diet and the lack of activity.

RECREATION AND MENTAL HEALTH

A formidable task confronting society is that of aiding the mentally ill, who exist in large numbers. One out of ten persons may expect to spend time in a mental hospital, with women outnumbering men at all ages and at a rate proportionately greater than their majority of more than a million in the population explains. Recreation may act as a preventative of mental illness or play a part in curing it; and many psychiatrists, social scientists, educators, and members of other professional groups have turned their energies toward discovering the nature of the relationship between recreation and mental health.

Good mental hygiene, a preventative approach to mental illness, requires individuals to recognize the dangers of a highly complex society and the limitation of demands that they can safely impose upon themselves. Doctors have pointed to diversions such as golf, tennis, and swimming as possible antidotes for nervous tension and mental overwork. Frustrations and boredom, which are also related to mental disturbances, may be outgrowths of the urge to express aggressiveness. Its repression without suitable outlets may endanger mental health; and it has often been pointed out that competitive games provide for some people the proper balance between the needs to express and repress, both of which exist.

Nor are mental problems peculiar to adults. The growing number of school and college students afflicted with tension, ulcers, and nervous breakdowns has dramatized the urgency of safeguarding their mental health. It is important that they have opportunities for both excitement and relaxation through participation in wholesome recreational activities. Indeed, life ought to be enjoyable and satisfying for people of all ages. They should ordinarily have no need to resort to sedatives and tranquilizers to escape mental and emotional stresses. In summary, the variety of avenues possible in recreational activities may make it possible for young and old to practice good mental health; but much needs to be learned on this subject and it should not be assumed that recreation acts as a panacea for all ills.

RECREATION AND PHYSICAL FITNESS

A prominent by-product of the Cold War between the United States and Russia is a deep interest at the highest levels of government in the United States in the physical fitness of the American people. This interest, in turn, has stimulated in individuals of all ages and professions an active appreciation of the values of recreation. President Kennedy communicated a sense of emergency when he declared: "The strength of our democracy is no greater than the collective well-being of our people. The vigor of our country is no stronger than the vitality and will of all our countrymen. The level of physical, mental, moral, and spiritual fitness of every American citizen must be our constant concern."[21] Even earlier, in 1956, President Eisenhower formed a cabinet-level Council on Youth Fitness and a Citizen's Advisory Committee on the Fitness of American Youth to help community groups, schools, and numerous recreation centers with the promotion of recreation and fitness programs for all age groups. Over the years, the Council and the Advisory Committee have aroused and sustained national interest in improved national fitness through publications, conferences, films, teaching, and other motivation aids.

Operation Fitness–USA, a program promoted by the American Association for Health, Physical Education and Recreation,[22] developed a national fitness test for use by teachers and recreation leaders in schools and on playgrounds. National norms have been established for children in grades five through twelve and for college men and women. Fitness insignia and certificates are available for distribution to those deemed physically fit. Other projects in this program include a nationwide chain of sports clinics, as well as festivals, demonstrations, movies on fitness, recognition for good existing programs, development of teaching progressions, and sports skills and knowledge tests.

[21]President's Council on Youth Fitness, *Youth Physical Fitness*, Parts One and Two (Washington, D.C.: Superintendent of Documents, 1961), p. 1.

[22]This highly important organization, frequently referred to as AAHPER, recently changed its name to American Alliance for Health, Physical Education and Recreation.

American businesses have responded to the call for increased emphasis on physical fitness. Thus, the Wheaties Sport Federation took shape, and Bob Richards, the Olympic Pole Vaulting Champion, became its director. It initiated projects to encourage an interest in fitness among the membership of various youth organizations such as church groups, park recreation centers, and the YMCAs. On the West Coast, the Union Oil Company founded the Union Oil's 76 Sports Club. And Mutual of Omaha has proposed underwriting the expense of a Youth Fitness Congress. This activity crowned a long record of achievement by industry in promoting recreation.

Despite the encouraging signs of a spreading interest in physical fitness, progress in developing the desirable level among American boys and girls has been uneven. Impressive and significant gains were recorded in the years from 1958 to 1965, to be sure, only to lose momentum in the next ten years. A study released by the Office of Education reveals that the level of fitness did not on the whole improve in the decade from 1965 to 1975.[23] The generalization is valid for both boys and girls, even though the girls displayed a higher level of endurance in the 600-yard run and walk than earlier. Just the same, the performance on the part of the girls was not the equal of the boys in five out of six tests that were carried out. The lone exception was a fitness test with differing requirements for the two groups. It required chinning for boys and flexed arm hang for the girls.

According to *The New York Times*, these reasons were being advanced for the lack of a general improvement in both groups:

1. The national interest in physical fitness, heightened by President Kennedy's personal support, reached a plateau in the schools.
2. Some schools may be dropping physical education for economic and other reasons.
3. American children reached their fitness peak in 1965.

A rather different position was taken by Simon McNeely, program officer for the study, when he suggested that the continuing spread of affluence in American society explained the results. He thought it possible that "with the continuous inroads of soft living in the United States, youth did well to maintain the gains made between 1958 and 1965";[24] and he discounted the theory that American children had reached a fitness plateau in 1965. Some school systems, such as those of Dade County, Florida, and San Juan, California, maintained vigorous physical education programs that had actually improved fitness scores in the decade in question.

[23]*The New York Times,* 19 March 1976.
[24]Ibid.

RECREATION AND INDUSTRY

Few modern companies would consider a new plant in a community without first surveying its recreational facilities, and countless concerns have assumed the responsibility of providing for the recreation of their workers. Management profits when workers are happy, and the provision of recreation is viewed as contributing to their satisfaction with their work. The view taken by management is shared by organized labor. George Meany, speaking for the AFL-CIO, has expressed the hope that labor will work with professional recreation for the growing numbers of older citizens, American youth, and the workers—these groups, of course, not being mutually exclusive.

A few examples of industry's efforts, which are for both management and workers, must suffice. Though bowling and baseball teams have long been sources of diversion, today companies expect to provide more elaborate recreational facilities. The National Cash Register Company of Dayton, Ohio, operates a 166-acre park for 12,000 workers; it includes swimming pools, golf courses, picnic grounds, and a fieldhouse for winter sports. The River Rouge plant of the Ford Motor Company has an indoor shooting range, lighted tennis courts, lighted baseball diamonds, and horseshoe pits. Country clubs and yacht clubs for workers are provided by International Business Machine Corporation and Standard Oil of California, respectively. And Corning Glass has automatic bowling alleys, dancing classes, etc. Presumably, the president of Bell & Howell spoke for industry, management, and worker alike, when he declared: "Everyone in the organization gains from a well-planned recreation program."

MASS RECREATION

Since World War II, recreation has become a family affair; and the more affluent the family, the greater the participation in sports and leisure-time pursuits. It is not too much to say that there is underway a regular boom in sports. Sports activity, which in the past varied markedly with the changing seasons, now plays a strong role throughout the year. Skiing, a glamorous and sophisticated activity, has extended the outdoor play season into the winter months. In less than twenty-five years skiing has been transformed from the practice of the few into the United State's fastest growing outdoor winter sport. Sales of winter sports equipment are growing at the annual rate of 10 percent a year, and the ski and sled market has reached $20 million annually.

Contrary to popular opinion, the American people are now more

**SPORTING GOODS: A 6-BILLION-DOLLAR
BUSINESS—AND GROWING**

Spending by Americans for most types of sporting
equipment—particularly for participatory sports—is on
the rise. Estimates for the 10 top activities—

	Spending in 1975 (millions of dollars)	Change in Past Two Years
Bicycles and supplies	$1,144.6	Down 6%
Firearms and hunting gear	$1,063.8	Up 37%
Equipment for organized teams	$689.3	Up 29%
Golf equipment	$543.5	Up 23%
Tennis equipment	$522.5	Up 85%
Fishing tackle	$461.7	Up 13%
Snow-skiing equipment	$378.0	Up 38%
Camping gear	$334.1	Down 13%
Baseball, softball equipment for individuals	$169.0	Up 21%
Billiard equipment	$115.5	Not available

IN ADDITION: Another 800 million dollars will be spent on a
host of other sporting activities, such as archery, hockey,
basketball, bowling and water skiing.

ALL TOLD: Americans will shell out some 6.2 billion dollars this
year for sporting goods, up 21 per cent in just two years

Source: National Sporting Goods Association

Figure 1–2   The Sporting
Goods Business

often participants in sports than spectators, though it is true that they continue to jam stadiums in a manner reminiscent of the best days of the Roman Colosseum. That more Americans every year are taking an active part in recreational sports opportunities can be seen from the following table, compiled by the National Sporting Goods Association, which reveals the amount of spending on sporting goods that took place in the year 1975, a year, it might be noted in passing, that was marked by a worldwide economic recession.

As recreation flourishes in American society, sports and sports items that were formerly the preserves of the wealthy have become the source of genuine leisure-time activities for great numbers. For example, playing tennis and golf and owning an expensive boat were once the distinguishing marks of privilege, separating the well-to-do from the great mass of the population. But as the table given above reveals, the numbers who play tennis and golf have swelled into the millions, and the rise continues. If the enthusiasm for tennis is due in large measure to the enthusiasm engendered by the very active American Lawn Tennis Association, the immediate impulse in the mid-70s was supplied by the nationally televised 1973 match in which Billie Jean King struck a great blow for women's rights by defeating Bobby Riggs before millions of viewers. "Riggs and King got tennis out of the country club and got cab drivers talking about it," declared Alan Schwartz, president of Chicago's Mid-Town Tennis Club. And this is to say nothing of the interest created on a continuing basis by the Virginia Slims tournament and through team tennis. Needless to say, the American public received a strong reminder of the charms of golfing from the publicity given to the interest of former President Eisenhower in the sport. Today, Americans own 9 million pleasure boats which reflect various degrees of affluence on the part of their owners; and, in 1961, some 6 million participated in water skiing, taking their cue, perhaps, from Mrs. John Kennedy, wife of the late president, and Colonel John Glenn, an astronaut who became one of the nation's heroes and, perhaps coincidentally, the senator from Ohio.

Among the sports on the current scene that are rapidly gaining new recruits are skindiving, bowling, billiards, and pool. The comparatively new sport of skindiving attracts people for a variety of reasons, some looking for hidden treasure, others for fish, and still others for aesthetic satisfaction. Bowling, billiards, and pool are older sports but have appeared in a new guise. In effect, they have been cleaned up and rendered attractive. Twenty years ago the American Bowling Congress began successfully to change the questionable reputation and environment of bowling alleys. They have since become one of the most popular family recreation centers. Pool is undergoing a renaissance in part because of the appeal of modern billiard halls for women. The former pool hall, renamed the billiard hall, attracts both men and women into air-conditioned, carpeted arenas; and billiard and pool tables are becoming permanent fixtures in bowling alleys, school and college recreation centers, and private homes.

TRENDS

In the absence of a major catastrophe, the population will literally surge ahead during the remainder of the century. The flow to the cities and suburbs and their continued growth will persist. If the present trend continues, white-collar workers (professional, technical, managerial, clerical, etc.) will outnumber the farm and blue-collar workers combined. One other important point is that the population will have more young people, who are among its most active members.

Numerous changes are also anticipated in the popularity of the various activities. For example, professional baseball may well be in serious difficulty by the end of the century. Television has drained vitality from the minor league system, and the colleges are not very effective farm systems for the major leagues. The relative decline of baseball is a facet of cultural change. Its movement is too slow to be of interest to a sophisticated, affluent society; and drawing the great audiences in the last quarter of the twentieth century, it is said, will be professional football, ice hockey, soccer, basketball, and tennis. This analysis is borne out by the growth of professional major league teams in the decade from 1965 to 1975 as seen in Figure 1-3.

The growth of interest in professional sports is by no means an isolated phenomenon. It is rather a national barometer of the national interest in sports generally. As interest grows in watching professional teams, it likewise expands in participatory sports in the college, school,

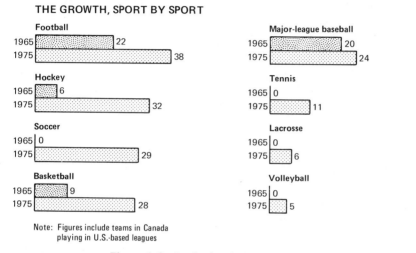

Decade of Explosive Growth _ _ _

A TRIPLING IN PROFESSIONAL TEAMS

Number of Professional Major-League Teams

1965 57

1975 173

THE GROWTH, SPORT BY SPORT

Football
1965 22
1975 38

Hockey
1965 6
1975 32

Soccer
1965 0
1975 29

Basketball
1965 9
1975 28

Major-league baseball
1965 20
1975 24

Tennis
1965 0
1975 11

Lacrosse
1965 0
1975 6

Volleyball
1965 0
1975 5

Note: Figures include teams in Canada
playing in U.S.-based leagues

Figure 1–3 Professional Major League Teams

and community. Interest in participation is expected to continue and even accelerate. Thus, the annual growth rate in the purchase of pleasure boats is expected to be 10 percent a year, and a parallel expansion is underway in camping and tenting. Bowling and golfing continue to gain in appeal, but the golfer will find it increasingly difficult to find a course within easy driving distance of a metropolitan area. Bicycling, now rampant in Europe, is expected to increase in the United States as traffic grows more congested. Cities may turn to constructing bicycle paths like those already begun in Boston because of the persistence of Dr. Paul Dudley White. The appeal of outdoor recreation will expand. An important limitation, of course, is the amount of recreational area available to the Americans who seek nourishment in outdoor recreation near urban and suburban centers.

OUTDOOR RECREATION: THE ROCKEFELLER REPORT

From the very beginning of American society an important current of thought has stressed the right of Americans to the outdoors and the desirability of retaining a natural environment as the wellspring of the nation's spiritual strength. This tradition was reflected in Jefferson's dream of an agrarian republic, free from what he considered to be the blight of cities; in Thoreau's flight from growing urbanization to the primitive beauty of Walden Pond; and in the emphasis on conservation by the federal government that dates from the days of the heroic Theodore Roosevelt. It inspired Congress to establish, on June 28, 1958, the bipartisan Outdoor Recreation Resources Review Commission, of which the chairman was Laurance S. Rockefeller. It reported to President Kennedy on January 31, 1962. In the letter of transmittal accompanying its remarkable report (cited hereafter as the Rockefeller Report) the Commission stated that "the report surveys our country's outdoor recreation resources, measures present and likely demands upon them over the next forty years, and recommends actions to ensure their availability to all Americans of present and future generations." Because of its depth, scope, lucid presentation, and the quality of its recommendations, the Rockefeller Report is a milestone in the history of outdoor recreation in the United States that will influence immeasurably the future of outdoor recreation.

The recommendations of the Commission fall into five categories: (1) a national outdoor recreation policy; (2) guidelines for the management of outdoor recreation resources; (3) expansion, modification, and intensification of present programs to meet increasing needs; (4) establishment of a bureau of outdoor recreation in the federal government; (5) a federal grants-in-aid program to states. A few months after receiving the report, President Kennedy announced the establishment within the Department of Interior of the recommended Bureau of Outdoor Recreation and the appointment of an Outdoor Recreation Advisory Council, which the report also recommended, to provide broad policy guidance for the activities and programs carried out by the Bureau.[25]

After giving a description of the action taken by cities, states, and federal agencies to make outdoor recreation available to the American people, the Rockefeller Report points out that the problem has taken on new dimensions in the twentieth century, particularly in the years since 1920. This is due to a combination of factors, such as the growth of population, the movement of people to the cities, the rise of incomes, and the mobility imparted by the perfected automobile and the completion of a great network of highways. The report remarks that "in their search for opportunities for recreation, urban dwellers now travel across states with the same ease with which they once crossed counties." As a result, large numbers of people now descend suddenly on outdoor recreation areas that are ill-prepared to receive them. The problem facing the country, which public policy has to solve, is stated simply: "There is a striking contrast between the demands for outdoor recreation on the

---

[25]John F. Kennedy, "Our Conservation Program," Message, March 1, 1962 (87th Congress, 2nd session), H doc. 348, p. 3.

part of urban populations and the limited supply of land and water resources readily accessible to them."

According to the Rockefeller Report, the most striking aspect of the supply of outdoor recreational areas is one of paradox. Seemingly, land and water are plentiful for this purpose, for public areas designated for recreation equal one-eighth of the land in the country. The difficulty arises not from the number of acres available, but from the number of effective acres (i.e., acres available to the public suitable for recreation). Either because of their location or because of administrative procedures governing their usage, recreation areas are not presently fully utilized. Few are sufficiently near the metropolitan areas, where more people live, for an outing on the weekend. In fact, much of the land set aside for recreational areas is in Alaska and the American West, while a large percentage of the potential users is in the East, especially the Northeast, which is fast becoming one long urban ribbon of dense settlement. Interest is everywhere. Management practices also affect the use made of the recreational areas. For example, if a given area were transferred from what is called a low-density use emphasizing natural environment to high-density use (mass use) emphasizing facilities, more recreation opportunities would be made available. The federal government manages most of the recreational areas—84 percent as against 14 percent for the states and 2 percent for local governments. The Fish and Wildlife Service manages on the federal level the largest number of acres, though the forest agencies surpass it if acres at both the federal and state levels are considered. The highway and fish and game agencies lead among the state agencies.

It is estimated in the Rockefeller Report that about 90 percent of American adults engage in some type of outdoor physical activity during the course of a year. In all segments of American society an interest exists in the outdoors. Studies show that the most popular activities are pleasure driving, walking, playing games, swimming, sightseeing, bicycling, fishing, attending outdoor sports events, and picnicking. Smaller numbers engage in sports requiring special skills or equipment such as skiing, mountain climbing, skindiving, and sailing.

Many more outdoor recreation areas are needed to meet anticipated needs. Most in demand are attractive paths for walking, bicycling, and horseback riding, along with swimming areas, and picnic sites. In the next two decades the federal government plans to increase swimming areas by 70 percent, picnic areas by 37 percent, camp grounds by 55 percent, and winter sports areas by 36 percent. Within the United States there are 95,000 square miles of inland fresh waters—an amount equal to the state of Oregon. But the demand for inland waters, if stated in terms of only fishing interests, will require a 50 percent increase by 1976 and a 150 percent increase by the end of the twentieth century. It can be met by creating artificial water areas, by improving existing waters, and by making greater use of salt-water areas. The planning will fall to the Bureau of Outdoor Recreation.

A key recommendation of the Rockefeller Report, one that has already been carried out, was the establishment of a Bureau of Outdoor Recreation. Its responsibility, the report ran, "should be to consider the needs of the American people for all phases of outdoor recreation—within cities, in rural areas, and throughout the country." It was considered necessary because there are in existence more than twenty federal agencies concerned with some phase of outdoor recreation, and a similar pattern exists on the state level. The need was evident for overall national direction, which the Bureau is to supply. The Bureau has six major functions: (1) the coordination of related federal programs; (2) stimulation and provision of assistance in state planning; (3) the administration of grants-in-aid; (4) the sponsorship and conduct of research; (5) the encouragement of interstate and regional cooperation; and (6) the formulation of a nationwide recreation plan. These are self-explanatory; and, if the Bureau functions as its sponsors hope, it will have the broad responsibility for averting what could otherwise be a crisis in outdoor recreation later in the century. It is to receive broad policy guidance from a Recreation Advisory Council, which has already been appointed. Members of the latter include the Secretaries of Interior, Agriculture, and Defense, with the Secretary of Interior as chairman. The aim of setting up such a council is to ensure that outdoor recreation policy and planning receive attention at a high level of government and to promote cooperation among the departments that have important responsibilities for the management and development of resources that have major values for outdoor recreation. Other departments and agencies of the government will be invited to participate on an *ad hoc* basis when the Council considers matters within their purview.

RECREATION TODAY

American society, equipped with abundant leisure, places a new value on recreation. An efficient economy makes work from sunup until sundown no longer necessary, and the leisure of an affluent society has produced a surge in recreation so extensive that the era has been named the "Golden Age of Sport." Groups of all ages and incomes seek recreational opportunities and skills, and both industry and government at all levels have provided their services. According to the Rockefeller Report, Americans are turning to outdoor recreation as never before, and their activity foreshadows a coming tidal wave. More people want to be more active; both time and money are available, and by the year 2000 the demand for outdoor recreation will have tripled. The forces at work expanding the demand for outdoor recreation will have the same effect on the field of recreation, generally; and a memorable passage in the

Rockefeller Report commenting on the variety of outdoor recreation activities and the values forthcoming from them applies in many ways to the whole field of recreation. "If the magnitude of outdoor recreation in America is great," ran the report, "so too is its variety. Some swim on, and others under, water. Some walk on the surface of the earth or dig for archelogical relics, while others descend into caves or go aloft in gliders or planes. Some go camping for silence and isolation. Others seek out campsites where they can be with other people. This variety reflects the values which Americans seek from outdoor recreation—sociability as well as solitude, the serenity of the forest and the excitement of physical activity on the water."[26]

RECREATIONAL SPORTS PROGRAMS

Running through organized recreation like a major stream at floodtime pouring into a sheltered lake, recreational sports seem at times almost to overwhelm the spectrum of leisure-time activities found in organized recreation today. Undeniably they impart to organized recreation its dominant tone and theme. But the dominant position achieved by the recreational sports program did not come all at once, and it is desirable now to turn to its historical evolution. For a list of receational sports, see the Appendix of this book.

DISCUSSION QUESTIONS

1. What is meant by the statement "The U.S.A. is now a post-industrial society"?

2. How has the development of a post-industrial society shaped present-day cities and suburbs? What are the implications of these social and economic developments for recreational sports programs?

3. Why did the Rockefeller Report recommend the establishment of a Bureau of Outdoor Recreation and what are the functions of this Bureau?

4. What trends may be anticipated in recreation during the remainder of the twentieth century?

[26]Outdoor Recreation Resources Review Commission, *Outdoor Recreation for America: A Report to the President and to the Congress* (Washington, D.C.: U.S. Government Printing Office, January 1962), p. 25.

5. Distinguish between "leisure" and "recreation." What differing views exist?

6. Is leisure a dynamic force in the American way of life? Explain your answer.

7. Sebastian de Grazia believes that "the great and touted gains in free time since the 1850's . . . are largely myth." What is the basis of this belief? Is there contrary evidence?

8. Define "cybernation." What good effects may be forthcoming as it spreads? What potentially harmful effects?

9. What are the educational values of recreation? Are these found in recreation outside the schools and colleges? Why or why not?

10. What contribution may recreation make to physical and mental health?

BIBLIOGRAPHY

DEANE, PHYLISS, *The First Industrial Revolution.* Cambridge: Cambridge University Press, 1965, reprinted 1967.

DE GRAZIA, SEBASTIAN, *Of Time, Work, and Leisure.* New York: Doubleday and Company, Inc., 1964. This was originally published in 1962 by The Twentieth Century Fund, Inc.

KAHN, HERMAN, *The Next 200 Years.* New York: William Morrow & Co., Inc., 1976.

KAPLAN, SAMUEL, *The Dream Deferred: People, Politics and Planning in Suburbia.* New York: Seabury Press, 1976.

KRAUS, RICHARD G., AND BARBARA J. BATES, *Recreation Leadership and Supervision.* Philadelphia: W. B. Saunders Co., 1975.

"Leisure Today—The Leisure Revolution: Its Impact on Culture," *Journal of Health Physical Education and Recreation* (October 1976), a special editorial insert, pp. 1-31.

"Leisure Today: The Concept of Life Style," *Journal of Health, Physical Education, Recreation* (November-December 1974), a special editorial insert.

MICHAEL, DONALD N., *Cybernation: The Silent Conquest.* Santa Barbara, Calif.: Center for the Study of Democratic Institutions, 1962.

MICHENER, JAMES A., *Sports in America.* New York: Random House, 1976.

OUTDOOR RECREATION RESOURCES REVIEW COMMISSION, *Outdoor Recreation for America: A Report to the President and the Congress.* Washington, D.C.: U.S. Government Printing Office, January 1962. This is the Rockefeller Report.

RAWSON, WYATT, TRANS., GEORGE FRIEDMANN, *The Anatomy of Work: Labor, Leisure and the Implications of Automation.* New York: The Free Press of Glencoe, Inc., 1961.

ROCKEFELLER, JOHN D. 3rd, *The Second American Revolution.* New York: Harper & Row Publishers, 1973.

SNOW, C.P., *The Two Cultures: And a Second Look.* Cambridge: Cambridge University Press, 1965.

STALEY, EDWIN JR., AND NORMAN P. MILLER, *Leisure and the Quality of Life.* Washington, D.C., American Association for Health, Physical Education and Recreation, 1972.

WEISKOPF, DONALD C., *A Guide to Recreation and Leisure.* Boston: Allyn & Bacon, Inc., 1975.

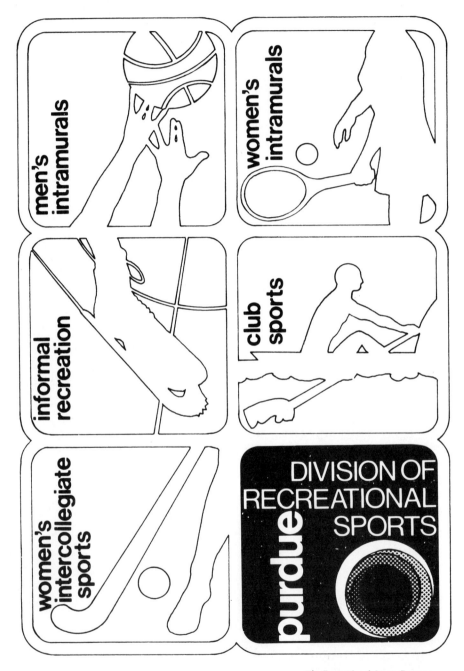

The Recreational Sports Program.
Purdue University: Division of Recreational Sports. Courtesy of George W. Haniford.

2

The Evolution of the
Recreational Sports Program

From the converging of two streams—physical education and organized recreation—has come the recreational sports programs of American schools, colleges, and communities. Though much of recreation is also a part of physical education and much of physical education is recreation, each field, as a whole, differs from the other in important ways. Indigenous to both, however, is participation in sports and games as a wholesome and constructive leisure-time pursuit that contains values for the all-around development of the human personality.

Traditionally, voluntary programs of physical education have been viewed as consisting of physical education activity classes; recreational sports; intramural sports; and varsity athletics. Participation in recreational sports takes place when students voluntarily engage in activities as leisure pursuits without the competition necessarily being organized into a formal program. Varsity athletics, on the other hand, are highly organized but participation is limited to the gifted few. In that the recreational sports program provides organized competition and recreational sports activity for the mass of students, it is, in important ways, different from physical education and varsity athletics. Administration of programs of recreational sports should be in the hands of a professional staff, who provide facilities and equipment, officials, and supervision. The provision of facilities and equipment means making available handball and squash courts, archery ranges, bowling alleys, golf courses, swimming pools, volleyball and softball areas, etc. In recent years voluntary programs have been enlarged to include co-recreational activities, sports clubs, extramurals, and school-community recreation.

The evolution of recreational sports programs is directly related to the rise of organized recreation, a term that encompasses more than sports and games associated with physical education. Thus John L. Hutchinson defines recreation as "a worthwhile, socially accepted leisure experience that provides immediate and inherent satisfactions to the individual who voluntarily participates in an activity."[1] The following categories of activities, in the view of the National Recreation Association, form the core of the well-balanced recreation program: sports and games, dance and drama, arts and crafts, reading and writing, music, hobbies, special events, social recreation, and outdoor recreation.

RECREATIONAL SPORTS ON THE COLONIAL FRONTIER

Long in the making, recreational sports programs are the products of the American past. Indeed, recreational sports have always been woven into the fabric of American society. Even though the forbidding nature of the colonial frontier placed obvious obstacles in the way of engaging in recreational activities, the early routine of the settlers fostered the sense of competition that is associated today with recreational sports. Competition formed part of their daily activity in securing food, clothing, shelter, and protection in the face of the hostile environment of an often inhospitable continent.

The struggle for survival compelled the early settler to choose between the necessities of life and the pursuit of leisure and purely recreational sports; and it was the former that won in this period. Other obstacles to the early development of recreational sports programs are attributable to the Calvinist or Puritan ethic that frowned on play as a mischief-breeding idleness and extolled the moral and ethical values of labor at the expense of play and recreation. The rise and spread of these programs depended on very different prevailing assumptions.

Yet one should not overemphasize the lack of recreation in colonial America. The early settlers were an active people, who enjoyed much of the work required in making a new way of life. Fishing and hunting to provide food for the family appear in early accounts as "a pleasure in the life of the pioneer settler." Considerable enjoyment also flowed from racing events, water sports, skiing and skating, snowshoeing, horseback riding, and logrolling. Then, too, simpler pleasures often accrued as by-products of barn raising, husking bees, quilting parties, and transportation activities.

Gradually the settlers organized the recreational sports that formed part of their European heritage, although these activities were not usually legally sanctioned in the local communities. Bull and bear baiting, cock fighting, trap hunting, wrestling and boxing, tests of strength and physical skill, and horse racing—all of these occupied many hours of the early settlers' time.

[1]John L. Hutchinson, *Principles of Recreation* (New York: A. S. Barnes and Company, 1949), p. 2.

THE SECOND CENTURY OF SETTLEMENT

As pioneer settlements evolved into the towns of the eighteenth century, the climate of opinion slowly became more favorable toward leisure and recreation. Yet a working day that lasted from daylight to dark meant that most recreational activities would continue, of necessity, to form part of the daily routine. The Puritan condemnation of leisure found important strongholds in the schools and colleges, where authorities seem to have expected students to shun pleasurable activity. As late as 1771, President Wheelock of Dartmouth warned against engaging in idle diversion: students must use their leisure hours from study in the "practice of some manual arts, or cultivation of gardens and other lands." It could be said that agricultural and mechanical labor were the accepted leisure-time pursuits for students. The same distrust of recreation pervaded a determined statement of the Methodist College in Maryland. It asserted grimly that "the Methodists have wisely banished every species of play from their colleges."

RECREATION FACILITIES AND SPORTS CLUBS

As late as the first decades of the nineteenth century, recreational sports struggled to progress in the face of suspicion and hostility. By that time progress was slowly being made in the construction of recreation facilities and in the organization of sports clubs. In the two decades between 1820 and 1840 a small number of outdoor gymnasiums were opened in schools and colleges to provide organized recreation programs for students. This forward step, largely the result of the German influence, had the effect of publicizing German gymnastics and, likewise, the early American programs of physical education. Many leaders in the field of sport believe that the movement of organized school and college athletics and recreational sports and games programs is directly attributable to the arrival of German gymnastics in the United States. As a result of German gymnastics an outdoor gymnasium was built in 1821 at the Latin School in Salem, Massachusetts; and in the same decade gymnasiums were built at the Round Hill School in Northampton, Massachusetts, and at Harvard, Yale, Bowdoin, Amherst, and Brown.

Sports clubs were being organized at about the same time. The Cincinnati Angling Club was formed in 1830, and many cities had such clubs by the middle of the century. A year after the formation of the Cincinnati Angling Club, a Sportsman's Club in the same city organized shooting matches for wild pigeons. The Yacht Club of New York, established in 1844, scheduled annual regattas; a year later the Knickerbocker Baseball Club was organized; and in the following decade the National Association of Baseball Players was formed. And so it went.

The beneficiaries of these advances were men. By the late nineteenth century, however, recognition of the woman's need for organized physical activity was gaining ground.

WOMEN'S EARLY PARTICIPATION IN PHYSICAL ACTIVITY

Although physical education, exercises, and dances for women were introduced in eighteenth-century America, it was only in the late nineteenth century that participation in physical activity by girls and women won social acceptance. Their emancipation for exercise and activity was due to the expanding educational system and the influence of the Industrial Revolution. Proclaimed needs for the protection and improvement of health gained popular support and justified the physical-activity-for-women movement. A worthy cause, it came at a time when women were advancing demands generally for more rights; it also paved the way for women attracted to recreational activity by personal interest. Leaders of the women's physical education and recreation programs included Catherine Beecher of Hartford Female Seminary, Helen C. Putnam of Vassar, Dr. Delphine Hanna of Oberlin, Senda Berenson of Smith, Elizabeth Burchenal of New York, Elizabeth Bates of Brown University, Blanche Trilling of the University of Wisconsin, Winifred E. Tilden of Iowa State College, and Maude Cleveland of the University of California.

There were numerous signs of the new interest in physical activity for girls and women. By 1890 public opinion supported public gymnasiums for women, and most women's colleges provided the necessary facilities. Co-recreation was the rule in large cities, and physical education was not uncommon. At first, gymnastics dominated the programs; but the dance, an improved balance of activities, and athletics soon began to gain in influence. Sometimes both gymnastics and a variety of sports formed part of the physical education programs in women's colleges. By 1902 women were forming clubs for such popular activities as bicycling, walking, tennis, and boating. Bryn Mawr, by uniting the various sports clubs into one organization, instituted the first women's athletic association. Later, high school Girls Athletic Associations (GAAs), patterned after the college model, gained organizational strength in the formation of state leagues.

RECREATIONAL SPORTS IN SCHOOLS AND COLLEGES

The lead in the rise of recreational sports was taken, not by the schools and colleges, but by the students themselves. Although the students participated in the sports that became popular in local communities, education authorities refused steadfastly to include recreational sports in their educational programs. Wherever physical education programs were required, the activities were usually formal in nature with a heavy concentration on gymnastics. Two of the best-known of such programs are associated with the work of Edward Hitchock and Dudley A. Sargent in Massachusetts. The nineteenth century saw considerable success attained with German and Swedish gymnastics and the American versions of formal activity programs, even though the students displayed little interest in these activities. Yet advancements were made in school recreational sports in this period by the vacation school and the settlement house. The vacation schools that were organized because of the long vacation periods stressed in their curricula both practical subjects and play, the latter usually consisting of a variety of English sports and games. And the settlement houses, organized along the lines of Jane Addams' famous Hull House in Chicago, provided a diversified program of education, recreational sports and games, and welfare services.

THE BATTLE OF THE SYSTEMS

The late nineteenth century was distinguished by the Battle of the Systems, a term that refers to the competition for supremacy among the various programs of physical education. The main contenders were the German and Swedish gymnastics, the Hitchcock and Sargent programs of physical education, and the spirited English sports and games. It was the contention of school and college administrators that a formal system of gymnastics and physical education contributed to sound educational principles, whereas the English sports and games still suffered from the stigma attached to them as a result of the earlier Puritan distrust of leisure and recreation.

The rivalry engendered among the competing systems of physical education led to the now famous Boston Conference of 1889, which enabled leaders in physical education to compare their systems to learn whether agreement was possible on the type of program that schools and colleges should adopt. No agreement, in fact, was reached. The more neutral leaders present concluded that each system had merit, although each was marred by weaknesses; and no advocates at all were present for the student-preferred sports and games. The Battle of the Systems continued into the twentieth century until the English sports and games program was declared the winner.

THE RISE OF INTRAMURAL SPORTS

It has been seen that the formal programs of physical education, largely gymnastic in nature, were the programs in the schools and colleges, even though the students themselves universally preferred the English sports and games. The refusal of educational authorities to include the latter in the curriculum compelled the students to organize their own recreational sports activities outside formal channels. By forming their own teams and engaging in competition within the confines of the institution, they made the early programs of competitive sports largely intramural in nature. Thus, the early competitive sports activities were actually early programs of intramural sports. A student with a special interest in a sport joined the appropriate sports club for that activity, which was similar to the English university sports club. As the pattern of organization improved, the students planned the competition among the four college classes. Managers were chosen, leagues were formed, and the competition usually ended with a campus champion.

The beginnings of intramural activities in the colleges may be seen from the following events. In 1859 Yale University formed intramural boating clubs that later evolved into interclass crews; in 1865 Princeton formed intramural baseball teams, and within a decade numerous East Coast Colleges had similar teams. Intramural track and field competition also started at Princeton, largely as a result of the Scottish Caledonian Games. These early intramural activities flourished through the perseverance of the students. The school officials gave little support and, in fact, frequently voiced strong opposition on religious, moral, and ethical grounds. Several college presidents stated the view that such activity was ungentlemanly and certainly unhealthy.

Important changes took place in the early years of the twentieth century when student control of the intramural sports program was strongest. The class unit, which was predominant in the early growth of intramural sports, first encountered and then succumbed to the competition of the Greek letter societies, which provided a more permanent structure for intramural competition than the class units. The rapid expansion of the intramural sports movement raised questions, however, about continued control by the students, especially in view of the fact that they used mainly the same facilities and equipment as the intercollegiate teams.

EARLY DEVELOPMENTS IN INTRAMURAL SPORTS

The expansion of intramural sports programs in the first two decades of the twentieth century made it evident that the administrative control of the program would need to rest with a member of the faculty if satisfactory results were to be obtained. This took the form of a permanent faculty member in 1913 when both the University of Michigan and Ohio State University created the first departments of intramural sports under faculty direction. A few years later the University of Illinois and the University of Texas created similar departments; and by 1916 some 140 institutions had intramural programs. The director was assigned the administrative and supervisory duties for a program of competitive sports that would meet the needs and interests of the student body. As the directors of the early departments gained a broad perspective on their duties and responsibilities, they worked through intramural committees and intramural boards and councils to ensure a comprehensive program of activities that included such competitive recreational sports as baseball, basketball, football, swimming, handball, tennis, and track and field.

INTRAMURAL TERMINOLOGY

According to Elmer D. Mitchell, illustrious pioneer in the intramural sports movement, the term "intramural" was first used by Professor A. S. Whitney of the University of Michigan. When the Department of Intramural Athletics was created at the University of Michigan in 1913, Professor Whitney, who was Dean of the School of Education and a member of the Faculty Athletic Committee, was largely responsible for the title. Even though the word "intramural" had been used previously, it was the first time that a special department bearing this word in its title had been organized with a faculty member designated as responsible for organizing the recreational activities of the student body.

Originally the word "intramural" was two words. *Intra,* the Latin word meaning within, and *muralis,* the Latin word meaning wall, were combined to form intramural. The word was used variously to indicate a program of competitive and recreational sports organized and played by students within an institution. In the early period of intramurals it was common to see the following terms used: "intramural athletics" (as in the department title at Michigan), "intramural sports," and "intramural activities." The students disliked the double name, and administrators of the program found it unduly expensive to letter the awards. Ohio State University solved the problem by utilizing the single word "intramurals" for the name of its program. Intramurals quickly won the favor of students, faculties, and administrators and spread throughout the country.

A surge forward in school and college intramural and varsity athletics followed World War I. Many more intramural departments were established in the colleges, and by 1925 the high schools were starting intramural programs, although this movement gathered real momentum only after 1930. With the emphasis placed upon participation in recreational sports for the entire student body, many leaders judged the program by the number of students who participated. Gradually it was realized that the quality of the program was of primary importance, since the key factor was the educational values gained by each student participant.

Leaders of the intramural movement were essentially in agreement that intramural competition should be a voluntary and enjoyable form of recreation in the form of competitive activities that bring refreshment and satisfaction to the participant during his leisure hours. They concluded that, to be most effective, the intramural program should be a voluntary laboratory for the required program of physical education with the same relationship as the glee club and orchestra to the music department or the school paper and debating team to the English department. Directors of intramural programs were also becoming aware of the need for physical and medical examinations and more prone to stress a safe level of physical conditioning, especially in such vigorous activities as football, swimming, boxing, and racing events.

STANDARDS IN THE INTRAMURAL SPORTS PROGRAM

The setting of standards in the intramural sports program has progressed rapidly since the close of World War I. The colleges in the Western Conference have met annually since 1920 to formulate policies and programs. Professional associations have been active. The College Physical Education Association created an intramural sports section at its annual meeting in 1933, and five years later the division of Men's Athletics of the American Association for Health, Physical Education and Recreation set up an intramural athletic section.

A high point in the historical development of intramural sports was reached in 1950 when the National Intramural Association was formed. Its stated objectives are (a) to promote and encourage intramural and recreational programs; (b) to meet annually for professional growth; (c) to serve as a medium for the publication of research papers of both members and nonmembers; and (d) to work in close cooperation with the American Association for Health, Physical Education and Recreation; the National College Physical Education Association; the National Recreation Association; the American Recreation Society; and the National Education Association. Slow in developing, the National Intramural Association by the early 1960s had forged to the front, and included as active members many of the leaders in the field of intramurals.

GIRLS AND WOMEN IN SPORTS AND RECREATION

The history of sports and recreation for girls and women in the late nineteenth and early twentieth century has its own distinctive flavor. Their participation in physical activity ran a troubled course until a national leadership arose that could direct the programs of physical education into valuable acceptable channels. Unfortunately, these programs at first tended to follow the example set by men's varsity sports, though a strong current of opinion in support of intramurals soon arose among women leaders trained in the field. Nevertheless, in the early years winning a contest and developing the exceptionally skilled athlete became the overriding aims of participation, and a mannish female was often synonymous with recreation and sports for girls and women. The public reaction was one of cold disapproval and rejection, and participation in competitive sports was condemned as unladylike for females. It was thought that competitive activities made women more aggressive and masculine.

Other problems complicated the picture. Competition between schools made adequate supervision difficult, and this difficulty was compounded when the students handled the organization of sports, as they usually did during these years. Untrained women teachers often had little control over the girls, who traveled by themselves and played other teams at all hours of the night. Frequently there were doubleheaders, and the boys and girls divided the gate receipts. The excesses of the time are revealed in some letters, received in response to a survey of the situation that Gertrude Dudley and Frances A. Kellor made in the period just before the first World War. They stated that:

> these games were characterized by much unfairness and scrapping. Coaches ran up and down the side lines giving instructions, roughness was unchecked, and the players boasted of their ability to trip players and not be seen owing to their baggy suits, or afterwards described mean tricks that had won the game.[2]

The unfavorable publicity resulted in the cessation of intercollegiate athletics for women at Mills, Nevada, and Stanford; and some schools banned interscholastic competition. Leading women physical educators advocated competition between teams within schools rather than between teams of different schools, but social get-togethers or occasional friendly sports contests between pupils of different schools were deemed acceptable if they were supervised by parents or teachers.

THE RISE OF NATIONAL LEADERSHIP

The national leadership so badly needed in physical education and athletics for women was slow in developing. The beginning of efforts to protect and control sports and recreation for women dates from the end of the nineteenth century when Alice Bertha Foster of Oberlin, Senda Berenson, Director of Physical Training at Smith College, Ethel Perrin of Boston Normal School of Gymnastics, and Elizabeth Wright of Radcliffe served as a committee of the American Association for Advancement of Physical Education (later, the American Physical Education Association) to standardize rules in basketball for women. This committee was asked to become permanent, and it subsequently published the first

[2]Gertrude Dudley and Frances A. Kellor, *Athletic Games in the Education of Women* (New York: Henry Holt and Company, 1909), p. 71.

Women's Basketball Guide. In 1917 Dr. Burdick, then president of the American Physical Education Association, responding to proposals for a national committee to standardize, control, and give direction to women's athletics, appointed a standing Committee on Women's Athletics, of which Florence Somers of the Cleveland public schools was chairman.

Other steps were taken. College athletic associations grew in number as a result of increased interest in sports on the part of young women, and their responsibilities expanded beyond physical development to include field days, special athletic programs, and awards, as well as intercollegiate and intramural sports competition. A student group at the University of Wisconsin, deeply interested in women's athletics, organized in 1917 the first meeting of the National Athletic Conference of American College Women. Later, it became the Athletic and Recreation Federation of College Women (ARFCW). From the beginning, it took a firm stand against varsity intercollegiate athletics for women and sought to promote intramural programs and sports opportunities for all. National conferences were to be held every three years, and a subsequent meeting at Indiana University resulted in the adoption of a standardized point system and plans for a national directory and a newsletter.

As professional organizations grew stronger, opposition to domination of the sports for women by untrained individuals grew rapidly. Women physical educators stressed the differences in problems found in the boys' and girls' programs, and they advocated activities interesting to all girls, desirable from the viewpoint of health and recreation, and suitable for women's athletic ability. They recommended policies that promoted sports for their own sake, athletics suitable for girls that were not merely imitative of the programs for boys, competition within schools, team competition as opposed to individual, and the direction of athletics by women trained in the new profession. By 1920 the activities for women were being influenced by the Women's Athletic Committee of the American Physical Education Association, the Association of Directors of Physical Education for College Women, the National Athletic Conference of American College Women, and the State Leagues. Interschool athletics were being deemphasized in favor of a broader program of intramural activities, and a concerted effort was being made to stress the educational aspects of sport and to rescue athletics for women from the blight of commercialism.

THE WOMEN'S DIVISION OF THE AAHPER

The formation of the Women's Division of the American Association for Health, Physical Education and Recreation (AAHPER) was the result of a somewhat complicated procedure that may be briefly narrated. It began when the Women's Athletic Committee, responding to the pressures of the AAU and other groups, decided to seek sectional status in the American Physical Education Association as a means of asserting stronger leadership. In 1927 it became unofficially the Women's Athletic Section of the American Physical Education Association, the original committee being retained as an Executive Committee. Promising professional results were soon forthcoming. An Athletic and Rules Editorial Committee, functioning through work groups in the various sports, studied the rules and regulations of sports and games, published these, and acted as spokespersons for participants in sports and games. A Track and Field Committee developed a list of tentatively approved track and field events, and rules were standardized in basketball, hockey, swimming, and soccer. A Committee on Volleyball and the National Officials Rating Committee were added in 1929.

By 1937 another important administrative change had taken place, to be followed, twenty years later, by the formation of the Women's Division of the AAHPER. In 1937 the American Physical Education Association was reorganized as the American Association for Health, Physical Education and Recreation and affiliated with the National Education Association. At this time the Women's Athletic Section became an official part of the AAHPER, and it was known thereafter as the National Section for Girls' and Women's Sports (NSGWS). In 1950 a consultant in Physical Education and Women's Athletics was added to the Washington office of the AAHPER; and seven years later, in 1957, the NSGWS attained formal division status in the AAHPER and adopted the name Division for Girls' and Women's Sports (DGWS).

A major aim of the DGWS, from its inception, has been the formulation of guiding principles and aims for administrators, leaders, officials, and players responsible for women's intramural and recreation programs. A Standards Committee was appointed to initiate action, and a monograph was published in 1937 under the title *Standards in Athletics for Girls and Women.* It appeared in digest form two years later, and a revision was published in 1940. A second work, entitled *Desirable Practices in Athletics for Girls and Women* (1941), received wide distribution through the efforts of the American Association for Health, Physical Education and Recreation. Another helpful step was the publication of official guidebooks with approved rules for women in the various sports. The first rules committee was concerned with the standardization of basketball rules. Additional articles, as these were developed, were included in the guides over the years. In October of 1947, work was started on the formulation of statements of "desirable practices" and standards for specific sports, which were to be included in the sports guide. Items discussed as basic to desirable practices were as follows:

Women coaches and officials	Scholarships not awarded on athletic ability alone
National section policies	
Rated officials	Required medical examinations
Coaches' responsibility for developing good sportsmanship	College-level competition only
	Alternating games at home and away
Precedence of academic standards over sports demands	Encouragement of junior varsity games
No gate receipts	

The standards committee continued work, until by 1951 standards for all sports had been published in the guidebooks. A section on the Women's National Officials Rating Committee (WNORC) was also included, and the guides have continued to expand.

Today, each guide contains (1) a section on the Division of Girls' and Women's Sports which includes standards, personnel of the Executive Council, Sports Guides and Official Rules Committee, and State DGWS chairman; (2) committees working on particular problems related to a given sport; (3) feature articles relative to the sport; (4) an officiating section which includes personnel of the WNORC, standards, procedures for establishing boards, sources of information, and techniques of officiating; (5) standards and rules of the sport.

Women leaders of sports and recreation for girls and women continued to provide services in the tradition established in the nineteenth century of promoting and making possible the educational values of sports participation for all girls and women. The DGWS, as the spokesperson for women leaders, implements the mottos that over the years have been so closely associated with the efforts of the Division. "The game is for the good of those who play," "Play for play's sake," and "A sport for every girl and every girl in a sport." Services and leadership are directed toward the unskilled, the average, and the highly skilled.

In recent years leadership efforts have centered on cooperative working and planning with related recreation and sports organizations. One result has been expanded efforts to interpret the philosophy and purpose of the Division of Girls' and Women's Sports. At the same time, changing needs have been reflected in growing demands to provide greater opportunities for more highly skilled sportswomen and girls. Standards for extramural sports have been developed by the Extramural Sports Committee of the DGWS so as to provide leadership guidance, promote the welfare of participants, and increase the opportunities for challenging competition on the college level. The Athletic and Recreation Federation of College Women and a new consultant for the National Girls' Athletic Associations provide services for leaders of the school and college recreation programs for women. All in all, it is right to conclude that "no other Division of the AAHPER has had so much direct influence on the actual day-to-day functioning of its members as has the DGWS over the last forty-five years."[3]

But there are critics who contend that, even so, the role of DGWS has been rendered increasingly obsolete by the march of events, and they insist that a new framework and philosophy has to be developed for girls' and women's sports, especially in the area of interscholastic and intercollegiate competition. This was the note struck by Sandra Jean Stutzman and Charles McCullough when they wrote:

> Why have secondary schools decided to place their girls' interscholastic athletic programs in the hands of the various state athletic associations, and

[3]Ellen W. Gerber, Jan Felshin, Pearl Berlin, and Waneen Wyrick, *The American Woman in Sport* (Reading, Mass.: Addison-Wesley Publishing Company, 1974), p. 83.

the national federation of state high school associations? Why have many female athletic administrators renounced the capabilities of DGWS, and joined in the promulgation of state associations and the national federation?

The plunge by DGWS did not happen overnight, but instead occurred from a steady refusal to change a philosophy that no longer satisfied the needs of the girl athletes it was intended to serve. This philosophy contended that there should be complete homogenization of physical education, intramurals, and interscholastics—that the physical education teacher was expected to teach health classes and physical education skills, run the intramural program, and coach whatever 'extramural programs' might exist.[4]

TITLE IX LEGISLATION

A sweeping change in the financing of recreational sports programs for men and women has been introduced by what is known as Title IX legislation. The new federal legislation is so momentous in its implications for the conduct and functioning of recreational sports programs that the specific nature of Title IX legislation will be the subject of an extended and intensive consideration in Chapter 3: "The Recreational Sports Programs in Education."

TWO CONVERGING STREAMS: PHYSICAL EDUCATION AND ORGANIZED RECREATION

An understanding of the developments in the recreational sports programs in present-day schools, colleges, and communities is best attained by viewing the programs in relationship to organized recreation as it has evolved on the American scene. The foundations of recreation as a professional movement were laid in the late nineteenth and early twentieth centuries, and by the late 1920s and the early 1930s recreation was having a direct impact upon school, college, and community programs. During this period the intramural sports programs and the school recreation programs were converging in their principles and objectives. As leaders of both programs recognized, it was often difficult to determine where one program stopped and the other began. In the following sections, the developments in organized recreation will be outlined so that school, college, and community recreational sports programs may be seen in the broader context.

THE EMERGENCE OF ORGANIZED RECREATION

The recreation movement in the United States has followed the customary pattern of social development. Almost everyone has a need for rec-

---

[4]"Did DGWS Fail? Two Points of View," *Journal of Health, Physical Education, Recreation* (January 1974), p. 6.

reation, and the opportunity for it occurred as the Industrial Revolution changed the pattern of living, bringing urbanization and a shorter workweek, and thus creating a leisure for many in a fashion hitherto unknown in American society. It was also a period marked by the gradual breakdown of prejudice against play and recreation. Social and economic changes encouraged the growth of playgrounds, recreation centers, physical education programs, and a host of other recreational activities. The unusual expansion of sports activity was the most important and spectacular development in the field of recreation, and this expansion in turn raised a demand for extensive recreational sports facilities and equipment.

The first legislation for the purpose of creating playgrounds came in Brookline, Massachusetts in 1872. But this legislation did not result in the immediate development of playgrounds because the law remained a dead letter. Actually, the American playground movement originated in Boston in 1885 at the Children's Mission on Parmenter Street. A playground was built there after Dr. Marie Zakrquewska observed sand gardens in operation in Berlin and persuaded the Massachusetts Emergency and Hygiene Association to construct a large sandpile at the Children's Mission. So successful was the experiment that ten centers were in operation by 1887. Seven years later the sand gardens had officially evolved into playgrounds, and by 1901 they were being financed by school boards. The Boston experiment in turn had an important effect upon the opening of playground centers in cities throughout the country.

The recreation movement expanded. In 1898, the facilities of a public school in New York City were opened for recreational activities in the evening, and by 1907, twenty-six New York City schools were available in the evening hours as recreation centers. Three of them had recreational sports programs organized for the students, and during after-school hours these schools maintained the beginnings of a school-community recreation program. The New York City plan soon spread to Rochester, New York, where Edward G. Ward in 1907 supervised the opening of a public school building for school-community recreation. An intramural basketball league was formed among the school students with most of the games being played in the evening. The resulting Rochester plan, as it may be called, emphasized the central importance of "a social and civic center" to promote the use of school plants for community recreation programs. A National Community Center Association was organized to promote these school-community programs, and soon recreation directors across the country were trying to obtain school facilities and equipment for the programs.

One of the most significant events in the recreation movement occurred in April 1906, when a three-day meeting was held in Washington, D.C., to consider the recreational needs of children, especially in large cities. President Theodore Roosevelt gave his support and arranged for one meeting to be held at the White House. Out of this series of meetings grew the Playground Association of America. One of the basic beliefs of this new organization was the need for expanded recreational facilities and equipment in the schools of the large cities. This interest in school recreation was an important factor in helping the new organization to secure financial aid from the Russell Sage Foundation.

Joseph Lee, known as the father of the playground movement, became president of the Playground Association of America in 1910. He advocated a much broader interpretation of recreation. To him, recreation was worthwhile, constructive, and essential in the life of people of all ages; play and recreation were more than a concern for children and youth in the United States. Joseph Lee considered play to be the essence of recreation and a necessity in that it affords an outlet for stored-up energy and emotions, leads to worthwhile forms of leisure-time activities, provides an opportunity to become engrossed in activity and offers a respite from daily work, and releases a dynamic force that energizes the individual to constructive action. The Playground Association of America supported Lee's belief that recreation must be a part of the life of all people in the form of activities that are constructive, purposeful, worthwhile and enjoyable, and which lead to the fulfillment of desires through appropriate recreational activities that fit the needs of the individual.

A NATIONAL RECREATION ASSOCIATION

In 1911 the Playground Association of America was reorganized, taking the title Playground and Recreation Association of America; in 1930 it acquired the title of National Recreation Association. An important example of the influence of this new organization may be seen in the action taken by the National Education Association in 1911 when it sponsored a resolution to use school buildings as recreation centers following the close of the formal school day. A survey taken in 1917 showed that over 600 cities supported school recreation centers and many school boards were requiring special recreational sports facilities to be included in new buildings. This action by the National Education Association was the beginning of a sound and fruitful relationship among education, physical education, and recreation, and played an invaluable part in the development of school, college, and community recreational sports programs. In fact, the very next year (1918), a landmark in the history of intramural and recreational programs was established when the National Education Association listed the worthy use of leisure time as one of the seven cardinal objectives of education. This objective is the primary concern of present-day leaders in recreational sports programs.

The 1920s brought rapid changes in the intramural and recreation programs. In what proved to be an unprecedented period of leisure and prosperity, the scope of recreation continued to expand; and the American public itself attached a greater importance than ever before to constructive leisure-time activities. Both school and community recreation programs took rapid strides forward as the English sports and games became the activities of physical education programs in both high schools and colleges. There was a considerable increase in money spent on recreational facilities and equipment for both indoor and outdoor recreational sports activities.

President Calvin Coolidge summoned a National Conference on Outdoor Recreation in 1924 to call attention to the vast outdoor facilities. In its report, one section stressed the need to merge school recreation programs with community recreation programs, especially in such activities as swimming and waterfront activities, golf, tennis, bowling, and winter sports. The report made it clear that schools and colleges were expected in the future to prepare students better for recreational pursuits during their adult years. It inspired considerable action in the field of recreation. By 1926 the demand for recreation leaders was so extensive that the Playground and Recreation Association established a National Recreation School to train recreation leaders, supervisors, and administrators.

RECREATION IN THE GREAT DEPRESSION

While the late 1920s found recreational sports programs surging forward throughout the country, they were soon to face a national economic catastrophe that would, at first sight, appear to result in the curtailment of all recreational sports programs. In the early years of the Great Depression recreation budgets were slashed, recreation personnel dismissed, and a general feeling was created that play and recreation had no place in the life of the unemployed masses. This dismal prospect abruptly changed, however, because of the intervention of the federal government and leaders in the recreation movement.

The marked alteration in opinion was due largely to the well-known English educator Dr. L. P. Jacks, who toured the United States under the auspices of the National Recreation Association. He contributed importantly to a better understanding of the place of recreation in a country going through the throes of economic collapse. His comments, which received much publicity during the tour, reflected a deep concern for the great numbers of unemployed who had time to spare on their hands; and he repeatedly stressed that the recreational sports facilities of the schools, colleges, and communities should be better utilized in the face of the emergency.

Following Dr. Jack's tour, the New York Leisure-Time Committee of the National Recovery Administration gathered for a three-day hearing in 1933. At each session men like Alfred E. Smith, former governor of New York and an unsuccessful presidential candidate in 1928, and

Newton D. Baker, who had served as Secretary of War during the first World War, expressed anxiety as to how people would make use of their involuntary idleness. Baker suggested that the schools and colleges expand their physical education, intramural, and varsity athletic programs during the day and establish comprehensive school-community recreational sports programs for the evening hours. The Committee's report placed a special emphasis on the urgent need for public planning to help the population at large make constructive use of their overabundant leisure time.

As a result of detailed studies concerning recreation and leisure in the early years of the Great Depression, much keener interest was generated by the middle of the decade in supporting all types of recreation programs. More and more school buildings were opened after the formal school day for school-community and municipal recreational programs, and a number of cities sponsored school-community recreational sports programs during the evening hours. In the Depression years these programs proved to be invaluable in sustaining morale and providing a healthy, constructive, and worthwhile use of leisure time; and it would be difficult to overestimate the value of the lasting impetus thus given to organized recreation. Countless school and community recreational sports programs were saved by federal funds, which were applied essentially to facilities and equipment and the training of sports leaders. By 1937, twelve departments of the federal government were promoting and supporting recreation programs. The Federal Emergency Relief Administration and the National Youth Administration contributed to a financial plan making it possible for many college students to secure part-time employment in recreational sports programs; the effectiveness of the programs themselves was increased and frequently the departments were expanded. By 1938 the federal government had spent over a billion dollars supporting recreational enterprises. At one point the Recreation Division of the Works Progress Administration had some 50,000 people employed for recreation purposes, and the National Youth Administration had approximately the same number. In addition, the Forestry Service, National Park Service, and Department of Agriculture rendered much valuable service to recreational programs.

The example set by the federal government in promoting recreation was emulated by many segments of society. In 1937, the Congress of Industrial Organizations (CIO) established a Department of Recreation; and the American Federation of Labor (AFL) advocated programs of recreation for the masses of unemployed workers. As soon as recreation was recognized as a worthwhile and constructive force in society, even during a severe depression, nearly all types of youth organizations promoted the recreation movement.

Out of the Great Depression came the realization that recreation is vital to the well-being of people from childhood through the adult years, a virtual revolution in thought. Professional leaders in recreation accepted the premise that participants, if they are to benefit from recreation during their leisure hours, must be equipped with the necessary skills; and they pointed to the physical education programs in the schools and colleges as the appropriate means of acquiring these skills. The knowledge and skills thus attained can be used in the recreational sports programs and in community recreation, all of which serve as laboratories for voluntary participation. These programs supplement the academic programs in many ways, notably by giving the opportunity for participants to acquire desirable leadership qualities, attitudes, and social characteristics. To the leaders in recreation it seems obvious that the philosophy of recreation was shaped and molded into an indigenous program for the American people during the Great Depression.

PHYSICAL EDUCATION AND ORGANIZED RECREATION SINCE WORLD WAR II

As the United States struggled during the Depression years with manifold economic and social problems, World War II was generating in Europe. The storm broke in 1939; and two years later, on December 7, 1941, the United States became a belligerent. Recreation leaders were ready with their services, which were coordinated through the well-known United Service Organizations (USO). The latter organized and promoted recreation programs at home and abroad in an infinite variety of ways. Excellent use was made of the intramural sports concept at military bases; elaborate intramural sports programs were organized and carried out at home, on board ship, and on foreign soil. When the war ended in 1945, military leaders agreed that the leaders in intramurals and recreation had performed an invaluable service for their country.

After World War II intramural and recreation programs operated on the solid base that had been constructed during the Depression years. An unprecedented expansion took place in intramural and recreational facilities and equipment with new, modern designs and outdoor lighted facilities. One result of the wartime experience was striking. As returning servicemen and their wives stimulated co-educational activities in the colleges, the younger members of the student body adopted the practice.

In the postwar years the age-old dream of widespread leisure became a reality as the average workweek shortened steadily. Despite all good intentions of using leisure wisely, a large percentage of people seemed not to know how this could best be accomplished. In response to the need, physical education and recreation leaders tried to give leadership, especially in the area of facilities, equipment, and the professional preparation of personnel.

Three national conferences guided the postwar development of intramural and recreation programs when they set up specific standards that gave much-needed direction to the existing programs. The American Association for Health, Physical Education and Recreation sponsored in 1946 a national conference on facilities at Jackson's Mill, West Virginia. The discussions centered on the development of standards and guidelines for gymnasium construction and the planning of recreation areas; and the resulting recommendations were published in the influential *Guide on Planning Facilities for Athletics, Recreation, Physical and Health Education.* Two other national conferences set up standards for the professional preparation of teachers in health, physical education, and recreation: one at Jackson's Mill in 1948; the other at Pere Marquette State Park in 1950.

In recent years, intramurals and recreation programs have profited greatly from the active support of allied organizations which have promoted these programs in schools and colleges. For example, the Athletic Institute sponsored and financed a series of workshops that assembled leaders of the intramural and recreation programs to discuss problems of special concern to schools and colleges. And since the founding of the Federation of National Professional Organizations in 1954, it has displayed special interest in school and college intramural and recreation programs and in their being effectively coordinated.

Examples may be easily multiplied. The Advisory Council of the National Recreation Association gives special attention to the use of school recreation facilities and equipment. The National Recreation Association itself is rendering valuable service in supporting school and college intramural and recreation programs and in sponsoring research studies that will further effective school-community recreational sports programs. In November 1959, a National Conference on School Recreation was held at the headquarters of the National Education Association in Washington, D.C. It was co-sponsored by the United States Office of Education and the American Association for Health, Physical Education and Recreation; and its purpose was to discuss the role of the school in preparing students for the abundant leisure that they will have in the coming years. The delegates present, 125 in number, recognized that leisure was a positive force in American society and recreation a basic human need.

NATIONAL INTRAMURAL ASSOCIATION

The history of the highly influential National Intramural Association (NIA) may properly be said to have begun with its first annual conference at Dillard University, which was held in New Orleans in 1950. This organization arose largely through the efforts and activity of William N. Wasson of Dillard University, who received a Carnegie grant to study intramural programs in black colleges. His study bore fruit when he conceived the idea of a national organization that would center attention upon the problems of organizing and administering intramural programs and on facilities and equipment.

From the early beginnings change was at work. While the first two annual conferences of the National Intramural Association took place in the South and were concerned primarily with blacks in college intramural programs, the meeting rapidly took on a more national orientation and the focus of attention broadened. This appeared when the third annual conference was held at Howard University in Washington, D.C. in 1952. In attendance were white intramural directors and white recreation directors from colleges and communities. At this conference the members officially adopted the title National Intramural and Recreation Association for Men and Women with the title evolving later into National Intramural Association.

Among the many crises facing this new organization was one in particular that was extremely difficult to handle. The American Association for Health, Physical Education and Recreation (AAHPER) —currently titled American Alliance for Health, Physical Education and Recreation—extended an offer for the National Intramural Association to merge with the Intramural Section of the AAHPER. But the membership of the National Intramural Association voted overwhelmingly in favor of remaining a separate national organization. This action was taken at the twelfth annual conference held at Bowling Green State University in 1961. Thus the only national organization devoted exclusively to the advancement of intramurals continued as a national organization.

INTRAMURALS: NOT AN ISLAND UNTO ITSELF

As the National Intramural Association evolved through the years, the leadership became increasingly concerned about the proliferation of recreational sports groups that were arising in schools, colleges, and communities. The questions being asked increasingly were "How can we bring these diverse groups into the mainstream of intramural programs?" and "What is the most appropriate and effective terminology for this comprehensive recreational sports program?" The answers to these questions came closer as the recognition grew that the intramural program was not an isolated entity but rather a program that had to be considered in a larger context. This point of view was expressed by Kenneth H. Renner—Intramural Director at Florida Technological University—at the twenty-fourth annual conference of the National Intramural Association held in 1973 at the University of South Florida. He stated: "Intramurals can no longer be an island in itself, but must intentionally reach out and interact with other programs within the institution and even outside its walls into the community. In the past, our association and its directors have done very little to associate with the AAHPER and NRA and other related organizations which deal with similar programs. Today we're accepting the handshake from others as we find and sense the importance of the relationship. Tomorrow we must not only accept this interaction but be the one to instigate it."[5]

Leaders in the field of recreational sports in schools, colleges, and the community had been searching for a decade to determine the most effective organization, administration, and terminology that would include intramurals, extramurals, sports clubs, sports and games, and general recreational and voluntary recreational sports activities. This need was highlighted at the twenty-fifth annual conference of the National Intramural Association, which was held at Arizona State University in Tempe in 1974. In his "President's Report on the State of the Association in 1974," President R. J. "Ben" McGuire at the close of this address stated: "In closing, I believe we must look to the future and rewrite the objectives of the association and consider a possible name change."[6]

MOMENTUM FOR RECREATIONAL SPORTS

The terminology "recreational sports" had by this time gained a support among the leaders in the several organizations concerned with recreational programs in schools, colleges, and communities that was not to be denied. This can be seen most clearly at the twenty-sixth annual conference of the National Intramural Association, which met appropriately in New Orleans in 1975, exactly a quarter-century after the founding of the association. The momentum that had built up for several years for a change in name became so great that the members attending the twenty-sixth annual conference voted overwhelmingly in favor of a change of name centering upon "recreational sports." The keynote for the change was set by then-president Chuck Schelsky of Oklahoma University. And his words have the further interest of summarizing the steps involved in reaching the momentous decision. He declared: "We will be voting in our business meeting on a constitutional change to alter the name of our association. This topic has been discussed for several years by several of the members and studied at great length and [with] soul searching by your Executive Committee. Various combinations of terms were examined and re-examined. Your Executive Committee will be recommending a change in name for the association. Our reasons behind recommending this name were: 'Recreational Sports' better describes the programs we as individuals are directing and we as an association are serving—there will be sentiment to maintain the word

[5]Edsel Buchanan and Will Holsberry, eds., *24th Annual Conference Proceedings of the National Intramural Association* (N.p.: National Intramural Association, 1973), p. 120.

[6]Will Holsberry, ed., *25th Annual Conference Proceedings of the National Intramural Association* (N.p.: National Intramural Association, 1974) p. 8.

intramural—recreational does include intramural—and sports clubs —and unstructured or free play activities—and extramural."[7]

The detailed statement that explains most fully the reasons for the change in name came, however, from C. E. Mueller of the University of Minnesota, a long-time leader in the field of intramurals, with a national reputation for leadership in this area, and formerly president of the National Intramural Association. His statement is in the form of a position paper supporting the terminology of "recreational sports" that circulated at the conference meeting in New Orleans before the members of the twenty-sixth conference took their historic vote. Mueller's comments are of special interest, not only because of his position of conspicuous leadership in the field of intramurals but also because they explain at length the reasoning that lay back of the members' decision to adopt the terminology of "recreational sports." For these reasons, the Mueller position statement is reproduced below, exactly as it circulated to the members of the National Intramural Association:

> Perhaps N.I.A. members will feel a reluctance to change the name of the Association. Many of us have very fond attachments for the word "intramurals" because of our relationship to it over an extended period of time. Change is always very difficult, particularly when the change involves deeply rooted patterns. At the annual meeting of the Big 10 Intramural Directors, a motion was passed to change the name of the group to the "Big 10 Recreational Sports Directors." This body has been meeting since 1919, and indeed there was some hesitation to bring about this change.
>
> However, I submit that this is a "moment of opportunity" for our profession. In a time of re-examination and retrenchment in many areas of our lives, intramural programming and participation continue to expand in an exciting way. Much of this growth is taking place even with the difficulties of restricted finances and other programming problems.
>
> Traditionally, intramurals has been identified with male dominated participation and programs. Now we are on the threshold of sharing sports experiences among women and men at every level of programming. The Association needs a new image to neutralize "male" intramurals and to endorse and promote women's participation on and in the sports scene. A further point of consideration is that over the years, many of us have had difficulty explaining to people outside of our educational institutions what the term "intramurals" meant, and when the word "extramurals" was also defined, the confusion magnified.
>
> Under the new concept, recreational sports would be defined to include all sports programming at an educational institution, except for those sporting activities that take place within the varsity and physical education programs. The term "recreational sports" would include programs or units identified as intramurals, sports clubs, extramurals, mountain recreation, informal self-directed participation, etc. The recreational sports umbrella provides much greater coverage.

[7]Will Holsberry, ed., *26th Annual Conference Proceedings of the National Intramural-Recreational Sports Association* (N.p.: National Intramural-Recreational Sports Association, 1975), pp. 8-9.

Some may argue that the word "sports" should not be retained, but I submit that recreation is a very broad term that includes, according to some experts, everything that is done in a person's leisure time. There is already an association which oversees the affairs of recreation programs in the name of the National Recreation & Parks Association. By retaining the word "sports," it will identify a phase of the larger recreation spectrum for which intramural personnel are responsible. Although some intramural programs may include activities traditionally not thought of as sports, many of these activities are performed in a sporting manner. Also, retention of the word "sports" will help identify the kinds of responsibilities administered through the present intramural departments, as distinguished from those conducted by student union programs.

The Executive Council has included the term "collegiate" in their proposed name change, but this would impose limitations on the opportunities that are available to our profession. Although it is true that most Association members are collegiate at the present time, the trend is for these kinds of programs to expand—not only within the levels of educational institutions, but also in non-educational institutions. Eliminating the word "collegiate" would put our Association in a better position to serve elementary, junior high, and senior high schools; military, business, industrial, and community recreation programs.

Please keep in mind that adoption of the new name would not require individual departments and programs to change their titles. By adopting the term "National Recreational Sports Association," we will be better able to "serve people thru sports," and we will be in an excellent position to "grow together."[8]

RECREATIONAL SPORTS ACHIEVE NEW STATUS ON THE NATIONAL SCENE

If the statement from Chuck Schelsky set the stage for the decision taken by the twenty-sixth annual conference of the National Intramural Association and the position paper prepared by C. E. Mueller best explains the reasoning of the members of the conference, the final decision itself came in the business meeting of the Conference when the Constitution Committee proposed formally a name change from National Intramural Association to National Collegiate Recreational Sports Association. There were two lines of opposition to this proposal. First, the word "collegiate" did not allow for schools and communities to be properly represented. And secondly, those traditionalists present were opposed to leaving out the word "intramural." Finally, a compromise was reached and the membership at this twenty-sixth annual conference of the National Intramural Association voted overwhelmingly to change the name

[8]C. E. Mueller, "Position Statement for the Proposed Name Change of the National Intramural Association," in Will Holsberry, ed., *N.I.R.S.A. Newsletter* (N.p.: National Intramural-Recreational Sports Association, May-June, 1975), (no paging).

to National Intramural-Recreational Sports Association.[9] The new terminology has exceedingly great significance. Whatever the concession to the traditionalists, "recreational sports" has attained a new status on the national scene with implications for the future of great consequence.

ACCEPTANCE OF THE TITLE "RECREATIONAL SPORTS"

At the twenty-seventh annual conference of the National Intramural-Recreational Sports Association meeting in San Diego in 1976, leaders in the field were in general agreement that the terminology of "recreational sports programs" was being accepted very rapidly throughout the country in schools, colleges, and communities. Recreational sports programs are rapidly becoming inclusive of those recreational sports activities traditionally found in intramurals, extramurals, sports clubs, voluntary physical education sports activities, unstructured recreational sports, and the recreational sports activities of organized community recreation programs.

A statement of cardinal importance on "recreational sports" was presented by Rick Mull of Indiana University in a paper presented at the twenty-sixth annual conference of the National Intramural-Recreational Sports Association in New Orleans in 1975. Mull is currently a leader in this association. His paper is titled "Recreational Sport and the Future." In his presentation, he shows with precision exactly how and why the terminology "recreational sports" is surging to the front to describe recreational sports programs in schools, colleges, and communities. He stated:

> I would like to propose an encompassing phrase that is representative of our broad spectrum, philosophies, objectives, duties and responsibilities. This future term is Recreational Sports. This is a phrase or term that says exactly what we do. Recreational is a term that represents what we do. It encompasses our broad spectrum: intramurals, unstructured activity, extramurals and sports clubs. It indicates activity voluntarily engaged in during leisure and motivated by the personal satisfaction which results from it. It is also a word that means fun, enjoyment, relaxation, and diversion from daily routine. Sports is the limiting word (but in some circles still very broad). It indicates competitive games or play situations requiring varying degrees of physical ability, controlled by boundaries, strategies, rules, regulations and greatly influenced by chance. Combining the two terms, Recreational and Sports, we may define them, at least temporarily, as meaning: varying degrees of competitive structured sport and physical activity for everyone. It becomes apparent that Recreational Sports represents all areas of programming, making us identifiable to those less infomed on campus or in other social settings. The name can be understood, requiring no dictionary

---

[9]"Minutes of the Business Meeting, March 26, 1975," *N.I.R.S.A. Newsletter*, May-June, 1975, n.p. See also the report of the Constitution Committee, of which Kenneth Renner was chairman, in *26th Annual Conference Proceedings*, p. 279.

to get the meaning. Recreational Sports also separates us from the past and present and gives us a good start into the future.[10]

DISCUSSION QUESTIONS

1. Present a comprehensive definition of the following: intramurals; extramurals, sports clubs; physical education; athletics; recreation; and recreational sports programs.

2. Describe the evolution of recreational sports programs in schools, colleges, and communities.

3. Leaders in recreation consider that the philosophy of recreation was shaped and molded into an indigenous program for the American people during the Great Depression. What are their reasons for this conclusion?

4. In what ways have physical education and organized recreation converged?

5. Is there a direct connection between the development of recreational sports in colonial America and the development of recreational sports today?

6. Describe present-day developments and attitudes on competitive sports competition for girls and women.

7. Why did the National Intramural Association change its name to National Intramural-Recreational Sports Association?

BIBLIOGRAPHY

HUTCHINSON, JOHN L., *Principles of Recreation*. New York: A. S. Barnes and Company, 1949.

KRAUS, RICHARD, *Recreation and Leisure in Modern Society*. Englewood Cliffs, N.J.: Prentice-Hall, Inc., 1971.

NATIONAL INTRAMURAL ASSOCIATION, *Annual Conference Proceedings:* Annual Issues for 1971, 1972, 1973, and 1974.

NATIONAL INTRAMURAL-RECREATIONAL SPORTS ASSOCIATION, *Annual Conference Proceedings:* Annual Issues for 1975 and 1976.

NEAL, LARRY L., *The Next Fifty Years: Health, Physical Education, Recreation and Dance*. Eugene, Oregon: University of Oregon Press, 1971.

SIEDENTOP, DARYL, *Physical Education: Introductory Analysis*, 2nd ed. Dubuque, Iowa: Wm. C. Brown Co., Publishers, 1976.

---

[10]Will Holsberry, Ed., *26th Annual Conference Proceedings, of the National Intramural-Recreational Sports Association:* "Recreational Sport and the Future" by Rick Mull, pp. 103-104. National Intramural Recreational Sports Association, 1975.

FINAL TITLE IX

REGULATION IMPLEMENTING

EDUCATION AMENDMENTS

OF 1972

PROHIBITING SEX
DISCRIMINATION
IN EDUCATION

Effective Date: July 21, 1975

U.S. DEPARTMENT OF HEALTH, EDUCATION, AND WELFARE/Office for Civil Rights

Guidelines for Implementing Title IX Legislation.

3

The Recreational Sports
Program in Education

With the year 2000 looming nearer, the population of the United States is undergoing changes that are significant for the shape and content of the recreational sports program. This program includes what have been traditionally designated as intramurals, extramurals, sports clubs, recreation association activities, and unstructured recreational sports activity. Such programs will have to be adapted to the fact that the American population is on the average growing steadily older. By the year 2000, about 80 million Americans will be 19 years old or younger, whereas the age groups older than 19 will number 150 million by the end of the century.

As the population matures, important social change is at work. For example, the endemic violence on the social scene, which so often caught the attention of commentators in the 1960s and 1970s, is likely to recede or at the least reach a plateau if only because the numbers of teenage males will decrease by comparison with the numbers of young adults, middle-aged, and elderly in the population. The effect is bound to be sobering since the conduct of teenagers tends to be more aggressive than that of other goups in the population. Another attendant change is in the makeup of the college and university population, which is likely to be different in cardinal respects from that found in the 1970s. The number of college students in the age group from 18 to 22, it is anticipated, will decline, primarily because new population control techniques (such as birth control and abortion) permit smaller families than in the past; and this decline in the traditional college population will be offset by the enrollment of rising numbers of older adults, women, and part-time students. Larger numbers of people are expected to attend post-graduate institutions.

As the population mix in the colleges and universities, in particular, becomes more diversified, so will educational practice and procedures, the curriculum, and even the physical plants that are utilized for educational purposes. Many Americans, it is thought, will attend school from the age of 3 until they have attained at least the equivalent of two years of college; but their ways of doing so will have a greater flexibility than in the past. They are more likely to move in and out of the educational system as they update their job skills, study for new careers, follow out their interests in art, language skills, music, recreational sports, etc. There may be learning centers in offices, factories, and public buildings. These new possibilities are discussed in an interesting article in the *Wall Street Journal* (*"The Future Revised: Education's Big Boom Is Ending, But Studies to Get More Diverse,"* April 8, 1976), where it is likewise pointed out that the growing demand to cut back the rate at which expenditures are rising is probably going to result in an increased reliance on electronic teaching systems. Television will also supply a means of bringing general education on a larger scale to the public outside the educational stream. Another means of curbing the growth of educational expenditure is to build less expensive structures for housing the school population. With lives of about twenty years, such structures will be built of low-cost fiberglass, and their recreational facilities will be planned in such a way that they can be shared with community recreation departments, company athletic programs, and even private health clubs.

It also appears that the coming generation will see an attempt in the schools and colleges to strengthen the traditional values of American life. This emphasis was apparent in the remarks on the changing educational scene that were forthcoming from Ernest L. Boyer, Chancellor of the State University of New York, in the spring of 1976. First painting with broad strokes the lines of the developing curriculum, he then called attention to the relationship between that curriculum and the values in society. As he said, "there will be more of a connection between what you're studying and the vocation toward which you're pointing but with it will be renewed interest in liberal arts." And he added, "there will be a sharpening of the view that being an educated person has something to do with goodness and values. We're going to have to prepare better for the ethical and moral issues that grow out of our expected vocations" (Cited in the *Wall Street Journal,* April 8, 1976). A similar note was struck by Earl Pullas, Professor of Higher Education at the University of Southern California, who is quoted in the same issue of the *Wall Street Journal* as stating, "It's not enough to produce just knowlegeable or highly trained people. The American people are concerned with the deterioration of integrity. Higher education has abdicated in this area, even though one of its original purposes was to further develop values. We must regrasp that role."

VALUES IN EDUCATION

Learning values, whether on the part of the parents or students, is a complex process that requires continued study and thought from educational leaders. In 1962, the Joint National Conference of the Division for Girls' and Women's Sports and the Division of Men's Athletics at Interlochen, Michigan, examined the development of personal and social value systems. At the conference Seth Arsenian, psychologist and Director of Graduate Studies, Springfield College, summarized several ways of learning values when he asserted: "There are many illustrations of learning: Some learning is conditioning, some learning is identification, some learning is discovery." Another member of the conference stressed the importance of example and learning by identification with individuals in the comment: "If you are going to teach physical education you should exemplify it." The role of respect provided the theme for another speaker. "The verbal discussion of values has a place," he explained, "but only if you and the people with whom you are talking have some sense of mutual respect. It is in this area that the absorption and acceptance of values depends first on their acceptance of you as a person."[1]

That dedicated and exemplary leadership in developing worthy values is crucial was evident in the conference report. Youth, conferees indicated, are quick to recognize and respect sincerity. Stressed also were the dangers to society of a decay in moral and ethical conduct. A. O. Duer, Executive Secretary of the National Association of Intercollegiate Athletics, called attention to alarming breaches of ethical and moral conduct in high governmental places and unethical conduct in business, professional life, and sports which jeopardize the future of the American way of life. For the welfare of the coming generation, youth must develop a worthy set of leisure-time values, but adults must likewise learn the values of recreation participation. The conference members concluded: "If we are to restore high ethical values and habits in American youth, we must change the emphasis of our society, for no program can succeed unless supported by the adult society in which it is being generated."[2]

As early as 1918 the schools were entrusted with the task of developing a worthy set of leisure-time values and given the responsibility of seeing to it that adequate recreation was provided both within the school

[1]Joint National Conference of the Division for Girls' and Women's Sports and the Division of Men's Athletics, *Values in Sports* (Washington, D.C.: American Association for Health, Physical Education and Recreation, 1962), p. 38.

[2]Ibid., p. 72.

and by proper agencies in the community. The key document is the highly influential "Cardinal Principles of Secondary Education," issued by the Commission on the Reorganization of Secondary School Education of the National Education Association. The pertinent paragraph in the "Cardinal Principles" reads as follows:

> Every individual should have a margin of time for the cultivation of personal and social interests. The leisure, if worthily used, will recreate his powers and enlarge and enrich life, thereby making him better able to meet his responsibilities. The unworthy use of leisure impairs health, disrupts home life, lessens vocational efficiency and destroys civic-mindedness. The tendency in industrial life, aided by legislation, is to decrease the working hours of large groups of people. While shortened hours tend to lessen the harmful reactions that arise from prolonged strain, they increase, if possible, the importance of preparations for leisure. In view of these considerations, education for the worthy use of leisure is of increasing importance as an objective.[3]

That the trend set in 1918 has since continued became evident when twenty years later, in 1938, the Educational Policies Commission reformulated the objectives of education. The commission's statements of objectives reiterated the schools' responsibilities for leisure-time pursuits, sports, and recreation skills.[4] These were again supported in 1961 in the publication, *The Central Purpose of Education,* in which it was stated that education assumes the responsibility for helping individuals to develop knowledge, understanding, and capacity to choose worthy leisure-time activities. Its authors concluded that "an adequate physical basis for intellectual life must be assured."[5]

Schools and teachers have two major tasks. The first is the challenge of developing recreational interests and skills on the part of school children. The second is the challenge of developing a sense of leisure-time values. If these tasks can be accomplished, recreation activities can be the means for valuable and enjoyable self-improvement. If not, they can be the means to waste one's free time or to use it in a self-destructive manner. The young people of today need help in planning for present and future free time and in developing a discriminating sense of values with respect to recreation activities.

THE RELATIONSHIPS WITHIN THE TOTAL PHYSICAL EDUCATION PROGRAM

Historically, schools and colleges have attempted to meet educational responsibilities for physical development and leisure-time skills through

---

[3]"Cardinal Principles of Secondary Education," *Report of the Commission on the Reorganization of Secondary Education of the National Education Association* (Washington, D.C.: Department of the Interior, Bureau of Education Bulletin No. 35, 1918), p. 10.

[4]National Education Association, *The Purposes of Education in American Democracy* (Washington, D.C.: The Association, 1938).

[5]Education Policies Commission, *The Central Purpose of American Education* (Washington, D.C.: The National Education Association, 1961), pp. 6–15.

the combined offerings of the physical education department. Physical education has essentially three divisions: (1) the physical education instruction program; (2) the recreational sports program, of which the most important elements are intramurals, extramurals, sports clubs, and unstructured recreational sports activities; and (3) varsity athletics, usually referred to on the college scene as intercollegiate athletics and on the secondary school level as interscholastic athletics. In some schools and colleges intercollegiate or interscholastic athletics, as they have developed in the twentieth century, are viewed as separate from the physical education department; and until the middle of the 1970s they were largely the preserve of male athletes.

The characteristics of the physical education instruction program may be briefly given. Physical education classes are part of an instructional program established to teach physical skills of movement, and sports and games; to develop fitness; and to teach health, safety, and essential information characteristic of physical education. Classes are usually required in the schools but less commonly in the colleges and universities. Some schools require experiences in various sports areas. Others offer activities from which the student elects a program to meet the basic requirement. In a few instances, the program is completely elective. Instruction should be basic to all phases of the broad program of physical education and should consist of a balance of unique learnings valuable to all students.

THE INTRAMURAL PROGRAM

This phase of the physical education program consists of organized recreational sports competition for everyone desiring to participate. It has been described as an extension of the physical education instruction classes and as a laboratory. In recent years the intramural program has become broad in scope. At its best it includes a well-balanced assortment of team games, individual and dual sports, and co-recreational activities, conducted both formally and informally, and open to all students and faculty in the school or college.

The chief difference between men's and women's intramural programs, traditionally, has been in the administrative organization of the faculty-student leadership and in the program emphasis.

In the men's programs, although there are several administrative plans, one intramural staff member usually handles the major administrative and supervisory responsibilities. Students assist in the program, but overall organization is usually planned by a faculty member. Program activities have favored the traditional high school and college sports. The women's program is almost always administered by a student recreation association and a faculty advisor. Other faculty members often assist with the various sports activities, but students dominate the leadership. An intramural chairman or, in some instances, an intramural board, as an organizational component of the Women's Recreation Association, handles the sports competition. Other program activities include informal and social recreation and co-recreation.

EXTRAMURAL SPORTS

The extramural sports have general reference, in both high school and college, to those sports or programs that take place outside the confines or immediate surroundings of the school or college. The term "extramurals," although sometimes used in its broadest connotation to mean all competition outside the school or college, is usually reserved to describe intramural-type activities and programs not primarily concerned with the highest level of skilled players; and it is planned to include competition between two or more schools or colleges.

The extramural program is usually an extension of the intramural program, with few or no eligibility requirements and minimal practice periods. The activities are planned as a day of competition between two or more schools or colleges without gate receipts and with an emphasis on the social as contrasted to a scheduled season of varsity games played before a large spectator audience. The satisfactions are derived from playing one's best with a group of equal ability.

Extramural programs usually provide a higher skill level of competition than do intramural programs. Unlike the varsity program, extramural programs offer a number of planned interschool competitions for a variety of skill levels, including games between second and third teams in addition to those of the championship teams. This arrangement serves as a safeguard against an overemphasis and the possibility of using intramural games to produce champion teams for the extramurals. The extramural program has long been important to girls and women, who have enjoyed playdays, sports days, telegraphic meets, and informal competition between the teams of schools and colleges.

It should be added that historically women's sports competition between schools and colleges, called in men's programs interscholastic and intercollegiate athletics, was usually carried on under the heading of extramurals. And even extramurals, as found in women's programs, functioned under less competitive conditions than existed in men's extramurals. That is, the pervasive philosophy shaping women's programs was for many years much more hostile to the commercial aspects of competition in sports than the ideals governing men's programs. A change set in, however, around the end of the 1960s and at the beginning of the 1970s. The idea of competitive sports for women made gains, and with this acceptance of a higher level of competition for women's sports the extramurals for women tended increasingly to resemble extramurals for men. The trend was encouraged by the rapid rise of co-intramural programming, since developments in this important phase of the recreational sports program inevitably influence other phases, in this case extramurals and sports clubs. The intensifying interest in competition, now displayed in women's physical education generally, has also furthered interscholastic and intercollegiate athletics for women. According to modern authorities, sympathetic to the new trends in women's sports, "the ideals and principles of the earlier era are still unchanged in that the old overall standard, 'the one purpose of sport for girls and women is the good of those who play it,' is still a guiding concept. The belief that the welfare of the competitors is of overriding concern has not changed. The desire to provide for the needs of the college student still remains. What has changed are the beliefs of how to provide for these concerns within the context of competitive sport."[6] All of these trends, it may be anticipated, will accelerate as the Title IX legislation of the 1970s, which is discussed later in this chapter, bring men and women together more frequently in physical education, recreational sports, and varsity activities.

THE SPORTS CLUBS

An astonishing development in recreational sports has been the proliferation of sports clubs in the nation's schools and colleges. That proliferation was most notable in the 1960s, a period of ferment in the schools and colleges and indeed in the country at large; and it was rooted in the strong desire on the part of students, some of them graduate students, to participate on a continuing basis in athletics. Sports clubs afford a natural means of supplementing varsity athletics. The latter are for the gifted athlete, who is willing to undergo prolonged and rigorous training, whereas sports clubs are less demanding while providing an outlet for athletic interest. The decade of the 1960s stressed participation in government—doing one's own thing, as it was often described—and this aspect of sports clubs makes them very attractive to students. The appearance of a strong sports club movement was likewise welcome to the professional leadership in sports in education, as is evident from an article published by the National Association for Sport and Physical Education.[7] It laid down guidelines for the administration of sports clubs, a subject that will be discussed later in this book.

Just how widespread sports clubs had become in a few short years was revealed when D. F. Juncker, B. D. Anderson, and C. E. Mueller, all of the University of Minnesota, took a survey in the spring of 1974. Questionnaires sent to more than 2,000 institutions in the United States and Canada led to the conclusion in the report that perhaps as many as

---

[6]Ellen W. Gerber, Jan Felshin, Pearl Berlin, and Waneen Wyrick, *The American Woman in Sport* (Reading, Mass.: Addison-Wesley Publishing Co., 1974), p. 76.

[7]National Association for Sport and Physical Education, "Club Sports in Colleges and Universities," *Journal of Physical Education and Recreation* (October, 1975), p. 20.

10,000 sports clubs existed in North America. According to these authorities, a sports club is "any group of individuals organized about a particular sport or activity for the purpose of furthering interest in sports participation and socialization." It is typically under the jurisdiction of the intramural recreational sports division; and the sports are of great variety. The most popular are soccer, karate, sailing, skiing, judo, fencing, gymnastics, and rugby,[8] but sometimes a particular institution displays more than the usual amount of imagination. What else is there to say about a list such as that sponsored at the University of Idaho, in the year 1971–1972, which included Vandal Rider (Rodeo), Parachute Club, Sports Car Club, and Vandal Mountaineers, as well as the more traditional soccer team, bowling team, etc.?[9] One of the most interesting aspects of the new development is its association with the community. The trend was noticed by Juncker, Anderson, and Mueller in their account of faculty and community personnel now engaged as volunteers in the sports clubs at the University of Minnesota, who have begun to think "in terms of expansion of the sports club concept to lifetime community sports clubs programs, the hiring of full time coaches by the club and community, buildings associated with the educational institutions and park systems, and corporation-community funding for their programs."[10]

INTERSCHOLASTIC AND INTERCOLLEGIATE ATHLETICS

The terms "interscholastic" and "intercollegiate athletics" apply respectively to varsity athletics in the schools and colleges. With such programs go a season of scheduled competition, the rigorous training of gifted athletes, and the attempt to produce as often as possible a winning team that plays before a large audience of spectators, or even before millions through the instrumentality of television. To attain the highest degree possible of proficiency in a given sport, eligibility requirements ruthlessly eliminate all but the most talented and skilled athletes, and this athletic elite is given prolonged and intensive training with the best conditions attainable.

Since the belief is powerful in education that participants in the educational process should be developed to the maximum of their ability, it is not unreasonable to suppose that provision has to be made for the physically gifted through interscholastic and intercollegiate competition. And many observers of the current scene have reached exactly this

[8]"Sports Club Development—The 70's Community Involvement," *26th Annual Conference Proceedings of the National Intramural-Recreational Sports Association,* pp. 144–47.

[9]Clem Parberry, "Sports Clubs of the University of Idaho," *23rd Annual Proceedings of the National Intramural Association,* pp. 67–68.

[10]"Sports Club Development—The 70's Community Involvement," *26th Annual Conference Proceedings of the National Intramural-Recreational Sports Association,* p. 147.

conclusion. But the problem is more complicated than this observation suggests. It is also widely recognized that whenever interscholastic or intercollegiate athletics are staged for the purpose of entertaining spectators, it is very easy to lose sight of the individual as a participant; and the gifted contestant may be exploited in practice for the entertainment of others or for the financial gain of those who promote athletic contests. And this is to say nothing of what happens when organized gambling takes an interest in the outcome of a given contest.

What then is the situation? It is mixed. Many school and college administrators, along with the governing boards of educational institutions, have affirmed their belief in the educational potentialities of interscholastic and intercollegiate athletics. They may believe, as do many supporters of highly competitive varsity sports, that such competition prepares students for a complicated and competitive society. If so, they are likely to disregard the consideration that the number of gifted athletes is very small for the amount of attention lavished upon them. When conclusions of the type described above prevail, there are usually separate athletic departments with their own coaching staffs. On the other hand, leaders in physical education as a group are usually in favor of placing athletic departments and their coaches within the physical education program. It is not this point of view that has prevailed. In the 1960s and 1970s the trend has been toward separate athletic departments and separate coaching staffs, especially on the college and university scene.

These were the main features of the physical education program when the advent of Title IX legislation in the mid-1970s, as the direct result of rising feminism in the United States, set in motion a tidal wave of change in that very program. Back of Title IX legislation lay a movement for women's rights that had taken shape in the decade of the 1960s. There are many reasons that can be advanced for the appearance of a movement for women's rights at this stage of American history, but not least among them, surely, is the bald fact that women by this time constituted 40 percent of the country's working force. As the twentieth century began, only one woman in four was working outside the home. This movement from the home to the factory or the office coincided with advances in birth control that freed women for the first time from the fundamental tasks that had faced them from the time immemorial; that is, the tasks of having children and raising them to maturity. This changed situation, resulting in an unheard-of freedom for women, coincided with the appearance of large numbers of women as wage-earners. More than anything else, it was this conjuncture of circumstances that explains the strength of a movement for women's rights that has as a major goal amending the American Constitution to ensure full equality of opportunity for women. As of 1976, this amendment—the 27th Amendment to the Constitution—needed the approval of four more states before it could become the law of the land, but that this approval was likely to be forthcoming became evident when the Republican party

at Kansas City, in the summer of 1976, reaffirmed that party's support
for equal rights for women to which it had been pledged for a generation. Equally significant for women's rights was the passage of Title IX
legislation by the federal government, to which it is desirable now to
turn.

TITLE IX LEGISLATION AND WOMEN'S RIGHTS

Title IX is that portion of the Education Amendments (Act) of 1972
which prohibits sex discrimination against women in education, or, to
put the matter somewhat differently, protects the civil rights of women
in educational instiutions to which federal financial assistance is given.
This means most educational institutions, since about 16,000 public
school systems are affected and 2,700 colleges and universities. The
appropriate provision of Title IX reads that

> no person in the United States shall, on the basis of sex, be excluded
> from participation in, be denied the benefits of, or be subjected to discrimi-
> nation under any education program or activity receiving Federal financial
> assistance. . . .

As an editorial in *The New York Times* explains, "the crux of the matter is
the prohibition of any bias blocking equal opportunity for female students and teachers at any educational level."[11] Title IX applies to such
facets of school and college administration as admissions, financial aid,
and counseling and, in the case of teachers and other educational personnel, to such matters as employment, pay, and promotions, to name
but a few of the subjects on which it touches. It also applies to athletics
and physical education in a meaningful way. To grasp the full implications of Title IX, the guidelines must be considered that were drawn up
to describe how it is to be enforced and how it applies to educational
institutions. The task of preparing the guidelines was assigned to the
Department of Health, Education and Welfare (HEW), which Secretary
Casper Weinberger headed at the time.

These guidelines, which underwent public scrutiny as they took
shape, were incorporated in a regulation that was made public in June
1975 and went into legal effect on July 21 of that year. Entitled *Final Title
IX Regulation Implementing Education Amendments of 1972 Prohibiting Sex
Discrimination in Education,* this long-awaited and very important legislation centers on athletics and physical education, although other subjects
are dealt with. Indeed, one observer of Title IX legislation asserted that
the provisions regarding athletics and physical education were not, in
fact, the ones most likely to ensure equality of opportunity for women in
education; but whether this is a correct judgment or not, these are the
provisions that have excited the most controversy and aroused the most

---

[11]*The New York Times,* 5 June 1975.

comment. The significance of the *Final Title IX Regulation* of July 21, 1975 for recreational sports is simply stated. It defines a substantial part of the legal framework within which programs of physical education and athletics will function in the foreseeable future, and this means that whoever is involved in these programs must be informed about Title IX and the mechanism for its enforcement found in the *Final Title IX Regulation* of July 21, 1975.

In drawing up the *Final Title IX Regulation* HEW had to consider the outlook and philosophy of professional organizations in physical education and athletics and other interested groups such as those sponsoring women's civil rights, the final form of the Regulation being based in part at least on some 10,000 written comments from the public. There was bitter opposition to some of the provisions, and the final form was in the end more limited than was at first intended. Perhaps this opposition partly explains the period of delay that was allowed before full compliance was exacted. Colleges and secondary schools, where the opposition to reform was greater, were given three years to attain full compliance while elementary schools, where the situation was less complicated and controversial, were allowed but one year's delay. The existence of this opposition—found in particular in secondary schools and colleges where varsity athletics are so highly organized as to have at times a commercial flavor—may also explain the suspicion in some quarters that the enforcement of Title IX legislation is likely to be on occasion less than vigorous. The task of enforcement has been assigned to HEW's Office of Civil Rights; and that office, it was announced, even as the final Regulation was being made public, would henceforth cease to investigate automatically complaints of discrimination forthcoming from individuals. The new procedure leaves more flexibility with the Civil Rights Office, which plans to focus attention on patterns of alleged discrimination. The result has been to arouse the apprehension of civil rights groups, who foresee a weakened enforcement of the new legislation. According to the *Wall Street Journal,* they think the procedure calls into question the depth of President Gerald R. Ford's commitment to such causes as ending the discriminatory treatment of women and supporting racial integration in the nation's schools.[12] But the *Wall Street Journal* also reported, interestingly enough, that the provisions in Title IX legislation affecting athletics were stiffer than would otherwise have been the case had not President Ford, a former football player at the University of Michigan, opposed their watering down. If the report is correct, the final form, though more limited than was originally contemplated, was nevertheless more stringent with regard to big-time athletics than would have been the case if President Ford's intervention had not shaped the outcome.

While Title IX, and the rules for its implementation in the *Final Title IX Regulation* of July 21, reflect the strength of organized feminist

[12]*Wall Street Journal,* 4 June 1975.

groups concerned with women's civil rights and with athletics, the developments under discussion are also part of the earlier civil rights movement of the 1960s which had as its aim protecting the civil rights of blacks. This point is important since it is by no means obvious at first sight. Title IX and the mechanism for its enforcement grew out of amendments to the Civil Rights Act of 1964. That is, amendments to a law intended initially to protect the civil rights of the black minority, constituting about 13 percent of the population, have become a Magna Carta for girls and women, most of them white, who constitute more than one-half of the population. It is a curious outcome. These are the links. During the deliberations on the educational amendments of 1972 evidence was brought forward to the effect that women and girls were being persistently shortchanged in physical activities—i.e., denied their civil rights. Thus a school in a Midwestern district operated a program for girls known to be markedly inferior in quality to that provided for the boys in the same school. In another instance, the rules of a particular state compelled a certain high school to deny coaching to the best tennis player in the school and the opportunity to compete as a member of the tennis team because the athlete in question was female.

As was stated earlier, the *Final Title IX Regulation* of July 21, 1975 owed much to public participation in its formulation. At least, the opportunity for such participation was made available and the information widely disseminated about its nature before the Regulation took final form. A word about the procedure used will not be amiss at this point. The Regulation was issued in a tentative form as early as June 1974, and its contents were then given wide publicity when the Office of Civil Rights of HEW conducted extensive briefings in twelve major cities throughout the country. Comment forthcoming from the public centered on six issues, of which the first three are pertinent to the program of recreational sports in education. These were:

1. Sex discrimination in sports and athletic programs
2. Coeducational physical education classes
3. Sex stereotyping in textbooks

The last issue was left in the *Final Title IX Regulation* to the jurisdiction of state and local governmental bodies lest the federal government find itself acting as a federal censor. But the Regulation dealt at length with physical education (including health education) and athletics. And athletics were so defined as to include the recreational sports program as well as varsity athletics.

THE *FINAL TITLE IX REGULATION* AS INTERPRETED BY HEW

The guidelines in the *Final Title IX Regulation* were given wide publicity when HEW circulated its own interpretation. The new legislation, while falling short of requiring full equality, makes possible giant steps in that direction. The main theme running through the guidelines is that students are to be treated without discrimination based on sex. Thus grouping by ability is legal if there is no sex discrimination. The main points are quickly summarized. Coeducational classes are to be the order of the day in physical education unless the activity is a contact sport such as wrestling, boxing, basketball, etc. Where contact sports are involved, separate classes may exist for the two sexes. If health education is offered, classes are not to be conducted separately on the basis of sex unless the materials and discussion deal exclusively with human sexuality. If so, separate sessions on the elementary and secondary levels are legal. As far as athletics (defined as above) are concerned, separate teams are possible for males and females in contact sports, or there may be a single team open to both sexes. Here a qualification enters. That team must meet the test of accommodating "the interests and abilities of members of both sexes" or else separate teams must be provided. If separate teams are maintained, no discrimination on the basis of sex is permissible in providing supplies or equipment "or in any other way," but *"equal aggregate expenditures are not required."* This means among other things that athletic scholarships are to be offered to women in proportion to their participation in sports. HEW also listed a number of factors to be considered in determining whether equal opportunity is, in fact, being maintained; and these include the provision of supplies and equipment, expenditures for travel, quality of coaching, and others. But while equal opportunity must be provided, the *Final Title IX Regulation* stopped short of requiring equal aggregate expenditures in these categories (that is, the provision of supplies and equipment, etc.). HEW also discussed non–contact sports, the rules running on these lines. Whenever a team in a non–contact sport, such as tennis, has been previously confined to members of one sex and where athletic opportunities for the sex for whom no team is available have been previously limited, individuals of that sex must be allowed to compete for the team in question. If the provision of one team does not, however, meet the test of accommodating "the interests and abilities of members of both sexes," the institution must provide separate teams for men and women. This test, as was mentioned earlier, also applied to contact sports. But no summary of this legislation can replace the official interpretation offered by HEW, from which pertinent portions are printed in the following pages.

HEW ON PHYSICAL EDUCATION AND ATHLETICS

The statements on physical education and athletics that appear below are taken from HEW's interpretation of the *Final Title IX Regulation* and the information in brackets comes either from the same source or else from other HEW materials.

TITLE IX GUIDELINES

Treatment [of Students]

. . . although some schools [such as military schools] are exempt from Title IX with regard to admissions, all schools must treat their admitted students without discrimination on the basis of sex. . . . Specifically, the treatment sections of the regulation cover the following areas:

1. Access to and participation in course offerings and extracurricular activities, including campus organizations and competitive athletics;

2. Eligibility for and receipt or enjoyment of benefits, services, and financial aid. . . .

Classes in health education, if offered, may not be conducted separately on the basis of sex, but the final regulation allows separate sessions for boys and girls at the elementary and secondary school level during times when the materials and discussion deal exclusively with human sexuality. There is, of course, nothing in the law or the final regulation requiring schools to conduct sex education classes. This is a matter for local determination.

Physical Education

While generally prohibiting sex segregated physical education classes, the final regulations *do* allow separation by sex in physical education classes during competition in wrestling, boxing, basketball, football, and other sports involving bodily contact. Schools must comply fully with the regulation with respect to physical education as soon as possible. In the case of physical education classes elementary schools must be in full compliance no later than one year from the effective date of the regulation. In the case of physical education classes at the secondary and postsecondary level, schools must be in compliance no later than three years from the effective date of the regulation. During these periods, while making necessary adjustments, any physical education classes or activities which are separate, must be comparable for each sex.

Athletics [The term "athletics" encompasses sports which are a part of interscholastic, intercollegiate, club or intramural programs]

Where selection is based on *competitive skill* or the activity involved is a *contact* sport, athletics *may* be provided through *separate* teams for males and females or through a single team open to both sexes. If separate teams are offered, a recipient institution may not discriminate on the basis of sex in provision of necessary equipment or supplies, or in any other way, *but equal aggregate expenditures are not required.* The goal of the final regulation in the area of athletics is to secure equal opportunity for males and females while allowing schools and colleges flexibility in determining how best to provide such opportunity.

In determining whether equal opportunitites are available, such factors as these will be considered:

—whether the sports selected reflect the interests and abilities of both sexes;

—provision of supplies and equipment;

—game and practice schedules;

—travel and per diem allowances;

—coaching and academic tutoring opportunities and the assignment and pay of the coaches and tutors;

—locker rooms, practice and competitive facilities;

—medical and training services;

—housing and dining facilities and services;

—publicity.

[But while equal opportunities must be provided in each of these categories, equal expenditures in each category are not required.]

Where a team in a non–contact sport, the membership of which is based on skill, is offered for members of one sex and not for members of the other sex, and athletic opportunities for the sex for whom no team is available have previously been limited, individuals of that sex must be allowed to compete for the team offered. For example, if tennis is offered for men and not for women and a woman wishes to play on the tennis team, if women's sports have previously been limited at the institution in question, that woman may compete for a place on the men's team. However, this provision does not alter the responsibility which a recipient has with regard to the provision of equal opportunity. Recipients are requested to "select sports and levels of competition which effectively accommodate the interests and abilities of members of both sexes." Thus, an institution would be required to provide separate teams for men and women in situations where the provision of only one team would not "accommodate the interests and abilities of members of both sexes." This provision applies whether sports are contact or non–contact.

In the case of athletics, like physical education, elementary schools will have up to a year from the effective date of the regulations to comply, and secondary and postsecondary schools will have up to three years.

Organizations

Generally, a recipient may not, in connection with its education program or activity, provide significant assistance to any organization, agency or person which discriminates on the basis of sex. Such forms of assistance to discriminatory groups as faculty sponsors, facilities, administrative staff, etc., may, on a case-by-case basis, be determined to be significant enough to render the organization subject to the non-discrimination requirements of the regulation. . . .

Benefits, Services, and Financial Aid

Generally, a recipient subject to the regulation is prohibited from discriminating in making available, in connection with its educational program or activity, any benefits, services, or financial aid although "pooling" of certain sex-restrictive scholarships is permitted. Benefits and services include medical and insurance policies and services for students, counseling, and assistance in obtaining employment. Financial aid includes scholarships, loans, grants-in-aid and work-study programs.

Facilities

Generally, all facilities must be available without discrimination on the basis of sex. As provided in the statute, however, *the regulation permits separate housing based on sex as well as separate locker rooms, toilets and showers.* A recipient may not make available to members of one sex locker rooms, toilets and showers which are not comparable to those provided to members of the other sex. . . .

—A recipient school district may not require segregation of boys into one health, physical education, or other class, and segregation of girls into another such class.

—Where men are afforded opportunities for athletic scholarships, the final regulation requires that women also be afforded these opportunities.

Specifically, the regulation provides: "To the extent that a recipient awards athletic scholarships or grants-in-aid, it must provide reasonable opportunities for such awards for members of each sex in proportion to the number of students of each sex participating in interscholastic or intercollegiate athletics."

—Locker rooms, showers, and other facilities provided for women must be comparable to those provided for men.

—A recipient educational institution would be *prohibited from providing financial support* for an all-female hiking club, an all-male language club, or a single-sex honorary society. *However, a non-exempt organization whose membership* was restricted to members of one sex *could adhere to its restrictive policies,* and operate on the campus of a recipient university, *if it received no assistance from the unversity.*

—Male and female students must be eligible for benefits, services and financial aid without discrimination on the basis of sex. Where colleges administer scholarships designated exclusively for one sex or the other, the scholarship recipients should initially be chosen without regard to sex. Then when the time comes to award the money, sex may be taken into consideration in matching available monies to the students chosen. No person may be denied financial aid merely because no aid for his or her sex is available. Prizes, awards and scholarships not established under a will or trust must be administered without regard to sex.

—An institution which has one swimming pool *must* provide for use by members of both sexes on a non-discriminatory basis. . . .

THE EFFECTS OF TITLE IX LEGISLATION

Title IX legislation only reached the statute book in final form, then, in the summer of 1975; and only the passage of time will reveal its precise effects on physical education, athletics, and the program of recreational sports. What can be seen clearly is that intercollegiate sports is the area where the new legislation has initially aroused the greatest commotion and consternation. The male NCAA (National Collegiate Athletic Association), fearing the impact of the new legislation on the great revenue-producing sports of football and basketball, lobbied unsuccessfully to exempt intercollegiate athletics from its operation. According to *WomenSport* ("Shedding Light on Title IX: What You Need to Know to Make It Work," February 1976), the NCAA spent more than $200,000 in the enterprise. As that magazine reported crisply, "NCAA honchos, after spending more than $200,000 lobbying to avoid sharing a dime with women, went home to the unnerving prospect of revamping bloated football budgets." The asperity of the comment seems justified when it is realized that on a national basis women's sports budgets run at about 2 percent of the men's budgets. In any case, the NCAA was ready with its own reply if the comment credited in *WomenSports* (February 1976) to Walter Byers, the executive director of the NCAA, was actually his. Byers is said to have stated: "Two percent is enough." Whether it was unnerved or not, the powerful organization has filed in response to the *Final Title IX Regulation* a legal complaint against HEW in the effort to set aside Title IX legislation so far as it affects intercollegiate sports and scholarships at the college level. The outlook of the NCAA was also conveyed when its attorney, Michael Scott, attacked Title IX, stating, "This may well signal the end of intercollegiate athletic programs as we have known them in recent decades." Secretary Weinberger denied that this was the inevitable result. As he said, "I can't see anything in the provisions to put intercollegiate athletics out of business." And he stressed once more that equal opportunity did not "necessarily" require equality of expenditure though it might require "more, much more" than was presently being spent on women.[13]

But if the new legislation elicited the bitter opposition of the NCAA, this fact in the long run is less important than its implications for women in physical education, athletics, and recreational sports. It is realistic to recognize that the changing order does not mean equal expenditures for women in these fields, but this realism ought not to stand in the way of recognizing and appreciating that the future for women in education and sport has been virtually transformed. On this point it is well to note that Secretary Weinberger, in the statement cited above, had declared that equal opportunity did not "necessarily" require equality of expenditure, a choice of language surely that permits the possibility that in a given case HEW might well insist on equality of expenditure for women's programs in physical education, athletics, and recreational sports. It should also be noted that the important pace-setting colleges and universities are increasing the sports budget for women. Thus the University of California at Los Angeles, which perhaps spends more money on women's athletics than any other institution in the country, raised its budget of 1974–75 from $60,000 to $180,000 for women's sports, and in

---

[13]*New York Post,* 4 June 1975.

the first term of 1975–76 anticipated spending $265,000. Instances of this kind of progress can be multiplied. It may be concluded under these circumstances that whatever modifications were introduced into Title IX legislation, either in the process of its formulation or in the subsequent explanations given publicly by HEW, the way has been opened for a social revolution in the gymnasium and on the playing fields of this country as women recognize increasingly the possibilities in Title IX legislation for giving them a greater role in sport and education. Despite the severe adverse criticism of Title IX, found in the bitter appraisals forthcoming from groups as disparate as the NCAA, who think the legislation much too sweeping, and the keenly disappointed women's advocates and civil rights supporters, who believe that it does not go far enough, there is room for the solid middle ground taken by Marjorie Blaufarb, managing editor of *Update*, a monthly publication of AAHPER. This was her memorable statement: "The fact is Title IX is a very touchy subject all over the country. Right now, it's on a trial and error basis. Everybody will eventually do what the law requires; eventually equality will be achieved" (quoted in *WomenSports*, February 1976). The words are wise and perceptive. Whatever the degree of disappointment among those elements who dislike portions of Title IX legislation, or even all of it, one suspects that in the long run—and not in a very long run at that—"everybody will eventually do what the law requires; eventually equality will be achieved."

DISCUSSION QUESTIONS

1. Describe the values of a recreational sports program in education.
2. Do the "Cardinal Principles of Secondary Education" give special attention to leisure-time values? Explain.
3. Describe the specific divisions of physical education and illustrate how each division becomes an integral part of education in schools and colleges.
4. What are the major differences between an intramural program and an extramural program?
5. Describe the significance of Title IX legislation to each of the following: (a) the field of education; (b) the physical education instruction program; (c) the recreational sports program; and (d) interscholastic and intercollegiate athletic programs.

BIBLIOGRAPHY

American Alliance for Health, Physical Education and Recreation, *Update*. Washington, D.C.: Issues of 1975 and 1976.

BLAUFARB, MARJORIE. *Complying with Title IX of the Education Amendments of 1972 in physical education and high school sports programs.* American Alliance for Health, Physical Education and Recreation, Washington, D.C.: 1976.

"The Future Revised: Education's Big Boom Is Ending, But Studies to Get More Diverse," *Wall Street Journal,* April 8, 1976.

GERBER, E. W., J. FELSHIN, P. BERLIN, and W. WYRICK, *The American Woman in Sport.* Reading, Mass.: Addison-Wesley Publishing Co., 1974.

RONALD HYATT, "The Intramural Story," *Journal of Health, Physical Education, Recreation* (March, 1974), a special feature ed. pp, 39–60.

JUNCKER, D. F., B. D. ANDERSON and C. E. MUELLER, "Sports Club Development: The '70's Community Involvement," *26th Annual Conference Proceedings of the National Intramural-Recreational Sports Association,* April 23–27, 1975, pp. 144–47.

"Shedding Light on Title IX: What You Need to Know to Make It Work," *WomenSports* (February 1976), pp. 44–48.

U.S. Department of Health, Education and Welfare: Office for Civil Rights, *Final Title IX Regulation Implementing Education Amendments of 1972: Prohibiting Sex Discrimination in Education.* Washington, D.C.: U.S. Government Printing Office, July 21, 1975.

Memorandum to Chief State School Officers, Superintendents of Local Education Agencies and College and University Presidents: Subject: Elimination of Sex Discrimination in Athletic Programs, September 1975.

II

The Community
and the School

Community Recreation.
Courtesy Whatcom County Parks, Whatcom County, Washington.

4

Community Recreation
in Transition

Leisure-time sports and recreation activities have become in the course of the last two decades a recognized need within the ranks of all age groups. As these words imply, this has not always been the case. In the years before World War II, the emphasis was on youth as recreation leadership worked to heighten the interest of this group for community sports. Similarly, in the schools the time devoted to programs of recreation grew from a single hour after school to all the afternoon, to evenings, to weekends, to vacation periods, and to the summer months. By the early 50s, however, the ranks of active participants enlarged with the advent of a youthful adult generation devoted to the concept of recreation, recreational sports activities, and physical fitness.

EXPANDING NEEDS AND SERVICES

As the adult population turned to sports activity, the impact penetrated all aspects of recreation programs.

School

For the nonschool population, recreation had been traditionally viewed as a family and personal responsibility until the returning war veteran after World War II, the beneficiary of the armed services' recreation programs, spearheaded the adults' search for organized sports activity. Wage-earners, with the declining workweek, and relatively youthful retirees swelled the ranks of activity-minded adults who dropped in at local school "teacher-recreation" nights; and the doors now opened to include parents, families, and other groups in the community. The surge of increased recreation participation by the post-school adult moved many schools to expand offerings, develop new programs, and serve interests in physical fitness and lifetime sports.

Community

Recreation as a public and local government function was rooted in early municipal efforts to obtain and preserve open space, public parks, and picnic areas. As demands for more organized services were placed upon local governments by various age groups, justification for formalized recreation programs developed, was promoted and accepted.

The number of cities with public-funded recreation programs increased dramatically. Swimming pools, civic centers, tennis courts, golf courses, and playgrounds were developed by cities and municipalities. New programs and program directors reflected the citys' and taxpayers' willingness to provide recreation opportunities for all and for all to share the costs.

Voluntary, Private and Commercial

Whether the explosion in recreation activity came from a changed society or enlightened leadership or from both, the impact was not limited to school and community.

With evident support for a great variety of recreation activities, voluntary agencies expanded to reflect the thrust, as did the number of recreation-oriented private yacht clubs, tennis, golf, and athletic clubs. Commercial agencies and business ventures responded to new demands and new markets. Bowling alleys, billiard and pool parlors, golf courses and driving ranges, and ski centers expanded and began to look like big business.

Continuing Demands

The expansion in recreation activity is steady. School recreation programs move to serve community members of all ages. At the same time community recreation programs mushroom, growing out of their facilities and reaching into the school plant. Increasingly, the past decade has witnessed merging, overlapping, and duplicating on the part of community, school, voluntary, private, and commercial recreation. There is little separate identity, but there are many common problems. Providing services to meet the expanding wishes of the public is rooted in the respective roles and legal responsibilities either assumed by the federal, state, and local government or assigned to them. Their various agencies are only now beginning to move toward the kind of precise delineation of responsibilities that permits and facilitates the much-desired economic efficiency.

RECREATION AND THE FEDERAL GOVERNMENT

The explosion in recreation has brought pressure to bear on all levels of government to develop policy, clarify responsibilities, and promote public support for the evolving programs. Recent legislation has made the role of the federal government conspicuous.

A Growing Involvement

The Federal Inter-Agency Committee on Recreation was organized in 1946 to coordinate the activities of the many departments and commissions concerned with some aspect of recreation. This Committee subsequently developed a recommended general policy for the federal government relative to public recreation, and another important step was taken when the Bureau of Outdoor Recreation was established in the Department of Interior (for the details, see the Rockefeller Report discussed in Chapter 1). The interest in recreation was reaffirmed on the federal level with the passage of the Elementary and Secondary Education Act (ESEA) in 1965, which gave financial support to recreational sports programs and community recreation by means of a number of grants for innovative and exemplary programs. One such grant funded "Education Broadfront" of Ellenburg, Washington, with provision for specific projects in such areas as school health, physical education, the community-school program, school camping and outdoor education, and the special education program.

Under ESEA Title III Pullman, Washington was funded for an exemplary education program in lifetime sports. Programs in Florida, California, Michigan, New York State, Texas, and others give leadership to an expansive federal involvement in sports and recreation through education.

Today's scope of the movement is illustrated by the numerous federal agencies that have some recreation function or responsibility. The list in Figure 4-1 of concerned government bodies indicates the diversity of their major area of responsibility. Additional agencies, commissions, and councils hold functions related to the recreation movement.

A Federal Responsibility

The federal government has assumed responsibility in the area of recreation and has delegated to state, county, and municipal governments the powers needed to develop recreation programs at their level.

Department of the Army	Department of Health, Education and Welfare
Corps of Engineers	
Department of Agriculture	Children's Bureau
Forest Service	Office of Education
Extension Service	Public Health Service
Soil Conservation	Water Pollution Control Program
Department of Commerce	Department of the Interior
United States Travel Service	National Park Service
Bureau of Census	Fish and Wildlife
Bureau of Public Roads	Bureau of Indian Affairs
District of Columbia Recreation	Bureau of Reclamation
	Bureau of Outdoor Recreation
Federal Communications Commission	Bureau of Land Management
	National Capital Planning Comm.
Federal Council on Aging	National Capital Parks
Housing and Home Finance	Smithsonian Institute
Interdepartmental Committee on Children and Youth	Tennessee Valley Authority
	The Armed Forces
	The President's Council on Youth Fitness

Figure 4-1. Governmental Agencies Serving Recreation Functions

In doing so the federal government has acted on the basis of two well-accepted principles: (1) the Constitution mandates that the government promote the general welfare of the people; (2) recreation contributes to the health, safety, and well-being of people. Within the executive branch of government, presidential leadership has been exerted through the Inter-Agency Committee on Recreation, which has acted consistently to establish the point that recreation is important to the general welfare of people.

While Congress was slower in accepting this view of the government's role in recreation, that commitment came in the wake of the Rockefeller Report (see Chapter 1), which was followed by the creation of the Bureau of Outdoor Recreation. Congress now recognized that recreation was part of the American way of life by voting financial support for a great variety of related projects and services.

Thus substantial appropriations have been made for land acquisition, development, and long-range recreation planning. The Task Force on Land Use and Urban Growth was created in the summer of 1972 to serve an already existing Citizens Advisory Committee on Environmental Quality, a governmental body established by presidential order in May 1969. The subsequent recommendations of the Task Force are replete with implications for a continued and expanded governmental commitment in the area of acquiring land for recreational purposes. Its authors wrote: "Federal spending for open space acquisition should be maintained at levels commensurate with needs. We see particular merit in continuing to extend the network of parks, seashores, and lakeshores that are owned and managed by the federal government itself."[1] The report continued with a proposal for a National Lands Trust to be established to assist public bodies in the designation, planning, and conservation of expensive greenspaces in and around major urban areas.[2]

The federal government has also provided for:

1. Operational management of outdoor recreation resources through the services of national parks, national forest, and land management bureaus.

2. Promotional, technical, and financial resource assistance to national, state, and urban open-space programs through the Bureau of Outdoor Recreation.

3. Direct support of recreation programs in federal institutions such as hospitals, armed forces, and Veterans Administration.

4. Financial assistance to recreation education and professional training through grants to colleges, universities, extension programs, and individuals.

A very recent piece of legislation is the Community School Act of 1974, which assists with cultural, recreational, and social service community programs. Federal financial assistance is offered to local districts, state departments of education, and institutions of higher education interested in developing community education.

RECREATION AND THE STATE

Multi-organizational structures and approaches characterize the many state-assumed responsibilities and long-range planning efforts to meet recreation needs. Before World War II this kind of activity on the part of the states was usually limited to acquiring and developing park systems and to offering programs of recreation through university extension programs. There was little coordinated or overall developmental planning. But gradually the situation altered as state education departments, colleges, and universities turned their attention and services to recreation. Diverse agencies concerned with state forests, state parks, fish, game, highways, state hospitals, prisons, children's homes, etc., have moved in the same direction. A new landmark was reached when the Outdoor Recreation Resources Review Commission, chaired by Laurance Rockefeller (see Rockefeller Report, Chapter 1), successfully recommended in January 1962 that the Governors' Conference, which was

---

[1]William K. Reilly, ed., *The Use of Land: A Citizens' Policy Guide to Urban Growth,* A Task Force Report Sponsored by the Rockefeller Brothers Fund (New York: Thomas Y. Crowell Co., 1973), p. 19.

[2]Ibid., p. 22.

to meet in the following July, endorse a resolution by which each state would prepare a long-range plan for developing outdoor recreation facilities and programs. The results were impressive. State programs expanded, new legislation was introduced or old legislation revised, and federal grants-in-aid for recreation were made available. As the duties of the state agencies multiply, the states undertake to exchange information, coordinate their efforts, and solve their problems by means of an interagency committee or state-level focal agency.

A State Responsibility

Like the federal government, the states have assumed a responsibility to provide for the recreation needs of those living within their borders. As early as 1945, North Carolina established a state recreation commission; and other states, though not all, have followed suit. For the states that lack a single coordinating authority, existing agencies and commissions provide recreation services. They operate either independently of one another or else by means of informal channels of communication. As far as its relationships with local agencies within a given state are concerned, the state government may grant to districts, schools, or to other units of government the authority to administer recreation programs. Here too there is variety. Sometimes the state identifies the unit of local government that is to be responsible for developing a recreation program, and in those states where the legal authority for recreation programs is expressed in the state park code laws or the state school laws, the basic administrative relationships are firmly established. But administrative patterns are less well-defined and are dependent on local initiative when enabling legislation is passed. Such legislation grants general powers to a local governmental organization to conduct recreation programs. No one governmental unit or agency is identified to administer the program. These are permissive laws, not mandatory, but they do provide the legal base, and powers to spend public funds for recreation and permit local communities to determine their own best adminstrative and operational plans.

All fifty states have provided for delegation of power to local governments through a variety of state laws that are primarily concerned with

1. Authority to local communities and provisions for them to administer granted powers
2. The right to acquire and maintain land for recreational development
3. The right to raise money through taxes, bond issues, and grants
4. The right to assume financial reponsibility for programs
5. Authorization for cooperative agreements among all state and community agencies
6. The authority to hire staff and provide program services

New laws are constantly being introduced and old laws refined to provide for change, growth, and better ways of proceeding, coordinating efforts, pooling resources, providing for multi-use of facilities, determining and serving community needs.

Of particular import to the future directions of school community recreation are the precedent-establishing state laws identifying and supporting the concept of the community school. Included here is the recent action taken by the state of Alaska.

Alaska Community School Act of 1975

Chapter 36. Community Schools.

Sec. 14.36.010. **Purpose, Intent.**

(a) The Community School is an expression of the philosophy that the school, as the prime educational institution of the community, is most effective when it involves the people of that community in a program designed to fulfill their educational needs. The Community School promotes a more efficient use of school facilities through an extension of buildings and equipment beyond the normal school day. The purpose of this chapter is to provide state leadership and financial support to encourage and assist local school districts in the establishment of Community Schools.

(b) It is the intent of the legislature that

1. a program of Community School grants be established to provide assistance to local communities in the initial development and implementation of Community School programs;

2. technical assistance and coordination of statewide efforts to develop and operate Community School programs be provided by the department; and

3. the Community School program will become fully operational at the beginning of the second fiscal year following its authorization.

Sec. 14.36.020. **Community Schools Grant Fund Created; Limitations on Use.**

There is created a Community Schools grant fund as an account in the general fund. The fund shall be used to make Community School grants to local attendance areas or school districts under this chapter. Legislative appropriations for Community School grants shall be deposited in this fund. Community School grants may be used for planning, training, and operations.

Sec. 14.36.030. **Grants.**

A district operating an approved Community School program may receive a first-year grant up to one-half of one percent of its public school foundation support; a second-year grant of up to one percent of that support; a third-year grant of up to one and one-half percent of that support; and, a fourth-year grant of up to two percent of that support. The support provided shall be in the proportion that the number of schools in each district that are operated as Community Schools is to the total number of schools in the district.

Sec.14.36.040. **Community School Program, Application for Grants.**

Under regulations adopted by the state Board of Education, a local attendance area may submit to the commissioner, through the school district, an application for a Community School grant. An application shall include

1. a comprehensive plan for the Community School program including, but not limited to, before and after school hours activities for both children and adults, continued education programs for children and adults, and cultural enrichment and recreational activities for citizens in the community;

2. a provision for a Community Schools Advisory Council;

3. provision for Community School direction and coordination to include personnel requirements;

4. a statement as to the number of schools to be operated as Community Schools.

Sec. 14.36.050. **Application Review, Disposition.**

The commissioner shall review and approve, disapprove or return to the initiator through the district board for modification, an application for a Community School program grant.

Sec. 14.36.060. **Technical Assistance.**

On the request of a school district the department shall provide technical assistance to a school district in developing and submitting an application for a Community School program. The department may use its own staff or consultants that may be necessary to accomplish this purpose.

Sec. 14.36.070. **Definitions.**

In this chapter

1. "board" means the governing body of a school district;

2. "commissioner" means the commissioner of education;

3. "Community School program" means the composite of those educational, cultural, social and recreational services provided the citizens of a community, except those services normally provided through the regular instructional program;

4. "department" means the Department of Education;

5. "district" means a school district or the State-Operated Schools;

6. "local attendance areas" means an elementary or secondary school, or combination of these schools, which functions as a distinct administration unit.

Signed into Law by Governor Jay Hammond on June 3, 1975*

RECREATION IN COUNTIES AND DISTRICTS

At times exploding demands for recreation have best been met by identifying and working through administrative units smaller than the state itself but larger than a developed city. A workable unit that facilitates serving the unincorporated areas has resulted in many instances in a county or district administrative body. Most popularly known is the

*Section 2. This Act takes effect July 1, 1975.

county parks system, which commonly includes providing recreation programs, picnic and sports areas, hiking, riding, nature trails, mountain climbing, swimming, boating, and fishing areas.

This administrative unit broadens the tax basis for small communities, provides more possibilities for property acquisition and resources, and often serves those in sparsely populated areas who would not otherwise enjoy program benefits.

County park boards have laid the foundations for their programs on public interest concepts and objectives, as illustrated in Figure 4-2. In 1964 the National Association of Counties issued a statement that gave impetus to the county parks program in its statement "that the special role of the county is to acquire, develop and maintain parks and to administer public recreation programs that will serve the needs of communities broader than the local neighborhood or municipality, but less than statewide or national in scope."

A County Responsibility

County responsibility for recreation often evolves from the way authorization laws are developed. In many states, responsibility is assigned to a recreation board or commission and authorized under enabling acts. In some instances there is joint administration by county and local authorities. Whatcom County, Washington County Parks Board spells out its derived authority in its manual of policies and procedures as illustrated in Figure 4-3.

RECREATION IN COMMUNITIES—MUNICIPALITIES

The record growth of community and school recreation in a relatively short period of time is stimulating community and municipal concern to ensure complementary, multi-program services rather than duplication of efforts that limit quality and breadth of activities.

Playground and indoor sports conducted by a community parks and recreation department are essentially the same as school programs, except that the nonstandardized recreation department programs are responsive to locally expressed desires, and are very flexible and more subject to change. Facilities, equipment, leadership personnel, programs, and resource services of one, however, can duplicate or supplement those of another. Relatively alike are the recreation activity programs offered by many of the voluntary agencies, which include YMCA, YWCA, Catholic Youth Organizations, Jewish Community Centers, Boys' and Girls' Clubs, Settlement Houses, Scouts, and Camp Fire Girls.

Restricted-membership agencies and organizations provide common opportunities in the universally popular activities of golf, tennis,

SECTION   NUMBER

      II. BOARD OPERATIONS   A-1

SUBJECT

        OBJECTIVES

ASSUMPTIONS: 1. In order to be and to remain a useful and healthy member of
            society every individual needs some form of recreation.

           2. Providing some forms of leisure services is a legitimate re-
            sponsibility of government.

           3. In order to provide every citizen of the county with the
            opportunity to satisfy his recreational needs, public agen-
            cies should supply those facilities and services which are
            impossible or difficult for most individuals or small groups
            of people to provide for themselves.

GENERAL PURPOSES: The purpose of the Whatcom County Park and Recreation Board
            is to maximize recreational opportunities and thereby improve
            the Quality of Life for all residents of the county.

GOALS: 1. To adopt, support and cummunicate the philosophy that re-
            creation means any activity, voluntarily engaged in, which
            contributes to the refreshment, education, entertainment,
            physical, mental, cultural or moral development of the in-
            dividual or group attending, participating, or observing
            any activity which leads to fulfilling a sense of self-
            worth.

           2. To provide a variety of recreation opportunities for all
            citizens regardless of age, sex, race, or economic status.

           3. To maintain full awareness of environmental concerns in the
            development and use of public lands and in the implement-
            ation of programs.

           4. To develop and maintain a statement of goals and objectives
            which is understood by the Park and Recreation Board, ad-
            visory councils and staff, and communicated to the com-
            munity and governmental leaders. The statement must be
            ever changing and a reflection of the community's highest
            ideals.

           5. To establish and maintain written policies, practices and
            procedures that enable maximum opportunity for use and en-
            joyment of services.

           6. To be responsive to the recreational needs and desires of
            individuals and groups, and to actively seek citizen input
            in the operation of the Board. To create awareness through
            involvement.

           7. To attempt to acquire and preserve in the public domain--
            unique geographical areas.

           8. To create and maintain facilities that are aesthetically
            pleasing and provide open space for human need.

           9. To conduct and communicate Board business in a manner that
            earns recognition as a highly ethical, responsible and honor-
            able organization among employees, taxpayers, suppliers, gov-
            ernmental agencies, press and the public at large.

         10. To foster innovation by encouraging the Board, advisory coun-
            cils, and staff to search for new and more effective ways of
            improving the Board's operation.

         11. To keep abreast of trends and changes that affect the level
            of service and utilize that information to increase contri-
            butions to the Quality of Life.

         12. To develop and maintain effective leadership at the ap-
            pointed, professional, and volunteer levels.

         13. To maintain an awareness of the political process and to par-
            ticipate in the development of legislation and/or other gov-

ernmental regulations which affect the Board's ability to meet its service responsibilities.

14. To coordinate, cooperate, assist, support and otherwise interact with private and public entities so as to maximize recreational opportunities in Whatcom County.

15. To maintain the Board in a sound financial position by constantly monitoring revenues and expenditures to insure adequate cash flow for current expenses, to maintain a ready reserve for capital requirements and to prevent deficit spending.

16. Fiscally responsible to take full and prompt advantage of potential economies and to aggressively seek new ways to reduce operating expenses.

17. Cooperation and resourcefulness to improve the Board's ability to provide service by constantly seeking additional sources of income, by expanding opportunities for joint ventures, private assistance, grants, endowments, by eliminating duplicate services in the public, private or quasi-public sectors and by volunteer citizen involvement.

18. To establish and maintain a climate that will attract, motivate, and retain competent employees and that will foster their continuing growth and development and provide them satisfaction in the performance of their work.

Revised 12/16/75

Figure 4-2. Objectives of Whatcom County Parks. Excerpt from Manual of Policies and Procedures. Courtesy of Whatcom County Parks Board, Whatcom County, Washington.

DATE
January, 1972

MANUAL OF POLICIES AND PROCEDURES
Whatcom County Park Board
Bellingham, Washington

Page 1 of 3

SECTION   NUMBER
    I. LAWS & ORDINANCES   A-1
SUBJECT

    AUTHORITY TO OPERATE

RCW
36.68.010   COUNTIES MAY ESTABLISH PARK AND PLAYGROUND SYSTEMS - DISPOSITION OF SURPLUS PARK PROPERTY

    Counties may establish park and playground systems for public recreational purposes and for such purposes shall have the power to acquire lands, buildings and other facilities by gift, purchase, lease, devise, bequest and condemnation. A county may lease or sell any park property, buildings or facilities surplus to its needs, or no longer suitable for park purposes: Provided, that such park property shall be subject to the requirements and provisions of notice, hearing, bid or intergovernmental transfer as provided in Chapter 33.34: Provided further, that nothing in this section shall be construed as authorizing any county to sell any property which such county acquired by condemnation for park or playground or other public recreational purposes on or after such acquisition: Provided further, that funds acquired from the lease or sale of any park property, buildings or facilities shall be placed in the park and recreation fund to be used for capital purposes.

36.68.020   PROGRAMS OF PUBLIC RECREATION

    Counties may conduct programs of public recreation, and in any such program property or facilities owned by any individual, group or organization, whether public or private, may be utilized by consent of the owner.

36.68.030   PARK AND RECREATION BOARD

    Each county may form a county park and recreation board composed of seven members, of whom one shall be the county superintendent of schools and the remainder shall be appointed by the board of county commissioners to serve without compensation.

36.68.040   TERMS OF MEMBERS

For the appointive positions on the county park and recreation board the initial terms shall be two years for two positions, four years for two positions, and six years for the remaining two positions plus the period in each instance to the next following June 30, thereafter the term for each appointive position shall be six years and shall end on June 30.

36.68.050   REMOVAL OF MEMBERS - VACANCIES.

Any appointed county park and recreation board member may be removed by a majority vote of the board of county commissioners either for cause or upon the joint written recommendation of five members of the county park and recreation board. Vacancies on the county park and recreation board shall be filled by appointment, made by the board of county commissioners for the unexpired portions of the terms vacated.

36.68.060   POWERS AND DUTIES.

The county park and recreation board:

(1) Shall elect its officers, including a chairman, vice chairman and secretary, and such other officers as it may determine it requires.
(2) Shall hold regular public meetings at least monthly.
(3) Shall adopt rules for transaction of business and shall keep a written record of its meetings, resolutions, transactions, findings and determinations, which record shall be a public record.
(4) Shall initiate, direct and administer county recreational activities and shall select and employ a county park and recreation superintendent and such other properly employees as it may deem desirable.
(5) Shall improve, operate, and maintain parks, playgrounds, and other recreational facilities, together with all structures and equipment useful in connection therewith, and may recommend to the board of county commissioners acquisition of real property.
(6) Shall promulgate and enforce reasonable rules and regulations deemed necessary in the operation of parks, playgrounds, and other recreational facilities, and may recommend to the board of county commissioners adoption of any rules or regulations requiring enforcement by legal process which relate to parks, playgrounds, or other recreational facilities.
(7) Shall each year submit to the board of county commissioners for approval a proposed budget for the following year in the manner provided by law for the preparation and submission of budgets by elective or appointive county officials.
(8) May, subject to the approval of the board of county commissioners, enter into contracts with any other municipal corporation, governmental or private agency for the conduct of park and recreational programs.

36.68.070   PARK AND RECREATION FUND.

In counties in which county park and recreation boards are formed, a county park and recreation fund shall be established. Into this fund shall be placed the allocation as the board of county commissioners annually appropriates thereto, together with miscellaneous revenues derived from the operation of parks, playgrounds, and other recreational facilities, as well as grants, gifts, and bequests for park or recreational purposes. All expenditures shall be disbursed from this fund by the county park and recreation board, and all balances remaining in this fund at the end of any year shall be carried over in such fund to the succeeding year.

36.68.80   PENALTY FOR VIOLATIONS OF REGULATIONS.

Any person violating any rules or regulations adopted by the board of county commissioners relating to parks, playgrounds, or other recreational facilities shall be guilty of a misdemeanor.

Figure 4-3. Authority to Operate Whatcom County Parks as stated in Manual of Policies and Procedures. Courtesy of Whatcom County Parks Board, Whatcom County, Washington.

riding, sailing, and swimming. Industry, unions, religious groups, and organizations provide comparable employee and family activity programs.

Of the broad spectrum of commercial recreation activities, sports commands a large share when one considers the commercial tennis courts, swimming pools, bowling alleys, ice skating and roller skating rinks, boating moorages, pool and billiard halls, and innumerable other sports-participation business ventures.

The problem of duplication presents three major areas of concern: (1) What is a public responsibility and what is a commercial responsibility? (2) What is the best administrative plan for local government responsibilities? (3) What is the best way to insure serving all needs with limited duplication?

Any answer to the first question must insure that economics does not deprive the lower-income public of all recreation opportunities. The cost of participation is therefore important whether sponsored commercially or publicly. Regarding the second question, the public is generally not too concerned whether the tax-supported recreation is under the jurisdiction of the recreation department, park commission, or school board. Most people are concerned that their tax dollars are well spent by an efficiently managed administrative unit.

There is no one best way to serve a great variety of needs. The challenge exists for each community to strive for cooperation among all agencies and organizations. This requires a dedication to community service that aims at eliminating wasteful duplication of efforts and expense. The most economical and effective use of community resources is generally promoted through joint agency planning, exchange board representation, and interagency councils.

A Community Responsibility

Each community, when starting a public program, must grant legal authorization. This is usually done through an ordinance consistent with the state enabling laws or through an amendment to the local charter. Authorization defines organization, powers, duties, and responsibilities of the identified community-level administrative body, usually an existing department of local government.

Although some communities elect to have the program function under the direction of a newly created recreation board or commission, programs more frequently are administered by (1) school authorities, (2) park departments, (3) recreation departments, or (4) combined departments of park and recreation. The implication is that one department is responsible for the community program. The community school concept treated in the next chapter reflects this effort. More often than not, recreation programs are offered under several of the above-mentioned administrative units in addition to the many non-tax-supported associations and commercial ventures.

Community Recreation Administration Plans

Legislation on all governmental levels has an impact and influence on the development of community recreation programs. If a state encourages schools to assume responsibility for community recreation or vests authority in them to do so, management authority is responsible to the school authorities and school board. Some states authorize management as a responsibility of municipal government, which in turn has to decide whether to put the program under an existing agency structure or create a new recreation commission, board, or department. In some instances management authority is left fairly open, and authority emerges that is best able to raise its own support money.

The following discussion will focus on several different administrative approaches. Although discussed from the points of view of varied local government structures, the public usually participates through an appointed or elected board or commission which serves in a policy-making and advisory role to local government and the administrator hired to carry out the program.

Under the Parks Department or District. In this plan, the developed recreation program is housed as a division of a well-established and usually well-financed department of city government, the parks department. This department controls most publicly owned land with recreation potentials and, in many cases, already developed facilities, playgrounds, sports fields, and courts.

Traditionally, parks departments were developed with concerns for beautification, maintenance, and acquisition of lands. They bring this experience as well as park service experience in public relations and serving large numbers of people to new recreation responsibilities.

A new division of a large department responsible for major functions faces many challenges, not the least of which are priority of interests and financial support. The direction and interests of the parks department has been in horticulture, engineering, and operation of properties. The concerns of recreation leadership have been for the development of programs using facilities and serving needs of people. The differences in background priorities cannot be eliminated as a factor of concern at times of budget development and budget cutting.

The Recreation Department or Commission. This administrative unit usually functions as a separate department of the local government. Recreation is the prime concern. Qualified leaders hold full-time jobs. The department meets program needs, and coordinates use of all public recreation facilities and services.

Efforts of a separate recreation department that receive concerted attentions usually fall into identifiable services of: determining recreation needs, programming, interpreting the program to the public, finances and budgeting, building and maintenance. Financial support for these responsibilities can be greater when the department is not combined with or subordinated to some other service or function.

Those who oppose the concept of a separate department point out the effect of an expanding governmental hierarchy, possible duplication of park department work, and granting of power to a department that controls little property. Supporting the professional recreation leadership, however, are the citizen boards which have recreation as their prime interest. The board and professional leaders of a separate department uniquely speak to the public and city government with one voice and as recreation specialists.

Combined Parks and Recreation Department or Board. In this combined department, a pattern that has been gaining support, the parks division has major responsibilities for park beautification, land acquisition, and maintenance. The recreation division serves the program needs of people.

This trend toward a single agency has come about as the parks people, traditionally involved in landscaping, acquiring, and maintaining land, moved toward acceptance of that function to provide for recreational use of the public properties. At the same time recreation departments were able to gain greater acceptance of their people-oriented programs. Expanding concepts and broadening points of view increasingly are bringing these two professional groups together into unified cooperative planning and administration.

As the conflict between parks and recreation subsides with cooperative and unified efforts, a new challenge looms ahead because of exploding community recreation activities that are moving toward increased use of school facilities while the school programs are expanding to serve more than the school-age segment of the community.

Community Co-op Plans

Recreation in some communities has grown without an overall administrative plan or line of authority. As the many programs emerge, a need for solving common problems and projecting for the future draws the leadership into a sharing and cooperative effort.

Interagency Recreation Department, Council, or Federation. Interagency action has proved valuable as a means of pooling interests and resources of neighborhood councils, clubs, associations, and commercial enterprises. Moving in this direction requires a concerted organizational effort to mobilize all available resources—public, private, and commerical—and to coordinate leadership, facilities, and programs. To insure success there must be wide public support from both those being served and the multiplicity of sponsoring or contributing interests involved.

Reading, Pennsylvania has had a Playgrounds Federation for years. The representation in the Federation consists of two persons from each adult neighborhood playground association. The Federation has sponsored citywide recreation events and raised funds, managed the budget, and met the problems of personnel challenges and property acquisitions.

The Neighborhood Recreation Council or Association. In this plan a neighborhood council, committee, club, or association takes on a variety of roles and responsibilities. In small communities the leadership promotes public interest, helps raise funds, and actually plans and operates programs. As responsibilities expand, the supportive group often proves to be the forerunner of a recreation commission.

Neighborhood recreation associations have functioned as nonprofit agencies often financed by the Community Chest, local government, and gifts and endowments. The association operates programs, and a board of directors assumes responsibilities for direction, raising, and spending funds.

Neighborhood councils have been organized by public recreation departments to serve in fundraising, sponsoring recreation events, securing use of local facilities, distributing recreation materials, and assessments.

Small community councils have administered and operated recreation services without being responsible to any departments or authority. In some instances recreation is only one of several major responsibilities of a council that has other neighborhood improvement ambitions.

Recreation Boards. A proliferation of agencies providing recreation programs in some big cities recognized that they were growing independently and without a means of communication. Duplication of programs that led to competition for participants' time existed in some instances, while program voids existed in others. Inefficient use of facilities became evident. Economic squeeze and public demand for more services pressed leadership for innovative approaches that would enable them to expand programs at reasonable costs, eliminate duplication of efforts, and better serve areas of needs and interests. Out of this web of pressures some cities found relief in the formation of representative recreation boards.

Muncipal-School Administration. Small communities have looked to the school as the center of community recreation. Traditionally, varsity sports have dominated the activities and spectators' interests, but momentum has been mounting in a more recent trend. The schools are expanding existing programs to a community-serving level or are moving to joint planning with the municipal recreation departments.

Joint planning by school and municipality has a long history for some pioneering schools such as in Long Beach, California. In 1929, the year that ushered in the Great Depression, the citizens of that California city voted into its charter a provision for coordinated municipal and school recreation. Under the Long Beach coordinated recreation plan, the board of education has provided for free use of all facilities for public recreation except when these are in use by the schools. And a great building program, which saw over $22 million expended by 1952 for new recreation and physical education buildings, reflected faithfully the fundamental theme that "no single elementary, junior or senior high, or college plant was designed or built without adequate planning for use by school students and community groups of all ages." A few examples of how this was done are illuminating. All high schools provide, in addition to deep pools, the shallow-water pools that beginners and elementary school children require. Despite the moderate climate the pools are covered so that no moment may be lost to recreational swimming. Built to open directly into the gymnasiums are kitchenettes that may be used for community affairs of all types; and the gymnasium floors are constructed so as to accommodate the badminton and volleyball posts favored in recreation leagues and co-recreation play.

The building program at Long Beach demonstrated the effective manner in which school facilities could be constructed to accommodate both the school population and the community at large. The community set an example of making facilities and areas available to the schools and indeed, practiced other forms of cooperation as well.

Other schools have made use of municipal swimming pools, and some cities such as Chicago and Dallas have developed projects by which schools and municipal parks are located side by side with provisions for joint usage. Initiating a program in the early 50s, the city school district and the recreation department of Monterey, California together operated a camping and day-camping program in what was viewed as a summer school offering for elementary-school children. Acting on the basis of the California State Education Code, the authorities set up the camp and day camp under the title "Outdoor Science and Conservation Education." Administration of the program was divided. The recreation department had direct, on-the-spot control; and the school district, through the summer session principal, was responsible for the curriculum. Their cooperation was displayed in the choice of personnel. The director and two supervisors were drawn from the school: they possessed credentials for elementary education and were qualified to supervise camping and outdoor science instruction. The group leaders, on the other hand, were employees of the recreation department. Trained as camp counselors, they had worked for at least a year on the local playgrounds. The school district paid the first group; the recreation department, the second. Except for the salaries of the school personnel, the city of Monterey paid all bills through the recreation department; and the recreation department, through the school district, furnished bus transportation, and provided all other transportation and hauling. The various threads of cooperation contributed to a well-functioning whole.

To aid the reader in better understanding municipal-school programs the Long Beach City Charter Provisions and organizational charts for the Long Beach Recreation Commission are included.

Long Beach City Charter Provisions for Long Beach Recreation Commission

Sec. 202a. The term "public recreation" wherever herein used is hereby defined and understood to mean and include all public recreation activities in or upon playgrounds, athletic fields, ball parks, summer camps, recreation centers, swimming pools, beaches, streets, water fronts, waterways, public buildings, coliseums, play areas in parks, tennis courts and other suitable places or other public lands or public waterways used, owned, controlled or operated by the city of Long Beach, either within or without its corporate limits, and the activities in or upon them, and use of same for athletic sports, or contests, games, aquatic games, community leagues, pageants, dramatics, music, public amusements and entertainments and other recreational and play programs or activities, whether herein specified or not, excepting therefrom, however, the municipal golf links, civic auditorium, and the municipal band and the provisions of this article shall apply to adults as well as to minors.

Wherever the term "Board" is hereinafter used, unless it is otherwise expressly specified, it shall be understood to refer to and mean the recreation commission, as in this chapter constituted. (Amendment of 1929).

Sec. 202b. There is hereby created a recreation commission of nine (9) members, not more than six (6) of whom shall be the same sex, and all of whom shall serve without compensation, except that this shall not apply to the City Manager, the Superintendent of Schools, the member of the City Council and the member of the Board of Education sitting on said board. The City Manager, the Superintendent of Schools, a member of the City Council chosen by the City Council and a member of the Board of Education chosen by the Board of Education shall constitute four (4) of the nine (9) members of said Board, and shall serve until their successors are elected, and within thirty (30) days after this amendment takes effect, said four (4) members shall appoint the other five (5) members of said Board, subject to the approval of the City Council, who shall be residents of the City of Long Beach and none of whom shall hold office as members of the Board of Education or of the City Council during their term of office on said Board. . . .

All appointments of said other five (5) members shall be subject to the approval of the City Council. . . .

Sec. 202c. The director of health and physical education of the city schools of the City of Long Beach shall be the director of playground and public recreation of the City of Long Beach, and the council may pay such portion of the salary of such director as may be fixed by the recreation commission. He shall act as a coordinating director of the playground and recreation program of the city schools and of the City of Long Beach. (Amendment of 1929.)

Sec. 202d. The city manager, upon the recommendation of the director shall appoint such supervisors, assistants, and other employees as shall be necessary, and upon the recommendation of the director, he may appoint supervisors, assistants, or others in the employ of the city schools of Long Beach, and none of the supervisors, assistants, or others engaged in technical recreation work shall be under civil service. (Amendment of 1929.) . . .

Sec. 202f. The director shall manage and supervise the public recreation of the city within or without its corporate limits; shall, subject to the provisions of Article XXVI of this chapter, purchase the equipment and materials necessary for public recreation and shall aid and promote and supervise all public functions of a public recreation nature or character; shall, subject to the approval of the Recreation Commission, by order entered on its minutes, have charge of the construction, operation, sale, renting or leasing of concessions or privileges on playground and public recreation areas, and shall have exclusive supervision and control of all equipment, apparatus and buildings, or portions of buildings, devoted to public recreation; shall issue permits for the use of playgrounds and other public recreation equipment and facilities; and shall, subject to the approval of the Recreation Commission, by order entered on its minutes, adopt a schedule of charges and fees and rents for special or regular services and use thereof. (Amendment of 1931.)

Sec. 202g. The City Council of Long Beach shall establish a fund to be known as the "recreation fund." There shall be deposited to this and expended from this fund all fees or moneys received by the board, including the proceeds from all gifts, legacies, or bequests or other sources managed or controlled by the board and derived by it in connection with the operation of the public recreation activities and facilities under its jurisdiction. All moneys in said fund shall be used for the uses and purposes of public recreation, as in the article defined, and not otherwise, and if not used during any current year shall accumulate in said "recreation fund." (Amendment of 1929.)

Sec. 202h. The City Council of Long Beach shall annually levy and collect on all the taxable property in the City of Long Beach for the purposes of creating a special fund to be designated as the "recreation fund" at least five cents (5¢) on each one hundred dollars ($100.00) of the value on all real and personal property of the city for city purposes, and, in addition thereto, shall have power to appropriate such additional funds as it may deem necessary and proper. Said fund shall be exclusively maintained and used to meet the legal demands and expenditures of the board made for the purpose of public recreation. (Amendment of 1929.)

Sec 202i. The City Council of Long Beach shall have the power by ordinance to set aside either absolutely or for a definite period of time any lands, waterways or buildings, equipment or facilities belonging to it for public recreation under the jurisdiction of the recreation commission, and the same shall, when and so long as used by the board, be under its exclusive jurisdiction and control. (Amendment of 1929.)

Sec. 202j. The board may, for and on behalf of the City of Long Beach, receive legacies, gifts or bequests for the purchase, maintenance or improvement of grounds, buildings, equipment or facilities for the purposes of public recreation. All moneys received from such legacies, gifts, or bequests shall, unless otherwise expressly provided by the terms of said legacies, gifts, or bequests, be deposited in the treasury of the City of Long Beach in the "recreation fund." . . .

Sec. 202k. The board shall make a report every three (3) months of the activities thereof to the city manager, and an annual report of the activities thereof to the city manager and the city council, and which annual report shall be filed with the city clerk. (Amendment of 1929.)

Sec. 202l. The board may recommend to the city manager and the city council the acquisition of lands or waterways, buildings, structures, or other equipment and facilities for public recreation as it may, from time to time, deem necessary for the proper conduct of public recreation as in this article defined. It shall have exclusive jurisdiction and control of the operation and conduct of all public recreation activities. No area used for public recreation shall be abandoned or dispensed with without the approval of the board, and it shall pass upon and approve all plans for the improvement of lands

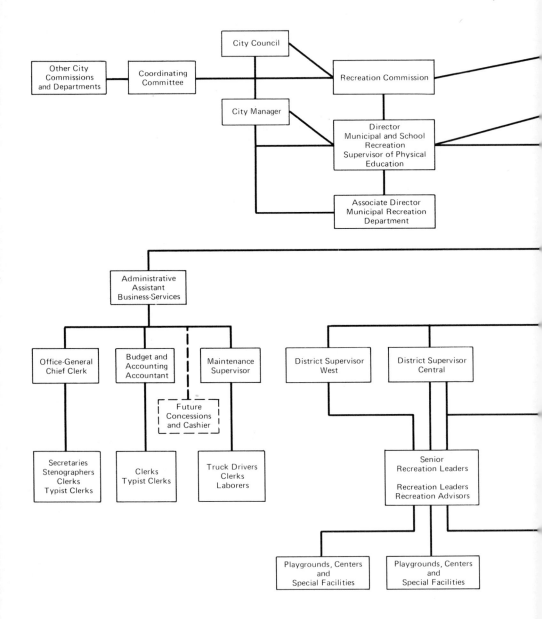

Figure 4-4. Coordinated Municipal and School Recreation Organization Chart. City of Long Beach, California.

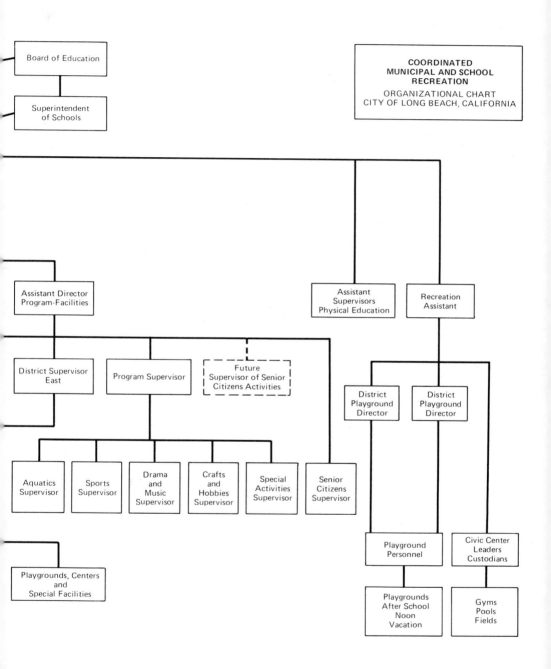

Board of Education

Superintendent of Schools

COORDINATED MUNICIPAL AND SCHOOL RECREATION
ORGANIZATIONAL CHART
CITY OF LONG BEACH, CALIFORNIA

Assistant Director Program-Facilities

Assistant Supervisors Physical Education

Recreation Assistant

District Supervisor East

Program Supervisor

Future Supervisor of Senior Citizens Activities

District Playground Director

District Playground Director

Aquatics Supervisor

Sports Supervisor

Drama and Music Supervisor

Crafts and Hobbies Supervisor

Special Activities Supervisor

Senior Citizens Supervisor

Playground Personnel

Civic Center Leaders Custodians

Playgrounds, Centers and Special Facilities

Playgrounds After School Noon Vacation

Gyms Pools Fields

for public recreation and for the erection, construction or improvement of buildings or other equipment, structures and facilities for the purposes of public recreation. (Amendment of 1929.)

Sec. 202m. The board shall elect one of its number as president, who shall hold office for one (1) year and until his successor is elected, and the director shall act as secretary of the board. It must hold regular meetings at least once every month, and shall establish such rules and regulations as it deems necessary for its government and for the faithful performance of its duties and which shall not be inconsistent with this chapter or with laws of the State of California. It shall provide for and do any other acts which may be found necessary and proper by it to carry out the provisions and purposes hereof, and to execute the duties imposed upon it under the provisions of this chapter.

Sec. 202n. Should it be determined by either the unanimous vote of the board of education or the unanimous vote of the recreation commission, or both, that it is advisable to discontinue the coordinated plan of playground and recreation and supervision and administration, as in this article provided, then written notice of such decision shall be given to the other board herein named by the board making such decisions, and one (1) year thereafter such plan shall be discontinued; then in that event, all the foregoing provisions of this chapter shall remain in full force and effect, except as follows:

The number of members of the recreation commission shall be reduced to seven (7), and the superintendent of public schools and member of the board of education shall no longer by virtue of their office be members thereof. The board shall select a director of recreation, shall fix his duties, tenure of office, salary, and his qualifications shall be the same as are required by the board of education of the City of Long Beach for its director of health and physical education, with the exception, however, that a state certificate from the state board of education shall not be required. (Amendement of 1929.) . . .

Sec. 202p. Anything in this Article to the contrary notwithstanding, the board herein shall hereafter be known as The Recreation Commission and the fund herein authorized shall hereafter be known as The Recreation Fund. . . .

DISCUSSION QUESTIONS

1. Illustrate with specific examples school recreation sports programs that have been expanded to serve post-school adults; preschool children.

2. Do expanding community recreation budgets and commercial recreation expenditures substantiate an "explosion in recreation activity"? Give statistics to support your answer.

3. How has the government become involved in the responsibility for public recreation? Through what specific legislation?

4. What generally accepted principles support government's role in recreation? Explain.

5. Do states follow a common pattern in their role of responsibility for recreation? Substantiate.

6. What are the implications of the Alaska Community School Act of 1975?

7. Are there advantages in a county recreation administrative body? Disadvantages?

8. How does a community obtain legal authorization to initiate a recreation program? How is the administrative body determined?

9. What are the advantages and disadvantages of recreation program administration by the (1) parks department (2) recreation department (3) public school?

10. How can the many cooperative recreation administrative plans be justified? What are the evolving dominant patterns of administration?

BIBLIOGRAPHY

BUTLER, GEORGE, D., *Introduction to Community Recreation.* New York: McGraw-Hill Book Co., 1967.

CARLSON, REYNOLD E., THEODORE R. DEPPE, and JANET R. MacLEAN, *Recreation in American Life.* Belmont, Calif.: Wadsworth Publishing Co., Inc., 1966.

CORBIN, H., and W. TAIT, *Education for Leisure.* Englewood Cliffs, N.J.: Prentice-Hall, Inc., 1973.

DRIVER, B. L., ed., *Elements of Outdoor Recreation Planning.* Ann Arbor, Mich.: Michigan Press, 1974.

GODBEY, GEOFFREY, *Leisure Studies and Services.* Philadelphia: W. B. Saunders Co., 1976.

JENSEN, CLAYNE R., and CLARK T. THORSTENSON, ed., *Issues in Outdoor Recreation.* Minneapolis: Burgess Publishing Co., 1972.

JUBENVILLE, ALAN, *Outdoor Recreation Planning.* Philadelphia: W. B. Saunders Co., 1976.

KRAUS, RICHARD, and JOSEPH E. CURTIS, *Creative Administration in Recreation and Parks.* St. Louis: C. V. Mosby Co., 1973.

KRAUS, RICHARD, *Recreation and Leisure in Modern Society.* New York: Appleton-Century-Crofts, 1971.

RODNEY, LYNN S., *Administration of Public Recreation.* New York: The Ronald Press Co., 1964.

Community School Program.
Courtesy of Washington Center for Community Education.

5

Community Recreation
in Education

The need for established channels of communication, cooperative planning procedures, and mutually acceptable definitions of programs and responsibilities becomes critical on local levels as schools and community recreation programs increasingly overlap, merge, duplicate, or supplement each other.

Title IX defines recreation as a school responsibility and directs that particular concern be extended to provide equal opportunities regardless of sex. State legislation or enabling acts in all states have spurred development of community recreation programs with expanding offerings of sports and leisure-time activities for both school-age children and adults. The Community Schools Act of 1974, implemented in February of 1976, offered $3.55 million in financial assistance for development of community education programs that provide a variety of cultural, educational, recreational, and related services.

As leadership is thus urged to action in serving recreation needs of the whole community, the questions are raised: "What is the difference between the after-school recreation program and the community program?" "When does one program end and the other program begin?" "What is a community school?" "When does education become community education?" Answers to these questions are being explored in developing cooperative efforts on the part of both school and community.

A common support for cooperative efforts between professional groups is provided in the 1974 American Alliance for Health, Physical Education and Recreation approved platform statement. Jointly supported by the National Recreation and Park Association, the National Community Education Association, and the American Alliance for Health, Physical Education and Recreation, the statement recommends a "strong formal system of communications," among school systems, public recreation, and park agencies to facilitate program development, prevent duplication, and benefit the community by thus better serving their needs.[1]

PARKS AND RECREATION

The parks departments have traditionally been concerned with land acquisition, landscaping, engineering, and maintainance of parks and historic sites, as we mentioned in the last chapter. Recreation professionals are people-oriented. Concern for "need of preservation" versus "needs of people" represents a philosophical anachronism of long standing.

> Some defenders of the National Park Service argue that there is an inherent conflict between urban recreation and the objectives for environmental and historic preservation that have typified the Park Service's primary mission since 1916. Other Park defenders are equally persuaded that the only way to strengthen and perhaps avoid the loss of a broad citizen constituency for the National Park system is to bring the system closer to where people live and work.[2]

As recreation programs have grown and expanded, land and facilities have become a vital need. Leaders concerned primarily with serving people have been quick to point out that the people need the parks rather than the parks needing people. The pressure for more public use of parks has had a resultant positive impact, as evidenced in the "marriage" of parks and recreation services in a variety of complementing administrative relationships.

The schools and parks and recreation functions have steadily moved to closer relationships as a result of exploration of the kinds of services mutually offered. Cooperative efforts increase in spite of some departments' struggle with the philosophical controversy of whether parks and recreation operational policy should include provision for cultural and educational services that would use community cultural centers and school facilities.

SCHOOL RECREATION

In many small communities the school offers the most comprehensive facilities, is most centrally located, harbors leadership resource person-

[1]"News," *Journal of Health, Physical Education and Recreation* (November–December 1974), p. 12.

[2]"The Urban Park Dilemma,," *Parks and Recreation* (July 1975), p. 17.

nel, and traditionally has been the natural recreation focal point. In many rural low-population districts the school continues in the role of "community recreation center." As communities expand into large cities, however, this identity is lost among the multitude of social organizations, agencies, and public service programs. Visibility is obscured among the "towers of centralized bureaucracy."

The 70s brought a change of direction away from centralization and concentration of power. The attack on big government was not directed solely at Washington, D.C. New York City in 1972 initiated an effort to reverse the trend by decentralizing administration of all major municipal services including recreation. Starting with four neighborhoods, a district manager, and district services cabinet, the idea soon expanded to twenty-four neighborhoods.[3]

The impact of the efforts of some governmental and dedicated public leadership to reverse the trend of centralization of power to more local control has not gone unnoticed: in fact, "the recent move to decentralization has inspired the development of both community schools and community-controlled schools."[4]

REVOLT AND CHANGE

Evolving administrative changes in parks, recreation, and school leisure services parallel a taxpayers' revolt. Rationales for increased taxes and seemingly less return for dollars spent. are being challenged. An increased public scrutiny of budgets and weak support for levies and bond issues reflects an audit-minded public. While demanding accountability, the public also presses for more services and more programs. Limited and inadequate facilities championed by schools, parks, recreation departments, and social service agencies represent either a four-way contest to win taxpayers' support or a bond of mutual concern. For some communities it has been a challenge met by innovative approaches, maximum use of public resources, and more efficient programming.

Evident Change

Philosophical change is not easily identified, but attention to several school and community occurrences warrant consideration for implications.

1. Evening adult education classes, catch-up programs for dropouts, even-

[3]Donald J. Middletown, "To Re-Create Urban Recreation," *Parks and Recreation* (April 1975), p. 58.

[4]Dee Scholfield, *Community Schools: School Leadership Digest* (Arlington, Va.: National Association of Elementary School Principals, 1974), p. 7.

ing recreation programs, tewlve-month schools, cooperative programs with community social agencies, and recreation departments—all indicate a growing acceptance by administrators that schools can no longer justify operating their plants for a limited 7–8 hour day for 180 days a year.

2. Joint ventures, cooperative use policies, and contractual agreements between school and community agencies can be seen as a partial acceptance that schools cannot do all things for all people.

3. Institutions such as community colleges, free schools, social agencies, and community recreation departments offer many additional alternate learning options. Brought into the school, these opportunities lend support to society's growing recognition that much learning takes place outside the formal structure of the school curriculum.

4. City government feasibility studies, independent consultant reports, fiscal audits of city services, impact statements, and community surveys of resource facilities and personnel required as part of project proposals seem to indicate a concern for more fiscal responsibility.

5. "Power to the People" is more than a slogan. It is a movement that is taking place, as illustrated by Independence, Missouri's 39 neighborhood councils started in 1971. Each council has direct communication links to the departments of city government. The voice of the people is just a whisper away from the governor, city adminstrators, and directors.

6. Experimental and new facility-planning concepts indicate efforts to provide more functional buildings to serve numerous programs, a mobile population, and a variety of lifestyles.

7. Coordination as a main thrust of effort evidences the recognition of overlapping and duplication of services, responsibilities, and resources.

A Variety of Efforts by Recreation Leadership

Increased community involvement in local issues, together with efforts of responsible leadership, has initiated a diversity of administrative change and innovation. The following summarizes efforts most generally attempted to facilitate efficiency and cooperative working relationships between the schools and the community:

1. Schools liberalize their "facilities use policies" with other governmental agencies

2. Verbal reciprocal agreements established between recreation council and school board for free use of playground equipment

3. Written agreements developed between school boards and city recreation authorities

4. Vacant buildings, churches, and empty warehouses used for expanded recreation programs

5. Programs expanded to include cooperative use of commercial facilities such as bowling, riding, golf, roller skating

6. Maintenance expense reflecting city programs in school facilities paid for by recreation department budgets

7. School personnel moved onto municipal recreation department payrolls as program leaders and supervisors of extended programs

8. School authorities sharing with the city on a formula basis relative to program expenses and salary of the recreation director

9. School-board-appointed representation on city recreation boards

10. Joint planning effected between school and community building programs

11. Twelve-month teacher contracts including one month paid vacation and requiring Saturday, after-school, and evening recreation responsibilities during the school year

12. Schools assuming major year-round responsibilities for the community recreation program and thereby serving as the community focal point

13. A "supervisor of youth services section" of the board of education assuming total responsibility for the recreation and activities program

14. Total program of physical education and recreation together with municipal recreation for all ages unified under one director and staff

SCHOOL AND COMMUNITY RECREATION ADMINISTRATION POSSIBILITIES

Recreation programs are administered by (1) schools and (2) communities or (3) school-community leadership.

School-Directed Recreation Programs

School recreation has traditionally been referred to as activities and programs planned for student leisure time within the school setting. Community recreation administered by the schools has evolved as the after-school and evening sports programs, classes, clubs, and activities expanded to serve the post-school community members. The concept of education as a lifetime experience implies school responsibilities to serve all ages in a variety of experiences including *lifetime sports and recreation activities.*

Proponents of recreation administrative responsibility being vested in the public school system point out that recreation is education. The school already administers as it provides leadership, buildings, and facilities for sports, recreation, and cultural activities. Furthermore, confidence in the board of education, teachers, and authorities is already established.

Because schools have had financial pressures over the years, it has been questioned whether school administration could provide adequate financial support. Without substantial resources and facilities, school leadership could limit expanded community-oriented programs. Inasmuch as school boards, with the legal power to develop recreation programs over the years, have done little, the questions are also raised

"What priorities would be given to programs not meaningful to the
established school curriculum?" "Would recreation be a subordinated
responsibility under school administration?"

Community-Directed Programs

Community-sponsered recreation programs are developed by a professional staff with a major interest in recreation and leisure services.
The program reflects the community's support of its proposed budget.
Activities are planned using the community-owned parks, playgrounds,
senior citizen centers, libraries, and museums. Because of the growing
diversity of leisure services there is substantial support for an administrative responsibility that is a direct arm of local government.

The scope of community-sponsored recreation programs has expanded to include an endless list of leisure-time activities, as illustrated
in the partial list of Figure 5–1.

Senior Citizen Center	Learning Classes	Free Play
Social Centers	Health Education	Roller Skating
Club Programs	Doing Classes	Quiet Games
Music	Art	Organized Sports
Crafts	Writing	
Garden	Acting	Aquatics
Hobbies	Singing	
Mt. Climbing		Fitness Programs
Sky Diving		
Cards	Auto Mechanics	Recreation for
		Handicapped
Chess		
Checkers	Retirement Planning	Hiking, Camping,
		Climbing
Dancing		
	Planned Travel	Playground Activities
Community Service Projects	Arts and Crafts	Area Sports
		Competition
Holiday Special Events		Championships,
		Tournaments,
		and Matches
Cultural Programs		Weight Training
Food Service		Summer Camps
		Bowling
		Pool

Figure 5–1. Scope of Community-Sponsored Recreation Activities

As community-sponsored programs multiply, YMCA, YWCA, Boys'
Clubs, and 4-H organizations reach out for the same blocks of leisure

time. Jaycee, Optimists, Lions, and others look for areas of service that could benefit from their help. Health and welfare provide an entire program of community services.

The multitude of community-sponsored programs often serve everyone's needs twice over. Critics are quick to point out that all organized recreation programs lack some type of systematic coordination and cooperation to eliminate the tremendous overlap and duplication of services that are so common.[5]

The community recreation departments have financial and personnel resources that enhance program development. The schools control the best space for recreation and community service programs. What is needed is joint efforts between school, recreation departments, service clubs, and social service agencies.

School-Community Leadership

A school that is transformed into a community civic and cultural center augmented by other resources is identified by a growing number of cities as a "community school." This emergence of the school as an education and recreation center for children and adults means that when the school is used after the traditional school day and year, it serves the needs of the community.

THE COMMUNITY SCHOOL

"Community schools are open both days and evenings year-round and become a place where people, children as well as adults, go both to learn and to enjoy themselves. Lifelong learning and enrichment opportuntiies for all ages are provided in the school facility, but are not confined to the building itself."[6]

Both the public schools and the parks/recreation departments have been effective as the responsible administrative agent for the community school programs. Regardless of ultimate responsibility, the most important key to success has been cooperation between city, county, schools, and involved social agencies. Justification for greater school-community coordination and planning includes the following:

1. Makes for more responsiveness to community needs
2. Eliminates duplication of facilities and supplies
3. Brings services to within neighborhood distance of the beneficiaries
4. Facilitates use of school and community leadership personnel

[5]Stephen L. Stark, "Community Education: Coordination and Cooperation," *Journal of Health, Physical Education and Recreation* (April 1974), p. 42.

[6]Larry E. Decker, "Community Education: Purpose, Function, Growth, Potential" *Journal of Health, Physical Education and Recreation* (April 1974), p. 39.

5. Forces a definition of teacher responsibilities and recreation leader responsibilities

6. Eliminates competition for community members' time when program duplication is removed

7. Enables improved facilities for the future because of the economy of efficient use planning, service programming, and consolidated maintenance

8. Enhances community support as taxpayers and beneficiaries

A school becomes a community school by administrative designation or is given title on the drawing boards of new construction. Administrative identity is the result of a community expression that leads to hiring a director and assistants. An inventory is made of all available resources and needs of the community. Existing programs and services are coordinated and facilitated. Where needed, new programs and resources are developed. Educative institutions are recognized. The community school, through its new leadership, serves as a unifying agent and center. It operates for community betterment. The program is unique and changes with changing needs.

Community schools that emerge from the drawing boards combine new school building plans with a community school concept to develop complexes of community recreation and education. These cultural centers, a reality in many cities, incorporate school, recreation, and social services. Harold B. Gores in 1974 projected today's reality in his "School House of the Future":

> The name school house may become redundant. . . . It is not unlikely that the newly emerging community center school may some day be known simply as the "center." . . . It will not be precisely designed to accommodate children; it will be designed for mass education for everybody. The center, held in common ownership by all the people, will be their school, their clinic, their town hall, their civic center, their country club."[7]

COMMUNITY EDUCATION CONCEPT

Community education has been described as a philosophical approach to community services that uses the community school as the facilitating agent. The emphasis is on implementing education as an ongoing lifetime experience for all ages.

Philosophy and Method. An excerpt from a statement by the superintendent of public instruction of the State of Washington enlarges on the foundations of Community Education:

> Community Education is. . . .: A Philosophy and A Method that:
>
> 1. extends the role of education from the traditional concept of only

[7]"Community Education: Schoolhouse of the Future," *Journal of Health, Physical Education and Recreation* (April 1974), p. 53.

teaching children to that of identifying the wants, needs and problems of the community and then assisting in the development of leadership, programs and facilities to fulfill those wants and needs and to attempt to solve those problems.

2. expands the traditional school role from a formal learning center for 5–18 year olds open 6–8 hours per day, 5 days per week and 36 weeks each year to a "Human Resources Development Center" virtually "round the clock all year long."

3. greatly increases the utilization of the largest tax dollar investment in most communities by making the facilties more readily available to those who have paid for their construction and maintenance.

4. provides a wide range of educational, social, recreational, cultural and community problem-solving opportunities without restriction as to clientele, facilities to be used, or time of day.

5. utilizes a community-wide "Needs and Resources Assessment" survey to determine program content and direction.

A Vehicle for Community Development and Involvement by:

1. reaching out to create opportunities for residents to belong, to learn, and to share, thus creating or revitalizing a "sense of community," and

2. stressing broad-based citizen involvement, inter-agency cooperation and coordination and greater utilization of local human and physical resources.[8]

Structuring. Community schools' administrative organizational charts that identify lines of supervision and responsibility reflect the desires of school and community or often emerge from a facilitating relationship. If authority for a particular program has been directive, coming from a specific administrative level, the diagrammed chart will reflect that line of authority. Figure 5–2 illustrates two organizational possibilities in which community and school establish a cooperative working relationship. Figure 5–3 illustrates an organizational plan within the school administrative structure; and Figure 5–3a presents a summary of the principal characteristics of a community school.

Programming. Dynamic programming changes to meet changing needs and problems are fundamental to the maximum use of educational and community facilities together with the coordination of community resources. Policy statements facilitate the cooperative effort as illustrated by Surrey Parks and Recreation Commission in one of its statements:

Policy
1. (a) Parks and Recreation Commission to use schools for part-time activities without payment of costs for heat, light, or janitoral and administrative services. The Parks and Recreation Department will use the same procedures and receive the same priority as the Adult Education Division.

---

[8]State of Washington Superintendent of Public Instruction Statement on Community Education. Courtesy of Washington Center for Community Education, Superintendent of Public Instruction, Olympia, Washington.

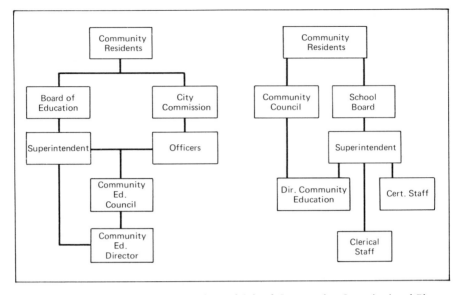

Figure 5–2. Community Education City and School Cooperative Organizational Plan

When schedules conflict, suitable arrangements will be made between the *Recreation Director* and *Adult Education Director*. If arrangements are in dispute, a decision of Superintendent of schools will be final and binding.[9]

Because most communities with multi-sponsored recreation and education programs conflict, compete, and tend to be self-serving, important to the success of the concept is its primary effort to coordinate services and thus prevent overlapping and duplication. Basic to community education is a "system of delivery" that should be developed to include the following:

1. Programs offered at the neighborhood level
2. Community needs established as the basis for services
3. Existing resources and services inventories

EVOLUTION OF THE COMMUNITY SCHOOL AS AN AGENT OF COMMUNITY EDUCATION

The community school was born in school recreation programs that extended the school day. To these programs were added enrichment activities such as arts, crafts, drama, and cultural programs. Expanded

[9]"Guidelines for Implementing Policy for Community Education and Recreation" (revised September 9, 1974), Surrey Parks and Recreation Commissions, Surrey, B.C., Canada.

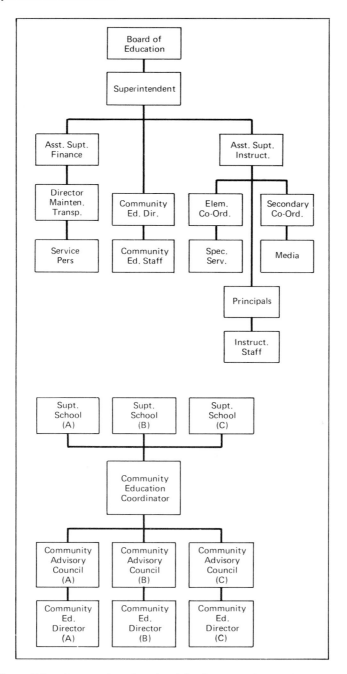

Figure 5–3. Community Education School-Centered Organizational Plan

SUMMARY OF PRINCIPAL CHARACTERISTICS OF THE COMMUNITY SCHOOL

1. Makes all facilities and trained personnel available day and night year around.

2. Adapts its facilities (building and grounds) to multiple use and to persons of all ages.

3. Develops much of its curriculum and activities from continuous study of people's basic needs.

4. Considers with due (equal?) importance the afternoon, evening, Saturday, and summer program - - and the regular academic daytime program.

5. Integrates insofar as possible the educational, social, physical, recreational, and health programs for children, youth, and adults.

6. Makes full use of all available resources, both human and material, in carrying out its program.

7. Is a source of initiative and gives initial leadership in planning and carrying out constructive community projects.

8. In all phases of its work it promotes democratic thinking and action.

9. Constructs its curriculum and activities creatively and is less reliant upon traditional education patterns.

10. Inspires its staff with a desire to be of service in real life activities and beyond the usual classroom responsibilities.

11. Expands and diffuses leadership throughout the community.

12. Is genuinely life-centered as a social institution.

13. Involves all persons concerned in planning much of its program.

14. Seeks to enrich all phases of the daytime program by use of community resources.

15. Aims to develop a sense of unity and solidarity in its neighborhood.

16. Initiates program of usefulness for persons of all ages, classes, and creeds.

17. Takes responsibility for coordinating living, learning and service activities of other agencies in the community.

18. Does much to establish confidence in the minds of people that they can solve cooperatively most of their own community problems.

Figure 5–3a. Summary of Principal Characteristics of the Community school from descriptive materials developed by W. Fred Totten. Courtesy of Washington Center for Community Education.

services included efforts to help all ages and levels of "school dropout or lifetime students" reach full learning potential. Most recently the community school has initiated efforts to serve social needs.

The Surrey, British Columbia (Canada) program patterned after Eugene, Oregon demonstrates that the concept of the community school is moving ahead in Canada, and there are about 10,000 such schools in the United States. Through departments and divisions of recreation, leisure services, parks departments, and institutions of higher education, which increasingly are promoting the development of leadership, more impetus will be added to developing progams.

Supportive federal legislation includes grants for college and university programs, funding for community school programs, and a charge to the commissioner of education to promote community education. A director of community education in the U.S. Office of Education implements community education legislation. On the state level many laws are also on the books to facilitate, operate, and fund community education on a shared basis. The Alaska Community School Act creates a statewide advisory council to coordinate activities and review grant proposals; a state coordinator of community education; and a process for funding local community school programs. Minnesota permits every school board to levy a community education dollar to be matched by a state quarter for every man, woman, and child in the community. Thirty states support full-time staff people assigned to community education.

The Mott Foundation of Flint, Michigan financially supports regional community education centers that serve every district. The centers provide assistance to local school districts planning to initiate programs, disseminate and develop materials, and provide training programs to help with the development of leadership (see Figure 5–4).

Three other promotional groups deeply involved in the movement include (1) the National Community Education Association, created in

State and Regional Community Education Centers	
Arizona, 85282	415 Farmer Education Bldg., Tempe
California, 94086	Sunnyvale School District, Sunnyvale
Colorado, 80521	Colorado State University, Fort Collins
Florida, 32233	1701 Davis Street, Jacksonville
Hawaii, 96821	360 G. Haleloa Place, Honolulu
Massachusetts, 02164	300 Elliot Street, Newton
Michigan, 48503	1401 E. Court Street, Flint
Illinois, 62901	Southern Illinois University, Carbondale
Minnesota, 55105	College of St. Thomas, St. Paul
New Jersey, 08071	Pitman
Ohio, 45056	Miami University, Oxford
Oregon, 97403	1736 Moss Street, Eugene
Texas, 77840	Texas A&M University, College Station

Figure 5–4. Community Education Centers

1966, which holds national conventions and regional conferences and provides consultant and leadership training services; (2) the *Community Education Journal,* which reports articles of interest to those involved in the effort; and (3) the Pendell Publishing Co., which in the early years of the movement published and promoted many related books and resource materials.

The National Joint Continuing Committee on Community Schools involves the National Community Education Association (NCEA), the American Association for Leisure and Recreation (AALR), and the National Recreation and Parks Association (NRPA). This committee has devoted itself to establishing guidelines of cooperation among education, community and state recreation agencies, college in-service leadership training programs, and other involved agencies.[10]

Flint Program

Evolution of the community school and the community education philosophy are best illustrated by the Flint, Michigan program. Here the model community education program had its early beginning before 1934 in a modest community school program of sports clubs for difficult boys. With the support of concerned citizens this program was expanded to include summer recreation. The federal work relief programs provided adult education classes and nursery schools, to be conducted in vacant buildings or whatever facilities were available, in addition to after-school recreation programs.

In 1936, philanthropist Charles Stewart Mott and public school physical education director Frank J. Manley proposed opening a few Flint schools after regular hours for supervised recreation for the young people. Mr. Mott agreed to fund the experiment if the school board would pay for heat, light, and janitorial services.

A bargain was struck. The concept caught on and the community became involved. By 1936 fifteen buildings were being used. Community-researched needs resulted in program expansions just before the war to include health, homemaking, industrial, and vocational education programs as well as various club programs, social services, and social work classes. After the war in 1947 the schools launched an update effort to determine how the school could best serve the community. A building program was launched, and in 1952 with community involvement, two community schools were built. A community school director was hired to coordinate and direct each school's programming.

Today all schools in Flint are community schools whose main objectives are to become the total human resource center for all age groups in the community, improve school children's environment, and ensure education as a lifelong process.

[10]The Charles Stewart Mott Foundation, "Letter," 2, No. 2 (December 1975), p. 4.

With the mobilization of community facilities and resources, the schools have become effective agents of social change. Flint and the Mott Foundation, with documented social improvement patterns since 1935, have shown improved preventive health, voting frequency, approval of bond issues, and a drop in vandalism. The schools reported fewer dropouts and an 80 percent enrollment in adult education, double the national rate.[11]

The intramural sports program is described by Tom Cole as "a cooperative effort between schools and the community education and recreation program." The junior high schools have citywide tournaments for nonvarsity players. Senior high has some citywide tournaments. Cooperative use of school facilities allows intramural and recreation programs to be run after school, nights, and weekends.[12]

The community school coordinator provides programs in adult high school education, occupational training and retraining, academic and leisure-time enrichment classes, recreation and social activities for all ages, family education and counseling, civic affairs and community action, health education and services, teen clubs, and youth and senior citizen acitvities.

A neighborhood council with broad representation that includes businesspeople, clergy, students, community leaders, and representatives of school organizations provides input guidance and direction for the school program and its operation.

Tulsa Program

Although evolving patterns of cooperation that mature into community school programs are unique unto themselves, the Tulsa story[13] highlights the growing-up process, which also started from a recreation program.

Tulsa recreation services were formalized by the appointment of a recreation director in 1952. As the program grew, authority for the services was redefined in a change of city charter which created a Tulsa Parks and Recreation Board in 1960. Program expansion led to requests for use of school facilities on a regular basis. Fees were established. Expenses were identified, but it soon became evident that interagency charges approximately canceled out. Fees were dropped; but the two public functions, the school and recreation board, continued to benefit

---

[11]Larry Malloy, *Community/School: Sharing the Space and the Action,* second printing (New York: Education Facilities Laboratories, 1974), p. 78.

[12]"Cooperative Recreation and Intramural Program Approach Through the Community Education Concept in Flint, Michigan," *Leisure Today: Selected Readings* (Washington, D.C.: American Association for Leisure and Recreation, an association of the American Alliance for Health, Physical Education and Recreation, 1975), p. 70.

[13]Everette E. Nance and Donna Pond, "Broad-Based Community Planning—Tulsa Model," *Leisure Today: Selected Readings,* pp. 74–75.

from mutual exchanges of facilities, personnel, and equipment. The
relationship set the stage for community schools.

By 1972 two pilot community schools were implemented. Interested
citizen groups supported the project and a community coordinating
committee was formed. The two schools became six by 1975. With expansion came professional staff, and more funds. The budget benefited
from revenue funds that supplemented the board of education and the
parks and recreation board appropriated funds. A community school
coordinating committee was brought into being as a policy-making
group. Representation included the mayor's office through the park and
recreation board, the school board, park and recreation department,
and the public school system.

An administrative director relates to the board of education, and the
park and recreation board oversees a staff of three professionals at each
site. Each school functions with its own advisory council, which gives
direction to program planning and leadership for its own school.

The professional staff of three at each school puts the program into
effect. A coordinator is responsible for the educational program. A recreation supervisor and recreation leader organize and supervise leisure-
time activities. Figure 5–5 illustrates the organizational structure of administration.

Architectural Design of Community Schools

As an evolving concept, for some, "community school" means use of
existing school premises during nonschool hours for recreation, adult
education, public gatherings, or just summer school. For others, it means
extended use of those facilities for fine arts, vocational education, and
social or preschool services. Most recently the term "community school"
has had reference to new structures planned, built, and operated
cooperatively by schools and agencies for the delivery of educational and
social services to the entire community. These services most significantly
reflect efforts for financial efficiency brought about by economic pressures combined with demands for more public services.

Variety best characterizes new plans, new building, new relationships of joint school-community ventures. Private industry and social
services have all been included in some of the new facility centers. There
have also been innovative approaches to joint financing, budgeting, and
operation. Coordination has been based upon agreements or contracts
between involved public bodies. Centralized administration usually acts
as liaison and mediator between agencies and users. Schools proceed
with education having more learning options, making better use of
community resources, and benefiting from more long-term financing
opportunities.

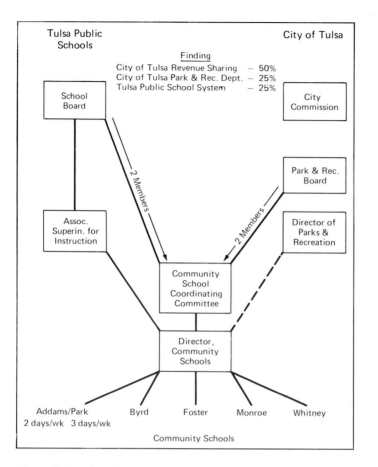

Figure 5–5   City of Tulsa Community Schools Organizational Chart

Examples of joint planning and operation illustrate the thrust of new community schools today.[14]

John F. Kennedy School and Community Center, Atlanta, Georgia

This center provides services for a well-defined city neighborhood. Initiated by the Atlanta Department of School Plant Planning and Construction, the $5 million facility opened in 1971 in the Nash Washington District

[14]Malloy, *Community/School.*

of Atlanta. Reflecting a comprehensive study of low socioeconomic community needs and services and the cooperation of the thirteen public agencies, two foundations, and the U.S. Department of Housing and Urban Development (HUD), the center proposes to take care of all community needs.

The school and many municipal and community agencies are housed under one roof. Forty-five percent of the space in the three-story center is used by agency offices, recreation, day-care, vocational, and rehabilitative service facilities. The community has free use of the facility at all times and full use after 3:00 P.M. All public services are facilitated by one administration. A community school director coordinates use, finances, and working alliances among the many federal, state, and city programs.

Whitmer Human Resources Center, Pontiac, Michigan

This community school, as the hub of the downtown renewal project, serves an entire city. Born out of a desperate effort to rescue a decaying urban core being abandoned by its inhabitants, Whitmer Center replaces four elementary schools and includes offices for ten community agencies.

Faced with devastating social, racial, and economic ills, thirty parents and community members with the consultant help of the Ford Foundation–sponsored Education Facilities Laboratory drafted and combined proposals that resulted in a human resources center building and operation concept. The community programs include medical and dental clinics, adult education, day-care services, recreation, arts, and a public restaurant for nearby workers, parents, teachers, and administrators.

An ongoing exchange of people and materials between schools and community agencies is encouraged by the center's director. Integration is brought about through a community executive board. Three teachers, eleven parents, and ex-officio agency representatives meet every two weeks with the director to solve problems and facilitate channels of communication. Interested citizens participate in program sponsorship through supportive subcommittee work.

Unique to the development of this facility was the struggle to secure a HUD grant. State statute prohibited school districts from receiving federal funds for construction of school facilities. Resolution was finally effected with an amended state law.

Thomas Jefferson Junior High School and Community Center

In 1972 a new building in Arlington, Virginia, brought together the board of education and the Virginia Department of Environmental Affairs. The facility united two previously segregated junior high schools with the planning and parks and recreation departments, which at that time then combined under the Department of Environmental Affairs.

Open from 6:00 A.M. to midnight seven days a week, for all ages, the joint-use building reflects changes of emphasis throughout the day. From 6:00 to 9:00 A.M. the Department of Environmental Affairs opens the canteen, clubroom, and some gym space. From 9:00 A.M. to 3:00 P.M. the field house space is used predominantly by the schools. After 3:00 P.M. the recreation program expands; and supervised by the board of education, an adult education program takes over a good part of the academic space.

A mix of age groups simultaneously uses various facilities and dining areas. Extension classes and sports programs keep the building in service well into the evening hours.

East Orange, New Jersey

East Orange, New Jersey, proposes for the future an education plaza of fifteen acres as a cultural, recreational, and enrichment center for the whole community. Recreational and park facilities would surround, complement, and serve a central "school" building, which, in effect, would become a school community center. Neighborhood schools would serve the outlying community areas and continue to make recreational facilities available.

THE FUTURE

As we have seen from the examples provided above, the community school concept offers variations of an old idea that is stirring from a "fitful sleep" for what might prove to be its "day in the sun."

DISCUSSION QUESTIONS

1. How has leadership been urged to serve more actively the public's recreation needs?

2. What is an after-school recreation program? How is it different from a community recreation program?

3. What has been the traditional role of parks and recreation departments? How is it changing?

4. School and community increasingly are becoming involved in recreation services. Discuss patterns of mutual involvement.

5. Duplication in recreation programs is being challenged. Discuss the pressures for change.

6. Should schools administer all recreation programs or should the community be the administratively responsible agent? Why?

7. Define the community school. Is there more than one kind of community school? Illustrate.

8. Define the community education concept. Is it a philosophy or method? Describe.

9. Discuss the evolution of the community school as an agent of community education.

10. Highlight the distinctive aspects of (1) the Flint Program; (2) the Tulsa

Program; (3) the John F. Kennedy School and Community Center; (4) the Whitmer Human Resources Center; and (5) the Thomas Jefferson Junior High School and Community Center.

BIBLIOGRAPHY

ARTZ, ROBERT M., *School-Community Recreation and Park Cooperation.* Arlington, Va.: National Recreation and Park Association, 1972.

CWIK, PER J., MARILYN J. KING, and CURTIS VAN VOORHEES, *A Monograph.* The Office of Community Education Association, 1975.

DECKER, LARRY E., *Foundations of Community Education.* Midland, Mich.: Pendell Publishing Co., 1972.

FAIRCHILD, EFFIE, and LARRY NEAL, *Common-Unity in the Community.* Eugene, Oregon: Center of Leisure Studies, University of Oregon, 1975.

HENRY, NELSON B., ed., *Community Education: Principles and Practices from WorldWide Experience,* the Fifty-Eighth Yearbook of the National Society for the Study of Education, Part I. Chicago: University of Chicago Press, 1959.

HIEMSTRA, ROGER, *The Educative Community Linking the Community, School, and Family.* Lincoln, Nebraska: Professional Educators Publications, Inc., 1972.

KERENSKY, VASIL M., and ERNEST O. MELBY, *Education II Revisited—A Social Imperative.* Midland, Mich.: Pendell Publishing Co., 1975.

MALLOY, LARRY, *Community/School: Sharing the Space and the Action,* 2nd printing. New York: Educational Facilities Laboratories, 1974.

MCCLOSKEY, GORDON, *Year-Round Community Schools: A Framework for Administrative Leadership.* Washington, D.C.: American Association of School Administrators, 1973.

MURPHY, JAMES F., *Recreation and Leisure Services.* Dubuque, Iowa: W. C. Brown Co., 1975.

Phi Delta Kappan, Community Education: A Special Issue, Bloomington, Indiana, November 1972.

SCHOFIELD, DEE, *Community Schools School Leadership Digest,* prepared by ERIC Clearing House on Educational Management, Arlington, Va.: Published by National Association of Elementary School Principals, 1974.

SEAY, MAURICE, *Community Education. A Developing Concept.* Midland, Mich.: Pendell Publishing Co., 1974.

III

The Human Dimension

Mt. Baker Ski Area.
(Courtesy Mt. Baker Recreation Co., Inc., Bellingham, Washington.)

6

The "New" Sports Participants

As the concept of lifetime sports wins increasing acceptance, the sports participant is drawn from all age groups in the population, from the child in the primary grades to the senior citizen. And education is spoken of as imparting lifetime skills, a point that may be seen in the minimum requirements for education that Oregon has imposed. The performance competencies set down in the Oregon goals include developing and maintaining a healthy mind and body and developing and maintaining the role of a lifelong learner.[1] In effect, the schools are made the instruments for serving community members of all ages, a role reinforced by the Community Education Service Act, which was funded in 1976. Accordingly, the sports participant is thought of as a lifelong participant to be served by the school and community. Such changing conditions and circumstances compel the directors of recreational sports to become familiar with sportspeople of varied ages, interests, and concerns: the elementary school student, the individual in the middle or junior high school, the high school–college student, and the sports-minded adult and senior citizen. But there are other reasons for thinking in terms of "new" participants. It will be seen that the traditional athlete has begun to reassess his values and that a "new" figure, the sportswoman, has made an entrance on the recreational sports scene.

STATISTICAL PROFILE OF POTENTIAL PARTICIPANTS

According to projections, the number of students enrolled in the elementary, secondary, and higher education system will decline from the 60 million of 1973 to 56 million in 1983. At the same time more

[1]*Oregon Graduation Requirements,* prepared by Graduation Requirement Task Force (Salem, Oregon: State Department of Education, 1973).

post-school adults will be looking to the schools and colleges to serve their needs.

Enrollment

The K–8 elementary school 35 million enrollment of 1973 is predicted to decrease to 31 million in 1979 and then begin to increase to 32 million by 1983. Grades 9–12, with enrollments of 15 million in 1971, are expected to remain about the same through 1979, then decrease rapidly to 13 million in 1983. Figure 6–1 illustrates the projections for elementary and secondary schools.

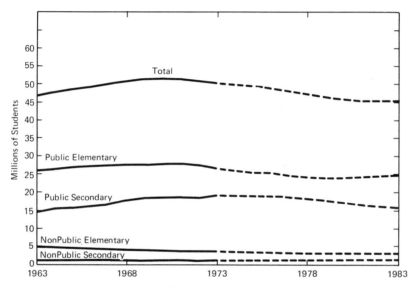

Figure 6-1   Enrollment in Grades K–8 of Regular Day Schools, by Institutional Control and Organizational Level: United States, Fall 1963 to 1983 (Washington, D.C.: National Center for Education Statistics).

The higher education enrollment is expected to increase by 700,000 students from 1973–1980 and then decrease by 200,000 students from 1980–1983, with the women accounting for over 75 percent of the increases.[2] Figure 6–2 illustrates this trend.

Post-School Population

The population profile of Figure 6–3 projects an increasingly dom-

[2]National Center for Education Statistics, *Projections of Education Statistics to 1983–84,* 1974 Edition, U.S. Department of Health, Education and Welfare/Education Division (Washington, D.C.: U.S. Government Printing Office, 1975), pp. 12–14.

inant middle-aged group of adults and a growing number of senior citizens.[3]

Confirming an already felt invasion of the schools by the post-school age group is Figure 6–4, which graphically illustrates the increased participation and projections of adult education programs.[4]

Educational Expenses

In spite of the anticipated decline in enrollment, educational expenses are predicted to continue to rise. Annual current expenditures for public elementary and secondary schools were $50.2 billion in 1973–74 and are expected to increase 33 percent to $67.0 billion by 1983–1984.[5] Figure 6–5 graphically illustrates this trend.

Institutions of higher education are projected to increase expenditures from the $31.3 billion of 1973–74 to $42.4 billion by 1983–84.[6] Figure 6-6 illustrates the projections.

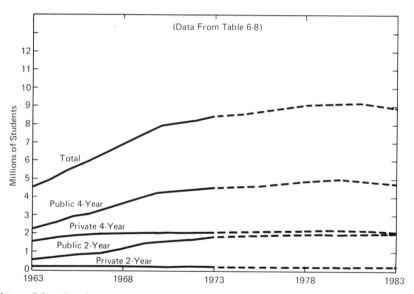

Figure 6-2   Total Degree-Credit Enrollment in Institutions of Higher Education, by Control and Type of Institution, Fall 1963 to 1983 (Washington, D.C.: National Center for Education Statistics).

[3]National Center for Education Statistics, *The Condition of Education,* 1976 Edition, U.S. Department of Health, Education and Welfare/Education Division (Washington, D.C.: U.S. Government Printing Office, 1976), pp. 10–12.

[4]Ibid.

[5]National Center for Education Statistics, *Projections of Education Statistics to 1983–84,* 1974 Edition, U.S. Department of Health, Education and Welfare/Education Division (Washington, D.C.: U.S. Government Printing Office, 1975), p. 81.

[6]Ibid., p. 83.

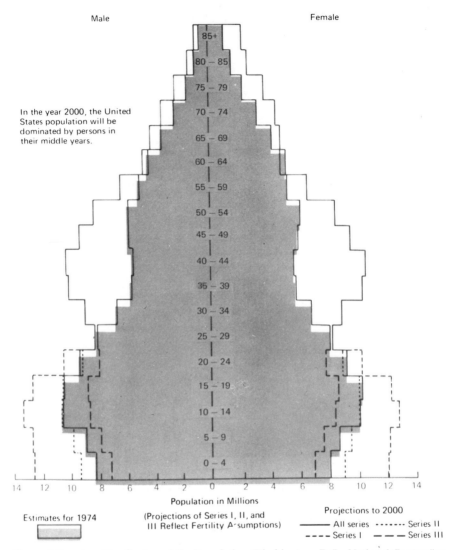

Figure 6-3   Age Distribution of the Population (Washington, D.C.: National Center for Education Statistics).

In terms of enrollees, it can be expected that schools will serve fewer school-age children and college students. At the same time a projected population bulge of middle-aged adults and a growing number of senior citizens parallel an increased interest in adult education. Evident implications are for new emphasis and expanded school-community services in an era of continued inflation, rising costs, and increasing expenditures.

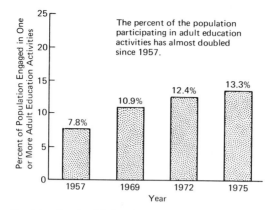

Figure 6-4 Participation in Adult Education (Washington, D.C.: National Center for Education Statistics).

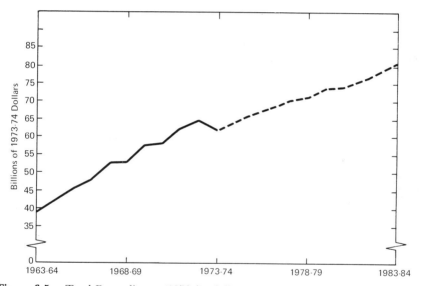

Figure 6-5 Total Expenditures (1973–74 dollars), by Regular Elementary and Secondary Day Schools: United States, 1963–64 to 1983–84 (Washington, D.C.: National Center for Education Statistics).

PARTICIPATING FOR FUN

(Primary Grades)

The 6- to 12-year-old youngster is an enthusiastic participant of almost any program that is fun. Organization, teammates, rules, final scores are secondary to fun and personal success.

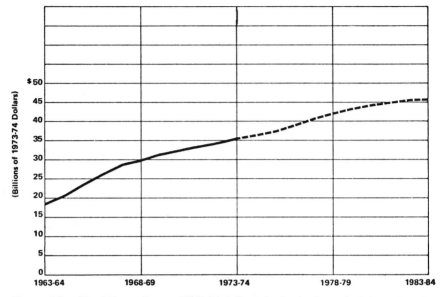

Figure 6-6 Total Expenditures (9773–74 dollars), by Institutions of Higher Education: United States, 1963–64 to 1983–84 (Washington, D.C.: National Center for Education Statistics).

Characteristics

Observed on the sand lot or in "pick-up" play with friends, the "fun participant" reveals traits that are somewhat different from those of the young competitor under winner-oriented adult leadership.

Likes Variety. This young sportsperson needs and enjoys a wide exposure to a variety of activities and games. This is the best answer for his or her short interest span, wide-ranging curiosity, and a capacity for learning that needs to be tapped.

A Competitor, Not a Champion. While exploring and refining skills, the elementary-school youngster likes to compete and to play hard but is not so dedicated to team or winning that a natural desire to quit when tired, won't end the activity. Competing to win has been an adult-imposed goal which in the real world of the elementary-school youngster is of little importance.

Loose and Unorganized. Loyalties are changeable and what is fair is important. Rules are for the moment and details of play are irrelevant. Games should be loose, flexible, and not miniature adaptations of adult activities.

More Individualistic than Group-Oriented With each year of social experience the elementary-school youngster moves from a totally individualistic personality to more of a group orientation. In the lower grades, team makeup is of little importance. Playing the game or indulging in the activity is important; team loyalty gradually develops in the upper grades.

Nurturing a Self-Image

At this age success nurtures self-confidence. The elementary-school youngster needs positive experiences through play. Susan Rockett, program planner of Georgia's Project Health and Optimum Physical Education, describes the dangers of overemphasized competition for this age group.

> Traditionally, the emphasis in physical education has been on competitive games and sports, with the gifted athlete receiving much of the attention to the neglect of his less agile friends who develop only a negative attitude about the entire idea of physical activity . . . the I'm a loser attitude developed on the playground often carries over into the academic and social life of the child.[7]

Play is for the fun of the moment and success, not defeat, is vital to the process of developing a positive self-image and fundamental inner self-confidence.

Learning to Handle Child-Size Pressures

The competitive urge, urge for excellence, and desire to test oneself become greater in the upper elementary years. The abilities to handle the accompanying pressures develop, and increasingly the elementary-age children involve themselves in agency-sponsored athletics as well as school programs.

Without proper and aware leadership the 6- to 12-year-olds may

1. Become sports specialists at a time when they should be learning a variety of basic skills
2. Subject themselves to emotional pressures they are not yet capable of handling
3. Become dominated by overzealous adult leadership when they should be developing their own social skills of independence and loyalties
4. Develop a distorted sense of values as a result of overemphasis on winning the game.

[7]Syd Blackmarr, "Every Child a Winner," *Journal of Health, Physical Education and Recreation* (October 1974), p. 15.

LITTLE AND BIG

(Middle and Junior High School)

Tall and short, skilled and awkward, the middle or junior high school youngsters represent wide extremes in weight and maturity. Boys are two years behind girls physically. Girls are advanced socially. Change to adulthood comes quickly, slowly, or is grossly delayed. Diversity best characterizes this participant, and a review of the sports programs serving the 6- to 14-year-old is a comparable mix.

Characteristics

On the brink or in the turmoil of change the junior high school and middle school youngster is developing social groups, loyalties, concern for details, and convictions of right and wrong.

Tries Everything. The 12- to 15-year-old emulates sports heroes whether in high school or the professional sports world. An extensive interest and curiosity is reflected in a desire to perform in many sports.

In addition to school programs the seventh-, eighth,- and ninth-grader also turns out for a variety of community programs that include

Little League Baseball	Junior ABC Bowling League
Pop Warner Football	Horse and Pony Club
Junior League Football	YMCA Gymnastics
Babe Ruth Leagues	Junior Power Squadron
American Legion Leagues	Community Tennis Tournaments
Pony League	Country Club and Community Swim Meets
Sandy Koufax Leagues	Community Junior Golf Tournaments
Biddy Basketball Leagues	Scouting Sports Activities
Connie Mack Leagues	Church Sports and Activities
Mickey Mantle Leagues	Junior Chamber of Commerce Skiing
Catholic Youth Organization	Junior Ice Hockey Leagues
YMCA Team Sports Leagues	AAU Sports Events

Testing Leadership. For boys and girls, testing leadership roles is one of the greatest challenges of this age group. Given the freedom they value, they can organize and manage their own activity clubs. An evolving interest produces a leader. Advisor control often functions through supplementary teachers, provided the program does not become over-organized or adult-dominated.

Organized in Many Ways. The middle school or junior high school without an intramural program is a rare exception in the United States, according to a survey conducted by Munson and Stafford.[8] In a time of transition and change, however, programs are organized and offered under a variety of names and approaches, such as (1) student clubs, (2) sports councils, (3) mini-courses, (4) interest groups, (5) interscholastics, (6) varsity, (7) school-community co-op programs, and (8) extramurals.

Activity Interests Unlimited. Activity interests are varied and numerous. Undoubtedly the direction programs take reflect leadership resources, interests, and budget possibilities. The list is extensive but some of the most popular include the following:

Dances, Games, and Contests	*Lifetime Sports*
Tug-of-War	Archery
Square Dancing	Badminton
King of the Mountain	Bowling
Frisbee Throw	Golf
Dodge Ball	Table Tennis
Medicine Ball	Skiing
	Tennis

Lifetime Activities	*Traditional Sports*
Camping	Basketball
Hiking	Baseball
Jogging	Football
Sailing	Soccer
Climbing	Hockey
Skindiving	Gymnastics
Snowshoeing	Volleyball
Spelunking	

Health and Safety

Exposed to and often unaware of health and safety dangers, the junior high school participant is physiologically extended by accelerated growth spurts. All too easily, the high school program of varsity sports is superimposed on the lower levels. Inadequate medical requirements, parental involvement, and physical conditioning pose health threats. Emulating sports heroes leads to playing their game and adopting their values and, if leadership imposes adults pressures, invites risk to health and safety.

Glenn Dickey, in *The Jock Empire,* challenges adult emphasis on statistics, recordkeeping, and winning.

[8]Corlee Munson and Elba Stafford, "Middle Schools: A Variety of Approaches to Physical Education," *Journal of Health, Physical Education and Recreation* (February 1974), p. 30.

Youth should be a time for experimentation, of trying different sports and different positions and of playing with different friends, instead of being tied down to one group.[9]

Overinvolvement

With the duplication of community and school activity offerings, this enthusiastic sports participant has to make choices. Overinvolvement is a threatening role for a physiologically fragile age.

THE ATHLETE: TRADITION-BOUND AND REASSESSING

The high school and college-age young man has been conditioned to compete to win. Some young participants are reassessing the cost of winning, and for some the fun of competing is assuming new value.

Questioning the Champion Image

Men and boys have traditionally and inseparably been aligned with sports. Highly competitive activities have alternately been praised and castigated by leadership, but the skilled athlete has loyally reported for practice in quest of his bid to become a champion.

Since the early 1900s sports, with an implied male connotation, have been given credit for character building, health insurance, and body building. Periodically, leadership has been attacked for condoning questionable behavior practices, instilling objectionable value systems, jeopardizing healthful well-being, and providing disproportionate advantages for a select few. Most recently, requests for investigations, the voices of dissenting coaches who speak out against the varsity system, and revelations of the sports world's business practices have raised questions that demand answers in the near future.

Words like scandal, crisis, and national shame flow freely from the typewriters of America's sportswriters and columnists. The American Council on Education in the first major study on College Sports conducted since 1929, has recommended that a National Commission be formed to look into the role of sports on America's College Campuses and hopefully, recommend major reforms.[10]

In spite of criticisms, however, support of the superior athlete has been continuous through the decades. Public school authorities and education policy-forming commissions have stood behind the athlete.

[9]*The Jock Empire* (Radnor, Pa.: Chilton Book Company, 1974), p. 171.

[10]Kenneth Denlinger and Leonard Shapiro, *Athletes for Sale* (New York: Thomas Y. Crowell Co., 1975), p. 248.

Leaders of the nation—presidents, judges, congressmen, and university presidents—have extolled the merits of competitive athletics, and the taxpayer has been willing to finance the pursuit of excellence by a few.

Today, although boys and young men are "turning out" as tradition dictates, the emulating imagery of amateur college sports and big-league professionals is becoming tarnished in the eyes of the aspirants. The champion and the environs in which he plays are becoming less attractive to the young athlete. Play and competition for many appears to be a rewarding experience for the present and less of a means of becoming a champion of the future.

Reassessing Values

Resisting total involvement, the athlete is less likely than in the past to accept as fact what he is being told by those around him. The new criticism is the outgrowth of cynicism about war and suspicion of big government. As he peers in the business world of sports, he perceives an industry of controlled competition; and he wonders whether players are not in fact pawns, manipulated to serve a variety of masters.[11] And he may also object to the nationalistic flavor of certain sports events. Questioning, noncommitting, and value seeking, he is reassessing his value judgments. As one authority wrote: "Coaches are dealing with a new breed of young people today. They are less willing to accept discipline, less willing to accept the establishment and less willing to accept the status quo."[12]

The values of society dictate, "that which is easy is good" and logic follows that the work ethic has little justifiable reason for being in an affluent society: "going out for a sport implies 'work' and the young participant is hesitant about his willingness to make a total commitment to disciplined play as contrasted to the freedom of the less 'win-oriented' recreation play. Many athletes drop from the team when rivalry means little and loyalty to other causes is more demanding than loyalty to school and team. Dedication also dims when the virtues of discipline and hard work are made to appear suspect, foolish, and the coach and the game he teaches appear to be no longer relevant."[13]

Today's contrast of values reveals that the coach is more win-oriented than the player. The young participant reflects a growing questioning of the concept of competition and in particular of the sacrificies demanded to win. Katherine Ley reaffirms that personality traits of male

[11]Roger G. Noll, ed., *Government and the Sports Business* (Washington, D.C.: The Brookings Institute, 1974).

[12]James Hansen, "Coaching in an Era of Increasing Individual Awareness," *The Winning Edge,* proceedings of the First National Sports Conference, May 18–20, 1973, Buffalo, New York (Washington, D.C.: American Alliance for Health, Physical Education and Recreation, 1974), p. 98.

[13]Ibid., p. 36.

coaches show on an average a much greater desire to achieve than their players have.[14]

As the public school sports programs have become more organized and college programs more dedicated to winning, young participants have seen themselves as losing their identity and their ability to control their own fate. Looking at themselves objectively, they see themselves as receiving little or no respect and treated as if they were numbers, not human beings. As one authority has explained, "Because they feel themselves to be victims of a system they distrust all institutions and authorities. They question, resist and deemphasize organization."[15]

A Paradox

Until recently athletics have firmly stood the test of time as a program in the educational system. Justification usually stresses their positive and constructive contributions to the goals of education. But some signs have appeared that a crumbling has set in, although the change ought not to be overstated.

All the same, supports appear to be waning as spectator behavior and commercialism threaten the philosophical foundations of athletics. Schools and communities at times are forced to discontinue programs because of the uncontrollable and riotous behavior of spectators. Others have been alienated by the description of sports as a means to financial wealth for a limited few. In some quarters an aversion to structured competition is leading to a growing appreciation for recreational and noncommercial competition.

There is an element of paradox in the situation in that the young male continues to be committed to sports and females are expanding at a great rate the ranks of dedicated competitors. Statistics also reflect a rising support for sports programs. According to one observer of the current scene,

> At the high school level almost four million boys and slightly over 800,000 girls participated in interscholastic programs. During the 1971–72 academic year 172,000 males and 32,000 females were members of collegiate teams at National Collegiate Athletic Association affiliated institutions. An estimated 100 million spectators attend high school basketball games annually.[16]

As the public, coaches, sociologists, and leaders explore the concept

[14]"Women in Sports, Where Do We Go From Here Boys?" *Phi Delta Kappan,* 56, no. 2 (October 1974), 129.

[15]Holmes N. Van Derbeck, "No Respect," *Development of Human Values Through Sports,* proceedings of National Conference Held at Springfield College, Springfield, Mass., October 1973, p. 12 (Washington, D.C.: American Alliance for Health, Physical Education and Recreation, 1974), p. 46.

[16]Charles R. Kniker, "The Values of Athletics in Schools: A Continuing Debate," *Phi Delta Kappan,* 56, no. 2 (October 1974), 116.

of "winning at all costs," young athletes are reassessing values and developing skills in the art of living in a society that is expanding leisure and championing equal rights.

THE SPORTSWOMAN:
VISIBLE, ACCEPTED, AND SUPPORTED

In an approving society young high school and college women in sports are more visible and their expressed interests more vocal than ever before. Play for play's sake and competing to become champions are new adventures and challenges. Within the excitement there is a leadership urge to break ground for new patterns of competition that will ensure a long life of wholesome experiences.

Experimenting with the Options

At a time when austere budgets threaten the very existence of some sports programs, girls and women, with encouragement and support, are projecting a new image. They are turning to sports and facing the pressures of competition for the sake of personal, social and financial gains. The signs of change are everywhere.

Women are enjoying a greater variety of professionally sanctioned meets and matches. Schools are providing more opportunities for the highly skilled as reflected "in many areas of the country where high school girls now have opportunities to play in up to eight to ten sports at the varsity levels."[17] Girls are working out with the boys in non–contact sports and competing on open teams. They are enjoying expanded co-recreation programs that mix and match partners in a variety of ways to *equate the competition* and strengthen the contest.

In spite of historic ups and downs in the professional educators' spectrum of acceptability of competition for girls, today's upswing reflects changing values, positive attitudes toward sports for girls and women, supportive court decisions, comparable funding, and elimination of discriminatory practices.

Freed of the Myths

The sportswomen of today have been freed of the many myths that have deterred them from sports participation in the past. Research in several fields of study give positive and encouraging support to the young athletes.

---

[17]Marjorie Blaufarb, "Equal Opportunity for Girls in Athletics," *Todays Education,* 63, no. 4 (November–December 1974), p. 55.

Physiologists and medical experts have promoted the importance of physical activity in building and maintaining good health and fitness; have reassured young women that rigorous sports activity does not harm childbearing functions or effect changes in menstrual cycle; have indicated that sports do not cause masculine behaviors in the female, and have presented a consensus that well-supervised athletic competition is not detrimental to the well-being of the female in good health.

Social scientists, warning of the growing delinquency problems, have supported opportunities to channel youths' need for activity and challenge socially acceptable recreation. They have also described possible benefits of involvement in sports competition (self-confidence, sense of achievement, self-discipline, and competitiveness) as non-sex-linked human values. The implication is that participation in sports can better equip women for personal security and independence.

In an era of experimental togetherness, young women are learning to be companionable hikers, campers, and sportspeople. They are learning to enjoy personal capabilities and the social values and satisfactions of playing, competition, and recreation with the family. They are developing rewarding relationships that are identified by sociologists as fundamental to enduring stability.

> For a happy union the prospective husband and wife must participate together in a sufficient number of activities that ensure companionship. Their mutual activities and interests may be in sports and games, literature, music and art or religion and a social cause.[18]

Women coaches and trainers express no doubt as to what girls may achieve through planned training programs. Patsy Neal reported at the National Sports Conference at Buffalo, New York in 1973 that women respond physically to training in the same ways that men do: (1) there is increased muscle size and efficiency; (2) the heart becomes stronger and beats more slowly; (3) the pulse rate and respiration returns to normal more quickly than that of the nonathlete after exertion.[19]

Educators and specialists in the area of child growth and development have declared that play is one of the fundamental and basic human urges. *Psychologists*, too, cite the potentials of recreation for good mental health.

Public Support

Until recently, women and girls in sport suffered a limited public image and indifferent support. This has been changed by school programs that equate opportunities for girls and boys, national and state

[18]W. Ernest Burgess, "The Wise Choice of a Mate," in Morris Fishbein and Ruby Jo Reeves Kennedy, *Modern Marraige and Family Living* (New York: Oxford University Press, 1957), p. 126.

[19]"Attainment and Maintenance of Championship Performance," *The Winning Edge* (Washington, D.C.: Alliance for Health, Physical Education and Recreation, 1974), p. 120.

legislation that reinforce this equality, and a growing desire on the part of young women to press for excellence in sports skills.

The idea of women in sports has become more and more acceptable. The traditional stereotype of the "masculine" woman athlete is being replaced by the more accurate image of a skilled participant aware of the potential personal satisfactions, career opportunities, improved fitness, competitive experiences, and recreation companionship possible through sports. The growing respect of peer groups, teachers, administrators, parents, and professional organizations has led to an awareness of the values of sports and recreation for girls and women.

The growth of fitness, conditioning, and commerical gymnasia, and the increased number of doors that have been opened to women in such male domains as the bowling alleys, golf clubs, yacht clubs, and hunting clubs point to the crumbling of old barriers and the recent acceptance of women as participants in sport.

The media are increasingly supportive. Although less than a token of space in the newspaper sports pages covers women's activities, news publishers are taking on women journalism graduates to report in their sports areas of interest and knowledge. And television is bringing in women commentators to cover sports events of all kinds.

A continued expanding acceptance is assured by efforts to educate men to appreciate the aspirations and achievements of women, to stimulate women to pursue excellence, and to expand culturally and personally acceptable behavior roles for both men and women.

Highly Skilled Competition for Women

Strenuous competition for women started in an extramural arena of student-organized interschool games early in the twentieth century. It grew in popularity until in the 1920s, when poor examples set by the participants led to a questioning of the healthfulness, respectability, and wholesomeness of the competitive experience.

As women developed leadership and standardized rules and regulations, however, the intramural program gained strength and support. Wars and an acknowledged absence of national fitness repeatly kindled added interest in vigorous activity. In the last decade there has been a strong movement for women's extramurals and interscholastics.

Women physical educators have been making pleas for more vigorous activity and more varied competition for the skilled girl. Interest and opportunity began to explode in the early 70s. Expanding intercollegiate programs for women at Cornell, for example, more than doubled in less than ten years.

Mimi Murray, Springfield College gynmastic coach, has observed:

> The woman in athletics is the result of a crying need for the highly skilled sportswoman to express herself. . . . The avenues of expression in

sport for women are opening in many varied sport areas, thus permitting more women to compete.[20]

On the public school level Washington State verifies the trend in its Interscholastic Association report of 1974, which indicates that over a four-year period there was a 342 percent growth in girls' sports participation. The National Federation of State High School Associations states that between 1970–71 and 1974–75, girls' track and field participation grew by 237,000; volleyball by 181,000; basketball by 175,000, softball by 100,000, swimming and diving by 57,000, and gymnastics by 44,000.

William P. Morgan, of the U.S. Army Research Institute of Environmental Medicine, has also observed the trend: "Recent widespread increase in physical activity and sports programs for girls and women represents one of the most significant developments in contemporary sports."[21]

Women's enthusiasm and growing involvement in sports is reflected in their improved skill abilities, calibre of team play, and the emergence of many superior athletes. Sports reporters repeatedly support these growing skills with printed observations—for example, the February 4, 1976 Bellingham *Herald* reported: "There is no question today's women athletes are far superior to those of a couple of years back."

Economic Opportunities

Young women participants now look to the sports world for financial assistance, career possibilities, and the economic rewards that were once reserved for men. They draw encouragement from court rulings that support equal pay for equal services. At the same time women coaches, teachers, and officials enjoy their new roles. As scholarships and financial assistance become more readily available in the academic world, vistas brighten on the professional sports circuit. Businesswomen of the sports world have evolved, most conspicuously, from the tennis and golf tournament circuits. Professional women competitors increasingly enjoy financial rewards similar to those of men, as illustrated in Figure 6-7, which lists incomes of several professional sportswomen.

Radio and TV are tending offers to women, as illustrated by Billie Jean King's two-year contract with ABC for a reported $200,000. Evonne Goolagong and Chris Evert, tennis professionals, are able to enhance their income through product endorsements. Many husband and wife teams depend on interests in sports for economic and career support in such fields as photography, writing, management, fashions, and sales.

[20]"The Woman in Athletics," *Journal of Health, Physical Education and Recreation* (January 1974), p. 65.

[21]"Female Athletes," *Journal of Health, Physical Education and Recreation* (January 1975), p. 45.

The Leading Women Money Winners 1975			
Golf		*Tennis*	
Sandra Palmer	$76,374.	Chris Evert	$323,977.
Jo Ann Carner	64,842.	Martina Navratilova	184,518.
Carol Mann	64,727.	Virginia Wade	138,576.
Sandra Haynie	61,614.	Evonne Goolagong	132,754.
Judy Rankin	50,174.	Billie Jean King	99,900.

Figure 6-7. Leading Women Money Winners in Golf and Tennis 1975[22]

IMAGES:
THE DAMAGING EFFECTS OF STEREOTYPING

Sex stereotyping has undoubtedly been an unrecognized force handicapping sports participation for men and women alike.

The Masculine Mystique

Lost in the shadows of aggrandized varsity sports and the accolades that come to champions, countless boys and men in years past have belonged to the group that described their aversion to sports with such statements as, "When I think of participating in sports, I lie down until the thought passes." Many factors have been cited to explain the view, held by many youth and adults, that there is nothing enjoyable or worthwhile for them in a recreational sports program. One of them is the proposition that boys and men who did not fit the masculine image of a champion athlete hold back from sports. In the scale of values to which American society subscribes, the champion athlete reigns supreme, and to appear less than a champion has been comparable to an effort to "self-destruct." And there are other factors. Fear may also be a deterrent. Men feel compelled in American society to win, whether the area of competition is business, courting, or recreational sports. That one might not win is a fear that erases fun and enjoyment from playing sports. The risk of defeat may loom so large as to remove the possibility of participation.

A masculine image of the sports participant has had an impact on women as well as men. While the nonathletic man has little reason to participate in sports, the athletically gifted woman has been cautious about expanding her abilities.

Girls and women have also struggled with society's views of their personal qualities and the roles that they should perform. In particular,

[22]Dan Jenkins, "Last Week They Held the Masters," *Sports Illustrated,* April 12, 1976, pp. 31–32.

they have been fearful that sport participation would give them a masculine image, that their showing a high degree of skill in sport would jeopardize their femininity. Such fears have been reinforced when men have been unwilling to participate in co-recreational activities and have subscribed to a set of values hostile to women skilled in sports activities.

But the greatest restraint on their serious participation in the world of competitive sports has come from their attempt to develop an acceptable self-image. It has been an uphill struggle as they contended with the traditional association of "skilled, masculine, and aggressive" or "unskilled, feminine, and submissive." There seems to have been no middle path. The intimidations rising out of the failure of peer groups to accept sportswomen and the low value assigned by men to a woman's skill in recreational sports when they seek marriage have until recently been further disrupting to the image-creating process.

The Sportsperson

The trend has reversed in recent years. Numerous factors have combined to encourage achievement-oriented individuals to foster their skill ability without regard for sex. The barriers imposed by stereotyping are falling, including the traditional labels of "masculine" or "feminine" in arbitrary reference to the skilled and unskilled.

Dorothy Harris has presented some queries that suggest constructive approaches to the struggles of men and women sports enthusiasts. "What standard of behavior is being used to determine what is desirable? Perhaps personality theorists have promoted a double standard too long. Maybe we should look at human behavior rather than feminine behavior and masculine behavior. This may be especially important in the sport environment where the behavior demands are generally the same for those who are participating regardless of sex."[23]

Lifetime Co-Recreation

With the shrinking workweek becoming a way of life and the minimizing of culturally induced sex differences in interests and abilities, the acquisition of a variety of lifetime recreation skills are social assets gaining in value for boys and girls, men and women.

The 1970 AAHPER gave the Life Time Sports Project its highest program priority. Progress was reported with expanded program offerings in both variety and skill levels that enabled individuals and teams to play opponents of equal ability and interest. A growing number of schools have been advised to revamp physical education programs to include lifetime sports. Continued success of the Life Time Sports Program has implications for substantiating the swelling demands for social-oriented activities. Similar substantiation can be seen in the fast-growing intramural activities such as "mixed murals," coeducation, and open

[23]Dorothy V. Harris, "Research Studies on the Female Athlete: Psychosocial Considerations," *Journal of Health, Physical Education and Recreation* (January 1975), p. 33.

tournaments, all of which with appropriate modifications allow men and women to play together.

Sports skills development are being recognized as prerequisites to enjoyable recreation with contemporaries, career associates, husbands, wives, and growing families. The pressure grows for opportunities to develop skills that will enable young men and women to enjoy outdoor sports such as golf, softball, or tennis; in the water: swimming, diving, or water skiing; in the winter: holiday sports, skating, skiing, tobogganing; on the beach: volleyball, medicine ball, or badminton; in the field: hunting, and target, skeet, or trap shooting. They will also want the strength, stamina, and endurance to enjoy challenging mountain climbing, rock climbing, or cave exploring.

David O. Matthews, intramural director at Illinois University, observes: "The direction that campus recreation is taking alerts the present day directors to the fact that free time recreation play is eventually going to overshadow the competitive program."[24]

THE ADULT

This account of the new sports participants concludes with a brief consideration of the post-school adult, whose primary interest is to participate in sports for enjoyment. His or her satisfaction is derived from informal competition, the social contacts that go with it, and the conviction that physical activity contributes importantly to maintaining health and physical fitness.

The Motivation

Exposed to a strong national physical fitness program and sustained support from the presidency over several decades, adults of all ages have a well-developed physical fitness consciousness. There are two main reasons for this that require mention. Adults now in their early twenties were the school-age children who were tested for physical fitness on a national scale in the 1950s. Poor results shocked the country and brought action in the form of the Council on Youth Fitness, which initiated a national physical fitness program in the public schools. Further, adults now approaching their senior citizen years are the inductees of World War II, the men and women who as members of the armed forces developed regular habits of activity on a day-to-day basis. It is not surprising, therefore, that the adults of today are strongly favorable toward activity and physical fitness.

Physiological Status and Concern

Post-school adults have in general peaked physiologically, and the aging process has started. Sometime between age 20 and 30, physical

[24]"The Next Fifty Years in College and University Intramurals," *The Next Fifty Years* (Eugene, Oregon: University of Oregon Press, 1971), p. 48.

and physiological functioning begins to slow at a rate that reflects heredity, way of life, and amount of activity involvement of the individual.[25]

Dr. Paul Dudley White's promotion of fitness over the years, the American Heart Association's endorsements for maintaining high levels of fitness, and the U.S. Public Health Service's recommendations for appropriate physical exercise have provided today's adult with the medical and health world's best advice for slowing the physiological declining process. Consequently, the adult sports participant is alerted and concerned about keeping fit through activity.

Activity Interests

Sport preferences of the post-school participant are as varied as those of students. They range from vigorous to only slightly active and reflect interest and motivation rather than age and prescribed programs. According to Rear Admiral William Lukash, White House physician, regular exercise is desirable for everyone, but especially for office workers; he points out that many ex-athletes such as former President Ford enjoy a variety of activities but prefer regimented workouts. He emphasizes daily activity whether it consists of an exercise program, jogging, calisthenics, brisk walks, swimming, or digging in a garden.[26]

Many adult participants take advantage of school and community programs that schedule special events such as:

Adult tennis	Senior citizen tennis
Adult golf	Senior citizen golf
League bowling	Senior citizen bowling
Ski bus weekly trips	Senior citizen skiing
Shuffleboard leagues	Horseshoe leagues

Other involvements reflect interests of a particular group such as at St. Petersberg, Florida where the Three-Quarters Century Softball Club, Inc. ignores age limitations. All members are 75 years of age or older and the team plays three times a week in season plus demonstrations out of season.[27] Eugene, Oregon is reported to be so excited about track that one out of every nine residents pounds the pavement daily.[28] At *The Bridge,* a senior citizen mini-affiliate of Fairhaven College in Bellingham, Washington offers "to those who are feeling older but not wise enough" a year-round academic curriculum that includes a variety of activities including slimnastics and skills in social and round dance for men and women.

[25]Anna S. Espenschade and Helen M. Ecket, *Motor Development* (Columbus, Ohio: Charles E. Merrill Publishing Co., 1967), p. 250.

[26]"How To Stay Fit," interview with Rear Adm. William M. Lukash, the President's doctor, *U.S. News and World Report,* November 10, 1975, p. 56.

[27]David Wilkening, "75 Plus Ball Club," *National Retired Teachers Association Journal* (September–October 1974), p. 6.

[28]"Resources," *Parks and Recreation,* 10, no. 2 (February 1975), 13.

Thus, many fitness-conscious, well-motivated, activity-oriented, tax-paying adults have a vested interest in the school and community programs of sport and recreation activities.

DISCUSSION QUESTIONS

1. The recreation sports director of today and the future is concerned with what age group? Why?
2. What are the statistical projections of school enrollments? Higher education? Adult education? Age distribution of population?
3. What is the trend in educational expenditure? Why?
4. Describe the primary-grade youngster. What are the implications for recreational sports programs for this age group?
5. Describe the middle and junior high school student. What are the implications for recreational sports programs for this age group?
6. Why is the image of a champion "tarnished"? Have changing values affected the importance of our image of a champion?
7. What sports opportunities are opening up for women? Are there any leadership concerns?
8. What have been the myths surrounding women in sport? How have the myths been destroyed?
9. How has stereotyping intimidated both men and women? Are there signs of change?
10. Why are the post-school adults of today particularly enthusiastic sports participants and concerned physical fitness aspirants?

BIBLIOGRAPHY

DENGLINGER, KENNETH and LEONARD SHAPIRO, *Athletes for Sale*. New York: Thomas Y. Crowell Co., 1975.

DICKEY, GLENN, *The Jock Empire*. Radner, Pa.: Chilton Book Co., 1974.

ELLIS, MICHAEL J., *Why People Play*. Englewood Cliffs, N.J.: Prentice-Hall, Inc., 1973.

GERBER, ELLEN, PEARL BERLIN, JAN FELSHIN, and WANEEN WYRICK, *The American Woman in Sport*. Reading, Mass.: Addison-Wesley Publishing Co., 1974.

HARRIS, DOROTHY V., *Involvement in Sport*. Philadelphia: Lea & Febiger, 1973.

LINEBERRY, WILLIAM P., *The Business of Sport*. New York: H. W. Wilson Co., 1973.

MILLER, D. M., and K. R. RUSSELL, *Sport: A Contemporary View*. Philadelphia: Lea & Febiger, 1971.

MURPHY, JAMES FREDERICK, *Recreation and Leisure Services*. Dubuque, Iowa: W. C. Brown Co., Publishers, 1975.

National Council of Secondary School Athletic Directors, *Crowd Control for High School Athletics*. Washington, D.C.: American Association for Health, Physical Education and Recreation, 1970.

NOLL, ROGER G., ed., *Government and the Sports Business*. Washington, D.C.: The Brookings Institute, 1974.

Family Recreation.

7

Professional Leadership and Socioeconomic Change

In the last quarter of the twentieth century professional leadership in the recreational sports program is faced with manifold problems rising out of social and economic change. Prominent among these problems are those rising out of a growing austerity in school budgets that is traceable to an incipient taxpayers' revolt. Even in wealthy suburban areas protest is mounting at the cost of schools, and if the schools are a target of wrath in this regard, the recreational sports program is inevitably affected. Other problems are a consequence of the social change set in motion by Title IX legislation with its insistance that the generally masculine world of athletics admit women to positions of consequence and leadership on a more equal basis than in the past. It is these two areas of social and economic change, with the problems that they pose for professional leadership, that are considered here.

FINANCIAL PROBLEMS: ADMINISTRATIVE ACCOUNTABILITY

Budget cuts have affected countless school sports programs in recent years. The failure of bond issues and tax levies, together with reduced gate receipts, has created difficulties for local school boards, school administrators, and college athletic directors. The Athletic Institute and Sports Foundation concluded that financial limitations have led to reductions in one out of every five elementary and secondary school physical education and athletic programs. The colleges and universities are also suffering. In some places the college varsity program has been eliminated and the emphasis is no longer on the less expensive forms of sports competition on the campus. The varsity programs that survive

REPORT OF A STUDY OF CALIFORNIA HIGH SCHOOL ATHLETIC PROGRAMS

To meet the provisions of Assembly Bill 3650, the California State Department of Education requested each of the 700 California public high schools to have the male and female athletic coordinators of each school complete a questionnaire designed to provide answers to certain questions raised by the California Legislature* Answers to 15 categories of questions were requested dealing with equality of athletic opportunity for boys and girls in numbers of teams, numbers of coaches, expenditures, sources of revenue, coaching pay, equipment and supplies, use of facilities, transportation, insurance, program needs, and suggestions for increased financing. The data collected were placed in two categories: findings and recommendations.

Findings of the Study of Athletic Programs

Of the 700 high schools asked to respond to the questionnaire, which was mailed on April 28, 1975, a total of 473 returned the form by the deadline of May 19, 1975. The responses, which covered the 1973-74 school year, were then compiled, and these were the findings of the study:

1. High schools were asked how many teams and coaches they provided for both boys' and girls' sports. The results revealed (a) that an average California high school fielded boys' teams in 11 sports; (b) that in these sports it fielded 21.5 teams representing varsity, junior varsity, and similar categories of players; and (c) that it provided 21 coaches for these teams. The results also revealed (a) that an average California high school fielded girls' teams in eight sports; (b) that in these sports it fielded 10 teams representing varsity and junior varsity categories of players; and (c) that it provided seven coaches for these teams.

2. Information was sought so that a comparison could be made of the number of boys versus the number of girls who were participating in California high school athletic programs. Statistics revealed that for every three girls who participated in such programs, seven boys participated; or that approximately two and one-third times as many boys as girls were participating in California interscholastic athletics.

*A copy of the questionnaire is available from the Administrator, Physical Education and Safety Programs, California State Department of Education, 721 Capitol Mall, Sacramento, CA 95814; telephone (916) 322-4985.

3. As an indication of public interest and potential gate receipts, data were gathered on the number of spectators attending home interscholastic athletic events. The data disclosed that the average high school has a total of 17,618 spectators in attendance for boys' events and 878 in attendance for girls' events.

4. Total gross expenditures per school for each of the two athletic programs indicated that expenditures for boys' programs totaled $14,227; for girls' programs, $3,271.

5. The sources of revenue to finance each of the two interscholastic athletic programs, by category of source, follow:

Source of revenue	Percent of support provided	
	Boys	Girls
District funds	44	56
Student body cards	10	14
Gate receipts	34.5	10
Booster clubs	2.5	2
School fund raising	3	8
Fund raising out of school	1	5
Other (wide variety)	5	5

6. In a typical California high school, the average extra pay given per coach per sport was $505 for coaches in the boys' program and $343 for coaches in the girls' program.

7. The amount spent on equipment and supplies in the average high school for each of the two athletic programs was $7,727 for the boys' program and $2,197 for the girls' program.

8. Two questions were asked in an attempt to determine how outdoor and indoor athletic facilities at the high schools were made available for use by boys and by girls. The percentages of time that such facilities were made available for use by each group follow:

Type of school facility	Percent of time available*	
	Boys	Girls
Outdoor courts, fields, and pools	56	42
Indoor athletic facilities	54	43

*Percents for boys and girls do not add up to 100 percent because in some high schools boys and girls have separate outdoor and indoor athletic facilities.

9. The data collected disclosed that little difference existed in the type of transportation used to transport boys and girls to interscholastic athletic events:

Mode of transportation	Percent of time used	
	Boys	Girls
School bus	77	74
Charter bus	5	5
Private auto	3	5
No response	15	16

10. Two questions were asked to determine the way athletic insurance coverage was provided, and the results disclosed the following:

Type of insurance coverage	Percent of athletes insured	
	Boys	Girls
Family policy	37	35
School policy paid by parents	32	31
School policy paid by district	14	15
Policy shared by school and parents	9	7
Other	8	12

11. Two questions were asked to determine whether the schools, in the opinion of the athletic coordinators, were providing enough athletic teams for the boys and girls. The data from those questions revealed the following:

Response of coordinator	Percent responding, according to type of team	
	Boys	Girls
Enough teams	53	33
Need one or two more	32	43
Need three or four more	9	18
Other	6	6

12. Of the suggestions made for obtaining additional revenue for high school athletics, approximately 30 percent favored revenue from the State General Fund, supported by sales and income taxes. Approximately 25 percent of those questioned favored a 5 percent tax on all athletic events in California. Approximately 18 percent supported an additional 5-cent local property tax. The remaining 27 percent of the respondents gave no opinion.

13. The athletic coordinators were asked whether their school districts had increased or decreased funds for high school athletics in 1974-75. A tabulation of their responses indicated that the school districts had increased funds for boys' athletics in 39 percent of the cases, decreased funds in 40 percent, and made no change in 21 percent. The districts had increased funds for girls' athletics in 69 percent of the cases, decreased in 16 percent, and made no change in 15 percent.

Recommendations for California Athletic Programs

On the basis of the findings of its study of the athletic programs for boys and girls in California high schools, the California State Department of Education makes the following recommendations:

1. That attention be focused on California high school athletic programs so that the ratio of sports offered, level of teams provided, and number of coaches assigned will become as equal as possible for boys' and girls' athletic programs.

2. That a special effort be made to encourage greater participation by girls in high school athletic programs.

3. That, in view of the existing practice of financing high school athletic programs, the importance of gate receipts be recognized and equal opportunity for earning these receipts be provided for both boys' and girls' athletic programs.

4. That evaluation of funding practices for athletic programs be made regularly in each high school so that adequate financing, in accord with sound educational standards, be provided for both boys' and girls' athletic programs.

5. That existing school district practice as to pay for coaching work be examined for the purpose of formulating a policy of equal pay for equal work; that is, a policy whereby men and women coaches who perform like services and hold valid California credentials for educational services will receive like pay.

6. That existing school district practice in athletics as to proportionate funding, scheduling of facilities and games, use of facilities, and travel and insurance be examined for the purpose of formulating a policy of providing equal opportunities in athletics for both boys and girls.

Figure 7-1 California High School Athletic Programs—Report of Study done by California State Department of Education.

often made adjustments in the length of the playing season or the amount of travel for athletic teams.

Demands for accountability that have resounded in the Washington political arena in the recent past are echoing at the state and local levels. Teachers' salaries, class loads, and benefits make headlines. Not so well known are the threats to sports programs, which increasingly have to be justified with accountability data. The leadership of sports programs continues to meet growing demands for substantiating evidence of program balance, effectiveness, and worth.

Accountability to the State

In the interest of strengthening accountability procedures, state departments of education have revised and refined the school district report so as to portray more fully the nature of the sports programs and to identify in detail staff roles and budget items. Earlier the demand for information had been met by one-page forms covering the kinds of activities and the number of participants, but increasingly a more extensive form is required that will provide greater data for the legislature and for study committees. Figure 7-1 is a summary report developed by the California State Department of Education.

Accountable to the School Board

Accountability on the local level, in an effort to retain public and school board support for programs, presses for more detail. Districts are

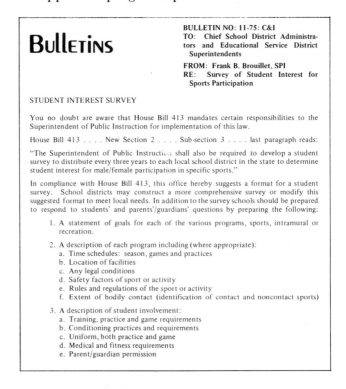

BULLETIN NO: 11-75: C&I

BulleTiNs

TO: Chief School District Administrators and Educational Service District Superintendents

FROM: Frank B. Brouillet, SPI
RE: Survey of Student Interest for Sports Participation

STUDENT INTEREST SURVEY

You no doubt are aware that House Bill 413 mandates certain responsibilities to the Superintendent of Public Instruction for implementation of this law.

House Bill 413 . . . . New Section 2 . . . . Sub-section 3 . . . . last paragraph reads:

"The Superintendent of Public Instruction shall also be required to develop a student survey to distribute every three years to each local school district in the state to determine student interest for male/female participation in specific sports."

In compliance with House Bill 413, this office hereby suggests a format for a student survey. School districts may construct a more comprehensive survey or modify this suggested format to meet local needs. In addition to the survey schools should be prepared to respond to students' and parents'/guardians' questions by preparing the following:

1. A statement of goals for each of the various programs, sports, intramural or recreation.

2. A description of each program including (where appropriate):
   a. Time schedules: season, games and practices
   b. Location of facilities
   c. Any legal conditions
   d. Safety factors of sport or activity
   e. Rules and regulations of the sport or activity
   f. Extent of bodily contact (identification of contact and noncontact sports)

3. A description of student involvement:
   a. Training, practice and game requirements
   b. Conditioning practices and requirements
   c. Uniform, both practice and game
   d. Medical and fitness requirements
   e. Parent/guardian permission

```
Survey of Student Interest in Sports Activities

Name _____ Male _____ Female _____ Grade _____ School _____

The following sports activities represent possible programs to be conducted for the
students of this school. The extent of actual offerings depends upon student interest,
school district financial capabilities, school and community facilities and available
personnel for coaching, supervision and officiating.

Directions:   Indicate your particular responses for each group of sports activities
by checking (   ) the appropriate box.

A. Interscholastic Competitive Sports

District Identify
```

Sport	I am not interested	*Interested but I need more information	*I will definitely participate
1.			
2.			
3.			
4.			
5.			
6.			
7.			
8.			
9.			
10.			

```
B. Intramural Sports or Recreational Activities

District Identify
```

Sport or Activity	I am not interested	*Interested but I need more information	*I will definitely participate
1.			
2.			
3.			
4.			
5.			
6.			
7.			
8.			
9.			
10. Other			

*Please refer to Items 2 and 3 in the bulletin.

Figure 7-2   Washington State Survey of Student Interest in Sports Activities (A format
suggested by Curriculum and Instruction Division of the Office of the Superintendent of
Public Instruction).

identifying physical education, intramural, extramural, and interscholastic budget items for girls and boys. Expenditures and services are being highlighted to facilitate public scrutiny through the local school board.

Student Interest Surveys

To discover whether the sports program activities are actually meeting the interest needs of students, school districts are providing school boards with student interest survey reports. The state of Washington mandates a student survey every three years. Figure 7-2 is the Washington directive.

TITLE IX LEGISLATION AND PROFESSIONAL LEADERSHIP

It is paradoxical that when budgetary considerations are imposing new restrictions on the recreational sports programs generally, social change is bringing more women into areas in the program which had earlier been masculine preserves. Customs are changing, and women are becoming directors of athletic programs and are developing skills in coaching, officiating, and athletic training. Their voices are heard more frequently in decision making and from the seats of power. As was just observed, this is a departure from the past. Before the enactment of Title IX legislation, the usual practice was for men to direct athletic programs, and they met the needs in overwhelming numbers for coaches, officials, and athletic trainers. To be sure, some economy-minded administrators have to a degree maintained the status quo by combining previously separate administrative units for women and men under a single administrative head and assigning women in such cases to assistantships or similar subordinate posts. But once this qualification has been made, the fact remains that Title IX legislation is fostering, overall, a social change in the recreational sports programs, and the women are the beneficiaries. They are increasingly assuming the title of director of athletic programs or recreational sports programs and undertaking the responsibilities for girls' and women's activities and in some cases for both boys and girls. Their functions make them analogous to the directors of the boys' and men's programs wherever the administrative structure is adequately funded. The movement toward greater equality can also be seen in the areas of coaching, officiating, and physical training, and if this type of skill is less impressive, from the viewpoint of leadership, than that required for directorship of a program, still these are positions and skills that suggest leadership ability to participants in the recreational sports program.

Coaches

Sport coaches are much in demand and short in supply. Reduced staff and increased teaching loads have cut into the resources for certified men coaches. As programs for highly skilled girls multiply, there has been a concerted effort to find and train qualified women who are willing to coach. This is not easily handled. A major coaching criterion is experience, and while most men coaches played on interscholastic teams at one time and benefited as well from professional course work, few women can cite such a record.

The belief is powerful that women must assume the long-term responsibility for coaching girls' sports, and a mindful professional leadership is moving rapidly to bring qualified women into the coaching ranks. But in the meantime other solutions have been necessary. Part-time coaches and the use of limited certification for specialists have met the short-term demands of the situation, while experienced coaches have shared their skills and knowledge with their aspiring counterparts. Workshops and clinics have been utilized to modernize coaching skills. Meanwhile, men have taken on interim responsibilities in coaching women's teams, and they have had the support of the National Association for Girls and Women in Sports (NAGWS).

The banding together of coaches within the structure of a national professional association to share and exchange problems gained identity in 1965 as the National High School Athletic Coaches Association (NHSCA). In its inception this group was predominantly male. The Association supports good coaching and promotes cooperation among coaches, administrators, the press, officials, and the public. It also sponsors clinics, provides the means of modernizing the profession, and facilitates the exchange of problem-solving ideas. It has a monthly publication entitled *Coach and Athlete,* and it grants special professional recognition by means of a Distinguished Service Award and naming a "National Coach of the Year." The female counterpart is NAGWS, which affords similar opportunities to its members. There are also strong state coaches' associations in Michigan, North Carolina, and Colorado; these are also stimulating interest and providing workshops. The state associations, organized with constitution and bylaws, board of control and officers, develop and promote a state code of ethics. The organizations function to serve the interests and needs of the membership and often develop as a structured affiliate of the state activities or athletic association.

More attractive remuneration for the services of women coaches is adding a positive impetus. Given support by court decisions such as that by Delaware's U.S. District Court, which identified a female coach's pay as a violation of the Equality Pay Act, discriminatory pay and promotion policies are gradually changing. Attention to underpaid women coaches, the volunteers used to keep programs alive, and those who have had to carry unreasonable teaching and coaching assignments is increasing. And equal pay for equal services is swiftly becoming the rule.

Officiating

In past years the efficiency of officiating services has suffered because officials have been obliged to enforce one set of rules for boys' games and another for the girls. But change is on the way. Working relationships have evolved on the state level that aim to eliminate the difficulties. The various state activities associations are finding mutually acceptable grounds of agreement, which are then adopted by constitutional amendment. These are the bodies that evolve officiating standards and leadership patterns, and typically there is only one such association or else the men and women have their own.

An example of such an association is the Washington Officials Association for Girls' and Women's Sports. An affiliate of the Washington Interscholastic Activities Association, it serves its membership in much the same way the Washington Officials Association serves the men. Reprinted here is the constitution of the girls' and women's affiliate.[1]

WASHINGTON OFFICIALS ASSOCIATION FOR GIRLS' AND WOMEN'S SPORTS CONSTITUTION

ARTICLE I
Name

The name of the organization shall be the Washington Officials Association for Girls' and Women's Sports.

ARTICLE II
Purposes

The purposes of this Association shall be to further the best interest of girls' athletics:

1. By aiding officials, coaches and players in acquiring a thorough knowledge of the playing rules of various sports through scheduling officiating clinics, workshops or classes;

2. By promoting uniformity in the mechanics of officiating through the use of National Association for Girls and Women in Sports-Associated Board of Officials (NAGWS-ABO) current rating procedures;

3. By encouraging observance of the spirit and letter of playing rules and ethical codes on all occasions;

4. By maintaining a central registry of all rated officials with current NAGWS-ABO national, state, local or apprentice ratings.

ARTICLE III
Membership

Section 1. Any person desiring membership in this Association must present his or her application, approved by the Chairperson of the local NAGWS-ABO Board, to the WIAA, with the stipulated fee.

Section 2. Qualifications for membership.

1. Current NAGWS-ABO National, State or Apprentice rating.
2. Membership in local affiliated NAGWS-ABO Board.

---

[1]"Washington Officials Association for Girls' and Women's Sports," *1975–76 Handbook Constitution Rules and Regulations* (Bellevue, Washington: Washington Interscholastic Activities Association, 1975), pp. 93–102.

3. Annual attendance at the WIAA-sanctioned regional, state or local officiating workshop or clinic in that sport.

4. Special cases will be reviewed by the Advisory Board.

Section 3. Members must regularly attend local Board meetings.

ARTICLE IV
Management

Section 1. The general management and operation of this Association shall be vested in the Washington Interscholastic Activities Association.

Section 2. A designated representative from WIAA shall serve this Association as Chairperson.

Section 3. The Advisory Board will act in an advisory capacity to the standing Girls' Athletic Activities Committee of the Washington Interscholastic Activities Association.

Section 4. Any issue involving WIAA member schools must be referred to WIAA through its Girls' Athletics Activities Committee.

ARTICLE V
Advisory Board

Section 1. The Advisory Board shall consist of a designated representative from the NAGWS Executive Board and the chairperson or representative from each of the NAGWS-ABO local Boards of Officials, and a representative from any subgroup as deemed necessary.

Section 2. Meetings to establish workshops, clinics and/or classes in the various sports and to conduct business pertaining to the Association shall be called by the designated WIAA representative.

ARTICLE VI
Amendments

Section 1. This constitution may be amended at any official meeting of the Advisory Board by a two-thirds affirmative vote provided the proposal has been presented to the local Boards at least 90 days prior to the meeting at which the vote is taken.

BYLAWS

ARTICLE I
Dues

Section 1. The annual dues shall be $5.00 for each sport, payable by July 1. All officials, with the exception of those who are new, will be charged an additional $5.00 for late registration. No registration for the current season will be accepted after November 1 for Volleyball, and February 1 for Basketball and Gymnastics. No refunds will be made after the competitive season begins.

ARTICLE II
Local Board Responsibility

Section 1. Each local Board Chairperson will be required to submit Board meeting attendance reports to the WIAA office.

Section 2. Each Board shall be responsible for assigning officials to contests within their geographic area.

Section 3. Each Board Chairperson will submit to the WIAA office a written annual report concerning the competency of their officials.

Section 4. Each Board shall be responsible for designating and enforcing an appropriate dress code for individual sports.

ARTICLE III
Advisory Board Expenses

Advisory Board members' expenses to all meetings called by WIAA shall be paid at the same rate allowed committee members of the WIAA when they are on official Association business.

ARTICLE IV
Formation of New Local Boards

Section 1. No new local Board may be formed in the immediate area where a recognized local Board now exists.

Section 2. All Boards must be 'recognized by the Girls' Athletic Activities Committee and the Board of Control of WIAA.

Section 3. Guidelines for formation of new local Boards shall be obtained from WIAA.

ARTICLE V
Amendments to the Bylaws

Section 1. These Bylaws may be amended by a majority affirmative vote of the Advisory Board provided said amendment has been presented in writing to the local Boards at least 30 days prior to change.

As with coaching, pressure has mounted for more qualified officials. As the women's sports programs expand, the needs increase. Men officials are serving in those areas lacking adequate women leadership and exceptions are being extended to accommodate deficiencies. State athletic associations are in some cases suspending for a year or two their requirements for certified officials as new programs are introduced for girls.

The National Federation of High School Associations sponsors committee meetings in various sports areas. The state associations send representatives who in turn report back rule changes, information, and ideas to the local groups. This has been the pattern under which the men officials have brought vitality to their state associations. An official certification procedure, unique to each state, has effectively served to enforce standards.

The National Association for Girls and Women in Sports (NAGWS) includes in its organizational structure an Associated Board of Officials (ABO), which is a volunteer committee of professionally interested personnel, together with supportive in-state district rating boards. The ABO functions to coordinate the services and needs of those individuals involved in officiating women's sports. Through district and local rating boards it conducts training sessions, workshops, clinics, demonstrations, and rating clinics for interested individuals, colleges, high schools, YWCAs, and various recreation groups.

The need for game officials is often met by "interning officials." For both boys' and girls' programs the resources of certified officials can be supplemented by an "Officials Club," which functions both within and outside the school programs. This leadership and training club provides excellent opportunities for potential young officials who are learning the skills and want to develop proficiency. It is also a resource of leadership when noncertified officials can add a positive influence on program management.

Athletic Trainers (AT)

The increase in competitive sports skill has drawn attention to needs and opportunities in athletic training. Care and prevention of athletic injuries of women athletics has developed as a major administrative concern as programs have expanded and leadership resources have been depleted.

Trainers have been firmly established as invaluable members of athletic staffs of major colleges, and although this is less evident, they also serve in an accepted role on the secondary school level. The need for women trainers is gradually being recognized by athletic and medical personnel. Towson State College (Maryland), Westchester State College (Pennsylvania), University of Maryland, Indiana State University at Terre Haute, and many others have women on the job. The search for qualified personnel, however, is exhausting those in the field and pressing the schools for more training.

But this is not the whole picture. Difficulties are in the process of being alleviated. Professional preparation programs for women trainers have appeared in education, while men's programs have, in some instances, expanded to accommodate women. In January 1974, an important step was taken when the National Athletic Trainers Association by means of an *ad hoc* committee on Women in Athletic Training established a liaison with NAGWS and WIAA to meet the demand. Internship programs are functioning in the high schools, and workshops featuring certified National Athletic Trainers Association (NATA) members are providing in-service training for the many in the field who are faced with new responsibilities.

As mounting cutbacks in budgets affect the staff, the coaches, directors, and sports managers have had to take some responsibilities in athletic training. It is no surprise, then, to find that both the sports leader and the specialists are learning such things as taping, conditioning, the immediate care of injuries, and the fundamentals of safe, sound programs of prevention.

DISCUSSION QUESTIONS

1. What are the main problems confronting professional leadership as the consequence of social and economic change?
2. How have reduced school budgets affected the recreational sports program? What are the implications for the future?
3. What is meant by "accountability"? In what ways does the concept affect recreational sports? The participants?
4. What are some ways in which Title IX legislation has changed the old customs? Discuss.
5. In what areas is there a shortage of qualified leadership? How is the problem being met?
6. If women are entering such fields as officiating and physical training in greater numbers, does this mean that the leadership role of women is expanding? Are these properly viewed as professions of leadership? Discuss.

BIBLIOGRAPHY

Association for Intercollegiate Athletics for Women, *AIAW Handbook-Directory 1975–76*. Washington, D.C.: National Association for Girls and Women in Sport, 1975.

BUCHER, CHARLES A., *Administration of Health and Physical Education Programs Including Athletics*. Saint Louis: C. V. Mosby Co., 1975.

BUCHER, CHARLES A., and RICHARD D. BUCHER, *Recreation for Today's Society*. Englewood Cliffs, N.J.: Prentice-Hall, Inc., 1974.

CRATTY, BRYANT J., *Psychology in Contemporary Sport*. Englewood Cliffs, N.J.: Prentice-Hall, Inc., 1973.

FROST, REUBEN B., and EDWARD J. SIMS, eds., *Development of Human Values through Sports*, proceedings of National Conference held at Springfield College, Springfield, Mass., October 12–14, 1973. Washington, D.C.: American Alliance for Health, Physical Education and Recreation, 1974.

HJELTE, GEORGE, and JAY SHIVERS, *Public Administration of Recreational Services*. Philadelphia: Lea & Febiger, 1972.

KANDO, THOMAS M., *Leisure and Popular Culture in Transition*. Saint Louis: C. V. Mosby Co., 1975.

KLAFS, C. E., and D. D. ARNHEIM, *Modern Principles of Athletic Training*, 3rd ed. Saint Louis: C. V. Mosby Co., 1973.

KRAUS, RICHARD G., and BARBARA J. BATES, *Recreation Leadership and Supervision*. Philadelphia: W. B. Saunders Co., 1975.

MILLER, DONNA MAE, *Teaching and Coaching Women in Sport*. Philadelphia: Lea & Febiger, 1974.

National Association for Girls and Women in Sports, *Women's Athletics: Coping with Controversy*. Washington, D.C.: American Alliance for Health, Physical Education and Recreation, 1974.

"Revolution in Women's Sports," reprint from *WomenSports* (September 1974), p. 18.

Competition.
(Courtesy News-Record of Maplewood and South Orange, New Jersey.)

8

Leadership Through
Democracy

For centuries the Judeo-Christian tradition has considered the human being unique and precious. Molded by this tradition, the American democratic system has sought to provide the framework within which the individual develops his potentialities to their maximum; and the ideal of developing mature, effective, intelligent, and happy individuals has long dominated American society, though Americans differ among themselves as to the best means of achieving it. The teachings of democracy may usefully be applied to leadership in the recreational sports program. These are most successful when leadership functions through democracy, carrying forward its ideals in formulating and implementing policies.

The scientific study of democratic leadership is comparatively recent. From this study the conclusion has emerged that the designated leader acts as the catalyst in the operation of the group, moving the whole to the course of action upon which it finally decides. The leader's role is particularly important in the recreational sports programs, where the leader serves as a guidance director who cultivates leadership qualities in students and channels their energies into constructive, effective action. It should be noticed that this leadership is democratic, the very opposite of autocratic and dictatorial.

DEMOCRATIC LEADERSHIP IN THE RECREATIONAL SPORTS PROGRAM

It is fitting that leadership in the recreational sports program fit the democratic mold, since this program grew up to meet some pressing social needs of a democratic society. Moreover, the total democratic pattern is strengthened when any one division of society uses democratic objectives and methods. Leadership through democracy in the recreational sports program has the dual advantage of making it possible for the program to function more effectively while enabling students to gain a better understanding of and preparation for taking their places in a democratic society. By practicing democracy the leader helps the student to learn self-government accompanied by respect for the rights of others, to accept more fully the importance of human dignity, to cooperate in attaining common goals, and to recognize that good citizenship is a daily need. Ordway Tead, one-time chairman of the Board of Higher Education in New York City, summed up the achievement of democratic leadership when he declared in *The Art of Leadership* (1935) that "leadership is known by the personalities it enriches, not by those it dominates or captivates."

Democratic leadership is exercised when the students in the recreational sports program help to determine policy. They should participate in choosing the sports in the program, selecting the time of year when these are to be played, scheduling hours, selecting playing rules and regulations, formulating officiating procedures, and shaping the procedures involving forfeits, awards, and eligibility for participation. Democratic leadership places a premium on the careful consideration of the opinions and suggestions of participating individuals; and, if properly exercised, it will leave each student with the recognition that one must work within a framework of responsibility. The democratic leader has the task of guiding the group in making an intelligent decision. Leadership, when it is successful, involves the group in problems and issues so that each individual has a feeling of responsibility for the solution; provides the intellectual setting for analyzing the logic of events; sets appropriate examples for the group to follow, and makes reasonable suggestions to help guide the course of discussion; fosters enthusiastic discussion of the goals desired; and opens legitimate channels of communication so that varying ideas and points of view may be expressed.

The recreational sports program affords unusual opportunities for encouraging the growth of leadership. Students enter the program as individuals seeking to understand the organization of which they are newly a part and to learn the rules, procedures, and group relationships that smooth their way. Even though each student continues to cherish his or her own individuality, retaining his or her own ways of thinking and acting, the democratic leader will encourage him to place the needs of the group ahead of his own. Effective group efforts produce a team effort that is productive, creative, and responsible in nature. As loyalty to the team grows, it brings in its wake a self-discipline that shapes a team out of what had formerly been only a group of individuals.

Leadership in the recreational sports program is the single most important factor in a successful program—more important than facilities, equipment, and supplies combined! Without good leadership a program with superior facilities and equipment will founder; with superior leadership a program with only ordinary facilities and equipment may surmount unusual obstacles. If the principles of democratic leadership are observed throughout the program, all concerned—the director and staff, the managers, the coaches, and players—will, in all probability, view the results with a high degree of satisfaction and with the pride that comes from achievement. Certainly the likelihood of success is greater with democratic leadership than with any other type.

SYMBOLS OF LEADERSHIP

"Leader" is a magical word, evoking different mental images to different persons, and sometimes even to the same person, depending upon the circumstances. A leader is thought of variously—as someone to be admired, as a director of others, as the wielder of influence, as a prop upon whom the weaker lean, or as an intelligent, strong, and talented person. But usually a leader is thought of as someone who has gained prestige by presenting ideas and programs that are soundly conceived and effectively executed. Some personal symbols of leadership are expressed in dress, manners, strength of character, emotional adjustment, self-confidence, faith, and convictions.

Other symbols are derived from the leadership role itself. Such titles as president, director, chairperson, manager, supervisor, coach, and captain suggest leaders. Outstanding achievement may also reflect a position of leadership in a given field, as, for example, a Nobel prize winner like William Faulkner in literature, or some prominent artist, sculptor, musician, surgeon, teacher, or athlete.

Still other symbols are derived from significant statements. The examples that follow are taken from athletics. When General Douglas MacArthur, the great American general of World War II, was earlier Superintendent of the United States Military Academy at West Point, he had this striking inscription placed in the entrance hall of the cadet gymnasium: "On these fields of friendly strife are sown the seeds which, on other fields, in other times, will bear the fruits of victory." Another example is the statement made by Bishop Daniel Poling of Philadelphia, who, speaking of the value of recreation, declared: "Give me the direction of the play life of the youth of this generation and I shall dictate the world's path tomorrow." Possibly the most famous slogan of all is the one attributed to Napoleon that "the Battle of Waterloo was won on the playing fields of Eton."

In the recreational sports program it is the director who symbolizes leadership; and to him falls the responsibility of stimulating its qualities among members of his staff, boards and councils, managers, team captains, and all participants.

QUALITIES OF LEADERSHIP

When a group chooses a leader, it acts on the assumption and with the hope that that person can lead its members with a minimum of friction along the lines on which they wish to move. In other words, they have concluded that one possesses the qualities of leadership required to guide them in a successful, united effort. This reasoning lies back of the election of a captain of a team or the choice of a director for the recreational sports program. Opportunity for a particular individual to become a leader arises largely from a specific, given situation.

The leader's success will be determined substantially by the degree to which one is able, through mastery of the art of human relations, to help the group attain its goals with unity, awareness, and self-satisfaction. Understanding the needs, interests, motives, and impulses of the group, the superior leader works toward the goals of the whole group. Such a leader brings its members into an evaluation of the pertinent issues and gives ample time for their consideration so that before any decision is reached the group is fully informed and aware of the implications of the matter at hand. In addition, the superior leader will help each member of the group to discover his or her own potentialities, for such a leader realizes the importance of cultivating with care the inner qualities of the individual.

The crucial test of leadership in the recreational sports program is met when leadership qualities are stimulated and cultivated in the participating students. What are these qualities of leadership? The following are frequently found among persons who have demonstrated outstanding leadership ability: intelligence, high moral and ethical standards, good judgment and common sense, integrity, belief in human dignity, drive and energy, endurance and vigor, courage and perseverance, maturity, insight, poise, patience, loyalty, resourcefulness, wisdom, vision, enthusiam, good physical and mental health, attractive personality, keen understanding of human relationships, and an awareness of the needs and interests of those involved in the program.

Few individuals possess all the qualities just listed, but identifying the qualities of leadership makes it possible for leaders to cultivate these qualities in themselves and in those under their guidance. In short, the director will seek to develop these qualities in the students in the program: The cliché "a leader is born" is a myth, since to a very considerable degree one may be created. Sometimes the important qualities lie dormant within an individual, springing to life in response to a particular situation in which just the right combination of circumstances has occurred. More often they reach fruition in a fertile soil prepared for their growth, but the cultivation must be careful and delicate.

The inner resources of the student are more likely to be cultivated if the student respects the director and staff. A climate of cooperation is created when the director upholds high standards of health, safety, and moral conduct and exercises proper standards of judgment. Wholesome and constructive actions should combine with good personal conduct and hygiene, appropriate dress, proper body mechanics, and a clear and effective speaking voice. A student cannot be expected to develop desirable qualities of character and gain worthy attitudes and social characteristics unless the director and staff not only possess these qualities in full measure but demonstrate them as well.

Since the recreational sports program is voluntary, the director should be endowed with strong leadership ability if the program is to flourish. Democratic leadership fosters in students personal standards of judgment that facilitate their acquiring the values inherent in the program. Accordingly, the director will seek to present effectively the philosophy, objectives, goals, and type of program needed in a particular situation. The leader must also utilize the latest research in education, psychology, biology, and sociology so as to understand individual and community needs in recreation and leisure. In understanding individual needs the director should be aware that research studies show that, all other qualities being equal, the person of higher intelligence will become the superior leader. Mental ability is an important quality in determining how high a person should attempt to rise in leadership positions. If one is promoted to a position too high for mental capacity, harm may be inflicted, whereas success at a lower level of responsibility would have had a beneficial effect. In understanding community needs the director should be aware of the great growth of leisure time among the mass of people in the twentieth century and tailor the program to give students the needed skills for leisure-time pursuits.

It is imperative that the director of the program be inspired by its goals. In addition, the director must give students the reassurance that the staff cares about them as people. They want to feel that the director has a concern for them arising from personal as well as professional considerations. A friendly attitude and an inspiring personality foster an esprit de corps among students—a friendly attitude gains a like response. Students differ greatly in their responses to a program leader, perhaps because local social groups value particular leadership qualities. By other standards one may meet the test of being a leader of high quality. If so, then one must compensate for weaknesses by using more effectively one's strengths. A difficult situation may be handled effectively on the strength of a particular quality of leadership such as imagination. Through participation in the recreational sports program under the right leadership, students can learn to win and lose graciously, to be loyal, competitive, courteous, unprejudiced, considerate of others, and to repress selfish desires.

THE DIRECTOR AS CONFERENCE LEADER

Conferences traditionally serve several major purposes. They may be used to inspire a group to greater action and solidarity, to present information to each member in a planned group situation, to negotiate and coordinate affairs, and to promote the group's goals through educating each member. Overall, the unity of the group is heightened; for the modern democratic conference requires those present to pool their viewpoints and arrive at a policy that may differ from the preconceptions of the members of the group when the conference began. To have a successful conference, participants must subordinate their own special interests to the greater good of the whole, working toward decisions that contribute to the overall goals of the school and college. The process of creative group deliberation provides a forum in which the group may analyze controversial questions and alert its members to their implications; and all must share responsibility for a decision reached by this means.

In the recreational sports program a typical conference includes the director of the program plus members of a board or council representing students, faculty, and administrators. If the conference includes fifteen persons or less, the democratic technique is to gather with the leader who encourages each member to become an active participant in the making of decisions. If the conference is to include more than fifteen, it is often advantageous for them to meet earlier in small groups to discuss the agenda before the regular conference is held. This procedure encourages independent thinking by each member, breaks down prejudices, enables a member to understand better another's viewpoint, and gives each member an overall understanding of the issues.

The preliminary preparations made by the leader will go far to set the tone of the conference. An agenda should be prepared as a guide for the discussion of items. It must be planned in advance and distributed to the members at least one week before the conference so that each member will have time to think about the issues and obtain additional information as desired. The perceptive leader is also aware that a pleasant physical environment is essential for a productive conference. He will want to be certain that room temperature is normal, lighting adequate, and the conference room quiet and free from interruption. A recommended procedure is that the department secretary inform visitors of the approximate length of the conference, and that he or she inform those who call by telephone that the call will be returned after the conference is terminated (except in emergencies).

When the conference convenes, the leader must clarify all the ground rules that may have a special bearing on the agenda. For example, what authority does the group have in making decisions that determine policy? Will there be a vote to determine a solution? If so, will *Robert's Rules of Order* prevail? If not, what procedures are to be used to guide the business meeting? Will some items on the agenda be discussed at the meeting with a vote on a decision postponed until a later meeting? Such details must be clearly understood by all those present if the meeting is to move along with each member feeling that he is actually a policy-making member.

The conference procedure considered most successful is to have the leader outline each issue to be discussed, present specific information that has a direct bearing on it, keep the meeting on course with each member's point of view stated, draw the entire discussion to a focal point, and then work toward a policy decision as soon as the full impact of a given issue is thoroughly understood.

The conference leader must use careful judgment in determining the amount of time to be devoted to an issue. While each member should have the opportunity to express his opinion, the discussion, nevertheless, should not run on until the group becomes restless because time is being wasted. As the conference proceeds, the wise leader constantly studies the members of the group to determine their reactions to the proposals under consideration; and he will want to generate within each member a concern for the success of the program that leads to a readiness to exchange information and experiences in the group effort to arrive at a sound conclusion. For optimum results the meeting should run no more than one hour and thirty minutes. If more time is required, then the conference should be adjourned for at least thirty minutes. The art of leadership is exercised successfully if this situation and timing are effectively handled.

Sometimes serious difficulties arise. A forceful speaker, holding strong views, may threaten to lead the group in a direction incompatible with the educational goals of the program and institution. At such a time, the conference leader should strive to keep the group attentive to the essence of the matter at hand while he stabilizes the meeting and seeks to develop an atmosphere that will encourage the free expression of views on the part of all present. Admittedly, this is difficult to do in view of the individual differences among the members of the group.

When highly controversial issues are discussed, fatigue increases, with resulting emotional outbursts. These are more likely to erupt near the end of the conference when members who are highly excited about an issue lose their composure. Yet skillful conference leaders recommend the placing of controversial issues at the bottom of the agenda. In this way the bulk of the business may be handled quickly and effectively; and, in the process, a healthy climate may be created for settling the more difficult issues that have been postponed. If a leader is reasonably certain that a crisis is building up on a given issue, he may want to explain on the agenda itself that the decision on this issue may be delayed until a later meeting. This procedure still permits a decision at the current meeting if the discussion moves along effectively.

Even the best-laid plans for a conference may fail to prevent a serious emotional outburst. If it occurs, the leader should refrain from rebuking the offending member in the presence of others. A rebuke may have a chilling effect upon the meeting, for members of the group are quick to read from such a display of power that actually they have very little opportunity to make policy decisions. Research studies made of executives in the Standard Oil Company of New Jersey indicate that two methods of handling the emotion-packed situation have proved to be highly successful. One method is for the leader to declare the meeting adjourned at the moment the crisis occurs; another meeting should not be called until the following day at the earliest. A second method that has proved to be very successful when the situation is less explosive is for the leader to declare a minute of silence. Tempers may cool and the atmosphere clear with the possibility of continuing the meeting in an orderly manner. At the close of the moment of silence it is advisable for the leader to summarize the thinking of the group to this point and then to invite a member known as a stabilizing influence to speak on the issue. The member whose emotions had caused the difficulty should be allowed to speak again, if he wishes to do so, before the vote is taken. After judging the degree of emotion still present in the meeting the leader may decide to postpone a vote on the explosive issue until a later meeting. An issue that conceivably could create a crisis of this proportion in a recreational sports conference is deciding whether or not to give awards to winners in the program. When official action is to be taken in any conference, it is extremely important for the conference leader to follow *Robert's Rules of Order*. The conference leader should make certain that the latest edition of *Robert's Rules of Order* is being used.

Despite the fact that conferences are frequently time-consuming and may be filled with difficulty, they are becoming the accepted means for gaining group communication and making decisions in education, business, industry, and even the military services. As a procedure or technique, the conference permits its members to take a more active part in the organization in general. The rising esprit de corps promotes not only the goals of the program and institution but also the personal and professional satisfactions of each member. When these results have been achieved, the art of leadership has been skillfully attained.

EXECUTIVE AND ADMINISTRATIVE LEADERSHIP

Many leadership functions of the director of the recreational sports program are almost wholly executive and administrative. In addition to such technical details as the handling of budgets, records, and reports, he has the task of giving tone and temper to the whole program. He will do this through the impact of his personality and character, but other ways include the assembling and directing of a competent staff, providing facilities and equipment, and making certain that these are properly cared for. In addition, the director has the function of maintaining cordial relations with the officials of the school or college and the members of the community interested in the program.

As far as the recreational sports program is concerned, the director is the key executive; but he must work with other executive and administrative leaders whose attitudes may well determine the type of recreational sports program that can be established. In the public schools the keys of power are found, in descending order, in a school board or board of education, the superintendent, and the principal; the comparable structure in the colleges consists of the board of regents or a like body, the president, the deans, and the departmental chairperson. Within a community, a variety of administrators from recreation agencies and commissions are in liaison with the school and college administrators to establish the administrative framework for a school or college and community program.

The personality and educational philosophy of the director may well determine the tone and temper of the program. A successful director, using the techniques of leadership through democracy, guides students into experiences in the recreational sports program that complement their academic work while promoting their interests and abilities in a program of recreation. Possessing a well-reasoned philosophy, an awareness of his responsibility to his students, and an ability to transmit ideas, he can move human energies toward desirable channels of expression and transform passiveness into vital action by tapping the deep-lying motives of the individual. In particular, the director will seek to inspire in students in the program a recognition of their responsibility for fair play and sportsmanship, a willingness to make equitable arrangements affecting the group, and a desire to take proper care of facilities and equipment.

But the director must also have humility. A fundamental weakness on the part of many a leader as administrator is derived from his belief in his own infallibility. He may have had many years of experience in his course of action, but he should be prepared to discover that some of his views no longer fit conditions. In converting others to his ideas he should also remember that these have evolved from a long, slow process, and he should not expect conversion in others to come overnight, if it comes at all. Patience is a requisite. For ideas have to germinate; and in a group program, where democratic leadership exists, these ideas have to be accepted by a variety of individuals, each of whom needs time for analysis and cogitation. Ideas and suggestions are seeds that must be planted, and their growth requires careful cultivation. But it cannot be too many times repeated: if the director, as executive leader, provides the opportunity for those involved in the program to have a meaningful part in policy making, he will be rewarded by the group's formulating sound ideas and judgments.

The primary purpose of the director as executive and administrative leader is to make the program a satisfying experience for the students. One important way of doing this is to select competent teachers, assistants, and officials. Working through this staff he will seek to guide the students into assuming their own leadership responsibilities. If his leadership is effective, students in the program will achieve levels of skill, interest, pride, and solidarity otherwise unattainable. The director, as executive and administrative leader, must keep in mind that organization is like team play in that each participant needs to understand what the program is organized to do. The students blend into a smoothly functioning program when their individual ideas, beliefs, and aspirations combine to give an effective performance. A striving for group goals accompanies individual growth. The process can be stimulated by effective executive leadership, particularly through the selection and direction of a competent staff.

Good administration also depends upon the staff and the students being acquainted with the rules and regulations governing their tasks and responsibilities. The director, working within the framework of these rules and regulations, should act constructively and courteously, taking cognizance of the studies that reveal how praise, when judiciously meted out, results in a better satisfied group working up to its capacity. If, on the other hand, penalties have to be administered, the necessary action should take place in private. Should reproof be needed, the director, in a courteous way, should discuss the entire situation with the person affected in a constructive attempt to discover the cause of the difficulty and the point at which it began. He should avoid violent language and sarcasm as weapons that may inflict irreparable damage. If a reprimand has to be administered, this should be done in a simple, straightforward manner with penalties that are thoroughly known to all concerned.

A further executive and administrative function falling to the director of the recreational sports program is that of maintaining harmonious relationships with other administrative officials in the school, college, or community. If he builds the necessary bridges, he will have established a solid foundation for the recreational sports program. The best publicity is, of course, an excellent program that brings educationally sound experiences to the student; but more is needed. The values of the program must be publicized among the faculty, the administration, and members of the community. Wherever and whenever possible, the director of the program must secure support for the program through new ideas and techniques, initiative and creativity, and a program endowed with both strength and quality.

THE LADDER OF LEADERSHIP

Many realize today that play and recreation in leisure hours can be wholesome and constructive. While the impulse to play is natural, the forms of play and recreation are not. Play without leadership and instruction is merely the imitation of adult activity by trial and error methods. The play and recreation leader adds vitality and a deeper meaning to the activities. Effective leadership eliminates discouraging experimentation and arouses within the student a desire for self-improvement and self-discipline, as it helps him to attain a maturity in judgment.

The ladder of leadership begins on the level of the elementary schools, where the least has been done up to this time in imparting a professional tone to the programs of recreational sports. As soon as the elementary schools are equipped with full-time teachers in physical education and recreation, the entire structure of education from that level through the colleges will have, in theory at least, one person available who is a specialist in recreational sports. He will be in a key position for influencing favorably the students so that they may gain the full measure of contributions from the program.

The present structure and philosophy of the typical elementary school make it very difficult, indeed, to secure the needed professional leadership for a recreational sports program. The self-contained classroom, in which the classroom teacher has almost complete charge of the students, places severe restrictions on physical education and recreation. It would be different if elementary school teachers were qualified in all areas of education. But so complex is modern education that few of them acquire all the professional knowledge, skills, and methods necessary to give elementary-school students the rich experiences needed for maximum development in the modern industrial age.

In practice, the self-contained classroom system, which lingers from the days of the little one-room schoolhouse, has to be supplemented by specialists in specific areas of education, notably in art, music, and health and physical education. This system is slowly yielding throughout the United States—especially in the large elementary schools—to a more modern system in which the teacher is limited to his academic specialty. Under the latter system a specialist in physical education and recreation is available, on a full-time basis, to direct physical education and intramural and recreation programs.

The elementary classroom teacher is not the only source of leadership in the recreational sports program. In the public schools, generally at all levels, the board of education, the superintendent, the principal, and guidance counselors are all in a position to influence the effectiveness of the program. Usually in the elementary school the classroom teacher sets the tone after administrative decisions have determined the emphasis to be placed on physical education and the voluntary laboratory of recreational sports. As has already been noted, he may call upon the help of a physical education specialist in developing the programs.

The typical pattern in the junior and senior high schools is to have a full-time person in physical education working under the administrative direction of a hierarchy of public school officials. Since the school is the outgrowth of the local community and reflects its needs, interests, and demands, school officials must not only understand these needs but also seek to meet them. Increasingly, American communities are realizing that the recreational sports program is a valuable investment. It should be in operation after the end of the academic program and merge into a school-community recreational sports program.

In the college and universities the program of recreational sports is a division of the physical education department. It is most successful when a director is appointed to have responsibility for its administration. But he himself works within a larger administrative structure that may be briefly described. The college or university president executes policies set by a board, which is usually a board of regents or trustees. Between the president and the director of the recreational sports program there intervene usually one college dean and the chairperson of the department of health and physical education. The specific arrangement of a given college or university will vary according to its administrative structure. It may include recreational sports council and boards, interfraternity and sorority councils, college masters, official student organizations, committees, and representatives.

That the leadership role of the administrators in the recreational sports program must be shared with the students in the program has been a major theme in this chapter. They will benefit from the manifold values of a well-conceived and executed program and in turn will relate their experiences to their parents and friends. If students are to benefit to the utmost from the program, the director must understand the complete range of recreation under his jurisdiction. In addition, he must have the necessary experience to permit him to conduct a complex program with several divisions operating at one time. For its varied tasks and responsibilities he will need to exercise sound judgment in providing for safety, discipline, and rules and regulations and in fostering mutually advantageous relationships with administrators, faculty, students, and parents. At all times he will seek to exercise his leadership through democracy.

DISCUSSION QUESTIONS

The question section in this chapter will be specifically aimed at helping to determine whether the principles and techniques of democratic leadership are used by the leader of the recreational sports program.

1. Is there evidence to show that the participants share in organizating and conducting the program?
2. Is there a feeling of respect and cooperation between the leader and the students? Do the students appear to enjoy their association with the leader of the program?
3. Does the leader set a personal example in integrity, sincerity, and courtesy? Do the dress and appearance of the leader suggest a professional program?

4. Does the leader appear to be just and fair in making decisions?

5. Does the leader create an atmosphere of respect for the rights of each student and give credit and encouragement as deserved?

6. Does the leader appear to be more concerned with the winning of games than with the welfare of the participants?

7. Is the main emphasis on winning or on providing a program that allows all students to participate?

8. Does the leader regard sportsmanship as a vital concern in the program?

9. Does the leader encourage individual initiative?

10. Does the leader attempt to create situations for the students that will facilitate the development of desirable leadership qualities, social characteristics, and healthy attitudes?

11. Does the leader show imagination?

12. Does the leader plan ahead so that the program moves smoothly and effectively?

13. Is there evidence that the students are learning the principles and techniques of democratic leadership?

14. Is there evidence of teamwork among the students and a proper observation of rules and regulations?

15. Does the leader interpret the values of the recreational sports program to the students?

16. Is there a well-balanced program of recreation suited to the needs and interests of the students?

17. Is there evidence that the recreational sports program is preparing students for leisure-time recreational pursuits?

18. Do the students appear to be skilled in recreational sports?

19. Is the program an outgrowth of the activities learned in a physical education program?

20. Does the leader give special attention to periodic evaluations of the entire program?

21. Does the leader give proper attention to the health and well-being of the participants?

22. Does the leader plan ahead for emergenices such as accidents?

23. Does the leader create within the students a feeling of respect for facilities and equipment? Are they maintained in a safe condition?

24. Does the leader develop the recreational sports program through committees, boards, and councils?

25. Does the director in schools and colleges consult teachers and administrators in other areas who may be able to bring valuable information to the program?

BIBLIOGRAPHY

BANNON, JOSEPH J., *Problem Solving in Recreation and Parks.* Englewood Cliffs, N.J.: Prentice-Hall, Inc., 1972.

BOUTON, ROBERT E., *Effective Supervisory Practices.* Washington, D.C.: International City Management Association, 1971.

CORBIN, H. DAN, *Recreation Leadership*. Englewood Cliffs, N.J.: Prentice-Hall, Inc., 1970.

DOELL, CHARLES E., and LOUIS F. TWARDZIK, *Elements of Park and Recreation Administration*. Minneapolis: Burgess Publishing Co., 1973.

EDWARDS, MYRTLE, *Recreation Leader's Guide*. Palo Alto, Calif.: National Press, 1967.

GOBLE, FRANK, *Excellence in Leadership*. New York: American Management Association, 1972.

KRAUS, RICHARD G., and BARBARA J. BATES, *Recreation Leadership and Supervision*. Philadelphia: W. B. Saunders Co., 1975.

STEINER, IVAN D., *Group Process and Productivity*. New York: Academic Press, 1972.

IV

Organization
and
Administration

Indoor Recreation.
(Courtesy: Dr. Steven Sherman of Brooklyn College.)

9

Patterns of Organization and Administration for the Recreational Sports Program

The recreational sports program in schools, colleges, and communities functions through several patterns of organization and administration. While the program has operated successfully under a variety of arrangements, the most successful have followed the practice of assigning the recreational sports program to a highly qualified director, who has this program as his primary responsibility. Such an administrative plan treats recreational sports as an important part of the overall field of health, physical education, recreation, and athletics. As was earlier noted in this book, the terminology "recreational sports program" is rapidly emerging throughout the United States in schools, colleges, and communities as the appropriate name for a program that includes intramurals, extramurals, sports clubs, girls' and women's recreation association activities, unstructured or free-play recreational sports activities, and school-college-community recreational sports activities. The recreational sports program usually includes each of these specialized programs, such as intramurals, as a subdivision of the recreational sports program. In the vanguard of the movement to bring all of these elements under the heading of recreational sports are such leading institutions as the University of Texas and Purdue University. For a comprehensive discussion of these developments and, in particular, a discussion of the position paper prepared by Pat Mueller in favor of the new terminology, see Chapter 2 ("The Evolution of Recreational Sports Programs").

The recreational sports program in the colleges and universities is the product of a longer, more extensive evolution than that found in the public school, and it is no surprise to discover a great variety of organizational and administrative patterns. To pick one's way through the variety, it is helpful to take as the point of departure the recreational sports program as it functions within the department of physical education. This is the most common and successful pattern, and it is likely to have the greatest staying power. Consequently, this program has been given a detailed analysis in the following pages. It then becomes possible to consider more briefly other patterns of organization and administration for the recreational sports program, those that have long been part of the educational scene and others that are by comparison innovative newcomers with the promise of altering that scene drastically in the future if their advocates are successful. This chapter will conclude with a brief examination of the administration of sports clubs and community recreation and the structured recreational sports handbook which is essential to the successful functioning of the recreational sports program.

THE DIRECTOR OF THE RECREATIONAL SPORTS PROGRAM WITHIN THE DEPARTMENT OF PHYSICAL EDUCATION

The most effective plan of organization and administration for a program of recreational sports—and the one that is most likely to receive an increasing amount of attention—is the one by which a highly qualified director has the recreational sports program as his (or her) primary responsibility, that program functioning within the department of physical education. Figure 9-1 illustrates graphically the position of the recreational sports program when that program is an integral part of the total offerings of the physical education department. Institutions vary somewhat in organizational pattern. Usually a college or university is organized so that this program falls into one of two categories. If the combined field of health, physical education, recreation, and athletics is merged into one department, there will be a chairperson for the total unit and a director for each division, of which recreational sports will be one. If the combined area is structured and designated as a school or college division of the entire college or university, then the chief administrative officer is usually a dean and each subdivision, a department. Under these circumstances, the recreational sports program should be a department of the division with a chairperson for the recreational sports department. On a small scale, public and private schools are beginning to develop this pattern of organization and administration. As the director of the recreational sports program prepares to work with students to coordinate schedules with facilities and equipment, to select competent officials, and to work out a satisfactory system of awards, he must be ever-mindful of local factors such as customs, traditions, special interests, and geographic conditions.

The director of the recreational sports program must have a thorough knowledge of physical education and recreation. He must

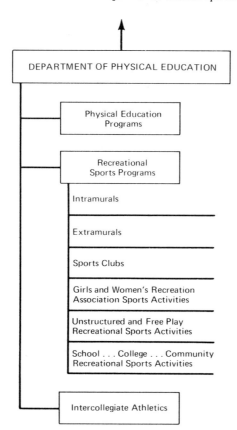

Figure 9-1   The Division of Recreational Sports in the Department of Physical Education at Brooklyn College.

maintain excellent personal relations with students and staff, organize and administer with adeptness, and meet the students' needs and interests with appropriate recreational sports opportunities. This program should function as an integral part of the total program of physical education, and it requires an appropriate budget that is independent of athletic gate receipts. The budget should be based upon standards similar to those required for the budget for any academic department.

As soon as an effective program is organized, the director will find that the number of participants will multiply, the amount of clerical work will increase, and additional officials will be needed. Consequently, he will need both full-time and part-time personnel. As director of the program he has the administrative responsibility for the staff and program as delegated to him by the administrative officers of the school or college. Recreational sports as an integral part of a physical education department are illustrated graphically in Figure 9-2.

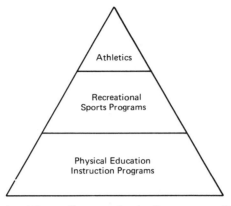

Figure 9-2   Recreational Sports Programs in the Department of Physical Education at Brooklyn College.

Recreational Sports Council

The success of the program is greatly enhanced by a recreational sports council. It should contain student representatives from all organizations such as dormitories, fraternities, sororities, college houses, off-campus organizations, and independent units. At regular meetings, operating with an established agenda, the recreational sports council will usually discuss forthcoming sports events and tournaments, eligibility rules, awards, forfeits, protests, officiating, and facilities and equipment for scheduled events. The council bridges the gap between the director of the program and the manager and supervisors of the program. The development of this council has created a need for a faculty advisor. Faculty members from other departments who are especially interested in the recreational sports program are usually willing to take an active role as an advisor. It is highly recommended that at least one such faculty member be named to this council as a participating member. Faculty representatives can help to formulate policy and also to shape and mold the program so as to enhance its educational values.

Recreational Sports Supervisors

Recreational sports programs in schools and colleges need supervisors to administer the details concerning facilities and equipment, schedules, officials, and miscellaneous arrangements. The most effective plan is to assign an adequate number of staff members in the department to the program; but if this is impossible, it may be necessary to appeal to allied departments for additional staff.

Graduate Assistants and Supplementary Staff

Where graduate programs in health, physical education, and recreation exist in colleges and universities, provision is often made for graduate assistants to teach in the program or give aid in other ways. A graduate assistant in this program is usually a highly skilled athlete, older than the students, whose presence lends stability to the program. Another possibility of supplementing the staff is through recruitment of public school teachers who are highly qualified in sports and games and have an interest in the recreational sports program. They often contribute markedly to the program.

Student Managers

Student managers are also an essential part of the recreational sports program. To it they bring interest, enthusiasm, leadership, and cooperation. In essence they are of two types—program managers and team managers. The first represents an organization such as a fraternity, dormitory, or independent unit. A student team manager has the task of organizing a given team, entering it in the program, and making allied arrangements for the season. Only students with a genuine desire to be team managers should be selected for this position.

Department Secretary

A full-time secretary is mandatory for a large recreational sports program. Duties are manifold: keeping office records and files; answering inquiries from the public; giving telephone service; preparing reports, schedules, copies of rules, minutes of meetings, and other materials that are to be distributed to students, staff, and administrators outside the department; preparing requisitions; checking medical reports, etc.

Because of a variety of responsibilities, the secretary should be pleasant and capable, inbued with an understanding of the value of the recreational sports program, and a person of sufficient tact in personal relations to maintain cordial relations with the staff, the students, the administration, and the public. A telephone should be installed at the equipment issue window so that reservations for handball, squash, tennis courts, etc., may be made without recourse to the secretary.

OFFICIATING IN THE RECREATIONAL SPORTS PROGRAM

Participation in recreational sports should be an enjoyable, wholesome experience. Sports officials have a responsibility to help provide an atmosphere conducive to it. The behavior of both officials and participants reflects the entire philosophy of the program. Participants must respect the sports officials; and, in turn, the officials must warrant this respect by gaining a full knowledge of the rules, appearing on time and in neat attire, officiating impartially, and using every available means to promote good sportsmanship.

Sportsmanship is one of the most cherished values emanating from a recreational sports program. Its importance as a quality of character and personality received striking emphasis in a speech by Senator Stuart Symington of Missouri, former businessman and Secretary of the Air Force, when he stated, "I think America's most cherished national possession is sportmanship. I choose to define sportsmanship as honest rivalry, courteous relations, and graceful acceptance of results. As a businessman I can vouch for how badly we need those traits in industry; and as a member of government, I can vouch also for their need in Washington. When a young American, though burning up inside, quietly turns away from a called third strike, or accepts without grimace, moan, or mutter, the foul called on him for basketball overguarding, he is learning those traits which later make him an asset to his community, to his future business or profession, and to his nation."

Most activities require competent officials, but some, such as ice hockey, touch football, and basketball, are more demanding than others. Generally, officials should receive compensation for their services. Where students are used as officials, they often receive a game fee, which, in many ways, is more satisfactory than payment on a per-hour basis. Whereas it is occasionally difficult to secure competent student officials in junior and senior high schools, students are most readily available in colleges and universities, especially in those with graduate programs in health, physical education, and recreation.

It is desirable that the recreational sports participants, managers, officials, and staff meet as a group before the start of the playing season for a sport to discuss rules and regulations, officiating, and other matters concerning the competition. An arrangement in many schools, colleges, and communities that has proved satisfactory is holding clinics for specific sports such as basketball, touch football, and swimming. It is the height of folly to assign officiating duties to students without first preparing them for what is a difficult assignment. They, too, must learn the rules and officiating techniques as a necessary preliminary to their assignment to a game. Some schools, colleges, and communities appoint a supervisor for each sport, whose duties include checking all details of officiating.

MISCELLANEOUS DUTIES AND DETAILS

Administrative duties and details are very nearly the same in school, college, and community recreational sports programs regardless of size. The magnitude of detail, however, will be in direct ratio to the number of activities, participants in the program, and available staff members and voluntary assistants.

While the recreational sports program lacks the spectator appeal of varsity athletics, its intrinsic value in education is being realized more and more. Such a program has great potential. To realize this potential the director must attend to much administrative detail. The specific categories of responsibility are as follows:

1. Timely and appropriate meetings of the staff, managers, and officials, etc., must take place to ensure all directly concerned that specific duties and details have been carefully worked out and to inform them of the rules and regulations that govern all activities.

2. An effective office procedure must be maintained to ensure proper handling of all records, reports, notices, public relations and publicity, photography, bulletin boards, pamphlets and brochures, business forms, and requisitions.

3. Medical records must be carefully checked to make sure that all participants are medically qualified for the activities in which they are planning to engage. First aid procedures must be ready for effective operation by staff members and assistants.

4. Awards and certificates in the recreational sports program must be administered so as to please the participants and conform to accepted practices in the school, college, or community program.

5. Effective plans must be drawn for scheduling, league formations, and the handling of point systems and forfeits.

6. Officiating procedures must be worked out that include the selection, training, and assigning of officials to contests.

7. The most satisfactory method of settling protests on procedure in competitive activities must be determined. It is imperative for the good of the program that protests be settled to the mutal satisfaction of those involved. While most schools and colleges require that protests be filed with the recreational sports council within twenty-four hours, the requirement of a "cooling off" period has merit. A twenty-four-hour waiting period may be required before the

protest can be filed. Another successful procedure requires that protests involving games played on a specific day not be accepted by the recreational sports council until the following morning.

8. Periodic evaluation of the entire program is necessary. In addition to improving current programs, the entire staff must be cognizant of the changes needed for forthcoming programs.

9. An effective arrangement concerning facilities for the recreational sports program is mandatory. They are at a premium since athletics and the program of physical education customarily receive first choice in schools and colleges.

FACILITIES FOR THE PROGRAM

A highly qualified staff for the recreational sports program is the single most important element in the program. But good facilities, readily available, are also essential. As soon as a staff is assembled, attention should go to arranging facilities and equipment to accommodate the participants in a large number of events. Programs are becoming more comprehensive each year because of new construction of gymnasiums, field houses, stadiums, and separate recreation buildings.

Since heavy scheduling of recreational sports activities occurs between 4 P.M. and 6 P.M., it is frequently very difficult in this period to find the necessary facilities to accommodate the program. The 4–6 P.M. period is also a peak period for athletic team workouts. Athletic teams take prime hours and are likely to continue to do so as long as the athletic division of physical education wins the greatest support from the general public. The alternative is to schedule the recreational sports program over a greater number of hours.

Activities can be scheduled very effectively between 7 P.M. and 10 P.M. on well-lighted courts and fields in schools, colleges, and communities. Leagues are frequently conducted during these hours in such activities as touch football, ice hockey, softball, volleyball, basketball, field hockey, swimming, handball, squash, tennis, archery, and bowling. This arrangement proves difficult in cases in which the student body must commute to classes from a considerable distance. These schools and colleges may achieve a great deal of success with recreational sports activity on Friday from 7 to 10 P.M. and on Saturdays and Sundays.

Studies made at the University of Michigan concerning participation in recreational sports activities reveal that a major concern of the students is to have playing areas available according to predetermined schedules. Facilities that are attractive, located near the students' living quarters, and easily accessible facilitate recreational sports participation.

If a student wishing to use facilities finds them frequently unavailable when his interest is growing in an activity, he will turn to some other form of recreation. The situation is eased if students are kept informed about availablility of facilities and program schedules, perhaps through the use of reservation sheets for activities such as tennis, golf, handball, squash, badminton, touch football, field hockey, and softball. An efficient system requires that reservations be made only on the day of play.

When two or more programs use the same facilities, it is imperative that the scheduling of events be supervised by one person who maintains the responsibility for coordinating all events that are scheduled on such facilities. Unless the recreational sports program has its own building and outside courts and fields, scheduling problems will arise. Since the athletic program, as was stated earlier, has first choice of facilities, and physical education classes have the second choice, recreational sports activities must be scheduled to accommodate these divisions of the total program. Title IX legislation may change this prevailing philosophy.

Facilities must be readily adaptable to a variety of sports activities. They must be properly lighted and ventilated and maintained in a safe condition. Modern building construction makes use of light units in the floor to mark lines for court dimensions. An appropriate light switch controls the floor-light units for the boundary lines of a specific sport. This plan eliminates the maze of multicolored lines that frequently appear on court floors. Electric scoreboards and public address systems facilitate the orderly handling of sports activities. Modern net holders and standards are available that permit multiple use of courts with very little time needed to change from one sport to another. These innovations may be seen at Purdue University and the University of Illinois at Urbana.

RECREATIONAL SPORTS GYMNASIA

Any account of the administration of recreational sports programs would be incomplete without at least a reference to the programs presently in operation at the University of Illinois at Urbana and at Purdue. These programs are many years ahead of their time and will, in all probability, set the pace for planning in recreational sports on the school and college levels. Directors of recreational sports programs everywhere will want to gain an understanding of the Illinois and Purdue programs, as they evaluate their own programs and prepare to make changes. The directors planning new facilities will need to be informed about the impressive recreational sports gymnasia that have been erected at Illinois and Purdue. These gymnasia provide the center for administering the recreational sports programs at the two institutions.

ALTERNATIVE PATTERNS

There are other patterns of organization and administration in the recreational sports program in addition to the one that has just been described. But the recreational sports program within the department of
physical education, it should be stressed, is, and is likely to continue to be
in the forseeable future, the one that sets the tone of administration
generally for programs of recreational sports in schools and colleges.
The others will now be described. In describing them, attention has been
given, though at times very briefly, to their strengths and weaknesses.

THE PHYSICAL EDUCATION DIRECTOR AND RECREATIONAL SPORTS

When the recreational sports program is the administrative responsibility of the physical education director, it loses its identity as a separate
program. If the physical education director is responsible for a required
program, intramurals, recreation, and athletics, the recreational sports
program is bound to be subordinate to interscholastic or intercollegiate
athletics. Although athletics appeal much more to the general public, the
recreational sports program is valuable to a much higher percentage of
the student body. The major advantage in having the director of physical education serve as director of recreational sports is that he can easily
reach all students in the service program with information about the
sports opportunities available through the program to the entire student body and faculty. In addition, he can effectively coordinate the use
of facilities and equipment within the department. It should be realized,
however, that when the director of the department of physical education
himself administers the recreational sports program, it is to him only one
of several programs in the department and not necessarily the most
important.
     Nor should the responsibility for directing the program be thrust
upon a physical education teacher. It may weigh on him to such a degree
that he loses his efficiency and effectiveness. The procedure should be in
reverse order. If a well-qualified physical education teacher receives
appointment as the director of the recreational sports program and has
any time available to teach physical education classes, then the teacher
may be assigned physical education classes to complete his professional
teaching load.

The Athletic Director and Recreational Sports

While the layperson would assume that varsity coaches in charge of recreational sports programs are the ideal choices for administering such programs, in point of fact, this is one of the weakest arrangements. When there is a separate athletic department in a school or college and the recreational sports program is under the director of athletics, the customary plan is to have a coach handle recreational sports in addition to his varsity assignment. This practice is rarely successful since the coach, very busy during a given season coaching the varsity team, may neglect the recreational sports assignment. Even if the coach has the best of intentions toward the recreational sports program, the history of assigning varsity coaches to these responsibilities reveals that the coach devotes nearly all of his time to the varsity team. After all, a winning season is a prerequisite for a new contract and a salary increase. Even varsity coaches who make a strenuous effort in the recreational sports program are, in most cases, only moderately successful since they are actually outside the program and, moreover, often become involved with difficulties in scheduling, curriculum changes, awards, and operational procedures. The most successful use of varsity coaches in the recreational sports program is made when they are assigned responsibilities entirely independent of varsity coaching duties—in other words, during a segment of the year when the coach is not in season with an athletic sport.

STUDENT LEADERSHIP

Two schools of thought about student control of the recreational sports program exist among directors of these programs. Some directors believe that a professional staff should exercise almost complete control; on the other hand, some assert that the students should have the control. Perhaps the best approach, under these circumstances, is to examine more fully the contending arguments before offering a solution.

Those hostile to student control argue that, despite the seeming democracy, good administration suffers. Experience reveals, they assert, that students lack the time needed to properly administer a recreational sports program; and they are only beginning to learn how to do it when they graduate. If they are given the responsibility, the inadequate amount of time at their disposal frequently results in poor scheduling, inadequate officiating, and chaos in working out a system of awards. Other objections are advanced. Proper safety measures and legal liability factors receive little attention. Student control of the program reflects the desires of the more interested athletes with much less attention given to the remainder of the student body. Controversial questions arise; and when they do, students are ill-equipped to handle them. And so it goes.

The proponents of complete student leadership and control of the program believe that this procedure provides the students with a much greater opportunity to develop leadership, sportsmanship, individual responsibility, and initiative. They argue that school and college students mature and learn faster in direct proportion to the amount of initiative and leadership that they experience. This school of thought recognizes that, though students will make mistakes, doing so is part of life. They need to have an opportunity to evaluate situations and to make intelligent reassessments, these experiences being a part of the education that is essential in a democratic society. (See Chapter 8: "Leadership through Democracy.")

By combining the two viewpoints, the solution may be discovered. It should be stressed that student leadership in the organization and administration of recreational sports programs contributes importantly to the success of the program. But this student leadership ought to supplement the work of the professional staff, not replace it. The means for doing this is the establishment of a recreational sports council through which the director functions. Students who have experienced this relationship with a capable director usually comment on it approvingly. For optimum results the director should create a climate in which the students feel that they have an opportunity to achieve professional goals. Students who have experienced only autocratic procedures will be slow to accept the challenge of leadership. It is the responsibility of the director to provide a program in which leadership enriches the personalities of the students rather than dominating them. Examples of colleges and universities that make student leadership a pleasant and rewarding experience are Purdue University, Brooklyn College of the City University of New York, Louisiana State University, and the University of Illinois at Urbana.

THE DEAN OF STUDENTS, DIRECTOR OF A STUDENT UNION, OR DIRECTOR OF EXTRACURRICULAR ACTIVITIES

The program of recreational sports that is under the direction of a dean of students, the director of a student union, or a director of extracurricular activities suffers serious disadvantages. While these specialists may have good intentions, they usually lack the proper qualifications for administering this program; and they are far removed from the evolving program and facilities and equipment which are instrumental to the success of the program. Hence they delegate a large measure of the work to others who have no direct connection with the specialists themselves. The securing and assigning of officials, the organizing of well-balanced teams, and the coordinating of team schedules with available facilities and equipment require a full-time recreational sports director at the center of the program.

THE DIRECTOR OF CAMPUS RECREATION

One of the most interesting administrative plans on the current scene is the proposal to place responsibility for the recreational sports program in a director of campus recreation. Indeed, the proposal is actually a practice in a number of institutions. The chief advocate of this administrative plan is David Matthews of the University of Illinois, and the details have been set forth in the highly readable and influential essay "Blueprint for Structuring Campus Recreation," that Michael J. Stevenson of the University of Michigan published in 1976.[1] This essay is compulsory reading for anyone concerned with the organization and administration of the recreational sports program. Stevenson's challenge is bold, the language unmistakable. Deeply concerned by what he sees as the tendency in colleges and universities to assign the control and funding of campus recreation either to physical education or athletic departments, he rejects these administrative patterns as inherently unjust to recreation and detrimental to its proper role on a campus.

To Stevenson, recreation encompasses much more than recreational sports. He would extend it to encompass other areas such as "theater, music, student union activities, arts and crafts, outing activities, and special-interest recreational clubs of a nonphysical nature."[2] The blueprint calls for centralizing the organization and administration of all these aspects of recreation, including recreational sports, in a coordinated single administrative unit, which he speaks of variously as "a division of campus sports and recreation" and "campus recreation."[3] The director of campus recreation, which is the more favored term, would be a high-level administrator, responsible directly to a university vice-president of finance or of student services. According to Stevenson, there are precedents; and he cites the examples of such trend-setting Big Ten institutions as Iowa, Michigan State, and Purdue, which are said to have transferred administrative responsibility for campus recreation

---

[1] James A. Peterson, ed., *Intramural Administration: Theory and Practice* (Englewood Cliffs, N.J., Prentice-Hall, Inc., 1976), pp. 20–29.

[2] Ibid., p. 26.

[3] Ibid.

from physical education and athletics to "a unit of the division of student services."[4]

A number of reasons are advanced for this sweeping change, usually adduced, as might be anticipated, from the standpoint of a supporter of campus recreation as against physical education and athletics. These are, in essence, the failure under the existing pattern of administration to give recreation sufficient funds relative to its importance on the educational scene, to give recreation access on an equitable basis to physical facilities, and to recognize the separate identity of recreation generally within the department. Stevenson explains:

> Most of the bargaining leverage has rested with interests other than campus recreation. A committee of section chiefs, for example, would typically include only one voice for intramurals. The other individuals—

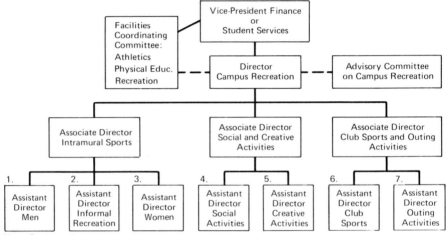

Note: See Legend

Legend for Model

(1) = Responsible for team, dual, and individual competitive intramural programs for men.

(2) = Responsible for informal / "free-play" activities program.

(3) = Responsible for team, dual, and individual competitive intramural programs for women, and for competitive co-recreational intramural program.

(4) = Responsible for social activities such as nonphysical recreation, dances, parties, and so forth.

(5) = Responsible for music, dance, drama, lectures, and so on.

(6) = Responsible for organization and administration of physical recreation-oriented sports clubs.

(7) = Responsible for orienteering, hunting, fishing, sailing, skating, skiing, and similar activities.

Figure 9-3   Model for Structuring a Division of Campus Sports and Recreation

[4]Ibid., p. 21.

possessing higher salaries, greater faculty rank, and typically, more departmental esteem—would fight for their own vested interests. Without question, this competition has frequently restricted the growth and development of recreation on college and university campuses across the country.[5]

To Stevenson, what was needed, then, to liberate recreation from these confines was a new administrative plan by which a director of campus recreation would have access to the necessary funds and be in a position to secure equity in the disposal of facilities. These conditions would be met if the director of campus administration was a high-level administrator in continuing contact with the vice-president of the university for finance or student services, on the lines given in Figure 9-3.[6]

Whatever one thinks of this diagnosis of the condition of recreation on the college or university scene, Stevenson's remedy is on realistic lines if the necessary support is forthcoming on a given campus. Here a note of caution must enter. To many an observer the doubt will occur that, all things being equal, departments of physical education, athletics, drama, speech, music, etc.—all of them affected by this blueprint for structuring campus recreation—are willing to accept with equanimity changes of this magnitude. In short, a major administrative restructuring on this scale is unlikely to occur unless some kind of consensus is reached among the departments that would be affected. And this is to say nothing of the point of view among those who hold that the program of recreational sports belongs, by any standard of judgment, more properly in a de-

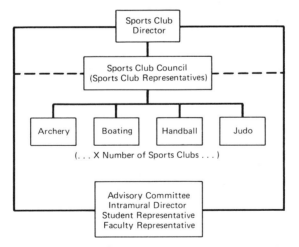

Figure 9-4   An Administrative Model for Sports Clubs

[5]Ibid., p. 22.
[6]Ibid., pp. 26–28

partment of physical education than in the field of recreation, grouped with nonphysical activities.

ADMINISTRATION OF SPORTS CLUBS

Sports clubs have long formed an integral part of the recreational sports program and, as was pointed out in Chapter 3, are usually found within the physical education department of a school or college. For the best results, the administrator of the sports club program should be responsible directly to the director of the recreational sports program; and his responsibilities should include budget and finance, eligibility, scheduling, medical examinations for participants, insurance, legal liability, etc.

A few practices will help ensure a smooth operation. The advisor of a sports club is, preferably, a full-time member of the faculty but on occasion may be a highly qualified graduate student or a member of the community. He should be chosen by the members of the sports club, with the approval of its director. Usually the advisor works with an advisory council that represents the school or college. Figure 9-4[7] illustrates graphically the administration of sports clubs at the University of Illinois (Urbana).

Essential to the success of the sports club is the formulation of a charter or constitution, which governs its operations. A superior model of such a charter or constitution was prepared by Ronald Hyatt, a recognized leader in recreational sports.[8] Hyatt's model is indispensable to anyone interested in establishing a sports club or in improving the operation of a sports club already underway.

SCHOOL OR COLLEGE RECREATION COORDINATING COUNCIL

A recreation coordinating council in schools and colleges will bring about effective recreation planning. Such a council makes it possible to have a systematic plan of recreation activities. The diversity of recreational offerings—which may range from art, music and theater through sports and community activities—makes a recreation coordinating council mandatory. It is influential in shaping philosophy, programs, policies, and procedures for recreation activities for the entire school or college. The director of the recreational sports program should be a voting member of the recreation coordinating council.

[7]Ibid., p. 228.

[8]Ibid., pp. 234–42.

ADMINISTRATION OF COMMUNITY RECREATION

The organization and administration of community recreation, usually structured within a department of recreation and parks, focuses upon providing recreational activities and services for all the people of a specific community. Methods of organization and administration will vary according to the size, geographic location, and special needs of a particular community.

A recreation and park department receives its mandate from the government of a community in the form of an enabling act. Generally, the department is administered by a commission or policy-making board appointed by a mayor with the approval of a city or community council. The board in most cases consists of five to seven members and has, as its primary responsibility, the operation of the department of recreation and parks. More specifically, the board formulates basic goals and determines policies for the department programs. The superintendent of recreation implements the policies formulated by the board.

Administration is more efficient and functions more smoothly if a department manual is developed for the board members and if additional community administrators become directly involved with the recreation and park department. If the best results are to be achieved, the manual includes state and local legislation concerning recreation and parks, the constitution and bylaws of the board, current budget materials, and a description of the administrative responsibilities of the superintendent of recreation. The excellent organizational and administrative chart presented in Figure 9-5[9] was prepared for the recreation and parks program in Topeka, Kansas. Not only does this chart, a model of its kind, reveal with clarity the administrative arrangements in the program but it also makes apparent the scope and dimension of a well-developed program of community recreation. The recreational sports program forms an integral part of the total recreation program, and the basic and fundamental principles of organization and administration of recreational sports programs are remarkably similar for schools, colleges, and communities.

RECREATIONAL SPORTS HANDBOOK

One of the most valuable administrative actions undertaken by the director of the recreational sports program is the preparation and distribution of a carefully prepared handbook for the information of partici-

[9]George D. Butler, *Introduction to Community Recreation* (New York:McGraw-Hill Book Company, 1976), p. 465.

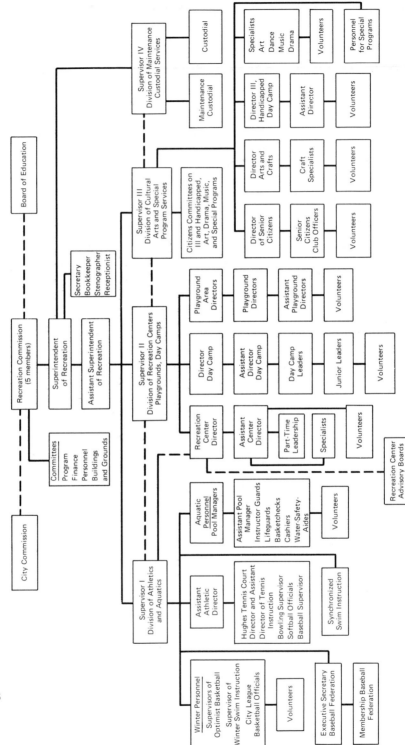

Figure 9-5 Organization Chart of the Recreation Department, Topeka, Kansas

pants. It is a valuable asset in helping to give structure and shape to a recreational sports program in schools, colleges, and communities. The handbook should be kept up to date, reflecting important changes that develop every year; and its contents should be readily available to those involved in the program. Copies should go to all participants in the recreational sports program, all staff members, and to others closely aligned with the operation of the program. (See Figure 9-6.)

An infinite variety of recreational sports handbooks are available to school, college, and community programs. These handbooks have been developed through the years primarily in the colleges and universities; and changes in their titles reflect those that have been going on in the program themselves. Since the handbook is the outgrowth of a recreational sports program that has traditionally been called "intramurals," the name of the handbook has traditionally been titled "Intramural Handbook" or else "Intramural Sports Handbook." But more recently, the

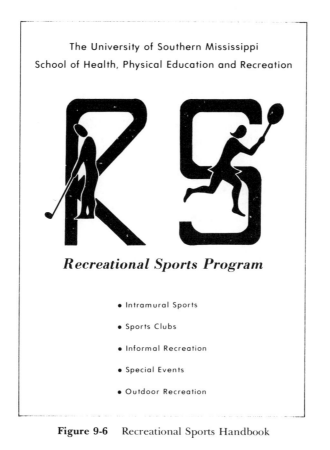

Figure 9-6   Recreational Sports Handbook

name "Intramural-Recreational Sports Handbook" has been used by many schools and colleges to give the actual program involved a more comprehensive name. Nor has the change in title stopped here. Since 1975 more and more leaders in the recreational sports program, who have been traditionally involved in programs known as "intramurals," "extramurals," "sports clubs," etc., are moving to name the handbook "Recreational Sports Handbook." In short, in this period of transition in terminology within the recreational sports program, the two words "recreational sports" are appearing increasingly in the title of the handbook.

The preparation of a "recreational sports handbook" requires a wide range of very specific information that focuses upon the broad and well-established principles of organization, administration, policies, and procedures in recreational sports programs. As was stated earlier, not only should such a handbook contain the most recent information available, it ought also to undergo examination every year and be brought up to date. There is no substitute for a continual review of its contents and their being kept current. Moreover, the handbook should give special attention to the needs of the local geographic area. One example of an exceedingly good recreational sports handbook is that of Purdue University. It is titled "Division of Recreational Sports" with subdivisions on informal recreation, club sports, men's intramurals, women's intramurals, and women's intercollegiate sports.

DISCUSSION QUESTIONS

1. Describe the basic principles of organization and administration that are essential in a recreational sports program.
2. What are the advantages of an effective recreational sports council in school, colleges, and communities?
3. What are the duties and responsibilities of recreational sports supervisors and program managers?
4. Describe the specific types of information that are essential in a recreational sports handbook.
5. Describe the importance of officiating and officiating clinics in recreational sports programs.
6. What are the advantages and disadvantages of removing the recreational sports program from the department of physical education and placing it within a "campus recreation" division in a school or college?

BIBLIOGRAPHY

BUTLER, GEORGE D., *Introduction to Community Recreation,* 5th ed. New York: McGraw-Hill Book Co., 1976.

HYATT, RONALD W., *Intramural Sports Programs: Their Organization and Administration.* St. Louis: C. V. Mosby Co., 1976.

MEANS, LOUIS E., *Intramurals: Their Organization and Administration,* 2nd ed. Englewood Cliffs, N.J.: Prentice-Hall, Inc., 1974.

MUELLER, PAT, *Intramurals: Programming and Administration,* 4th ed. New York: The Ronald Press, 1971.

PETERSON, JAMES A., ed., *Intramural Administration: Theory and Practice.* Englewood Cliffs, N.J.: Prentice-Hall, Inc., 1976.

ROKOSZ, FRANCIS M., *Structured Intramurals.* Philadelphia: W. B. Saunders Co., 1975.

"C" League Baseball for 8-12 Year-olds.
(Courtesy W. David Carew, Maplewood Recreation Department, Maplewood, New Jersey.)

10

The Extramural
Sports Program

Confusion reigns today about the precise meaning of the term "extramural sports." The most commonly accepted definition uses as its point of departure the intramural sports program. The latter, it will be remembered, stresses competition in recreational sports within the confines of a school or college; and the participants are officially part of the institution involved. Extramural sports are usually viewed as the projection of the intramural sports program beyond the confines of a school or college. The extramural sports program is an organized recreational sports competition with participants of a given school or college competing with students from other schools or colleges in the immediate geographic area. Extramurals are not to be confused with interscholastic or intercollegiate athletics for men.

However, the women's program of extramural sports, historically, has focused upon such activities as playdays and sports days, which have essentially encompassed in large measure what men call interscholastic and intercollegiate competition. The philosophy of sports competition for women in extramurals operated until the early 1960s (when a change set in) to place much less emphasis on winning than was the case in the men's extramural program. The development of co-recreational activities in the extramural sports programs of the 1960s brought about programs of recreational sports in schools and colleges that are remarkably similar in philosophy, organization, and program. The spirit of competition in women's programs was nourished not only by co-recreational activities but also by the new self-awareness in women that rose out of the women's rights movement.

Intramural sports directors throughout the country are, for the most part, hostile to the extramural sports program when intramural teams are the units of competition. But it must be quickly added that leaders of intramurals are not opposed, however, to extramurals *per se*. Usually they approve of sports clubs, playdays, sports days, outing clubs, co-recreational events, and many other types of off-campus extramural competition that are separately organized into extramural programs. Representative of the portions of the extramural program that are approved by most directors of intramurals are playdays and sports days.

Playdays and sports days have the decided advantage that their organization is in no way dependent on intramural teams. This form of extramurals leaves the intramural program a self-contained division of physical education in its own right without the risk of exploitation that arises when intramural teams are extended into extramural competition. The main purpose underlying the playday is to provide the opportunity for students to become well acquainted. Participants are selected at random for the teams with players from at least two schools on each team. Many playday directors try to have every school represented on a team. Activities usually include recreational sports and games, square and folk dances, and other types of entertainment. The traditional sports day is also based on the concept of friendly competition for pleasure in an informal atmosphere. Teams are drawn from two or more schools, and the players may or may not have played together as a team before entering the program. The most successful sports days are administered on the Olympic plan, by which scores are kept and competitive units win and lose in individual contests but the schools themselves are not rated on the basis of the number of victories. A great variety of recreational sports and games and rhythmic activities comprise the program.

This chapter centers attention on the controversial aspect of the extramural sports program that concerns scheduling intramural teams, including sports clubs, against their counterparts from neighboring schools and colleges. The controversy, as was indicated earlier, has arisen from differing viewpoints as to the advisability of intramural teams engaging in extramural competition. What is its significance? Is the controversy really a mere storm in a teacup created by momentary irritation over essentially trivial points of difference? Or is the issue involved so far-reaching that failure to resolve it will have repercussions for the whole field of physical education? Many leaders in the field of intramural sports believe that physical education has indeed entered another period in its history so crucial that the choice of the right course of action will enable the profession to fulfill its destiny, whereas errors of judgment on the national level can cause untold damage.

Since, historically speaking, intramural teams have long engaged in extramural competition, the roots of the present controversy reach back into the early history of intramural programs in the United States.

INTRAMURALS WITH EXTRAMURAL OVERTONES

Intramural sports programs in the nineteenth century grew directly out of the interest and activity of students and alumni, who, finding formal gymnastics in the school program distasteful, turned for pleasure to organized sports clubs reminiscent of those in English universities. Through these clubs they engaged in early English sports and games. Gradually, classes and social organizations such as clubs and fraternities began to compete in the embryonic intramural sports programs; and sports-minded students elected committees, officers, and managers to arrange and carry out their programs. Their example proved contagious. Physical educators with vision realized the need for competitive sports programs in which a large number of students could engage, and they incorporated some recreational sports competition into their programs. The prime example is the bold pioneering of Dr. Edward Hitchcock at Amherst College in Massachusetts during the years from 1861 to 1880. His leadership received support and reinforcement in the late decades of the nineteenth century and the early years of the twentieth from such outstanding figures in the history of physical education as Dudley A. Sargent, William G. Anderson, Luther Halsey Gulick, Thomas D. Wood, and Clark W. Hetherington. Nevertheless, the general picture remained one of formal gymnastics in the typical program of physical education, while students, with some help from early leaders in the profession, were laying informally the foundations of intramural sports programs.

Even though the latter programs were almost wholly intramural, a campus team sometimes competed against its counterpart in a neighboring school or college. It could be said that intramurals at this point acquired extramural overtones. As these programs became more sophisticated, the participants developed athletic associations with the primary purpose of organizing a single team to represent the entire school or college in competition with a similar team in the area. From this plan of competition arose the highly competitive programs of interscholastic and intercollegiate athletics.

By the early twentieth century the intramural sports programs, organized and sponsored largely by students, had become too large and unwieldy to continue without direction and supervision from the institution involved. Sometimes the response was to organize departments of intramural sports as was done at the University of Michigan and Ohio State University in 1913; but more commonly the intramural sports program became part of the structure of a physical education department. In this way the intramural sports program secured an official academic affiliation. On occasion, intramural teams played their counterparts at a neighboring institution. Though terminology for this type of competition varied, apparently at this time the term "intramurals" was most frequently applied to programs that would now be described as extramurals.

Following World War I, "extramurals" became the accepted term for this type of competition after a brief flirtation with some other terms. The practice for a time was to use the name "intramurals" if no gate receipts were involved; but if paying customers passed through the turnstiles, then the same event became "interscholastic athletics." Still others used the term "intermural," which technically was apt but could be confused easily with intramurals though the meanings are very different. Finally, however, these attempts were all abandoned in favor of the triumphant extramurals.

On first sight extramurals closely resemble athletics. Dr. Elmer D. Mitchell, who was himself a pioneer in the intramurals movement, made the distinction clear in an article published in 1931 under the title "Intramural Relationships." He differentiated between extramural programs, on the one hand, and the intramural and varsity programs on the other, when he asserted that scheduling intramural teams with those of another school "is not varsity because there is no emphasis on crowds or on the display of the highest skill attainable by careful coaching. Neither is it intramural, because it is outside the boundaries of one school. By far the best title for this purpose," he concluded, "seems to be 'extramural.' "

EXTRAMURALS IN THE GREAT DEPRESSION

Extramural sports programs gained momentum during the Great Depression, partially at the expense of the elaborate athletic programs in which athletic teams had traveled great distances in order to compete against traditional rivals. Extramural competition in the local community often became the order of the day. The marked emphasis on extramurals was reflected in the comments of Dr. H. Harrison Clark in an article, "Extramural Athletics in the East," which was published in 1936. After pointing out that the prevailing method of conducting extramurals was for the championship intramural teams of various colleges and universities to play their counterparts in other institutions, he described briefly the first Extramural–Intramural Day, which was held in the East on March 21, 1935. Seven championship teams from Syracuse and a like number from Colgate had played each other in such sports as basketball, handball, swimming, track, fencing, and bowling. The most extensive extramural sports program at that time was at the University of Maryland, where eleven sports from the intramural program were extended into the extramural program. Moreover, the University of Maryland sent intramural championship teams to Southern Conference tournaments in swimming, fencing, and golf. The trend described by Dr. Clark continues to the present.

THE EXTRAMURAL SPORTS PROGRAM TODAY

The main features of the extramural sports program were surveyed some years ago by Ellis J. Mendelsohn, who published the results in the *Annual Proceedings* (1956) of the National College Physical Education Association. While the passage of time has brought changes in the program, his findings are still valuable for the insights that they provide; and his survey remains the most authoritative and comprehensive of its kind. Mendelsohn worked from questionnaires sent to colleges and universities in eight athletic conferences representing all of the United States. Of the 107 colleges and universities returning answers, 44 reported that they had extramural sports programs. These contained a great variety of activities: basketball, softball, touch football, volleyball, handball, soccer, tennis, table tennis, wrestling, bowling, fencing, track, badminton, gymnastics, golf, squash, skiing, archery, sailing, judo, hockey, pool, boxing, swimming, weight lifting, billiards, cross country, ice skating, cricket, crew, outing activities, Sigma Delta Psi, horseback riding, motorcycling, outboard motoring, hosteling, hiking, and tobogganing. The most popular team sport was basketball; among the individual and dual sports, handball. While basketball continues to enjoy the great popularity that Mendelsohn noted, by 1976 paddle ball and racquet ball had superseded handball as the most popular of the individual and dual sports.

The survey also supplied information about the administration of the programs and the nature of the competitive units used to organize extramural competition. A virtual mosaic of plans was in use in the organization and administration of the extramural sports program. The majority of such programs was administered by intramural departments, but others had fallen to a variety of authorities such as the physical education staff, the residence hall staff, a faculty adviser, athletic coaches, the student union staff, the dean of students, or student groups. The budget for intramural sports, supplemented by student fees, usually financed these programs. The most popular competitive units were the intramural champion teams, but others included sports clubs, all-star teams, dormitory teams, ROTC teams, outstanding player teams, extramural collegiate leagues, and individual efforts on sports days and playdays. In view of the pronounced popularity of the intramural championship teams it is ironic to learn that the great majority of intramural directors questioned in the survey were adamantly opposed to the practice.

ADVERSE CRITICISM OF THE EXTRAMURAL ASPECTS
OF INTRAMURAL TEAMS

Increasingly, directors of the intramural sports programs for men are growing critical of the practice of scheduling extramural competition for intramural teams. They frankly express fear that the end result may be a distortion of the goals of the intramural programs to approximate those of interscholastic and intercollegiate athletics. In their view, extramural sports impart to the intramural sports program a philosophy different from its traditions, while at the same time obscuring for students the legitimate goals of intramurals. They conclude that emphasis is now on the more gifted athletes rather than on the desires of all students to engage in sports activity without regard for ability. The distortions introduced into intramurals through extramurals, according to the intramural directors, may well lead in time to a small-scale varsity program with intramural champions pitted against those of other institutions. Thus, extramurals jeopardize the proper balance that the intramural program maintains in physical education.

The actual operation of extramurals often lends weight to the conclusions of the intramural directors. When the intramural staff, officials, budget, facilities, and equipment are utilized to meet the demands imposed by the extramural sports program, a departure has been made from the basic principles governing intramurals; and a chain of new responsibilities is forged. Very soon it is necessary to add more staff, increase the budget, secure more highly skilled officials, make careful checks to determine the eligibility of students, plan for awarding trophies, and provide generally the trimmings associated with the varsity program. Still other difficulties arise. Students in the extramual sports program are usually required to supply transportation. Yet schools and colleges are unwilling to assume responsibility for accidents and medical expenses. Finally, athletic directors are prone to view these developments as encroachments upon their private bailiwicks.

DANGER SIGNALS RAISED AT NATIONAL CONFERENCES

Directors of intramural sports programs for men have long been on record as opposed to scheduling intramural teams into extramural competition. Their hostility, which has existed since the practice began in organized physical education, has manifested itself repeatedly since World War II. Thus the intramural directors present at the 54th Annual Convention of the American Association for Health, Physical Education and Recreation, which met in Boston in April 1949, formally expressed opposition to extramural sports programs when intramural teams formed the competitive units. Six years later, in 1955, the Western Conference intramural directors registered a majority vote opposing the scheduling of intramural champions against their counterparts from other campuses. A more comprehensive stand was taken in 1957 when the intramural directors at the National Intramural Association meeting, held at Brown University, voted overwhelmingly against all extramural sports competition in schools and colleges when teams of the regular intramural sports program are scheduled in extramural competition. Again, at the National Intramural Association meeting at Bowling Green University in 1961, the intramural directors voted against extending intramural teams into extramural sports competition on the ground that extramural programs quickly encounter the problems and pitfalls of interscholastic and intercollegiate athletics. A year later, in December 1962, intramural directors who attended the National College Physical Education Association meeting in San Francisco expressed opposition in principle to extramurals whenever the scheduling of intramural teams with off-campus competition was involved, though they gave support to extramural sports programs that centered on playdays, sports clubs, field days, recreation clinics, co-recreational events, and school-community recreation. Finally, in March of 1963, intramural directors attending the National Intramural Association meeting at Delaware Valley College in Pennsylvania once more went on record in express opposition to scheduling intramural teams in competition "outside the walls" of the school or college; and once more they stated explicitly their support of extramural sports programs based on other types of competitive units such as sports clubs and playdays.

IN SUPPORT OF EXTRAMURALS

Those who value extramural sports programs in schools and colleges believe that these programs, including their use of intramural teams as units of competition, supplement the physical education program by filling a void that exists between the intramural sports program and interscholastic or intercollegiate athletics. They assert that intramural teams can participate in extramural competition without harming the program of intramurals, a point of view the majority of directors do not, however, accept. Advocates of extramurals point out that this program provides a wide basis of interschool and intercollege sports participation for a large number of students who deserve this type of competition but, for one reason or another, are unable to compete in varsity athletics. The varying degrees of athletic ability in students, it is said, make this type of competition especially valuable. And the need for it can be deduced from the fact that large numbers of students participate in the existing extramural programs and also in competitive sports programs of a similar nature offered by such community groups as the YMCA, the churches, industrial organizations, little leagues, and municipal recreation centers.

Advocates also urge that the extramural sports program broadens and deepens the entire physical education program because it offers competition in a variety of individual and team sports and rhythmic activities organized through intramural teams, sports clubs, and individual efforts on sports days, etc. Those participating for enjoyment have the opportunity to gain social values and advance in leadership qualities. They may also learn to win fairly and lose graciously, to cooperate in a team effort, and, above all, to understand more fully the objectives of a democratic society. The program of extramurals, it is also said, has the advantages of requiring very little coaching, either a few short practice sessions or none, a limited amount of traveling, and a small budget allocation.

EXTRAMURAL PROGRAMS WITH INTRAMURAL TEAMS

Since the Great Depression, and noticeably since World War II, extramural competition based on intramural teams has been on the increase. Examples may be seen in the public school systems of Billings, Montana; Flint, Michigan; Lincoln, Nebraska; Denver, Colorado; Norfolk, Virginia; and, notably, in Shaker Heights High School in a suburb of Cleveland, Ohio, and in the school system of Providence, Rhode Island. Colleges and universities, especially in the eastern United States, have also extended intramural teams into extramural competition. Among those claiming successful programs are Syracuse, Colgate, Columbia, Princeton, Harvard, Yale, Amherst, Purdue, De Paul, and Illinois.

Shaker Heights High School has developed an extensive extramural sports program for high school boys, in which intramural teams participate. Robert J. Rice, Chairman of the Department of Physical Education, reported in 1959 on the nature of the extramural basketball program, which he praised as providing wholesome experience for the participants and as beneficial to the intramural sports programs in the schools involved. At one time six of the intramural basketball teams played visiting intramural teams from a neighboring school on the same day that the two high schools played an interscholastic basketball game. Two teams had been selected from each of the sophomore, junior, and senior intramural basketball leagues of their respective schools. Later, these intramural teams played again, this time at the neighboring school.

This success led to an extramural all-day tournament with all six schools in the interscholastic league of the area meeting at the Shaker Heights High School. Sports competition included basketball, volleyball, badminton, swimming, table tennis, and foul shooting. Each school was represented by a sophomore, junior, and senior team in each activity, and 450 boys participated. The event has since become an annual affair with each school taking its turn as host.

An even more ambitious extramural sports program is carried on in the junior and senior high schools of Providence, Rhode Island, where the intramural program in selected sports is automatically extended into extramural competition. Schedules are arranged in such intramural sports as swimming, basketball, baseball, track, and handball so that three-fourths of the sport season is devoted to intramural competition, one-fourth to extramural. The best intramural players in a given sport compose the extramural team that represents the school in rivalry with another school.

POSSIBILITIES FOR CHANGE IN EXTRAMURALS

Informed speculation about the future course of extramurals might well center on the implications of the "metroversity" concept for extramurals. The term refers to an arrangement for pooling the resources of a number of educational institutions in a given geographic area so as to offer to their respective student bodies more courses, increased library facilities, and such benefits as access to a more varied sports program. As Ellis Mendelsohn, University of Louisville, has explained, "while each student profits from the program he has chosen to pursue at his home institution, he may also consider the entire metropolitan area as a campus which he may use to satisfy his education interests."[1] If the concept at first sight seems more readily applicable to intramurals, the extramural aspect emerges with the realization that the effect is to bring students together from a number of institutions for the purpose of engaging in sports activity. This could mean that some of the social gains of extramurals are secured while the element of competition among contending institutions is minimized. The metroversity concept has been applied, for example, at the University of Louisville in Kentucky and to five of its neighboring institutions. Two state universities, two independent universities, and two theological seminaries have organized into a consortium of institutions that pool their resources on the lines earlier mentioned. Among the extracurricular benefits are certain selected intramural sports. As might be anticipated, this has not been done without qualifications and conditions; but the point to be noted is that the arrangement has led to establishing a student activity advisory board, which determines what sports are to come under the novel arrangement. In 1974, table tennis, bowling, chess, and volleyball were selected. The advantages of metroversity are clear. Financial savings is a distinct possi-

[1] *25th Annual Conference Proceedings of the National Intramural Association*, p. 80.

bility, but without damage to curricular and extracurricular offerings, which if anything are enhanced.[2]

An equally ambitious enterprise in the District of Columbia, the success of which depended on institutional cooperation, was described by J. Dutch Usilaner, of Montgomery College, writing in the *26th Annual Conference Proceedings of the National Intramural-Recreational Sports Association* (1975). This account brings out clearly the importance of institutional cooperation in extramurals as a means of bringing new and unexpected sources of financial support to the program. The story in a sense began when Greg Schultz was made director of intramurals at Georgetown University in 1971. Arriving at a time when physical education classes were being curtailed, Schultz invited twelve colleges within a ten-mile radius to form an association with extramurals as one of the objectives; and the response was warm and instantaneous. A constitution was prepared, by which the direction of the association was placed in an executive committee; and the newly formed corporation was a speedy success when the member colleges were able to prepare rules for touch football to which all could agree. The stage was now set for a new entrant on the scene in the form of the Schaefer Beer Co. The executive committee mentioned above was contacted by a public relations firm called Sportsplan, which represented Schaefer; and the way then opened for the new association to participate in a basketball and volleyball tournament that Schaefer was sponsoring in such metropolitan centers as New York, Boston, and Philadelphia. Washington was later added as one of the metropolitan centers in which an extramural tournament in volleyball was to be held. Commercialism was kept to a minimum. Sportsplan worked closely with the association's executive committee to minimize problems rising out of the local situation, and Schaefer did not interfere with the operation of the tournament, the colleges' regular programs, or the rulings of the executive committee. Usilaner was enthusiastic. "My suggestion would be to get the community behind you, get a sponsor and still have control of your program. It does not take anything away from the varsity. It is merely a showcase play day by athletes who get recognition without going through a regimen of practice."[3]

THE SPORTS CLUB

Long an integral part of the extramural sports movement in school and college throughout the country, sports clubs since the early 1960s have steadily multiplied because of the unique way in which they meet the

[2]Ibid., pp. 79–81.

[3]*26th Annual Conference Proceedings of the National Intramural-Recreational Sports Association, p. 142.*

needs and interests of a rising number of students. While the sports clubs were earlier a traditional appendage of intramural programs, they are now in the process of becoming increasingly a separate entity in the recreational sports programs of schools, colleges, and communities. For a discussion of sports clubs in education, consult Chapter 3. And for a discussion of the organization and administration of sports clubs, consult Chapter 9. As for the individual sports clubs, there are materials on them throughout the book; and here the index to this book is the best guide.

THE EDUCATIONAL VALUES OF EXTRAMURALS

Until recently, intramural directors hostile to the use of intramural teams in extramural competition received considerable support for their position from educators, physicians, psychologists, sociologists, and others who have studied the effect of competition on school children. Agreeing that competition in a sports program is valuable, they nevertheless seriously question the advisability of the degree of competition often found in extramural programs when intramural teams compete. Even on this point, however, some qualification is required since their concern about the deleterious effects of competition is, on the whole, limited to school children below the level of the senior high school. Behind this competition, it may be remarked, are social pressures that often grow out of parental strivings for recognition through the achievements of children or even for their swifter social development than professional opinion deems wise.

DESIRABLE ATHLETIC COMPETITION FOR SCHOOL CHILDREN

A chorus of professional and authoritative voices has been raised in objection to a high degree of competition for school children, whether it exits in varsity programs or in the extramural programs that have been discussed in this chapter.

The American Association for Health, Physical Education and Recreation and the Society of State Directors of Health, Physical Education and Recreation joined forces in 1949 to study organized sports competition for children. Consultants were drawn from the Department of Elementary School Principals of the National Education Association and the State Consultants in Elementary Education. Members of the four groups formed the influential Joint Committee on Athletic Competition for Children of Elementary and Junior High School Age. Its report, entitled *Desirable Athletic Competition for Children,* was the product of three years of study.

The report condemned a high degree of competition for school children. Its authors wrote that "interschool competition of a varsity pattern and similarly organized competition under the auspices of other community agencies are *definitely disapproved* for children below the ninth grade." Intramural directors welcomed the report as clearly revealing that extramurals based on intramural teams were unsuitable for the age groups designated. They could also agree with another comment in the report that "activities such as play days, and sports days, and occasional invitational games which involve children of two or more schools, and which have social values are to be encouraged."

A similar position was embodied in a statement on competitive sports programs in elementary and secondary schools which received unanimous approval on December 22, 1953 from the Educational Policies Commission and the American Association of School Administrators. The statement, published under the title *School Athletics*, read that "no junior high school should have a 'school team' that competes with school teams of other junior high schools in organized leagues or tournaments." Developing a team to represent the school, it was asserted, distorts the principle of an opportunity in sports for all students. The Educational Policies Commission believes, however, that high school boys can profit from competitive sports programs with other schools as long as adequate safeguards "prevent overemphasis, exploitation, and other possible abuses. . . ." Its recommendation is to allow all high school boys "to take part in occasional informal extramural competition."

The voice that perhaps commanded the widest public audience, however, was that of James B. Conant, former President of Harvard University. He completed in 1960 a comprehensive study of education in the junior high school that was published under the formal title, *A Memorandum to School Boards: Recommendations for Education in the Junior High School Years*. It is known more familiarly as one of the Conant Reports. Dr. Conant strongly recommended physical education and intramural sports programs for boys in junior high school. Concerning interschool competition, he stated that "interscholastic athletics . . . are to be condemned in junior high schools; there is no sound educational reason for them and too often they serve merely as public entertainment."

AN HISTORIC REVERSAL OF POLICY

In the years since World War II nearly all research studies completed on school athletics have warned against interscholastic activities for students in elementary and junior high school, and by implication against the use of intramural teams in extramural competition when the pattern is similar. But suddenly in June 1963, a history-making report entitled *Stan-*

dards for Junior High School Athletics was published that would permit interscholastic athletics in the junior high schools on the grounds that this form of competition could provide a valuable experience for many students if proper safeguards were maintained. The sources of this report make it authoritative. It emanated from the Junior High School Athletics Subcommittee of the Joint Committee on Standards for Interscholastic Athletics, sponsored by the American Association for Health, Physical Education and Recreation; the National Association of Secondary-School Principals; and the National Federation of State High School Athletic Associations. This astounding reversal of policy, for as such it must be described in the light of recent history, will have far-reaching effects on junior high schools and eventually on elementary schools where interscholastic athletics already flourish.

The reversal of policy came only after much thought and effort on the part of the subcommittee, which made a careful study of school athletics in education. Its members held open meetings at a number of appropriate national conventions, conducted investigations by mail, and evaluated the latest research findings on the subject. The resulting materials were then submitted for further study and evaluation to such groups as the Committee on the Medical Aspects of Sports of the American Medical Association and the School Health Section of the American Public Health Association.

A PLATFORM STATEMENT BY THE DIVISION OF MEN'S ATHLETICS, AAHPER

Almost simultaneously with the publication of the *Standards for Junior High School Athletics,* the Division of Men's Athletics of the American Association for Health, Physical Education and Recreation published a platform statement that reflects the same astonishing reversal of historic policy. Entitled *Athletics in Education* (1963), this platform statement contains recommendations not only for the required physical education and intramural and recreation programs but also for athletics under carefully controlled conditions. Though the comments apply to all levels of the educational system, the statement nevertheless provides a philosophical background for the *Standards for Junior High School Athletics* and supplements it. Two of the pertinent paragraphs in the platform statement that apply to athletics in the elementary and junior high school read:

> In Elementary Schools: Athletics between schools should be limited to informal games between teams from two or more schools and to occasional sports days when teams from several schools assemble for a day of friendly, informal competition. At such events, emphasis should be placed on participation by all students. The attendance of spectators (particularly students as spectators) should be discouraged. High-pressure programs of interscholas-

tic athletics, in which varsity teams compete in regularly scheduled contests that are attended by partisan spectators, should not be allowed under any circumstances.

In Junior High Schools: Limited programs of interscholastic athletics that are adapted to the capacities and the needs of junior high school boys are desirable. The physical and emotional immaturiy of the junior high youngster requires that such programs be controlled with extreme care to ensure that primary emphasis is placed on providing educational experiences for the participants rather than on producing winning teams and that the physical welfare of the participants is protected and fostered.

Despite the stated limitations on competition found in these two paragraphs, it can hardly be doubted that a fundamental alteration has taken place in professional opinion and that the door has swung open for more competition on these levels of the schools. For the history of interschool and intercollege competition in this country is replete with examples of theoretical limitations on competition that in practice have crumbled.

CONCLUSIONS

At this point in the controversy over the extramural sports program, it is difficult to predict confidently what the future holds. In following out the lines of its historical evolution since World War II, the keen observer might well have forecast ultimate victory for the directors of intramural programs who placed on record so persistently their opposition to intramural teams being used in extramural competition. But the trend suddenly reversed in the summer of 1963 with the twin publications of *Standards for Junior High School Athletics* and *Athletics in Education*. It would appear at this time that the advocates of the extramural sports program based on intramural teams, including sports clubs, have won a resounding victory over the opposition. That victory was in a sense underscored by the events of the 1970s, when a new emphasis on competition appeared in recreational sports for women and became prevalent. In short, the signs are plentiful that extramural sports now have a place in the recreational sports program from which they are unlikely to be dislodged in the foreseeable future.

DISCUSSION QUESTIONS

1. How is Title IX legislation, which became law in 1975, affecting the extramural sports program in schools and colleges?

2. What are extramurals and why has controversy arisen about the extramural sports program?

3. What are the advantages of extramural programs? Disadvantages?

4. Evaluate extramural programs from the viewpoint of their place in the overall physical education program and their educational value.

5. Why are the directors of intramural sports programs adversely criticial of extramurals?

6. Why were extramurals popular during the Great Depression?

7. Draw a composite picture of present-day extramural sports programs.

8. Why may it be said that until 1963 the intramural directors appeared to be winning the controversy over extramurals?

9. Discuss the recommendations of *Standards for Junior High School Athletics* and explain why this publication may be considered authoritative.

10. Why may the year 1963 be said to have marked an "historic reversal of policy" with regard to extramurals?

BIBLIOGRAPHY

HYATT, RONALD W., *Intramural Sports Programs: Their Organization and Administration.* St. Louis: C. V. Mosby Co., 1976.

MEANS, LOUIS E., *Intramurals: Their Organization and Administration,* 2nd ed. Englewood Cliffs, N.J.: Prentice-Hall, Inc., 1974.

PETERSON, JAMES A., ed., *Intramural Administration: Theory and Practice.* Englewood Cliffs, N.J.: Prentice-Hall, Inc., 1976.

Standards for Junior High School Athletics. Washington, D.C.: American Association for Health, Physical Education and Recreation, 1963.

Outdoor Activities Program of Campus Recreation Department.
(Courtesy of Associated Students, Washington State University, Pullman,
Washington. Photography by Christopher J. Tapfer, Program Supervisor.)

11

The Recreation Association: An Organizational Approach

Many sport and recreation programs have traditionally been carried out through volunteers. Their activity has been formalized under many names, but the chief organization with volunteer leadership is the recreation or athletic association (RA or AA) or council. Functioning within this predominantly volunteer organization, professional staff in the role of director, advisor, or manager provides leadership and stability. Administrative patterns with appropriate modifications or in combination with the other organizational structures as discussed in Chapters 5, 9, and 10 can serve as a framework for program management. The accomplishment of outlined detailed responsibilities makes the program potentially operational in both schools and communities with limited staff.

PLANNING THE PROGRAM

Planning and carrying out the functions of a recreation association is done by the membership with the advice and guidance of an experienced director who serves as a resource person, motivator, and consultant. In order to best establish priorities, an association initially and periodically investigates participants' interests. This can be done by questionnaire, discussion, mass meetings, or surveys. In light of interests, objectives are determined or revised, and a program is designed to meet these objectives. Activities then reflect participants' interests and abilities and are not perpetuated merely by inertia or tradition nor offered because of director preferences or dictates of other programs. Generally speaking, the program is planned to serve the greatest number rather than a select few. Associations with volunteer leadership can expand program offering to include team games, individual or dual sports, dance, swimming, co-recreation activities, and more to serve a great variety of expressed interests, limited only by available facilities and scheduling time.

VARIATIONS IN LOCAL ORGANIZATIONS TO MEET LOCAL NEEDS

Because recreation association programs have been developed to meet the needs of specific situations, many aspects of their organization are characterized by variety and flexibility.

Programs

Some organizations have a limited program, offering only competition in the major team sports. Others offer a broad program of team, dual, and individual sports; club activities; unorganized recreation; and co-recreational activities. The RA organizational framework thus serves primarily as an "administrator facilitator" for the program interests of its membership.

Membership

RA membership in many situations automatically includes all interested individuals. In other instances payment of dues or initiation fees are required. Another variation is illustrated in those cases where membership is extended upon fulfillment of certain participation requirements. Membership privileges are in some instances expanded upon payment of a flat fee or dues.

Advisor-Director

An advisor or director who lends enthusiasm and mature guidance while assuming the role of consultant is a necessary and vital part of all RA programs. The degree to which this person directs an association varies a great deal with the ability of the volunteer leaders. An effective advisor develops participant initiative, leadership, and involvement. Advisor-directors are usually hired or appointed by the department or administration. In some instances they are elected or requested to serve in an advisor role.

Leadership

Leaders within the recreation association usually are elected by the association membership. Elected officers then name the appointed officers. The elected and appointed officers; chairpersons; managers; club, house, and class representatives; and advisor basically make up the governing board of the association.

In addition to a relatively large board, most organizations have a smaller, more workable group called the executive board. It includes a limited number of the major officers and the advisor or director. This board facilitates and streamlines the business to be handled by the association, carries out routine details, and makes recommendations to the general board. Ideally, the executive board meets alternately with the general board. In this way, problems come before the smaller group for careful consideration and then are presented to the general board with recommendations. Often, the executive board also develops an agenda for the general board, which enables efficient handling of the business.

Officers, Managers, and Representatives

The members included on the RA board vary according to the local organization, but basic are those in the job management descriptions covered later in this chapter.

ORGANIZATIONAL STRUCTURES OF LOCAL ASSOCIATIONS

A small recreation association may have a comparatively simple organizational structure. The number and kind of officers, the representatives and appointed chairpersons, as well as the composition of the general and executive boards, may vary reflecting different emphasis, facilities, and other factors. A small association might have an organizational structure similar to that shown in Figure 11-1a, which includes sports managers, or club representatives.

It is wise administrative planning to make the organizational structure as broad as possible to avoid domination by one interest group. Representation by those of a great variety of interests, skills, and needs will ensure participation and support by many different groups. A program that has been expanded to serve increased needs is exemplified in Figure 11-1b. As the administrative organization increases and the board becomes larger, it may be desirable in some situations to combine areas

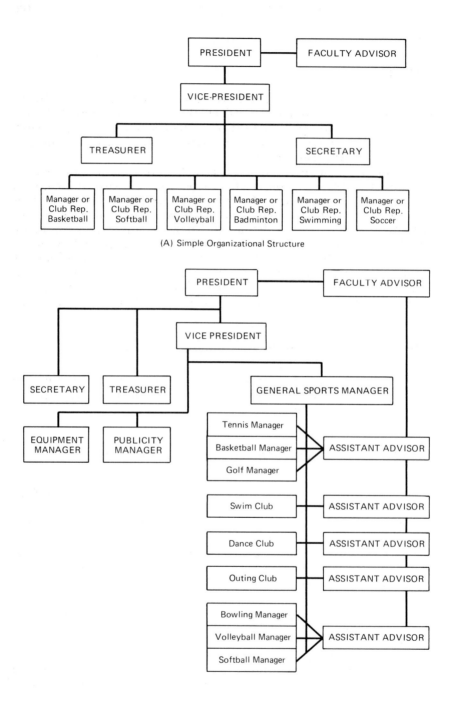

(A) Simple Organizational Structure

of interest, which could then be represented by a single head. In this way, the executive board can be kept small and workable. At the same time it does not have to devote time to the details of planning each activity. Instead, results of committee meetings can be reported regularly at board meetings. An expanded organization might also include officials from other districts, schools, or communities which sit in on the meetings and thus ensure coordination, planning, and exchange of ideas that are to the advantage of the total program and related scheduling problems (see Figure 11-1c).

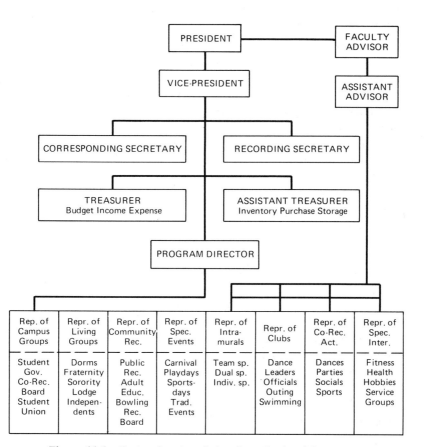

Figure 11-1   Recreation Association Organizational Structures

ORGANIZATIONAL PROCEDURES OF LOCAL ORGANIZATIONS

Interested individuals will ordinarily express a desire to develop a plan for a program of sports. An awareness of other recreation associations, and of their aims, purposes, and organizational structure, will stimulate thinking with respect to the potentials of a similar association. In order to develop a plan of organization, a meeting should be called involving a small group of the most interested individuals. At this meeting certain fundamental questions should be considered and decided upon:

What interests and needs will a recreation association serve?

Can an already existing organization serve the recreation and sports interests?

How highly developed an organization is necessary?

What activities could and should this organization offer with the available space, facilities, and equipment?

What regulations should govern membership?

What kind of meetings are necessary for the association to function effectively?

How can the organization and its various activities be financed?

What elected and appointed officers are necessary for the organization's management?

What procedure should be followed in initially electing and appointing the officers?

How should a constitution and rules of procedure be developed?

What plans are necessary to ensure safety and good health practices?

What staff personnel would be available to assist and serve as advisor-director and assistants?

What administrative approval is necessary for the organization of a recreation association?

What will be the relationship of the organization with the administration?

What plan should be used for presenting the proposed organization for approval and support?

What will be the tentative leadership organization and responsibility?

A follow-up meeting should be called shortly after the initial meeting. A temporarily appointed chairperson and secretary should preside at this meeting and the same considerations and recommendations made at the initial meeting should be presented for evaluation and discussion by this group. At a later general meeting a constitution should be voted upon. Officers should be elected, and managers appointed to initiate the program.

CONSTITUTIONS AND BYLAWS OF LOCAL ORGANIZATIONS

Constitutions are a vital part of every organization and require a great deal of time to develop. Each constitution is unique in meeting the needs of the situation it serves. It must reveal the philosophy of the specific association, and it has to be developed within the framework of available facilities, leadership, and existing regulations.

A constitution committee should develop regulations concerning the following.

The organization name, officers, managers, chairpersons, executive board, general board, and meetings

Purpose of the organization

Membership eligibility, fees and dues, voting privileges, affiliated membership, club membership, honorary membership

Officers, managers, club and living group representatives

Qualifications: general board, officers

Elections, appointments, and installations

Association procedures

Amendments to constitution

Bylaws

Sample constitutions are helpful in developing a good constitution; and, for this reason, reference to the constitutions of other local organizations as well as state athletic activities associations is helpful.

RECREATION ASSOCIATION JOB MANAGEMENT

A strong association reflects good organization, a well-defined program, and complete job functions. If the advisor-director is the only one who can answer questions and make decisions, that person in effect completely controls and dominates the organization. Volunteer leadership must be allowed to handle the reins of responsibility to thus develop competencies and ability to assume delegated administrative responsibilities. The following code of operations may be used as a resource to adapt for a particular situation or may be developed as an association officers' manual using an outline comparable to the following:

Preface

Statement of purpose of program, use of and responsibility for manual.

Table of Contents

JOB MANAGEMENT DESCRIPTIONS

Each officer's position should be described with specific statements of general qualifications, specific requirements, initiation date, training period, and time of assumption of duties.

President

The RA constitution charges the president to call to order and preside at all meetings of the RA board and of the executive board; appoint necessary chairpersons and committees; be an ex-officio member of all committees; and perform such other duties as are customarily delegated to a president.

It shall be the duty of the president

—to call and preside at any necessary special meetings of the general board, the executive board, or any of the various functioning committees

—to arrange weekly meeting with advisor-director to develop next meeting agenda, consider present or future problems, business, or ways to improve the organization

—to keep in contact with officers and committee persons, check program and activities progress, and call for oral and written reports for general board meetings

—to ask and receive guests at RA board meetings and activities, welcome and introduce new board members

—to attend meetings called by administration or send a well-informed substitute

—to supervise orderliness in RA office and files

—to stimulate officers and general board to positive action and continued improvement of the organization

—to supervise election procedure

—to keep a notebook of meeting agendas for reference for the next president

The president shall keep a calendar-guide for the year's activities to include a monthly "time-line" of responsibilities. The example given here reflects a school-year calendar but could be adapted for any twelve-month period.

June (1) Vice-President and committee publish RA handbook to be available for summer and fall information packets; (2) vice-president to complete plans and submit report for fall get-acquainted party; (3) appoint exhibits committee to plan for fall activities display during first week; (4) appoint sports managers, publicity managers, newspaper representatives, and committee chairperson for the following year

Summer (1) Keep in touch with officers and fall managers to insure preplanning, make appointments for any developed vacancies; (2) request reports from fall party committee to insure good planning; (3) prepare speech for orientation week

September–October (1) Orientation week; (2) fall party publicity and final check on program; (3) orientation of general board to purpose, activities, and RA organization; (4) review of job descriptions of club, district, house, or class representatives; (5) general manager, sports managers, and advisors meet to plan season's sports program; (6) participation lists for health, eligibility, and insurance; (7) invitations sent out for swim meet; (8) make appointments for any vacant offices or positions

November–December (1) Constitution committee submits any necessary revisions to general board for consideration; (2) intramural and interscholastic swim meets; (3) plans for winter party and Christmas project well formed before Thanksgiving; (4) complete volleyball and bowling sports seasons; (5) winter party including oral and written reports on season's sports, cost, participation points earned; (6) general manager meets with sports managers of winter season sports: basketball, bowling, badminton, skiing

January–February (1) Badminton, basketball tournaments started; (2)

playday committee develops plans; (3) ski programs planned and held; (4) co-rec bowling tournaments held; (5) inventory equipment and develop purchase list; (6) prepare budget

March–April (1) Determine delegates to conferences, if any; (2) present slate of new officers to board; (3) submit equipment and office-supply purchase list to board for approval; (4) vote for new officers and constitution revisions; (5) written reports on season sports programs including cost, participation credits earned; (6) general manager, sports managers, advisors meet to plan spring sports program; (7) complete playday report and association budget; (8) spring banquet committee begins work, request report, order awards; (9) installation dinner for new officers, orientation and training period; (10) start spring sports: tennis, softball, and golf; (11) choose representatives to attend area playday; (12) playday invitations sent out the first week of spring season; (13) committees and sports managers appointed for next year; (14) next year's calendar and handbook started by vice-president

May (1) Publicity for spring banquet: (2) playday report; (3) spring banquet, installation, awards, guests; (4) next year's calendar of RA activities submitted for approval; (5) handbook completed; (6) advanced planning of fall party started

Vice-President

The RA constitution charges the vice-president to perform all necessary duties in the absence of the president; act as social program chairperson, appointing assistants and committees necessary for conducting the traditional and social activities; keep permanent records of all such events.

It shall be the duty of the vice-president

—to meet periodically with the president to discuss the problems, purposes, and news of the organization

—to become familiar with *Robert's Rules of Order* and procedures of the RA executive and general board meetings and periodically take over running of these meetings

—with the help of the ex-vice-president, to develop a calendar of events for the upcoming year including dates of traditional and social activities, sports seasons, and special events; present calendar to executive board and administration for approval

—each spring quarter, with executive board's approval, appoint chairpersons for all social and traditional functions, and advise them of their responsibilities in carrying out the following:

time and clearance with administration

RA budgeted monies and review of old reports

committee appointments and help with: program and entertainment, invitations and name tags, food and clean-up

—review traditional events which include:

fall get-acquainted party

winter co-ed ice skating party with bonfire, caroling, and food

installation, initiation, and training dinner party for old and new officers

spring steak fry for all RA members including entertainment and awards

playday planned for various like-interested groups in area or state

—insure that periodic progress reports of the various chairpersons' activities are made to the general board and that written reports with respect to planning, finances, and program are in the files within three weeks after each function (see Figure 11-2)

Event _____   Permanent Record
                                   Typewritten or in ink. Use other side of sheet
Chairperson _____   when necessary.

Date of Event _____   Date of Report _____

Committees _____   _____

            _____   _____

            _____   _____

            _____   _____

Theme _____

Program of Activities

Entertainment

Food and/or Refreshments

Publicity

Special Equipment, Decorations, Prizes

Budget

Appropriation   _____   Itemized Expenses

   Total Expense   _____   _____ _____

                                            _____ _____

                                            _____ _____

   Total Income   _____   Itemized Income

                                            _____ _____

                                            _____ _____

Profit or Loss   _____   _____ _____

Recommendations:

                                            _____ Chairman

Figure 11-2   RA Social Activities Report

—to develop and have printed and delivered by June 1st the RA handbook—mock-up to include:

> purpose of handbook, statement of RA and its aims, list of association officers, managers, club presidents, and the various chairpersons

> message from president and advisor or administrator

> description of the sports and recreation activities, eligibility, means of participating, and persons to contact

> pictures and last year's tournament winners

> point system and constitution

> general information including location and use of RA office, suggestion box, constitution and publications, mailboxes and communication channels, equipment room and use

> calendar of events including executive and general board meetings, social and special events, sport seasons including deadline dates for tournaments, meets, election dates, and award banquets

Secretary

The RA constitution charges the secretary to keep a permanent record of all RA and executive board proceedings; conduct all association correspondence; and notify board members of date, time, and place before each meeting.

It shall be the duty of the secretary to

—become familiar with *Robert's Rules of Order* to facilitate taking and reading minutes at board meetings; mimeo and distribute minutes

—handle all RA correspondence including business letters, thank-you notes, and invitations, and keep a date order file of original and carbon replies

—develop and distribute letter explaining RA election and appointment procedures including candidate qualifications (see Figure 11-3)

—distribute slate of candidates, eligibility list, date, time, place of voting (see Figure 11-4)

Treasurer

The RA constitution charges the treasurer to take charge of association funds and maintain permanent records of same; pay out monies upon approval of president and board; present to executive board for approval an annual association budget; and act as chairperson of the finance committee.

It shall be the duty of the Treasurer to

—act as custodian for: association's fiscal budget, account books including

---

RECREATION ASSOCIATION
ELECTIONS

Nominations for the Executive Offices shall be made by a committee composed of senior class active members.* not to exceed two from each living group. This committee shall present a slate of nominations to the RA Board meeting within the last four weeks of the winter quarter.

Elections shall be held the week preceding the final week of the winter quarter.

Election of Executive Officers shall be by secret written ballot of active members. Candidates receiving the highest total of votes shall be considered elected and the presidential candidate receiving the second highest number of votes shall automatically become vice-president.

EXECUTIVE OFFICERS	QUALIFICATIONS
President	second quarter' sophomore or junior C average active member of RA one term on RA Board
Vice-President	same as above
Secretary	active member
Treasurer	active member
Recording sports manager	active member
General manager	active member

House groups are advised to select members to serve on the nominations committee. RA offers excellent opportunities to develop real leadership—make your suggestions known to the senior class members. Support your candidates (candidates from your house or other houses) through the voting membership of the RA. All persons on campus are automatically members of RA; however, voting members are those who have participated in RA activities—Aquai, Intramurals, Playdays, etc. Reference List.

*Active members are those individuals who have turned in participation credits during the current year.

Figure 11-3   RA Election Notice

accounts-receivable and accounts-payable; monthly statements; and forms folder including requisition, payroll, and inventory forms

—attend all RA meetings and, when called upon, give a report of the financial situation of the association

—keep record of accounts-receivable and accounts-payable and spread to budget item accounts

—at the end of each month balance and prove all accounts and budget items

—have large expenditures approved by executive board and small bills cleared through the appropriate chairperson or manager upon submission of approved requisition form (see Figure 11-5)

—assume responsibility for record keeping, salary schedules, and payroll

—make up budget in light of current year's expenditures, plus anticipated expenses of the coming year, and present to funding source (see Figure 11-6)

—at the end of year balance and close books, indicating working balances

---

RECREATION ASSOCIATION
ELECTIONS

Date . . . . Friday, April 26

Time. . . . . All day

Place. . . . . Student Union

Who can vote . . . . All RA members

RA SLATE

Date _____

Slate of Officers:

PRESIDENT	TREASURER
M. Kolstad	P. Neil
C. Lillie	B. Clardy
H. Harlan	K. Harris

SECRETARY	GENERAL MANAGER
A. Hamilton	M. Dickson
K. Anderson	C. Fairbanks
A. Shea	J. Rickert
G. Huntley	T. Brown

RECORDING SPORTS SECRETARY

J. Baker
E. Sievers
R. Greene

AMENDMENTS:

1. For those sports having a round robin preliminary to the elimination tournament, it will be necessary for a member to participate in the tournament to receive a participation credit.

2. A competitor must participate in at least one (1) round robin game before being eligible to play in the elimination tournament.

3. To participate in any sport a player must be approved medically.

4. To be an active member of RA and to be eligible to vote or run for office, you must have earned at least one participation credit in quarters previous to election quarter.

5. The eligibility list is to be turned into the staff member handling the medical program one week prior to the date of the first scheduled game of that sport.

Figure 11-4   RA Slate and Notice of Elections

for the new treasurer, and submit to board a complete report of year's term of office with recommendations and suggestions for next year

Publicity Manager

The publicity manager must know how to use the various means of communicating such as newspapers, posters, notices, pictures, scrapbooks, radio, and TV. This manager must be able to delegate responsibility to committee members and have self-starting initiative and originality.

```
┌─────────────────────────────────────────────────────────┐
│              RECREATION ASSOCIATION                       │
│                  REQUISITION FORM                         │
│                                                           │
│                                    Check No. _____     │
│   Authorization for the expenditures of funds            │
│                                    Am't of check _____  │
│                                    Date _____ 19 ___  │
│                                                           │
│   Check in favor of _____ │
│                                                           │
│         Mailed to  (  )  _____ │
│                                                           │
│         Pick-up    (  )  _____ │
│                               (Address)                   │
│                                                           │
│   List Items to be paid for                    Cost      │
│                                                           │
│         _____     _____         │
│         _____  -  _____ -      │
│         _____     _____         │
│         _____  Total _____     │
│                                                           │
│   Organization _____ Signed _____  │
│                                                           │
│   Countersigned _____ Title _____   │
└─────────────────────────────────────────────────────────┘
```

Figure 11-5 RA Requisition Form

It shall be the duty of the publicity manager to

—attend all RA general and executive board meetings and contribute thinking and experience with respect to all RA problems and planning

—promote and supervise all publicity relative to RA activities and manage the program within the appropriated budget

—provide publicity in the following media through appointed chairpersons:

(a) publications—newspaper articles, news service releases, RA mimeographed newsletter, articles in national organizations

(b) pictures—RA photographer to cover all RA activities, picture file, procedure for obtaining copies of pictures taken by news service and local papers

(c) scrapbook—collect and assemble RA scrapbook

(d) displays and posters—develop permanent and portable displays and seasonal posters

(e) bulletin board—keep sports center bulletin boards up to date with current activities, announcements, and appropriate information

—coordinate the responsibilities of the various chairpersons; help with promotion ideas and techniques and periodically give progress reports to executive and general board

—at end of term of office make available sample posters, displays, and recommendations for the next year

—submit oral and written reports of year's activities

RECREATION ASSOCIATION
PROPOSED BUDGET 19

Carry Over $

INCOME:

Budget Appropriation . . . .
Transfer from other Funds. . . . .
Playday . . . .
Picnic Collections . . . .
Miscellaneous . . . .
Total Income

EXPENDITURES:

Awards	150.00
Rent	240.00
Dues	50.00
Equipment (sports)	300.00
Equipment (capital).	900.00
Payroll	
Office Secretary (part time)	500.00
Officials	400.00
Office Supplies	150.00
Program	
Association meetings	
Fall.	100.00
Winter	100.00
Officer Training	50.00
Spring Installation	100.00
High School Playday	150.00
College Playday.	150.00
Meets	100.00
Co-recreation	300.00
Publicity	
Handbook	300.00
Newsletter, Scrapbook.	60.00
Supplies, Posters	80.00
Reserve	
Contingency.	300.00
Total	$4,580.00

Note: Recreation Assoc. Reserve Fund balances are as follows:

(1) Reserve for Equipment . . . .
(2) Reserve for College Playday. . . . .
(3) Reserve for Convention Travel . . . .

Recommended for approval   Approval:

_____   _____

Manager   Business Manager

_____   _____

Advisor or Director   Auditor

Figure 11-6. RA Proposed Budget

Equipment Manager

The equipment manager often has the responsibility to check on the building, open it, lock it up, "cover" the office, and issue and collect RA equipment.

It shall be the duty of the equipment manager to

—keep informed regarding RA personnel and activities and be effective as a good office public relations ambassador

—have all score sheets and clipboards ready for games and activities and check them in the manager's mail box at end of activities periods

—check RA and department equipment "out" and "in" according to an accountable procedure

—do any incidental office work or errands, answer the phone, and secure the building

—take equipment inventory, make recommendations for new purchases, and upon board approval make necessary purchases (see Figure 11-7)

Recorder

The recorder keeps records of points earned by membership, awards won in the past and those to be ordered for the future, and equipment inventories.

It shall be the duty of the recorder to

—keep a permanent file of all participation credits (PC) submitted by the sports managers and recorded on each member's record card

		INVENTORY AND PURCHASE RECOMMENDATIONS								
		July ___ to July ___			July ___ to July ___			July ___ to July ___		
Item	Where stored	On hand	Recom. purch.	Actual purch.	On hand	Recom. purch.	Actual purch.	On hand	Recom. purch.	Actual purch.

Figure 11-7. RA Inventory Record

—keep the active membership file and record cards for each member up to date, and just before elections, send an eligibility list to the secretary

—keep a record of group and individual standings and notify the general sports manager of those individuals and groups that become eligible for awards

—prepare summary reports of association participation to show interest, growth, and budget justifications for association activities (see Figure 11-8)

—interpret the RA awards system at appropriate and opportune times

The General Sports Manager

The general sports manager is responsible for the sports activity program and therefore has to help each sports manager promote and organize his or her particular sport.

It shall be the duty of the general sports manager to

—coordinate the entire sports and intramural program, and act as consultant and supervisor of the sports managers; distribute and interpret managers' job descriptions

—delegate authority of securing officials for the programs and insure safekeeping of the permanent records of all activities

—act as eligibility chairperson and confirm that all participants meet health requirements by the second week of each sports season (see Figure 11-9). (A team may request defaults from teams playing with ineligible players.)

—call and preside at a meeting of sports managers and advisor-director two weeks before beginning of each sports season to get a successful program underway

—confirm that each manager at the beginning of the season posts lists and encourages team signups

—be responsible for visiting programs to keep informed

—plan a meeting with the club presidents in order to keep informed of their activities and also to insure cooperative planning with respect to the many individual programs

—meet with the co-recreation manager as the need arises

—assist the particular sports managers or club presidents with the organization of interschool competition such as playdays, sportsdays, or invitation days and with the organization of clinics, master lessons, or demonstrations

—call a meeting of the managers of the sports within a week after each season to set deadlines for written and oral reports; review job management and possible suggestions for the next year

—compile a participation hours report at the end of each season, summarized from participation reports received from the sports managers

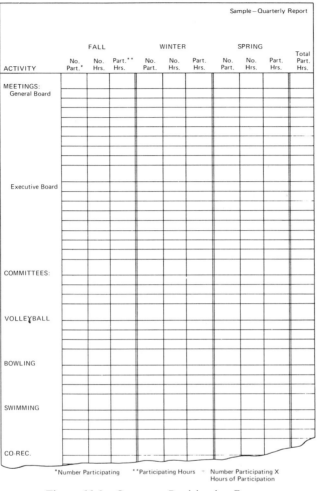

	FALL			WINTER			SPRING			Total
ACTIVITY	No. Part.*	No. Hrs.	Part.** Hrs.	No. Part.	No. Hrs.	Part. Hrs.	No. Part.	No. Hrs.	Part. Hrs.	Part. Hrs.
MEETINGS: General Board										
Executive Board										
COMMITTEES:										
VOLLEYBALL										
BOWLING										
SWIMMING										
CO-REC.										

Sample—Quarterly Report

*Number Participating   **Participating Hours ⁻ Number Participating X Hours of Participation

Figure 11-8   Summary Participation Report

—report officals' monthly hours and wages to the treasurer
—prepare end-of-season oral and written reports for board

The Sports Manager

The sports manager is responsible for developing a sports promotion campaign for a particular activity at the beginning of the year, to be initiated not later than three weeks before the beginning of the particular sports season. At this time a meeting is scheduled with the general

RECREATION ASSOCIATION

ELIGIBILITY LIST

_____PARTICIPANTS

House _____   Date _____

The following individuals have indicated an interest in participating in RA activities and meet the necessary qualifications. Physically fit as indicated by a medical examination.

Transfers desiring to participate after this house list has been submitted will assume the responsibility of getting medical approval before they will be qualified to participate.

1._____   17._____
2._____   18._____
3._____   19._____
4._____   20._____
5._____   21._____
6._____   22._____
7._____   23._____
8._____   24._____
9._____   25._____
10._____   26._____
11._____   27._____
12._____   28._____
13._____   29._____
14._____   30._____
15._____   31._____
16._____   32._____

Figure 11-9   RA Eligibility List

sports manager to review organizational plans. Thereafter the manager assumes full responsibility for the sport.

It shall be the duty of the sports manager to

—make signup sheets the first week of the sport season for all groups, houses, or living units. (Representatives are asked to post these sheets and encourage signup. After one week they are collected and the tournament schedule is worked out by the manager. The game schedules are posted and printed in the paper as soon as possible and the first game is scheduled for the second week of the season. A tournament chart is posted and kept up to date indicating winners, scores, and playing rules.)

—put into effect promotion campaign. Publicity should be sent out through varied media before and during the season, and as follows:

newspapers—the sports editor or reporter should be contacted and given a pre-season article for publication (this could include the winners of last year's tournament, dates and time schedules, sports manager's name, place of tournament); frequent articles should appear during the season reporting the progress of the tournament and team standings; a final outlined article should be submitted for publication giving team standings, the number participating, and related information

posters—the manager should have a committee to make posters and see that they are well placed (RA publicity chairperson may be asked for help)

notices—the manager should pass out announcements and notices to the representatives at board meetings (if representatives are absent, the manager must deliver the information—it is wise to check occasionally to see if the notices are conspicuously posted)

pep campaigns—campaign skits are very good and effective in stimulating interest

sports captains—appointed sports captains, in some instances, stimulate interest and insure enthusiastic leadership

—insure that all sports and tournaments observe defined regulations, rules, and standards

—insure that participants comply with eligibility requirements

—advise the front office of the details of the sports season to facilitate answering all questions intelligently and carrying out such details as insuring that the dates are put on the score sheets as well as names of teams and that tournament schedules and eligibility lists are posted

—be available at stated times to assist with tournaments or matches and to answer questions (hours should be posted beside the tournament chart, together with a contact telephone number in case of emergency)

—provide score sheets for the RA front office; after the game or match turn these in to the desk, together with the names of players or teams

—tabulate PCs (participation credits) in preparation for the final report to be given to the general sports manager; tabulate the number of hours each participant has played in the tournament (it is best to summarize every two weeks), give total to general sports manager at the end of the season (see Figure 11-11)

—obtain and schedule officials for the particular sports season (see Figure 11-12)

Co-Recreation and Challenge Games Manager

Co-recreation and challenge events are becoming an expanding part of the program. Signup, scheduling procedures, and promotion should pattern that of the other managers.

It shall be the responsibility of the co-rec manager to

—plan and organize events so as to be compatible with rest of program

—assume leadership role comparable to that of other managers

SIGN-UP SHEET

RA Intramurals _____
                              (Sport)
(Basketball) is scheduled this quarter, on
MTWTH afternoons. Each group is urged to
sign up as many teams as possible. A team is
composed of ( ) players, and ( ) officials.

   Game time is 4:15, defaults are declared
at 4:30. Game schedules will be sent to each
living unit and posted. Watch the dates for
your games.

RA INTRAMURALS

JOIN THE FUN

NEXT WEEK

IT'S TIME TO SIGN UP

SIGN UP YOUR TEAMS

Team 1   Team 3

Players _____ _____   Players _____ _____
        _____ _____   _____ _____
        _____ _____   _____ _____
        _____ _____   _____ _____

Captain _____   Captain _____
Officials _____   Officials _____

Team 2   Team 4

Players _____ _____   Players _____ _____
        _____ _____   _____ _____
        _____ _____   _____ _____
        _____ _____   _____ _____

Captain _____   Captain _____
Officials _____   Officials _____

Figure 11-10   RA Sports Signup Sheet

—turn in season reports to include manager's report, participation report, tournament schedules, and winners' comments and suggestions for next year (see Figure 11-13)

The Club President

Club presidents represent the leaders of interest groups affiliated with the RA. As such, they are enthusiastic and usually highly skilled in a particular activity area. Officers are elected by the club membership in accordance with its constitution, and a representative is usually required to attend RA general board meetings to contribute thinking and experience to RA activities. The club president keeps the board informed of its program, membership, and financial position. The club functions as an affiliate of the RA, observing its constitution and both benefiting from and contributing to its financial position when necessary and when possible.
It shall be the duty of the club president to

—develop a constitution consistent with the club's purposes and its affiliation with the RA

```
┌─────────────────────────────────────────────────────────────┐
│              RECREATION ASSOCIATION      To be turned in to the│
│                                          General Sports Manager│
│                PARTICIPATION REPORT      at the end of the season.│
│           (to supplement "sports manager's report")            │
│                                                                │
├──────────────────────────────────────────┬───────────────────┤
│ NAME OF ACTIVITY:              DATE:                           │
├──────────────────────┬──────────┬─────────────────┬───────────┤
│ List alphabetically  │ Check if │ Total No. partici-│ Write     │
│ the names of everyone│ in tourn.│ pation hours    │ "P.C." if │
│ who turned out for   │ or demon.│ completed       │ earned    │
│ this activity.       │          │                 │           │
├──────────────────────┼──────────┼─────────────────┼───────────┤
│                      │          │                 │           │
│  (blank rows)        │          │                 │           │
├──────────────────────┴──────────┴─────────────────┴───────────┤
│          Signed _____              │
│                          (Manager)                            │
└─────────────────────────────────────────────────────────────┘
```

Figure 11-11   RA Participation Report

—conduct meetings and develop program plans

—continue representation on RA board and cooperate with and promote its program

—submit a financial statement

—submit an end-of-year report with respect to the club and its activities

DISCUSSION QUESTIONS

1. Can a recreation association administrative framework function in a community program as well as a school program? How are volunteers obtained? What are the advantages of this administrative approach?

OFFICIALS FOR (   ) INTRAMURALS

The persons listed below will be the OFFICIALS for Intramural games on the days indicated by a check (✓) mark. The SCORERS and TIMEKEEPERS will be furnished by each team playing.

OFFICIALS should report to the Center at 4:10 p.m. and be ready to get the assigned game under way as near 4:15 p.m. as possible. Teams not ready to play by 4:30 will be called a default. However, you may call the game if there are enough players who wish to stay and play a practice game.

If for some reason you can not be present for your assigned game, will you please select and ask one of the SUBSTITUTES from the list to take your place as the OFFICIAL. It would be appreciated if you would also notify the Volleyball Sports Manager of the substitution.

At the end of the day's game each Official will turn in hours worked to the Equipment Manager in the front office. You will be paid at the rate of _____ per game. Checks are made out at the first of each month.

Thanks and good officiating.

Name	Phone	Mon.	Tues.	Wed.	Thurs.
B. Chaffey	LI 9-7664	x			
G. Gray	LI 3-3623	x			
P. Cameron	LI 3-6964	S	x	S	x
D. Johns	LI 9-1735		x		S
V. Rhinehardt				x	
M. June				x	
D. Burns		S			x
J. Whitten			S		S
S. Newton				S	
L. Palin			S	S	
D. Leary		S	S	S	S
T. Nertel		S	S	S	S
M. Brown					
R. Childs					
T. Gilbert					
A. Payne					
M. True					
N. Hill					
G. Budd					
G. Donnally					

x—Official
S—Substitute

Figure 11-12   RA Sports Officials' Schedule

2. How would a participants' interest survey be conducted for school programs? Community programs? Besides activity interests, what other information should be sought?

3. What membership requirements would you recommend for school programs? Community programs?

4. Outline a personnel organizational chart for a defined situation, indicating channels of communication.

5. A recreation association constitution should be developed around what major concerns or procedures?

6. How valuable is a recreation association officers' manual? What are the potential uses of a manual?

7. In broad classifications of responsibility, what are the duties of the recreation association officers?

8. What are the duties of managers? What are the effective lines of responsibility?

9. What are the potential financial resources for a recreation association? How should an association budget be developed?

10. How would you carry out the annual equipment inventory and purchasing procedure? The day-to-day purchasing and payment of bills?

```
                                              To be turned in to the
                                              General Sports Manager
                                              at the end of the season.

                 RECREATION ASSOCIATION

                   SPORTS MANAGER REPORT
                (to accompany "Participation Report")


   Name of Activity _____ Date _____

   Total number participating _____ Number earning P.C. _____

   Requirements for receiving P.C. (list all regulations, rules, etc.)




   SUMMARY: (Give here type of tournament, or demonstration, etc.; other arrangements for
     practice and participation; winners of tournament, if any; procedure of recording "hours";
     and any other information that should be helpful to those in charge for the succeeding
     seasons. Attach a copy of the tournament schedule, with dates, if there was one).














   PLEASE: Type or ink!            SIGNED _____
                                            (Manager)
```

Figure 11-13   Sports Manager Report

BIBLIOGRAPHY

BROWN, JOSEPH, *Planning for Recreation and Parks.* Englewood Cliffs, New Jersey: Prentice-Hall, Inc., 1976

BUTLER, GEORGE D., *Introduction to Community Recreation,* 5th ed.. New York: McGraw-Hill Book Company, 1976.

FISK, MARGARET, ed., *National Organizations of the United States,* Vol. 1: Detroit, Michigan: Gale Research Co., 1975.

HYATT, RONALD W., *Intramural Sports Programs: Their Organization and Administration.* St. Louis: C. V. Mosby Co., 1976.

MEANS, LOUIS E., *Intramurals: Their Organization and Administration.* (2nd ed.). Englewood Cliffs, New Jersey: Prentice-Hall, Inc., 1974.

PETERSON, JAMES A., Editor, *Intramural Administration: Theory and Practice.* Englewood Cliffs, New Jersey: Prentice-Hall, Inc., 1976.

V

Operational
Policies
and
Procedures

Mt. Baker Ski Area.
(Courtesy Mt. Baker Recreation Co., Inc., Bellingham, Washington.)

12

Financial Support
and Management

If its administration is efficient, a recreational sports program is fairly inexpensive to operate, especially when viewed in relationship to the relatively large number of individuals who benefit from it. Yet expenses have to be carefully watched and controlled for the program to yield maximum benefits. Here a sound plan of business operation is the essential condition, one that is simple yet comprehensive. A sound plan calls for the study of anticipated income and expenditure, an annual budget, and efficient methods of bookkeeping and auditing. Of these items the budget is of paramount importance, and it is necessary that it should be realistic while sufficiently flexible to permit planning for future needs and taking care of emergencies. It is more likely to be realistic when provision for maintenance, facilities, and capital equipment are made in the general funds of the school or college or provided for by student fees. Of the two sources, student fees are seen as providing better for an ideal program in recreational sports, with general funds and physical education budgets in second and third place, respectively. A recent survey of the recreational sports program on the college level reveals that a little more than half of the directors of recreational sports programs believe that their funding is adequate, with dissatisfaction more typical of large-college directors. Interestingly, the directors of programs in junior colleges believe their funding adequate.[1]

[1]Gerald M. Maas, C. E. Mueller, and Bruce D. Anderson, "Survey of Administrative Reporting Sequences and Funding Sources for Intramural-Extramural Programs in Two-Year and Four-Year Colleges in the United States and Canada," *25th Annual Conference Proceedings of the National Intramural Association*, (1974), pp. 122–26.

INCOME AND EXPENSES

Successful recreational sports programs attract great numbers of students, which means providing more facilities and equipment than those demanded by the class programs. Financing an expanding recreational sports program thus means additional expenses. Many small schools and colleges have inadequate equipment money for classroom needs, not to mention needs for growing recreational sports programs. Frequently, therefore, these programs have to be supported by supplementary finances.

Sources of Income

As suggested above, sources of income are varied in both high schools and colleges. One of the following plans may provide an adequate source of income, though some are clearly more productive than others.

Percentage of Activity Fee. A percentage of the student activity fee is the most popular form of supporting the recreational sports program. The plan is feasible wherever there is a blanket student activity fee for all students. All men and women are entitled automatically to share in the recreational sports activities, and the program has a guaranteed income. Problems arise, however, if buying a student activity ticket is optional. Income figures cannot be projected, and all students are not automatically entitled to participate in the program. Solutions may take the form of basing the budget allocation on the fee income for the preceding year and requiring an activity card of all participants.

General Funds. Another popular form of funding is a provision for the recreational sports program in the college's or school's general fund. It should include money for publicity, personnel, equipment, facilities, and all expenses necessary to the program.

Department of Physical Education. The department of physical education often provides funds for the recreational sports program. This is a good plan if a specific budget item ensures a stable income that cannot be usurped for other expenses. Some departments assume financial obligations for recreational sports as routine expenses and furnish equipment and supplies.

Student Government Allocation. An annual allocation from the student association or student government may support the recreational sports program. In this situation, activity incomes are turned over to a student association, which, in turn, makes up its own budget of allocations.

Appropriation from Department of Athletics. Financing all or a part of the recreational sports program by appropriations from the department of athletics is a practice found more frequently in the men's program than in the women's. This practice has the disadvantage of depending on varying gate receipts. Development of the program is limited or interrupted because of resulting fluctuations in the available budget monies. Title IX Legislation is gradually providing equal opportunities for all students.

Dues and Initiation Fees. Students often have to earn participation points to establish eligibility for membership in the recreation association. They then pay dues and an initiation fee. This source of income provides operating money for the association, although objections have been raised because this procedure tends to limit participation to just the membership.

House Membership, Entry, and Forfeit Fees. Some recreational sports programs require houses to pay membership fees and/or team entry fees. Those teams desiring to compete in sponsored tournaments pay an entry and a forfeit fee. The forfeit fee is reimbursed if the team plays all the games. This fundraising plan again tends to limit participation and is in conflict with the fundamental principle that there should be free, elective recreational sports opportunities for all.

School Help. In those situations where the money has to be earned for the annual budget, help is often given by various departments, and the school may provide facilities without charge. The department of physical education furnishes equipment and supplies. The building and grounds department and security department provide maintenance and security services, etc.

Rental Income. Many recreational sports associations have supplies or rental equipment such as bicycles, skis, golf clubs, canoes, sailboats, and tennis racquets, which they rent to students for a nominal rate. Sometimes a cabin is owned that is rented to other groups. In these instances, rentals provide an additional source of income.

Spectator Income. Synchronized swim clubs, modern dance clubs, gymnastic clubs, fencing clubs, and similar groups often sponsor productions, meets, demonstrations, or lessons. There are admission charges and instructional fees to cover operational expenses. In some cases a profit is realized, and often a percentage of this goes to support the recreational sports programs.

Fundraising Campaigns. Some schools have to resort to sponsoring various shows or activities as a means of raising funds. Often these are very time-demanding, and there is the question as to how justifiable fundraising is as a student responsibility. The following activities are usually successful: selling clothing, sports equipment, flowers, collegiate felt items, cosmetics, balloons, programs, magazines, cake and pastries;

sponsoring dances, contests, plays, circuses, carnivals, movies, professional entertainment, and publications; providing services such as skill lessons in sports, car wash, house cleaning, baby sitting. Parent groups or the parent-teacher association often lend financial help through cake sales, rummage sales, and bazaars.

Items of Expense

In contrast to the income sources, which are usually few in number, the expenses of a recreational sports program are many. Because programs differ with respect to their dependent or independent relationship with the physical education department, the expenses assumed do not always accurately reflect the financial obligations of the after-school program. The following list presents typical expenses:

Maintenance
(Upkeep of owned or rented
facilities)

    Cabin repairs
    Equipment repairs
    Repairs to buildings
    Care of field, facilities, and areas

Equipment
(New equipment)

    New sports equipment
    Recreation equipment
    Rental equipment
    Office, lounge, or cabin furniture
      and equipment

Personnel
(Payroll and student help)

    Office help
    Equipment manager
    Officials

Transportation and Conventions
(Association representation)

    Travel expenses for representatives
    Convention host or hostess expenses
    National, district meeting expenses
    Sports participants' travel

Programs
(Miscellaneous)

Decorations
Food
Entertainment
Guests
Clinic specialists
Club program expenses
Sports days

Dues and Subscriptions
(Association affiliations and
publications)

National dues
District dues
Subscriptions to magazines

Supplies and Office Work
(Supplies and clerical work)

Paper supplies
Typewriter ribbons, Scotch
  tape, masking tape,
Paper clips, thumbtacks,
  staples
Pencils, pens, ink
Stencils
Mimeographing and printing; xeroxing

Operating Expenses
(Service charges and overhead)

Electricity
Telephone
Service charges

Insurance
(Short- and long-term)

Accident insurance for team
  members
Travel insurance for delegates
  to conferences

Publicity

Handbooks
Pamphlets
Posters
Picture in yearbook
News sheets

Awards

Recognition awards
Playday and sports day awards

BUDGETS AND BUDGET MAKING

Efficient financial management of an organization is based upon a carefully developed budget. A budget should be the best possible estimate of probable income and expenditures and should serve as a complete financial plan for a defined period. It should be based upon the anticipated and known income, the estimated and known needs and expenses for the next year, and those estimated for the next three years. The plan should be carefully developed by the treasurer in light of past records and, if handled by a student treasurer, with the help and approval of a faculty advisor.

A carefully developed budget is the most effective method of ensuring wise spending. It provides for the most valuable and equitable distribution of available funds to the various divisions of the recreational sports program. It facilitates analysis of the various costs and gives direction for necessary revisions. It eliminates the possibility of spending more money than is available and is a means of checking questionable buying. With a well-developed budget, and adequate records upon which it is based, the need for increased appropriations can be shown and justified easily and effectively. At the end of the school year, responsible personnel can authoritatively show how all the budgetary money was spent. A program that is thus guided by sound budget practices is one that observes good business practices.

Developing the Budget

In order to develop a satisfactory budget, background information must be obtained from several sources. Immediate and future needs must be considered and possible income must be known.

First, it is necessary to summarize possible expenditures. A review of the past several years, and the last year in particular, is essential. This is accomplished by comparing previous years' proposed and actual budgets. Next, recommendations of the current staff, officers, managers, and chairpersons should be summarized. Projected estimates of increased participation and resultant increased needs should be required of the responsible people. Also, the recreational sports program board should be consulted with respect to future plans. Current inventories of equipment, supplies, and recommended purchases must be considered. Information from these sources should make it possible to estimate immediate and future expenses.

Next, possible future incomes should be estimated. A review of previous budgets serves as a guide to anticipated incomes and appropriations. Consultation with responsible persons, a review of records, and the advice of the boards should provide guidance in anticipating additional sources of income. It may be the procedure to determine financial needs and then to present these needs to a school organization, which in turn provides an appropriation.

With systematic and reliably developed estimates of income and expenses it should be possible to determine financial needs and possibilities for the ensuing year as well as for several years ahead. Whether the budget is for one or two years, it has been found practical to plan it on a fiscal-year basis, beginning on July 1 and coinciding with the activities of the school year. Before drafting an initial budget, income and expense budget items have to be decided upon. If a budget has been drawn up in past years, it is customary procedure to develop the new budget using the same classifications of items. This consistency facilitates comparisons and analyses that may be necessary.

The budget items should provide for some flexibility and need only be detailed enough to reveal incomes and control expenses. They should be general enough to permit supervisors and student officers to render judgments and develop ability and integrity in financial management. The detail that is required is often determined to some extent by the business office or the supervising authority. There are many ways of preparing budgets, and obviously it is impossible to devise one that is applicable to all situations.

ADOPTING THE BUDGET

Approval of the recreational sports budget will be dependent upon the sources of income. If it is appropriated by the physical education department, it will have to be presented to the department chairperson for action. In other instances it may have to be approved by the athletic department. If part or all of the recreational sports program income is earned by an organization such as the student government, it usually has to be presented to this group for approval. Further, if the budget includes a school or school board appropriation, it has to be approved by the principal and the superintendent. In these cases, sometimes the business manager of the college or high school approves the budget before it goes to the board of education or board of trustees.

After the budget is adopted and approved, it becomes the financial program of the one- or two-year period, and expenses for the new period are permitted. The care and thoughtfulness with which the budget is developed is reflected in the degree to which it can be followed as a financial plan.

Because unexpected expenses inevitably arise, practically all financial plans make provision for some readjustment in the allowances. An emergency fund may be included as an original budget item to provide for such possibilities. The difficulty here, however, is in trying to antici- pate the size of unforeseen emergencies. The fund may be too small to serve its purpose; or if large and unused, it may become a catchall item and encourage waste. Emergencies can also be handled by transferring funds from a budgetary item of less need to one of greater need. These transfers usually require special approval; and, if the amount is super- vised by another authority, his or her approval is also required. The budget should allow flexibility in handling emergencies.

Financial Control

One of the important functions of a budget is that of controlling the finances. In order to make this possible, after the budget is adopted, each individual responsible for a program area should be advised of the budget allocation for the year. In addition, the treasurer should make monthly reports of the expenditures incurred and the remaining ba- lances of each budget item. Those individuals responsible for the specific items then have a current book report of money spent and money still available in their yearly budget.

Common practice today does not require the treasurer to handle actual money. This individual makes out the budget and approves ex- penditure requisitions, but the school handles the money in the general business manager's office. In this way, responsibility for the money is less worrisome and the possibility of misuse of funds is reduced to a minimum.

At the end of the year, the treasurer adds up the expenditures of each budget item as a means of accounting for the expenses of the year. Most responsible individuals or associations then provide for a regular audit of the books. This is usually carried out by any one of several people. In some situations, the faculty administrator or advisor does it; in others, this financial check is carried out by the business manager. It is advisable to have someone not connected with the association conduct the audit. An independent external annual audit is the best budgetary procedure. The person placing the final stamp of approval on the budget should be a certified public accountant.

MANAGEMENT OF FUNDS

Efficient management of funds necessitates systematic procedures for keeping records.

Bookkeeping

A good bookkeeping system includes methods of keeping a record of the income and expenses. Often the school business office will help the faculty administrator or the association treasurer to set up a bookkeeping system.

In order to facilitate bookkeeping procedures, it is suggested that the budget items be used as a basis for classifying income and expense transactions. Whether the recreational sports personnel handles the money or not, it is essential to keep a set of books and an accounting of all financial activities. This is a valuable experience for student assistants as well as a safeguard for responsible action. If the money is handled by a business manager or treasurer, a monthly statement should be requested showing how much has been spent under each budget item and, if possible, the balance on hand of each budget item. The treasurer should then compare these reports with his or her own books.

Accounts-receivable are entered by date, description, and amount. The amount is then listed under the appropriate budget column. The accounts-payable are entered by date, description, and amount and are also broken down and recorded in each budget account column. The anticipated revenue or budget appropriation is recorded at the top of each of these accounts. At the end of the month, the items under each account may be totaled to show the amount of income or expenses for each item. The difference between the total of the expense items and the amount appropriated at the top of the column indicates the amount remaining in each of the budget items.

Purchasing Procedure

Purchasing in those situations in which the money is not handled requires a paper procedure. According to this plan, stores and equipment companies are requested to bill the recreational sports association. At the same time, the individual making the purchase turns in a copy of the bill to the treasurer. Charges indicated on the bills are entered in the account book. If these are recorded promptly, the treasurer has an up-to-date record of expenses, which is most helpful for comparison with the business office statements or for references if the office statements are delayed. In a few cases where it is necessary to pay cash for approved purchases, a requisition for reimbursement is sent to the business office, which in turn sends a check to cover the amount spent.

Payment of Bills

In the situation in which a business office handles the money, bills are usually paid once a month for the department. Some organizations, however, have their own banking and checking accounts. In this case, the treasurer approves expenditures, and receives and pays all the bills. Usually expenditures over a designated amount require the advisor's approval. If a board or association handles its own finances exclusively, it is essential that bills be paid promptly, that checking accounts are balanced and approved periodically, and that audits are conducted periodically.

DISCUSSION QUESTIONS

1. The financial support for the recreational sports program may come from the general school budget. What are some of the advantages of this plan? Are there any disadvantages?

2. Do you consider gate receipts an acceptable and adequate means of financial income for the recreational sports program? Would you accept gate receipts as a source of income with certain qualifications?

3. Is the typical student adequately trained and experienced to act as treasurer and to manage the finances of the total recreational sports program?

4. Is an organized financial plan necessary to handle all monetary transactions of the program?

5. What are several of the more acceptable sources of income for the recreational sports programs?

6. What are several of the common expenses of this program? Which of these should be assumed by the department?

7. Describe the steps considered essential in developing anticipated expenses for a proposed budget.

8. Describe the steps considered essential in developing anticipated income for a proposed budget.

9. Procedure for adopting a budget is usually unique for each school situation. Discuss several common procedures.

10. Outline a system of purchasing, payment of bills, and bookkeeping that is practical in a recreational sports program in (a) schools, (b) colleges, and (c) communities.

BIBLIOGRAPHY

BUTLER, GEORGE D., *Introduction to Community Recreation,* 5th ed. New York: McGraw-Hill Book Co., 1976.

MEANS, LOUIS E., *Intramurals: Their Organization and Administration,* 2nd ed. Englewood Cliffs, N.J.: Prentice-Hall, Inc., 1974.

National Intramural-Recreational Sports Association, *Annual Conference Proceedings*. Annual Proceedings from 1975 to present.

PETERSON, JAMES A., ed., *Intramural Administration: Theory and Practice.* Englewood Cliffs, N.J.: Prentice-Hall, Inc., 1976.

Publicity Media.

13

Publicity and Public Relations

Favorable publicity is often basic to the successful promotion of the recreational sports program. To use it most effectively is as great a challenge as developing a variety of effective and unique publicity techniques. When a structured plan is organized with the aim of establishing favorable attitudes and responses as well as serving as a medium of communications, it is by definition a good public relations program.

PUBLIC RELATIONS POTENTIALITIES

The potentialities of a public relations program for recreational sports challenges creativity in many unexplored areas. Contacts with people who can give media time or space are important, as is skill in writing a news item or television script. A specific ability is required for focussing the public relations effort, one that is uniquely adapted to a given situation.

Sometimes the development of effective publicity suffers neglect because such terms as "publicity," "advertisement," and "sell" have acquired a commercial connotation offensive to some directors and educators. And there is some tendency on the part of administrators to lessen their activity in this direction because they believe that a good program serves as the source of its own publicity.

Commercialism should be sought out in promotion as well as in programming and controlled when identified. It is important to realize that a planned program of publicity and communications can serve either itself or the recreational sports program. The first results in measuring success by the amount of material put out (lines of news coverage, time on the television or radio, number of printouts, booklets, or handouts) or total expenditures. But this is not the proper measure of success for the recreational sports program. What matters here is the positive impact of the program of publicity on the community and on the participants.

An in-depth dimension can be added to the design of publicity techniques if the public relations program is supported by a fundamental philosophy that places the interest of the participants first. Specific targets such as increasing participation, gaining public support, and stimulating interest and attendance can be related to interpretations of the basic principles of a particular sports program.

Because public opinion decides the importance of programs, this opinion often needs to be influenced to effect support of worthwhile recreation activities. That public relations programs can bring about such support is best illustrated by the success the national physical fitness effort has had on promoting an awareness of the need for improved physical and health fitness.

Although the influence of well-organized publicity cannot be underestimated, it must be constantly evaluated to ensure use of the most effective techniques for a particular situation. Coverage of only one segment of a program, such as team sports, to the neglect of individual sports may lose program support. Or a predominance of varsity sports publicity may discourage less skilled participants. Daily newspaper coverage may be good for community recreation programs but of little value for college programs. Certain techniques may become ineffective, as in the case of bulletin boards that gradually become overused and cluttered. With continued assessment and "retooling" of the techniques, the potentials for public relations are limited only by leaders' imagination and good judgment.

PUBLIC RELATIONS STRUCTURES

Structured public relations programs design action and maximize efforts. Designs that diagram action from a national to district to state and local level can also be adapted for a variety of organizational levels: community to districts to neighborhoods; or school boards to administrators to individual schools or PTAs; or student councils to clubs to interested groups. Success reflects the involvement of people.

PEPI of AAHPER

The Physical Education Public Information (PEPI) program of the American Alliance for Health, Physical Education and Recreation reflects the success of a well-structured program. A national program, it is implemented on the local level through a network of volunteers to inform the public about the "new physical education," its concepts and activities. The aim of the program is to "stimulate professional leadership to share with the public the worth of their programs."

A coordinator functions on the national level. A PEPI Action Corps (PAC) serves six districts (S, NW, SW, MW, E, and Central) as regional liaisons, voices, and directors of workshops. State PEPI Coordinators (PCs) stimulate public relations and promotion efforts on the local level and work with the district coordinator.

"PEPI-Grams" from the national level serve as an in-house communications media to keep the coordinators informed on various projects and programs supported by PEPI.

Industries have been involved to lend support to various aspects of the program. E. R. Moore has provided substantial funding for films. The Gillette Company supports expense-paid trips to study physical education abroad. TV spots have been sponsored by a variety of organizations and associations.

PEPI projects also include two 16 mm color films: *All the Self There Is* and *Every Child a Winner*; bumper-sticker logo "Physical Education—The Best Health Insurance"; animated PEPI badges; visual aids; speakers' bureau; weekly news columns; and concerted efforts to stimulate action on the local level.

The successful efforts of PEPI can serve as a model for local programs and can also be a part of those programs by using its available resources.

PUBLICITY RESPONSIBILITIES

Publicity is a prime responsibility. Handled properly, it serves to secure and retain popular respect, to attract members, to help the participants themselves, to teach an appreciation of the values of activities, and to provide a basic communications device by which to publicize the dates and times of events.

Public Respect. Recreation and intramural boards, financed by fees, student funds, and by taxpayers' money have a responsibility to report their activities to involved supportive people, participants, and potential participants—all of whom make the programs possible. Supportive individuals are entitled to know what services their money is providing. An understanding of the many program aspects will also ensure a more sympathetic attitude toward financial problems when and if they arise. Interpreted to the public, a philosophically founded program of varied activity offerings, one that is financially well-managed and accountable, will gain invaluable respect.

Increased Participation. In a public service role there should be an inherent obligation to publicize the "good life." If an organization has something good to offer and something educationally valuable, all prospective participants and individuals should be made aware of it. It is true that the most effective means of "selling" recreation to men and women is through the silent agent of a good program. As the only medium of publicity and interpretation, however, the exposure is limited to those already participating. There is also an obligation to ensure that all potentially interested individuals are informed about the "what, when, where, and how" of program activities. Communicating this information should be done using all practical publicity means within the limitations of the controlling budget. At the same time all media should be honest and accurate and prepared in an effective yet dignified manner.

Appreciated Values. Program values can be enhanced by a public relations program. Vitally interested, participating groups and individuals made familiar with recreation activity program offerings, aims, and purposes will respect and support the value of its services. Potential participants reached by the publicity program often are awakened to recognize that the offerings are valuable to them. Effective communications will also gain support and appreciation from the nonparticipant who better understands the program. It is a responsibility of communications to gain support of these varied groups and thus ensure the program's future.

Communications Devices. Publicizing recreation events, including the date, time, and place, by using the most effective device is essential if the participants are to grow in number, to appreciate the program, and to take advantage of participation opportunities. This responsibility can be assumed by maximizing the effectiveness of well-selected communication devices as exemplified by (1) well-placed posters, (2) good timing of news articles, (3) effective distribution of pamphlets, and (4) selective audience time for radio and TV.

ELEMENTS OF EFFECTIVE PUBLICITY

Publicity intended to change thinking, develop positive imagery, stimulate interest, and announce events for many people has to be organized as a plan to be carried out over a period of time. The reluctant public or participant is effectively reached by a publicity plan that functions over a period of time through a steady flow of information covering a broad prospectus of the recreation program. Included as part of the plan, however, should be short-term publicity directed at immediate goals and including posters, notices, and flyers to attract supporters for a particular event or activity. Although limited in affecting student and public opinion, short-term publicity may be effective in a particular situation.

Interpretation. A special effort should be exerted to interpret the educational and recreational value of activities to the community, administration, teachers, and youth. If these groups are enlightened and helped to realize the increasingly important role of recreation in the American way of life there will be greater appreciation of the program and more vigorous verbal support, both of which would ensure favorable public judgments.

Motivation. There is a large segment of our population—boys and girls, young men and women—who will always take the initiative and take advantage of recreational opportunities of which they are aware. For these individuals, the recreation leadership has merely to assume the responsibility of prominently displaying activity schedules, dates of special events, and the extension of an invitation to participate.

There is another group of potential recreation beneficiaries. This group is composed of people who have to be convinced that it is worthwhile to participate and that they in particular should become active, participating members. They present a real challenge because they have to be educated and motivated through publicity.

Involvement. The most effective kind of publicity is that generated as a result of involving people. A creative publicity program should strive to involve board members, officials, teachers, administrators, and citizens.

Participation. What is the activity? Where is the action? When does it take place? Notices are vital to the schedule, and they have to be timely, accurate, and conspicuous. The participants will arrive only if they know what, where, and when.

PUBLICITY COVERAGE

The following items based upon the public's interest and need for information are suggested as being most valuable coverage for publicity purposes.

Promotion. Publicity should include promotion material that arouses interest in the program. This is particularly important in the beginning of the season, before special events, and at the beginning of a tournament, meet, or competitive contest.

Activities. Prospective participants will want to know the particular program of activities, the details of organization, game schedules, progress reports, results of the games, and team standings.

Program Objectives. Constitutions contain abbreviated statements of the aims and purposes of an organization. These should be elaborated upon and presented in a concise and easily understood manner for the interest and information of the present and potential membership.

Administration. The administrative organization of the program should be interpreted; the responsible personnel need to be made known to the public; rules, regulations, and required procedures should be publicized.

Standards. Professionally respected recreation programs are based upon recognized standards and should be made known to the public.

Finances. The membership and financial supporters of the program are interested in the operating costs. They should be provided with budget information and an accounting of expenses and income in some interesting and, preferably, pictorial way.

Personnel and Personalities. In many situations there are members and/or personnel who have had unusual recreational experiences or have had to overcome handicaps in order to enjoy participation. These experiences should be shared with others through publicity.

Instruction and Supervision. Often, outstanding leaders in the field provide instruction or act as consultants in the recreation programs. Publication of this information is valuable, attracts members, and is justly due those specialists who devote time and energy to the association.

Novel and Unusual Occurrences. Funny or uniquely newsworthy stories, feats, or incidents often take place at recreation activities. They are of general interest and should be shared with the public.

Participation and Growth. Everyone is interested in figures and numerical pictures of fellow participants who enjoy the activities or programs with which they are familiar. It is also interesting to see the growth of the program through an increase in participants, activities, and funds. Furthermore, all people like to be associated with a growing department or organization.

Participation Values. Although most individuals have a vague notion of why they participate in physical activity, it is worthwhile to point out these values to them in some form of publicity. This lends status to the program and enhances the participating members' satisfaction in doing something worthwhile.

Programs. The yearly program should be presented to the public; then the seasonal programs, and, more specifically, the program highlights should be publicized.

THE PUBLICITY COMMITTEE

Because publicity is the backbone of popular interest in the program, the intramural board and recreation administrators should concentrate their efforts on developing a strong publicity committee. Success in ob-

taining well-trained and interested personnel for publicity responsibilities is often achieved by cooperating with school departments such
as journalism, English, art, and similar related areas. Students specializing in these areas are often able to combine their work with an interest in
sports.

One of the first tasks for the committee is to decide what to publicize
and at whom to direct its energies. Next, the committee should organize
its activities on several levels. (1) The internal leadership should be well-
informed and convinced of the value of the recreation program.
Further, it should be aware of and support the public relations program.
(2) Short-term campaign publicity should be aimed at getting individuals
out for a particular tournament, party, or recreation function. (3) Seasonal publicity should stimulate interest in a broad offering of seasonal
activities and their values. (4) Long-term educational publicity should
interpret the value of recreational activity and present the objectives of
the association and the standards that are practiced and observed.

Publicity on these levels should then be directed at a wide span of
individuals and groups. The publicity committee should direct some
publicity to the following:

Leadership Personnel	*Local*
Elected officers	Administrators and chairpersons
Appointed chairpersons	Community interest groups
Assisting staff	Parents and civic leaders
Assisting community members	Students and student organizations
Participating members	Teachers and faculty
District	National professional organizations
District interest-related organizations	National publications
District recreation publications	National recreation associations
Other schools	
District professional organizations	

It is advantageous to outline the kind of publicity for each level and
to indicate how it is to be directed to the specific individuals and groups.
Once outlined, it becomes the committee members' responsibility to
carry it out.

Excellent guidelines for a publicity committee are available in the
publicity handbook published by Sperry Hutchinson Company. It proposes the following four steps:[1]

---

[1]*Publicity Handbook,* copyright by The Sperry and Hutchinson Company (Fort Worth,
Texas: 1972), pp. 3–5.

FOUR STEPS TO GOOD PUBLICITY

Step One: Contacts

As publicity chairman your most important allies will be newspaper editors and broadcast personnel. If your predecessor didn't give you a list of these people, start right now to build one for yourself and your successor. Such a list may include several contacts at large newspapers, where special interest departments are edited by different people.

You are important to the people you need to know. Editors and program directors are interested in getting to know you as a news source.

Try to determine by an advance phone call what is the least busy day and hour for those you wish to call on in person. Go to them well prepared with facts about your club. Type your name, address and phone number and the name of your club on a sheet of paper to leave with each person you call on. Make your get-acquainted visit brief. Media people are very busy.

Ask what their deadline is, how they like to have copy presented. Be prepared to answer their questions about the general aims and specific program of your club for the coming year.

Before you leave, write down your new contact's name, title, phone number and exact mailing address. The inside back cover of this handbook is a good place to keep such a list.

Newspaper editors and program directors in large cities should be contacted by phone. When you've reached the proper person, get and give the same information as in a personal visit. Then confirm it all in a brief note, saying that you look forward to working with him.

Step Two: Tools

Effective publicity is easier when you have good "tools" for the job. You'll get them from several sources.

This handbook is one.

Many news media people will supply you with guides to follow in preparing copy for them.

An important tool from your club secretary is a complete membership roster. Make sure it is accurate.

A well-outlined program of important events and special projects for the whole club year is a *must*.

A date book with lots of room to note deadlines and plans is an invaluable tool. School supply stores sell September-to-June datebooks, perfect for the club year!

Typing your publicity is important. If you don't own a typewriter try to arrange for the use of one for your publicity work. (Perhaps a member will donate a used machine?)

Assemble a scrapbook of your year's publicity as you go along. Paste in it clippings of every newspaper story. Add your own notes of radio and television publicity and any other media used. Such a record will help you avoid monotony as you work through the year. It will also be a valuable tool for your successor.

Keep all your tools in one place. You are then ready to meet with club officers at a moment's notice, prepared to suggest the next step in the year's publicity program.

Step Three: Decide What Is News

Newspapers used to carry reams of what they call "chicken dinner news." Whole columns were devoted to reports of routine meetings, names of those attending, refreshments served and other matters of interest only to members. Today's newpapers carry little of this sort of copy. World news has crowded it off their pages. The same is true of broadcast media.

Your club secretary is expected to notify members to pay dues, or to bring a covered dish, or that a baby sitter will watch the members' tots.

You must learn to recognize and use for publicity only those things that interest others.

Will your news interest non-members in the community? The state? The whole country? Or are you asking the editor or broadcaster to tell people something they couldn't possibly care about? If so, they won't use it. They needs NEWS. Their job is to capture the attention of their audience and hold it. Editors like reliable sources of lively copy.

You can be the originator of a more interesting club program if you issue a tactful challenge to the club officers. "Give me something to publicize," is a request that often works wonders. When members are made aware of the need to *do* newsworthy things they are apt to develop programs and projects that have good news value.

What do you do if something totally unexpected happens? What if an otherwise routine meeting suddenly develops into news that will interest outsiders?

Jot down accurate notes of what was said and by whom, or what club action was taken. Get in touch with your newspaper or broadcast contact immediately after the meeting. Tell briefly what took place and why you think it's news. Then let the media person be the judge of its usefulness.

Step Four: Focus On the Right Audience

It has been said that the difference between amateur and professional publicity is that the amateur thinks of his *story* while the professional thinks of his *audience*.

Decide first what audience you want to reach:

> *Do you want to build membership?*
> *Do you need public support for a special project?*
> *Would you like to draw people from another area to your town or neighborhood for a fund-raising event?*

What group of people will be most interested in your news? As you plan your publicity campaign always keep in mind the special-interest newspaper departments and the radio and television shows prepared for specific audiences. These include:

Religion	Men's Clubs	Fashion
Civic affairs	Women's Clubs	Food
Sports	Teens	Recreation
Education	Travel	Conservation
Fraternal	Gardening	Health and Medicine

When you've decided which audience you want to reach, develop a "news peg" for your publicity. Relate your story to the interests of the audience you hope to influence.

Then seek the cooperation of newspaper, radio and television professionals who reach that audience.

These Things Can Be News:

Club elections	Benefits that need public support
New projects	Awards won, or awards given
Outstanding speakers	Anniversaries of club
Unusual action or occurrence	milestones
at club meetings	Athletic events
Entertainment	Craft and hobby shows
Tours, study sessions,	Competition with other groups
demonstrations	Civic events that
Fashion shows	involve club members
Resolutions on matters of	Member participation
public interest	in local, national
	and world affairs

PUBLICITY METHODS

Many techniques can be used by a publicity committee. The following pages describe some of the practical ways of circulating information and publicizing a recreational sports program.

Bulletin Boards and Displays

Bulletin boards and displays are the most widely used media of publicity, yet undoubtedly are the most misused and abused. Neatness, timeliness, and attractiveness are necessary for effectiveness.

Bulletin Boards. This publicity medium is an easy yet effective means of announcing events or calling students' attention to particular activities. The boards need to be conspicuous, neat, eye-catching, and up to date. Arrangements that are well-organized, attractively prepared, and changed frequently will cause students to look and read. Harmonious color combinations, printed headings, pictures, and neatly typed notices contribute to making bulletins attractive. A responsible person should take care of the board, develop new ideas, collect pictures, and make attractive arrangements of the materials. All notices should pass through the hands of the person in charge and approval for posting should be required.

Tournament charts, activity posters, and alphabetical letter sets are available from commercial concerns. Often these are attractive, and their use facilitates keeping calendars and tournament scores posted as part of a permanent bulletin display.

Bus Ads. Publicizing in school or public buses is often used with great originality and success.

Charts and Pictorial Displays. Usually the various managers' reports are a part of a larger summary of the board's or association's activities. Often an annual report is summarized and presented in the form of graphs, pictures, charts, and diagrams. This material, along with descriptions and interpretations, can be very effectively used for special informative bulletins.

Daily Sports Bulletin. A habit-forming means of notifying students of daily recreation events is that of posting a daily sports bulletin. Such a notice, if always posted in the same place, soon becomes known, is watched by potential participants, and serves as a daily reminder.

Exhibits Displays. The major advantage of this form of publicity is that it enables the public to see and handle equipment, costumes, books, or to be a part of a "do-it-yourself" exhibit.

Permanent Displays. A work-saving publicity device is that of developing permanent displays that can be used year after year and for several purposes such as freshman orientation, playdays, PTAs, and conferences. These displays can consist of permanent posters or charts kept in folding display cases. Trophy cases and similar permanent exhibits also stimulate interest.

Posters. With permission of faculty and store owners or the help of alumni and friends, timely posters can be placed in strategic locations such as department or dorm bulletin boards, store windows, theater lobbies, and restaurants. Posters, however, must be original and attractive to be noticed. They should be put up about a week before an event and afterwards taken down promptly. General posters need to be changed often. Something new will attract people's attention; but if the posters are the same day after day, they will be ignored.

Mail and Flyers

The unique advantage of direct mail as a publicity technique is its complete control of the audience. This can be a great advantage if it is important to get material to a particular group.

Flyers. Flyers can be used in a number of ways: to call attention to a particular activity, to stimulate interest in elections, to present schedules of events, or to introduce the program to the students. If used to present the organization to new students, it should answer such questions as these: What is its purpose? How does one participate? How do you learn about the agenda? In what sports can one participate? What are the benefits of the program?

Packets. It is the custom of various schools to mail to students and alumni packets of literature. The literature tells about the campus and campus activities and lists events and activities in the new year. Each of these packets could also include appropriate literature about recreational activities and opportunities.

Postcards. Letters, postcards, notices, and flyers may be used effectively when mailed on a group basis to sororities, dormitories, rooming houses, clubs, and individuals. Many organizations develop a mailing list of prospective participants. Each one on the mailing list is then sent a card with valuable information, appropriate pictures, or drawings. Often this information includes the season's or year's schedule of activities, officers, directors, special events, and pictures of the activities and/or responsible personnel.

Movies and Photography

Movies and photography represent a very effective publicity medium. The motion picture, an extremely potent force in molding public opinion, has not been used extensively by recreation associations. However, reduced costs of operation over the years may make it more practical.

Association Movies. Some sponsors of recreation programs, with the help of experienced photographers, have made motion pictures, filmstrips, or slide series of their activities. Such publicity aids can be designed to acquaint freshmen and new students with the opportunities and activities offered by the association.

Commercial or Rented Movies. Sports activities, competitive events, and recreation activities are increasingly being recorded on film. Since recreation-minded individuals usually have a broad interest in these activities, use of films proves a valuable publicity technique. Appropriate films can be rented from numerous college or commercial film libraries.

Photographs. Action photographs of students participating in sports are valuable in attracting interest. Often students with their own candid cameras can get excellent action publicity shots. A student or amateur photographer might assume the responsibility of taking publicity photographs. A most effective way of stimulating interest is the use of large, good, clear photographs on posters, in publications, and on bulletin boards as graphic descriptions of the program activities and personnel.

THE THREE B'S FOR GOOD NEWS PICTURES

1. In general, the three B's for good news pictures are: Babies, Beasts, and Beauties. To which we'd add a fourth: *Be doing something.* Don't just have your models sit or stand there. Work out action plans in advance, either through consulting with the editor or the photographer.

2. Be sure to check the editor to find out how many models he likes in any one picture. Two or three persons are generally the limit. Follow his wishes to the letter.

3. When you choose your models, do use the prettiest or best-looking members. Honor your leaders and hard workers in some way if they are not photogenic. They will live to bless you for it even though they may be offended at the moment.

4. Have your models wear simple, classic clothes. Wear light colors for a dark background, dark colors for a light background. Never photograph mature women in short sleeves or in profile. Avoid white gloves; they detract attention from faces in the picture.

5. Follow the photographer's suggestions for picture composition. A good photographer has this special knowledge; he may also have definite orders from the editor, if sent from a newspaper.

6. Be ready to work quickly. Have everything ready so the photographer can get to work quickly on arrival. The publicity chairman should be his contact, ready to answer his questions and identify by name and title the people he photographs. A typewritten list which he may keep is most helpful to a photographer.

7. If the photographer comes from a distance, send him written instructions how to find the place. Also give him a telephone number where he can reach you in case of delay.

8. Photographers, like reporters, are always treated as guests at any function they cover. If food is served, be sure to offer it to them.

9. When you send them pictures editors will tell you how to prepare and attach captions to any photographs you submit.

10. As a general rule, the caption (identification of the models) is typed on a piece of plain white paper. Leave paste-up space at the *top* of the sheet.

Then paste about one inch of the caption sheet to the *bottom* of the picture, attach it on the back, or reverse side, with the typing up. Fold the caption up over the face of the picture.

11. NEVER use a paper clip, and NEVER write on the back of a picture. Either of these will likely damage the print finish, spoiling it for reproduction.[2]

Photo File. Photographs, pictures (of officers, managers, board members, and outstanding events), cuts, illustrations, and artwork should be kept for ready use. A file should be developed and added to each year.

Personnel and Programs

Example and good programs often "speak louder" than words and mechanical means of publicity.

Orientation Week. Orientation week or freshman camp is very often included as part of the introduction program for new college students. One part of this program is usually devoted to an introduction of the campus organizations. The recreational sports program should be presented to the students at this time. Leadership of the activities might present the various aspects of the program through talks and a variety of appropriate publicity techniques.

Participating Membership. The public obtains many impressions of recreational sports through the participants. Each student forms an opinion of the program and passes it on to friends and family. It is important, therefore, that this avenue of publicity be developed. The participants should be given an understanding of what is being attempted through the program offerings, the problems involved, and the progress being made.

Personnel. The board members, officers, and managers represent the organization and often by their example contribute a great deal of good publicity. These leaders should be well-liked people, whose speech, dress, walk, and attitudes naturally command respect and admiration. Leaders who carefully plan meetings, making them interesting and helpful, who encourage members to exercise initiative in carrying out their responsibilities, and who give credit to others instead of claiming it for themselves, develop a strongly supported organization and good public relations. Board members frequently discuss recreational sports activities with their roommates and dormmates. If these individuals reflect

[2] Ibid., pp. 3–5.

enthusiasm and loyalty to the program, they, too, will gain public support for the program.

Program. The program itself is the best single means of continuous and reliable publicity. A good program with "sold," enthusiastic, and satisfied participants is a fundamental for all publicity and the best technique an organization can use to promote its program. The daily or yearly program provides objective publicity that can be seen or experienced at any time.

Talks by Athletic Leaders. The officers, managers, and directors of the program should take advantage of all speaking opportunities to interpret the values, activities, and accomplishments of their organization. Good public relations is dependent upon commendable presentations. Speeches, therefore, should be well-prepared. The topic and material should be carefully selected and should be of interest to the listeners. An inexperienced speaker will reflect a better mastery of subject if the speech is written out in full, with careful consideration in the choice of words, rhetoric, and thoughts. It should be developed with an interesting beginning, a clear, dynamic summary or conclusion, and a delivery time of about twenty minutes. After experience in presentation only notes should be used, and progressively less and less written material. A sincere interest and enthusiasm in the subject will be reflected in a more effective presentation.

Publications

Publications represent many media that can be used to alert and inform a large audience about the recreation program. In order to ensure consistency in the publicity program and observance of policy, the content of all publications should be approved by someone in a position of authority. This should be handled by approval from the advisor, director, or a member of the physical education department.

Alumni and School Bulletins. Administrations often send out alumni news bulletins or official information bulletins as a means of keeping interested personnel informed of the school's activities. The recreational sports program should be adequately represented in these publications.

Association Rap Sheets. Many departments and associations publish their own weekly, monthly, or quarterly mimeographed news sheets. A great variety of news stories, notices, and reports can be included in these publications. Income-producing advertising can also provide some financial support. Such a paper is valuable for keeping staff members and students informed of the planned activities.

Bulletins. Some large recreation departments send out colorful bulletins to periodically announce coming events, give end-of-season reports of winners, supply entry blanks, and give a calendar of the upcoming season. Small schools use bulletins to distribute to classroom bulletin boards.

Calendars. Mimeographed or printed calendars developed as schedules for the year are very popular and do a fine job of presenting the program to the public. Calendars have been used as orientation materials for new students and have included information such as (1) the names and addresses of directors, officers, and sports managers; (2) a day-by-day schedule of recreational activities completed for the year; (3) a list of open hours for informal sport, dance, and recreational participation; and (4) the seasonal sports tournament schedule.

Handbooks. Booklets, handbooks, and folders of information concerning seasonal or yearly activities are effective. Valuable and informative material can be presented in an attractive booklet form. Some departments publish intramural handbooks which are given to staff, managers, captains, houses, and interested personnel. However, the expense of printing and photographs has to be considered. To reduce the cost a much less expensive mimeographed booklet or handbook can be produced.

Local Newspaper Articles. The newspaper can be used effectively if it reports activities and schedules in a regular sports column. The public can be kept informed of worthwhile future events and results of championship playoff tournaments.

The best printed coverage will be the result of good relations with the local or school newspaper staff. Complimentary tickets or invitations to the various functions will encourage reporters to visit the activities and write the stories. Interviews with the necessary personnel should be arranged or scheduled for news reporters. Accurate facts, figures, and names should be quickly available.

In situations where the stories have to be prepared, the writer must know a little journalism and must be aware of the three kinds of news stories: (1) results of an event just concluded, answering the basic questions, "Who did what, when, where, and how?"; (2) an advance notice of something that is going to happen which answers the basic questions in the future tense; (3) feature stories that generalize over a period of time and in which the writer explains, interprets, describes, and develops a subject for the purpose of informing or giving practical guidance.

The writing reporter's style should be brief and accurate, including pictures when possible and using the correct and desirable newspaper format. In a newspaper story, the most exciting and important fact is in the headline, which is developed in the first paragraph. Each succeeding paragraph tells the remaining facts in decreasing order of importance. If an article has to be cut, the least important material is deleted from the end of the article.

BASIC B'S FOR PUBLICITY

1. Be the only person from your group to contact the news media. Two members calling the same newspaper editor or program director are bound to bring conflict or confusion.

2. Be quick to establish personal contact with the right persons at each newspaper, radio and television station in your area.

3. Be sure to write everything down. Train your memory, but don't trust it.

4. Be prompt in meeting every deadline.

5. Be legible. Type news releases. Erase and correct errors. Don't use carbons, except for your own file copy.

6. Be accurate. Double check dates, names, places before you submit your copy.

7. Be honest and impartial. Give credit where due.

8. Be brief. Newspaper space and air time are costly.

9. Be brave. Don't be afraid to suggest something new if you honestly believe you have a workable idea. Media people welcome original ideas when they're practical and organized logically.

10. Be business-like. Never try to obtain publicity by pressure of friendship or business connections. Never ask when a story will appear. Never ask for clippings.

11. Be appreciative of all space and time given your club's publicity. The media giving it also have space and time for sale.

12. Be professional. Members of the press are always invited guests. Never ask them to buy tickets or pay admission. Arrange a special "Press Table" for large banquets.[3]

News Service. Large programs are fortunate in having publicity departments. Such departments have experts who gather and write the news, take pictures, and organize and select the media in which it is to be published. Alert recreation directors or administrators will take advantage of this opportunity to keep the news service informed of their activities.

Pamphlets. All kinds of pamphlets, mimeographed bulletins, and handbills can be used effectively. Some of the following may stimulate new

[3]Ibid., p. 2.

ideas: seasonal sports announcements listing sports and activities for the particular season; names, addresses, and phone numbers of managers and other personnel who may be in demand; pamphlets in the shape of sports equipment, clothing, or sports figures; the purposes and activities of the association stated in poetry; pictures of officers, board members, and managers with cut-out, photographed heads and miniature stick figures symbolizing their offices; organization charts with pictorial representatives of the various offices.

School and Department Catalogues. Many schools and departments publish periodical information notices, which are sent to alumni and interested personnel. Editors of these publications may be approached to suggest the inclusion of information about the activities of the recreation program.

School Yearbook. A yearbook is a tradition in most high schools and colleges. Sections of this book are usually devoted to various school organizations. The recreation organization publicity committee may want to plan an attractive layout highlighting the year's activities.

Souvenir Programs. Programs of sports events often include sections devoted to pictures, statements of objectives, standards, values, or announcements of particular recreation events.

Student Campus Paper. Most schools have some kind of periodic publication. It may be a daily, or weekly, or even a monthly newspaper. Because the campus publication is a powerful factor in molding opinion and informing students and faculty, it should be fully utilized for disseminating news. Daily recreation and sport columns, feature articles, and weekly sports schedules should be included in these publications.

As is true for the town newspaper articles, the campus reporter for men's or women's sports should know what constitutes news stories and how news stories are prepared. This individual should assist the representatives of the campus paper in every possible way and should have a good understanding of the sports activities.

Windshield and Bumper Stickers. Reminders, slogans, or short campaign-type publicity often use this medium very effectively.

Radio and Television

Radio and television as communication techniques offer unparalleled opportunities, and should not be overlooked by any publicity committee.

Radio. The radio is becoming more accessible as an instrument to influence public opinion, and many local radio stations welcome educational programs or "shorts." Some stations set aside a certain amount of time for such programs, and the recreation association has merely to contact the person in charge of programming to be allotted some specific time. In other instances, established programs welcome guests or guest programs. If there is a broadcasting station in connection with the school, contact is easily made through the audiovisual department. Both students and teachers have opportunities to interpret and publicize their departments and organizations through radio.

Television. As a publicity medium, television has become as popular and as available as radio. Through local stations, closed circuits, and school stations, recreation associations and boards increasingly have opportunities to present various aspects of their organization to the public. This powerful publicity medium can be used for features on sports, sport announcements, demonstrations, powerful, live presentations of activities in action, or film clips of recreational sports programs. As a means of publicity it is quite within the ability of students and directors and affords valuable experience.

Talk, Drama, Demonstrations

Speech, as a primary method of communication, has a great personal appeal and serves public relations very effectively. Drama and demonstrations supplement oral communications.

Assembly Programs and Pep Rallies. School assemblies offer an excellent opportunity to educate pupils, parents, and teachers about recreation. These programs can feature such things as demonstrations of sports techniques, safety measures, talks by the school doctor, and fashion shows with an emphasis on posture and sport clothes.

Demonstrations. Representative and interesting demonstrations of physical recreation activities should be presented before the public, educational groups, student clubs and organizations, and before student gathering centers. If executed well, demonstrations are valuable visual representations of the organization's activities.

Dramatics and Skits. Drama and skits can be used most effectively to rouse enthusiasm, to put information across, or to obtain support for the program. These can be given in dorms, assembly programs, and meetings.

Exhibitions. Many recreation programs or clubs have developed exhibits. Some of those which attract interest and provide information have included exhibits of equipment, safety practices, clothes, facilities, and skills. These are generally displayed in public places such as store windows and public or school buildings.

Loudspeaker. In areas in which this is permitted, a traveling advertising vehicle with signs and/or loudspeaker can be very effective in getting students to turn out for a particular event.

DISCUSSION QUESTIONS

1. How may the potentiality of a good public relations program be fulfilled? What are the possible pitfalls?
2. Outline the structure of the PEPI program of AAHPER. To what do you attribute its unique success?
3. Does a recreation organization or board have an obligation to publicize its program? If not, why not? If so, what are some of the obligations?
4. Well-planned publicity may establish momentum for success in a recreation program. Discuss.
5. What are the elements of effective publicity? What are some of the elements of poor publicity?
6. If you were to plan effective publicity coverage, what aspects of the recreation program would you interpret to the public? What media would you use?
7. How can publicity responsibilities be delegated and administered? Should this be a responsibility of volunteers, students, or staff?
8. What is the role of an effective publicity committee? What levels of publicity should be developed?
9. Enumerate several publicity media and explain why they are particularly effective.
10. Outline a public relations program for a recreational sports program.

BIBLIOGRAPHY

ADAMS, ALEXANDER B., *Handbook of Practical Public Relations*. New York: Thomas Y. Crowell Co., 1965.

Administration of Athletics in Colleges and Universities. ed. by Edward S. Steitz, National Association of College Directors of Athletics and Division of Men's Athletics. Washington, D.C.: American Association for Health, Physical Education and Recreation, 1971.

BUCHER, CHARLES A., *Administration of Health and Physical Education Programs*. Saint Louis: C. V. Mosby Co., 1975.

PEPI-Gram # 9 "A Report of Progress." Washington, D.C.: *Journal of Health, Physical Education and Recreation,* October 1973, pp. 10-11.

Publicity Handbook. Consumer Services, Fort Worth, Texas: The Sperry and Hutchinson Co., 1972.

STARR, EDWARD, *What You Should Know About Public Relations.* Dobbs Ferry, N.Y.: Oceana Publications, Inc., 1968.

League Baseball Awards.
(Courtesy W. David Carew, Director, Maplewood Recreation Department, Maplewood, New Jersey.)

14

Awards, Point Systems, and Records

Whether points should be granted or awards made in the recreational sports program has created controversy. There are leaders who strongly believe that no awards should be made while others are equally convinced of the advantages flowing from the practice and argue unhesitatingly for awards in all forms of competition.

CONTROVERSIES OVER AWARDS

Award systems are intended to serve a variety of functions such as recognition, motivation, publicity, and rewards. These functions differ in importance according to each particular program, and to leadership has fallen the task of deciding where to place the emphasis. If a system is to be designed, a value must be assigned to these functions with respect to their potentiality in contributing to the program's objectives.

Potential Negative Values

Professional leaders who are opposed to the practice of giving awards have pointed out dangers that are worthy of consideration. It is contended that awards and point systems tend to place too great an emphasis on artificial goals. This practice directs the thinking of the participants to gifts and awards rather than the activities and their inherent values. There is a resultant distraction from the fundamental motives of participating for the joy and gratification of playing the game and from such personal benefits as improved physical, mental, social, and emotional fitness.

Acquisition or possession of awards, some observe, encourages rivalry so intense that "means to win" is sacrificed to "win at any cost," which leads to unethical practices. Others point out what appears to be a perpetuating possession of coveted awards by a few groups. Winning teams attract the highly skilled who thereby make it possible for those teams to continue winning the awards.

Some leaders have expressed the opinion that a program develops strength in its major emphasis—recreation for everyone—when there are no awards and no emphasis is placed on individual skill. If the primary purpose is to serve those of all skill levels, recognition of the highly skilled will discourage and, because of feelings of inadequacy, possibly turn away the unskilled.

It is also pointed out that development toward psychological and social maturity is characterized by less need for tangible awards. Therefore, the role of artificial goals should, through the grades, increasingly be minimized and more emphasis be placed on the values of intrinsic rewards as end goals in recreation activities.

Some individuals question whether awards are justifiable financially. Can the expenditure of a large portion of the budget for the benefit of a few award recipients be justified? Is the practice of recognizing a few as champions educationally good?

Potential Positive Values

Some people justify granting awards as a custom consistent with the cultural practice of honoring successful and outstanding performance. These proponents of an awards system contend that man has always competed for prizes and that the principle of awards should not be abolished just because in a comparatively few instances it is abused and overemphasized.

Supporters of an awards system point out that athletic awards recognize the exceptionally gifted in sports while enabling less-gifted individuals to compare their own records of achievement as these are compiled. The recognition extended to highly gifted athletes is said to be comparable to the honors, pins, or certificates granted for outstanding achievement in extracurricular and academic activities.

The warning is issued that competition without recognition and awards soon loses popular appeal. Other leaders believe that an awards system enforces team and individual dependability and they cite the reduction in game forfeitures. And there are those who insist that recognition should be forthcoming to athletes who have played hard and well. They need and deserve recognition, it is said.

Because individuals like to compare their performance levels, it has also been contended that a system of awards stimulates strenuous competitive sports participation, this participation contributing in turn to improved national fitness.

Finally, an awards systems is described as an educational tool that may be uniquely effective. Supporters praise it as a way to foster loyalty and spirit, motivate and increase participation, develop personal pride in accomplishment, and provide a means of setting high ideals of sportsmanship. Some leaders claim that a program will grow under a plan of awards and will die without them.

INTERPRETING THE FUNCTIONS OF AWARDS

An awards system reflects the fundamental philosophy of the program. Often it is a wise procedure for the administration to periodically assess fundamental beliefs and thus clarify program direction and purpose. Having done this, undoubtedly worthy considerations will be found in both the potentially positive and negative values of an awards program.

A practical, yet valuable awards system—one that represents a compromise between abolition and overemphasis—seems possible. Many objectionable outcomes could be minimized if awards were understood as a means to an end rather than as an end in themselves.

An awards system based on a worthy set of values can give team or individual recognition not only for winning but also for sportsmanship, service, participation, and leadership. Also, a well-planned system can grant recognition to outstanding individuals on a variety of skill levels, thus reflecting a belief that "championship" is not the only value worthy of effort and participation.

A sound awards system can use symbolic awards of little monetary value, such as chenille and felt letters, medals, pins, modest cups or trophies, certificates, or ribbons. An award of little or no monetary value will seldom become the major goal of an activity, nor will it threaten the spirit of amateurism.

Value and respect for symbolic awards can be developed if the purposes of the awards are interpreted to the participants, audiences witnessing recognition programs, or readers of news articles. The possibility of granting public recognition at assembly programs, banquets, or in newspapers is worthy of consideration if the interpretation is well handled.

Wise and respected leadership guidance is essential in contributing to the success of a sound awards program. The meaning of intrinsic values needs to be understood by the participants in order to ensure the most rewarding outcomes. Guidance toward these outcomes is a fundamental foundation for the program's development. Both of these requirements can be provided by a skilled leader.

Finally, to achieve an understanding of a good program the proper outlook toward awards must be developed on the part of participants, community members, and all influential leaders interested in the sports and recreation program. Positive attitudes are not possible if external pressures are pulling or pushing personnel in different directions.

The Middle Schools of Renton, Washington briefly interpret their awards program to students, staff, and parents as follows:

AWARDS

Intramural

Each middle school should establish an intramural award system based primarily on participation. An example follows. The example is based upon one point earned for each hour of participation, excluding sports team hours. The points may be cumulative for the two middle school years.

25 points	Certificate of achievement
50 points	School emblem
75 points	School letter
100 points	Pin

Sports Team

Each middle school coach should recognize sports team membership by the awarding of a certificate of achievement to each athlete at the end of the season.

Meet/Game Awards

Trophies are expensive and unnecessary for the sports team program at this level. Individual ribbons or certificates should be awarded to teams and/or individual members of the team.[1]

AWARD SYSTEMS

Tradition perpetuates award systems in many community, school, and college situations. However, if changing times dictate a different approach or an evaluation of the existing system reveals weaknesses or a director initiates a new program, the development or redirection of a

---

[1]Virginia Wyatt, Linda Penny, and Bill Martin, eds., *Middle School Intramural and Sports Activity Guide*, Renton School District No. 403, Renton, Washington, D.C., September 1975.

```
                          AWARD POTENTIALS

Individual Accumulative
        500 pts.            Letter
       1000 pts.            Numerals
       1500 pts.            Pin
       2000 pts.            Blanket or Stuffed Animal
Winners and Runners Up      Ribbons
All Sports Trophy           Presented to that individual who wins the
                            greatest number of 1st and 2nd place rib-
                            bons throughout the year.
Homeroom, District
Class or League Plaques     Presented to that group who wins the
                            greatest number of Place Ribbons.
Sportsman Participation     Presented to the group that accumulates the
Trophy                      highest number of points awarded on the
                            basis of participation, good sportsmanship
                            and fewest forfeitures.
Rotating Sports Trophies    Awarded to that team winning the cham-
                            pionship in a sport. The trophy is retained by
                            the winners until won by another group.
```

Figure 14-1   Award Potentials

system may evolve around acceptable answers to the questions: "Reward What, Whom, How, and When?" (Figure 14-1 illustrates award potentials.)

Reward What?

Place Winners—recognizes the first-, second-, and third-place (or more) winners. Tradition and respect for a champion usually dictate recognition of winners in sports activities.

Participation—recognizes those individuals who participate in a variety of sports activities. Not necessarily highly skilled, these award winners are recognized for the obvious value they place on participating.

Skill—levels attained by participants, and as evaluated by performance tests, have been used as part of an awards program. The evaluation used can also serve in determining improvement awards.

Improvement—by those individuals who work at and value self-improvement in sport skills can be recognized. Evaluation may either be subjective or objective.

Responsibility—assumed by supportive or participating individuals is often recognized by an award. Responsibilities taken on include team manager, captains, or program assistants who help with equipment, refereeing, or supervising.

Character—development of characteristics that are valued outcomes of the sports program can be given recognition.

Reward Whom?

Individuals—as award winners are judged by various criteria such as: the champion tennis, golf, or badminton players; that individual who has shown the greatest improvement, participation, or skill; or that one person who has, through responsibility or character traits, contributed the most to the program.

Groups—as a unit, are often recognized for one or more awards. A team, house, community, league, school, class, or homeroom may be singled out for recognition. Skill improvement, place, skill ability, participation, or any other specifically designated criteria may be used as a basis for identifying excellence of a particular group.

Area—awards can be granted in those situations where participants represent varied geographic areas. A city or county, for instance, may have participants from NE, NW, SE, and SW sectors. School or college programs may include participants from varied but easily defined areas.

Levels of Ability—can be treated as units within which awards are given for any one or more achievements deemed worthy of recognition. A beginners' or advanced unit might recognize first-, second-, or third-class place, participation, or achievement of individuals within the classification.

Homogeneous Classifications—such as age groups, height-weight groups, men's groups, women's groups, or co-recreation groups can be developed. An awards program may then be developed which recognizes achievements within these groups.

Reward How?

Letters—felt or chenille are universally popular. Letters most frequently used include "I" for intramurals, or letters representing the school, community, or particular program. Often a distinction is made by having plain or old English style letters.

Numbers—representing the year of graduation or year of award are well accepted and usually sewn on sweaters or blazers by the recipients.

Trophies—traditionally have had a meaningful role in the sports award program and have included traveling trophies, engraved display trophies, small or large permanently awarded trophies.

Plaques—whether traveling plaques, school or community display plaques, or small individually awarded engraved plaques, these are valued as symbols of recognition.

Pins, Rings, Medals, and Jewelry—of varying kinds used as awards. However, there is a danger that excessive monetary worth awards may obscure the represented goals.

Certificates—hand-printed artistry or commercial forms have been used in a variety of ways to identify winners or achievement (see Figure 14-2).

Figure 14-2   Salem Community Schools and Salem Public Schools Certificate of Award, Salem, Oregon

Ribbons—make excellent awards which the participants value to frame, display, or simply accept as a token of recognition.

Symbolic Awards—of insignificant dollar value are the symbolic or incidental awards that are a part of some programs that avoid establishing traditional items of recognition.

Patches—for varying accomplishments, championships, or participation serve as a part of or as the total recognition program.

Engraved Names—on permanent community or school plaques that are a part of a building or a room are basic to the awards program that grants recognition by adding names to an ongoing list that is preserved for posterity.

Reward When?

End of Tournament—is a popular time to plan recognition and awards ceremonies. This recognition period, however, is often a part of a larger program of awards that might be classified as seasonal, semi-annual, or annual.

End of Season—for those sports seemingly classified by nature into fall, winter, and spring activities is an opportune time to recognize excellence. Within this framework sports competitions and awards are often scheduled within fairly equal blocks of time. Each season is then treated as a unit with no potential award winners carried into another season.

Semi-Annually—is appropriate for those programs that are not identified by seasons. The holiday period often divides the sports year in half. A December and June banquet or wind-up of activities represents the culmination of a six-month season.

Annually—climaxes the year's activities. A yearly awards program, represented by any one of a variety of get-togethers, assemblies, banquets, picnics, or demonstrations is a means of granting recognition to deserving individuals or groups judged on year-long performance. This annual program in some instances is the only recognition given to participants. In other cases it is a program planned in addition to short-term or seasonal awards.

INTERPRETING THE FUNCTIONS OF POINT SYSTEMS

A system of earning points has to be developed if awards are to be included as part of the sports program. The obvious service of a point system is that of providing a basis upon which to grant awards. An overall plan thus must be compatible with the functions of the awards program.

Schools and communities differ in size, facilities, and opportunities to participate in sports activities. It is necessary, therefore, to recognize that point systems will have to be modifed and made appropriate for each situation. However, state associations that have set up point and award programs in which many different schools participate confirm that point systems will have to be modified and made appropriate for common interests.

An overly elaborate point system requires a demanding record-keeping system. Simplicity and numbers that are easy to work with are the keys to an effective plan.

Performance

Is the point system developed to recognize outstanding performance? Recognition of outstanding performance tends to increase the importance of superior skill and winning as a value and goal. The highly skilled are motivated to excellence. The winning of games becomes a dominant value, and performance often is judged by games won. The number of points granted for place winners thus reflects the importance of skill excellence and winning.

Participation

Is the point system developed to recognize a concentration of participation in a selected few activities, participation in many different sports, or primarily to recognize involvement in sports activity? Participation can be stimulated through participation points. Many interests can be encouraged through points awarded players in the many different sports.

Some individuals respond with greater enthusiasm to a program based upon a points and awards plan rather than a program designed only for self-satisfying intrinsic rewards. Defining units of participation and points earned thus reflects the importance of playing in the sports program, and stimulates a continuing interest.

Achievement

Is the point system developed to recognize or encourage skill improvement in particular activities? Some players like to have a representation or record of their improving skills. These individuals respond to the competitive element of improving skills rather than competing to win as an individual or team. Points granted for progressive levels-of-skill achievement reward those individuals who respond best to structured improvement.

Character Development

Is the point system developed to recognize leadership, service, or sportsmanship? If points are awarded for leadership, service and/or sportsmanship, these qualities assume importance. The moderately skilled, the physically limited, or the handicapped are able to participate actively in the points and awards program.

Criteria and procedures for evaluating character traits and services have to be established, and the number of points granted have to be unified. The greatest challenge to granting points for character development is to keep the procedure simple and the criteria standardized.

Equal Opportunities

Is the point system developed with a concern and provision for equal opportunties? Men, women, boys and girls, the handicapped, the unskilled, and the transfer student who would like to receive point recognition for previous participation can all be included as identified individuals in a point system that is designed to strengthen equal opportunties.

Program Growth

Is the point system developed to stimulate program growth? A point system may function to serve one or more participant goals. Of comparable importance is the incorporation of an inherent stimulation to the growth of the program. This can be accomplished by granting points to new participants, rewarding those who involve new participants, or giving point recognition to the expanded interests of individuals.

POINT SYSTEMS

Schedules for awarding points are seldom alike in all details because each program reflects its own environment and leadership. Activities and accomplishments to be awarded are identified and assigned points that reflect local values. In common, however, all systems should facilitate easy administration. The points should be in terms of numbers that are easy to manipulate such as 5, 10, 100. These, in turn, should be granted in accordance with the functions of the point system decided upon and the defined point schedules.

Determine Purpose

The proportion of points awarded for a particular accomplishment will reflect the purpose of the awards program. If, for instance, awards are granted primarily for participation but also for skill achievement, a greater number of points would be given for participation and fewer would be given for achievement. If winning is important, fewer points would be awarded for leadership or participation and more points for first, second, or third place. The number of points given for various activities will reflect the philosophical values of the association or department.

Definitions of Point Values

Refinement of the point system requires point-value definitions of (1) amount of time played, (2) kind of activity, (3) place won, (4) office held, and (5) kind of service rendered. The specificity of these definitions varies from very general broad groupings to a listing of specifically defined activities and their point values.

Classification of Sports

Awarding a specific number of points is often qualified by the classification of a particular sport. Activities are sometimes designated as Division 1, 2, or 3; team competitive, individual competitive; and noncompetitive activities (see Figure 14-3, Points and Awards Classifications of Sports).

SPORTS CLASSIFICATION		
Division 1 (team)	Division 2 (individual)	Division 3 (noncompetitive)
Crew	Gymnastics	Scuba Diving
Touch Football	Track	Spelunking
Soccer	Swimming	Skydiving
Basketball	Tennis	Rock Climbing
Volleyball	Golf	Bicycling
Baseball	Badminton	Hiking
Softball	Sailing	Horseback Riding
LaCrosse	Bowling	Jogging
Hockey	Archery	Conditioning
Rugby	Skiing	Skating

Figure 14-3   Points and Awards Classification of Sports

Under this plan individuals or teams are awarded points that reflect the weighting given to the various classifications of activities.

Points Schedule

The development of a points schedule usually encompasses the supportive roles of responsibility assumed by the many volunteers, as well as the place winners and participants. The specific number of points, the means of earning them, and the weighting (if used) for achievement, participation, and attendance have to be spelled out in easily understood and unitized criteria. The point schedule of Figure 14-4 can be modified to serve particular situations.

	Supportive Roles				Place Winners			
	Entry Partici-pation	Sports-manship	Achieve-ment	Leader-ship	Win. 1	Win. 2	Win. 3	Win. 4
Team Sports Div. I								
Season	10	5	5	5	5	4	3	2
Sports Events	2	2	2	2	3	2	1	1
Indiv/Dual Sports Div. II								
Season	10	5	5	5	5	4	3	2
Sports Events	2	2	2	2	3	2	1	1
Non-Competitive Div. III					Participation			
Season	10	5	5	5	5	4	3	2
Sports Events	2	2	2	2	3	2	1	1

Figure 14-4   Schedule of Points

Accumulative Points

Accumulative points that serve an aspect of the awards program help to maintain interest over a period of time as well as increasing participation by players interested in different sports. Participants' enthusiasm often cools if they lose a couple of games, but they are inclined to continue participation if, under an accumulative points plan, a variety of point rewards warrants their efforts. In order to win points it should be necessary to continue involvement in the activities scheduled throughout the season. In this way a team or individual may not win many sports championships but may earn enough points in all sport activities to gain award recognition.

Noncompetitive Points

With increasing participant interest in noncompetitive activities some programs benefit from a point system that gives due consideration to active participation in hiking, camping, canoeing, spelunking, mountaineering, conditioning, jogging, and similar individual recreational sports activities. Involvement in these activities must be defined in participation units and point-value equivalents.

Negative Points

Some program directors have incorporated negative or minus points as a part of the points system. Under this plan an individual or team earns points for entering a sport or recreation program and for completing the season but loses points for each forfeiture or for dropping out of the sport. Developing dependability on the part of the participants improves the quality of the total program and has a positive affect on all players.

Miscellaneous Points

Some programs have very elaborate plans, but simplicity is effective if the plan basically equates the inequities, gives recognition to worthy efforts, and includes a flexibility that allows for change that is reflected by periodic evaluation.

The awarding of points and awards for participation is gaining favor, particularly in programs aimed at the younger age groups, as illustrated by the certificate in Figure 14-5.

Figure 14-5   Participation Certificate, Fairhaven Middle School, Bellingham, Washington

Other considerations for awarding points might include some of the following:

Accumulative distance swims, hikes, jogging

Accumulative participation hours

Accumulative skill performance

Completion of fitness tests

Completion of skill tests

Service as official, referee, umpire, timer, lines official, scorer

Service as manager, captain, or office recorder

RECORDS AND REPORTS

Records should be kept of all participants and activities in a sports program. A well-designed record-keeping system serves the point and awards program, provides statistical data for accountability reports, becomes the basis for budget projections and purchasing plans, and can serve as a measurement tool for program evaluation.

Simplified Record Design and Filing

Standardized records and forms should be developed with simplicity and efficiency of use in mind. Students, staff, or volunteers who keep the records should be able to do the recording and tabulating with a minimum amount of time and expense. Because of the many uses of a good record-keeping system it will also become a permanent file, and space can become a problem. Forms, therefore, should be designed on standardized cards or sheets and should be as small as practical.

Kinds of Records

Diversity of record needs characterizes the many recreation and sports programs of cities, communities, and schools. It is difficult to suggest forms universally applicable. The following discussion covers several classifications of records, some or all of which might be considered for a particular situation.

Activity or Tournament Implementation Forms. These forms are usually used by the sports manager or team captain who is responsible for a sport or team and has to obtain a list of interested participants, means of contacting them, and their free time or preferences for scheduling activities. This information is usually obtained from a signup sheet that also includes conditions of participation, as illustrated in Figure 14-6.

Eligibility Lists and Attendance Sheets. Because of various participation requirements imposed such as (1) health, fitness, and medical approvals; (2) accident insurance coverage; (3) parental approval; (4) conditioning,

Activity _____

Season _____ to _____

Year _____

Name or Team Team Captain	Address/Contact	Phone	Indicate Available Times			Check Available Days						
			Morn.	After.	Even.	S	M	T	W	T	F	S

Game times will be:

Morning:	7:15 and 9:15
Afternoon:	1:15 and 3:15
Evening:	6:15 and 8:15

Defaults are declared 15 minutes after game time.
Game schedule will be posted at the center.

Figure 14-6   Sports Signup Sheet

practice games, or skill levels, eligibility lists are developed. This is done on an individual name or team basis and is often posted for verification. With the participants and teams "cleared" in the eligibility list, attendance sheets can be developed and the program is underway.

Participation Reports. These reports, for individual and team participation, are the basis for points and awards. Participation reports thus provide the data for the points and awards system. The reports also provide information for summaries of participation, championship performances, and data necessary for year-end accountability and budget reports.

Individuals' participation records (Figure 14-7) provide the data for summary reports that indicate numbers of participants (total girls, boys); and numbers of participation hours the program services in addition to winners and place positions. Team participation records (Figure 14-8) provide the data for summary team reports, activities, win/loss records, and standings.

Activity _____ Season Dates _____ to _____							
One Participation Credit (PC) = 1 hour of participation							
Names Alphabetically	Male	Female	Practice Sessions 2 hrs. Sessions	Tournaments 2 hrs. game	Demonstra- 2 hrs. event	Total Hr. Partici- pation	Place Winner
1							
2							
3							
4							
5							
6.							
7							
8							
9							
10							
11							
12							
13							
14							
15							
16							
Total Participants		Total PC's =					

Figure 14-7   Individual's Participation Record

Activity _____ Season Dates _____ to _____						
One Team Participation Hour (TPH) = 1 hour of participation						
Number on each team _____						
List Names of all Teams	Practice Sessions	Demonstr- ations	Tourna- ment game	Win	Loss	%
1						
2						
3						
4						
5						
6						
7						
8						
9						
10						
11						
12						
13						
14						
15						
16						
Totals						

Figure 14-8   Team Participation Record

Seasonal Summary Reports. For those point and award programs that include seasonal awards, summary reports similar to Figure 14-9 for each sport season are important. Annual long-term and ongoing records are developed from this data.

Davenport, Iowa Community Schools use a participation report form illustrated in Figure 14-10.

Continuous Annual Reports. Annual reports are important for annual awards, accountability, and long-term analysis of program effectiveness and participants' interests. Records of number of teams and participation hours, as well as male, female, and co-recreation participation patterns, provide the necessary data for accountability reports and future planning. A form similar to that shown in Figure 14-11 may serve this need.

A continuous annual report on individuals' participation patterns may be designed similar to that shown in Figure 14-12.

Hurst, Euless, and Bedford Public Schools in Hurst, Texas use the summary form shown in Figure 14-13.

YEAR _____

One Participation Credit (PC) = 1 hour of participation								
Activity	Club		Intramural		Interschool		Total	
	No. Participant	PC	No. Participant	PC	No. Participant	PC	No. Participant	PC
Archery Male__ Female								
Badminton Male__ Female								
Basketball Male__ Female								
Bowling Male__ Female								
Football Male__ Female								
Golf Male__ Female								
Gymnastics Male__ Female								
Soccer Male__ Female								
Softball Male__ Female								
Swimming Male__ Female								
Tennis Male__ Female								
Track Male__ Female								
Totals								

Figure 14-9 Seasonal Summary Report

Points, Awards, Performance Records. Permanent records of names, year's awards, and performance records are often kept for tradition, posterity, and challenge of future performers.

Individual Record Cards. These are basic to the point and award record-keeping system. Each card serves an individual for several years of involvement. Points are posted as earned and often in the case of a student transfer the record card and points are accepted and equated within the recreational sports program. Figure 14-14 illustrates several types of record cards.

State and Affiliate Records and Report Forms. Before leaving this section on reports, a word must be said about possible records for affiliate administration units. State or regional recreation associations may be interested in various aspects of local programs. State departments as well as local boards often request statistics to guide and substantiate decisions.

Evaluation Procedures

An evaluation procedure is an important aspect of planning that should be built into the overall program design. It produces the suppor-

SCHOOL _____ WEEK OF _____

STAFF MEMBER	AM	PM	EVE	G	B	CO ED		STAFF MEMBER	AM	PM	EVE	G	B	CO ED
Aerial Darts							Relays						
Archery							Rhythmics						
Badminton							Rope Activity						
Basketball							Self-Defense						
Free Throwing							Shuffleboard						
Battleball-Bombardment							Skating						
Bicycling							Soccer						
Bowling							Softball						
Cheerleading							Spectator						
Conditioning							Speedball						
Deck Tennis							Sports Days						
Football, T − F							Swimming						
Punt, Pass, Kick							Life Saving						
Frisbee							Synchronized						
Golf							Water Safety Aid						
GRA Activity							Table Tennis						
Gymnastics							Tennis						
Hockey, Field							Track						
Jogging							Cross Country						
Kick Ball							Trampoline						
Life Saving							Tumbling						
Modern Dance							Volleyball						
Officials - Aides							Water Polo						
Paddleball							Weight Training						
Recreational Games							Wrestling & Arm						

TOTAL PARTICIPATION COUNT FOR THE WEEK

Number of mornings used this week ____ ____ ____ ____
Number of afternoons ____ ____ ____ ____
Number of evenings ____ ____ ____ ____
Saturday used ____ ____ ____ ____

Initial Instructors

_____
Signed

Figure 14-10 Intramural Activity and Participation Report, Community Schools, Davenport, Iowa

Team Participation Hours or Number of Teams									
Activity		19 ___		19 ___		19 ___		19 ___	
		TPH	No.	TPH	No.	TPH	No.	TPH	No.
Archery	Male / Female / Co-Ed								
Badminton	Male / Female / Co-Ed								
Basketball	Male / Female / Co-Ed								
Bowling	Male / Female / Co-Ed								
Football	Male / Female / Co-Ed								
Golf	Male / Female / Co-Ed								
Gymnastics	Male / Female / Co-Ed								
Soccer	Male / Female / Co-Ed								
Softball	Male / Female / Co-Ed								
Swimming	Male / Female / Co-Ed								
Tennis	Male / Female / Co-Ed								
Track	Male / Female / Co-Ed								
Totals									

Figure 14-11   Continuous Annual Report—Team

tive data upon which directors and staff make decisions. It is facilitated with good records.

Program support and promotion is revealed in participation data.

Needs and interests can be determined from interest surveys of participants.

Staff effectiveness is determined by mutually developed evaluation tools and testimonies used in conjunction with carefully written job descriptions.

Facilities, equipment and budget needs can be calculated through analysis of the statistics available in the several reports.

Financial accountability can be interpreted in light of participant cost analysis for the various phases of the program.

DISCUSSION QUESTIONS

1. How do you interpret the values of an awards program? Relate the values to several basic philosophical beliefs.

2. Outline an awards system answering the questions "what? who? how? and when?"

3. What are several basic guidelines to be followed in developing a point system? Illustrate their importance.

4. Summarize the potential functions of a point system.

Individual Participation Hours (IPH) or Participants		19 ___		19 ___		19 ___	
Activity		Male	Female	Male	Female	Male	Female
Archery	Club						
	Intramural						
	Extramural						
Badminton	Club						
	Intramural						
	Extramural						
Basketball	Club						
	Intramural						
	Extramural						
Bowling	Club						
	Intramural						
	Extramural						
Football	Club						
	Intramural						
	Extramural						
Golf	Club						
	Intramural						
	Extramural						
Gymnastics	Club						
	Intramural						
	Extramural						
Soccer	Club						
	Intramural						
	Extramural						
Softball	Club						
	Intramural						
	Extramural						
Swimming	Club						
	Intramural						
	Extramural						
Tennis	Club						
	Intramural						
	Extramural						
Track	Club						
	Intramural						
	Extramural						
Volleyball	Club						
	Intramural						
	Extramural						
Totals							

Figure 14-12   Continuous Annual Report—Individual

5. When assigning point values for particular involvements or accomplishments, what definitions are important to develop?

6. Are there positive and negative points in an awards program? How may they be used?

7. What is the justification for record keeping other than for points and awards?

8. What kind of participation report forms would you propose using? Interpret the important features and their value to administration.

9. Describe a record-keeping and data-collecting procedure that would make possible continuous annual reports. What report forms are necessary? Who would complete the various forms?

10. Outline a proposed evaluation procedure for a program and its leadership. Indicate your sources of data.

BIBLIOGRAPHY

Beeman, Harris F., Carol A. Harding, and James H. Humphrey, *Intramural Sports: A Text and Study Guide*, 3rd ed. Dubuque, Iowa: W. C. Brown Co., Publishers, 1974.

Date _____

Name of School _____ Sponsor _____

Activities	No. of Indiv. Stud.	Percentage of Participants to Total Pop.	No. of Teams	No. of Games	Type of Tournament Organization	Number of Drop-Outs	Number of Protests	Number of Forfeits

Figure 14-13   Year's Activity Summary, Hurst, Euless, and Bedford Public Schools, Hurst, Texas

Name_____   Address_____

Telephone_____   Fr. So. Jr. Sr. (circle one)

QUARTER	FRESHMAN		SOPHOMORE		JUNIOR		SENIOR	
	Activity	No. Hours	Activity	No. Hours	Activity	No. Hours	Activity	No. Hours
FALL								
WINTER								
SPRING								
TOTAL			TOTAL		TOTAL		TOTAL	

Awards Given_____   Date_____

Figure 14-14   Individual Record Cards

BENNETT, BRUCE L., *Comparative Physical Education and Sport.* Philadelphia: W. B. Saunders Co., 1975.

BUCHER, CHARLES A., *Administration of Health and Physical Education Programs Including Athletics.* St. Louis: C. V. Mosby Co., 1975.

DAUGHTREY, GREYSON, and JOHN B. WOODS, *Resource Manual for Physical Education and Intramurals Programs.* Philadelphia: W. B. Saunders Co., 1976.

Name .... **Key for Recording Data**

Participation	Club	Intra	Adm	Club	Intra	Adm	Club	Intra	Adm	Club	Intra	Adm
Badminton												
Basketball												
Bowling												
Bridge												
Dance												
Fencing												
Golf												
Hockey												
Lacrosse												
Official												
Rifle												
Softball												
Sportsdays												
Swimming												
Table Tennis												
Tennis												
Volleyb'l (coed)												
Volleyball												
Other												
Total												

Composite Card

Committee	Year	Capacity
Election		
Ex. Board		
Publicity		
Others		

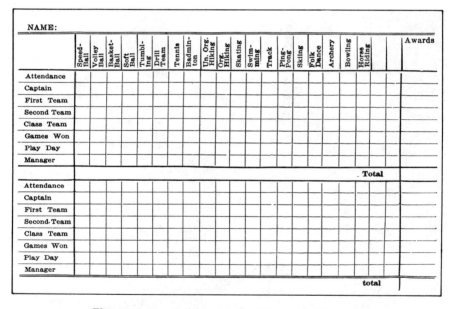

Figure 14-14 Individual Record Cards *(cont'd.)*

———, *Physical Education and Intramural Programs,* 2nd ed. Philadelphia: W. B. Saunders Co., 1976.

MEANS, LOUIS E., *Intramurals: Their Organization and Administration,* 2nd ed. Englewood Cliffs, N.J.: Prentice-Hall, Inc., 1974.

PETERSON, JAMES A., ed. *Intramural Administration: Theory and Practice.* Englewood Cliffs, N.J.: Prentice-Hall, Inc., 1976.

STRAUB, WILLIAM F., *The Lifetime Sports-Oriented Physical Education Curriculum.* Englewood Cliffs, N.J.: Prentice-Hall, Inc., 1976.

Health.
(Courtesy: Marjorie McLaughlin and Diane Feldman of New York City.)

15

Health, Safety, Accidents, and Legal Liability

The administration of the recreational sports program requires an intelligent concern for the health and safety of the participants and a knowledge of legal liability on the part of those who direct such programs if the best interests of both are to be served in an era of growing public awareness and understanding of health and safety. Although the unique aspects of the various programs mean that individualized solutions to problems often have to be sought, still good health and safety practices in all activities reduce accidents and legal involvements.

Health, safety, accidents, and legal liability are closely related administrative responsibilities. Improved well-being of the participants, one of the major assets asserted for a good program of recreational sports, is better assured when details are known of the individual's own health record. If the program is administered in accordance with sound safety practices, all participants are likely to have the best possible experience. However, even when the very best practices are observed with respect to health and safety, accidents will occur. It is important, therefore, that the directors of the recreational sports program handle accidents effectively and prudently and act with an understanding of their legal implications.

HEALTH PRACTICE AND PRECAUTIONS

To increase sports participation so as to ensure the benefits of a recreational sports program to as many individuals as possible is one of the prime responsibilities of leadership. Success of such a program is in part measured in terms of the number of participation hours, but no emphasis on increasing numbers should be allowed to obscure the fact that the program is conducted above all for the health and welfare of the participants. The paramount objective, giving direction and guidance to the recreational sports program, is that of improving, protecting, and conserving habits of good health and physical well-being in all participants.

Every encouragement should be supplied to young people to develop the proper exercise and activity habits needed to retain physiological youth and vigor. This means that a stimulating environment and atmosphere, with proper leadership, are requisites if good health habits are to be developed.

Environment

A healthy environment is conducive to a wholesome recreational sports program. Such facilities as the swimming pool, the gymnasium, locker rooms, showers, and lavatories should be kept sanitary and stocked with the necessary supplies. Adequate care and preparation of facilities for the school-community program require that adequate janitorial schedules be maintained.

Of equal consequence is a healthy mental and social environment. The recreational sports program functions best in an atmosphere where the participant develops the ability to adjust happily to the demands of everyday living. One pathway to self-confidence is successful achievement, and the route should be kept open to all participants, not just to highly skilled athletes. Credit and recognition should be granted to the less skilled individual just as generously as to the more highly skilled individual.

Competition should be planned and directed by trained and understanding leadership. Activity should be tempered by the age of the participant and the amount of exercise for which he or she has been conditioned. For the healthy individual, natural safety valves will normally end activity before any physiological harm can be done. Unusual emotional pressures, however, may influence the action of these safety valves. Medical examinations and signs of fatigue which are familiar to a trained leader should dictate the amount of activity appropriate for each individual.

Individuals should participate in activity to a degree consonant with the results of a sound medical examination. Some of the greatest benefits from physical activity accrue to those individuals who enjoy physically challenging activities. The general prescription of vigorous, strenuous activity for improved health is based upon the assumption that the participant is physiologically healthy and capable.

Precautions

Precautions to be observed by those responsible for the functioning of the recreational sports program include medical examinations, the proper training and conditioning of participants, and steps toward heightening parental understanding of the sports activities. The procedures described below are typically found in the schools, but the principles underlying them are applicable to the college and community scene and the practices themselves may be adapted whenever this is appropriate.

Medical Examinations. Individuals with physiological limitations should curtail the amount and vigor of their physical activity. Often handicapped individuals are unaware of their limitations. In other instances, unwilling to forego the challenge of the game, they do not reveal their restrictions. It must be stressed that those who participate in vigorous activity have to assume the responsibility for their own welfare. Nevertheless, supervision of individuals requires a health follow-up and medical examinations by a competent physician.

Most state high school athletic associations require a certificate of fitness for those pupils who engage in strenuous competition. In other instances, the departments of health and physical education and/or the recreation or intramural board require health checks for participants in competitive activities.

As for the medical examinations, they are often part of the school health service; if they are not, they may be given by family doctors. Whoever gives them, the examinations should be thorough enough to determine the student's physical ability to participate in various recreational sports activities. Just when the examinations are given, and how frequently, varies with different situations; but they should be administered so as to keep track of the participant's changing health status. They are usually given (1) at the beginning of the freshman year or (2) during the freshman and senior years or (3) at the beginning of each year or (4) just before participation in strenuous sports.

The usual practice in schools that administer medical examinations to all students is to keep confidental permanent record folders on them. With this information available, those responsible for administering programs of recreational sports are in a position to learn about individuals who are physically too limited for active sports participation. They may receive from the school health service lists of students who must restrict their physical activity. The notices sometimes include such materials as the doctor's view of the kind of activities suitable for a limited individual.

Training and Conditioning. Youth and young adults in good health may be able to tolerate intensive physical activity and have the capacity to push themselves to a supreme effort, even to the stage of exhaustion, without permanent harm. But proper training and conditioning are needed to minimize the possibilities of physical discomfort and harm. Although recreational sports participation is generally less strenuous than athletics, preliminary physical conditioning and training is important. Inactivity is a problem with respect to high school and college students. If the students have completed their physical education requirement, recreational sports participation is often their only vigorous physical activity. In order to condition the contestants adequately and safeguard their health, training periods or practice sessions should be an important part of the program. For particularly strenuous sports, a minimum number of practice sessions should be required before the scheduled competition. Eligibility could be dependent upon participation in a designated number of conditioning sessions.

In some instances restrictions may be necessary to prevent a certain type of individual from overparticipation in the recreational sports program. If sports participation is demanding too much time, or jeopardizes his or her health, a more balanced school program should be recommended in a personal conference.

Parental Permission. A wise procedure to help ensure good health practices is that of obtaining written parental consent before students are allowed to engage in strenuous after-school competition.

Consent slips often include statements releasing the school from any claims for accidents or injury incurred during the student's participation in the sport. These waivers are not valid before the law if a suit for negligence is instituted because a parent has no authority to waive the claim of a minor. The parent, in effect, waives the right to sue for damages; but the minor may still file suit.

Parents' permission or consent slips and waiver statements are helpful in that parents speak to their children with respect to behavior, dangers, and responsibilities. By implication, they also indicate that the child is physically able to participate. They tend to share with the teacher some of the responsibilities for the health and actions of their children.

SAFETY PROCEDURES

Safety in a recreation program has to be a united approach and a continuing effort on the part of directors, supervisors, student leaders, and participants. Proper safety precautions should be taken with respect to all aspects of the program. Leadership personnel should be aware of and practice good safety habits, taking care, for example, to keep playing areas and facilities safe and free of hazards. It has been estimated that 50 percent of all accidents could have been avoided if proper safety precautions had been practiced. In addition to the previously mentioned health precautions (medical examinations, training or conditioning periods, and parental consent), certain safety procedures should be practiced with respect to participation, competition, instruction, supervision, equipment, facilities, and transportation.

Participation

Since awareness of the requirements for safety helps reduce the number of injuries and accidents, administrators should think in terms of promoting health awareness on the part of all participants. Controlled participation is also important to safety. Injured students should not be allowed to continue. Proper dress and protective attire also have a part to play in taking precautions in a given activity, and the wise administrator will make certain that activities are tailored to the age and maturity of the participants.

Equitable Competition

A policy of planning as nearly equal competition as possible minimizes the dangers of accidents and injuries. Competition between high school students and junior high school students, for instance, increases the possibilities of injuries because of their differences in maturation.

Instruction, Coaching, Officiating

All efforts should be made to minimize accidents or negligence by anticipating possibilities revealed by training and experience. Instruction and coaching methods should include adequate explanations, preliminary exercises, and advice as to the difficulties of particular activities. Logical and necessary progressions should be followed in teaching new activities and new strategies as well as in programs of conditioning and fitness. Officiating should be done by professionally trained and experienced individuals. Play should be controlled. Unnecessary roughness should not be tolerated and participants should be required to wear proper protective gear.

Supervision

The best results are forthcoming from following these maxims. Provide adequate supervision for the activities scheduled at a particular time and see to it that supervisors are present at all times to help with problems and promote the safety of the program. Minimize the possibilities of accidents by constant application of rules and regulations designed to regulate conduct in the gymnasium, showers, swimming pools, dressing rooms, and on the playgrounds. Playgrounds and gymnasiums require supervision during practice or training sessions and all program activities, and it is necessary that those placed in charge be competent and sufficiently numerous to ensure effective supervision in all play areas. Healthful and sanitary practices should be required of all participants.

Equipment and Facilities

Good practices are of the first importance. To begin with, equipment and facilities should be authoritatively approved for safety, and storing should be in an appropriate area with adequate space for their use. Regular inspection will go a long way toward ensuring good working order and absence of defects. The following precautions will provide optimum safety. When a piece of equipment becomes unsafe it should be withdrawn from use immediately and repaired. Facilities should be safe and sanitary. Design should be based upon sound principles of safety. All hazards should be removed. Floors should not be slippery or dangerous. The various areas should be clean and well ventilated. Heat and light should be adequate (see Chapter 16). Play fields and areas should be safe, well drained, without mud and dust, level, and free of obstacles. The areas should be fenced or situated so that children will not run into the street. In those instances where different age levels use the same fields, the grounds should be divided into areas designated for the older and younger pupils. Dangerous facilities and equipment should be available only under specified safety conditions and should not be available to the unskilled. Safety protective devices should be employed where necessary. Adequate protective equipment such as archery arm guards, gloves or tabs, fencing protective weapon tips, plactrons, masks, glasses protectors, mits, shinguards, chest protectors, and similar gear should be provided and kept in good condition. Facilities and equipment should be adequate for the numbers, the age groups, and the activities for which they will be used. Building codes and fire regulations should be observed.

Transportation

Interschool activities such as playdays, sports days, and exchanges for a great variety of recreational sports activities involve teachers and students in transportation responsibilities. Common carriers or school buses should be used in preference to private cars because of their operators' experience in this area and the legal protection they afford. If it is not possible to contract transportation, only responsible and dependable individuals should be allowed to transport students and staff, and safety precautions require defined qualifications and procedures. Written rules of conduct for participants on away activities are equally important for safety. Trips from school seem to stimulate thoughtless or rowdy actions which lead to accidents.

ACCIDENTS

In spite of precautions taken, accidents do occur in the recreational sports programs and supervisors have to know what to do in this event. It is important that those in responsible leadership positions are aware of proper accident procedure, the details of which should be worked out in each organization and department. Appropriate accident policies and procedures should be developed for the various situations. Supervisors should have a thorough knowledge of first aid, including what not to do as well as what to do.

Any accident that occurs on the school grounds and under the jurisdiction of the school should be reported on suitable forms. This report is valuable in correcting causes of accidents and providing the teacher and the school with protection in case of litigation. A written report filed within twenty-four hours of the accident is exceedingly valuable.

Recreational sports directors should have appropriate forms developed by themselves, the school administration, or an insurance agent. Many schools use the form prepared by the National Safety Council. The report should include the following:

Name, address, date, time, place of injury

Circumstances under which accident occurred and how it occurred

Action taken: specific treatment, no treatment necessary, first aid, physician called, hospitalization

Part of body injuried, nature, description, extent, and severity

If possible, signed statements of information from witness or individuals concerned

Physician's recommendations concerning future physical activity: regular, limited, adapted, or no activity

Accident Expenses

Accident injuries usually involve medical expenses. Although the institution has a moral responsibility to handle injuries incurred in the program, actual practice varies because state laws necessitate different solutions to this obligation. Possiblities for paying expenses include the following: (1) the administration pays the bills; (2) an insurance plan paid for by the institution takes care of the expenses; (3) insurance paid for by the student takes care of the costs; (4) parents assume financial responsibilities; (5) legal action is initiated for financial recovery.

Liability. Many institutions observe a policy of paying for all injuries received in sports. Others take care of those injuries which can be handled by the school health services but assume no responsibility for hospital bills, operations, or other expenses. Some schools share the expenses on a fifty-fifty basis with parents. A few states have passed legislation defraying the cost of accident insurance. In other instances students are required to pay the premiums. Teachers, advisors, and recreation association leaders should become familiar with the policy of their school and state.

School Insurance Plan. Insurance has been the solution for many administrators desiring to provide some financial protection to pupils, teachers, and the school. Most state athletic associations offer insurance plans or have athletic benefit plans in effect; otherwise they usually recommend commerical insurance companies. Payment for the policies is by a state appropriation, the board of education, or the physical education or athletic department. Although these plans are usually thought of with respect to the varsity programs, the coverage of "all sports" includes the recreational sports program.

Teacher-Student Insurance Plan. In those institutions which assume no financial responsibility for accidents or injuries it is not uncommon for students and/or teachers to develop their own protective insurance plan through professional associations or commercial insurance companies.

Transportation Accident Expenses

Transportation problems to and from athletic events differ. If a bus company is contracted to carry students, the company's legal responsibility is a condition of the contract. But when transportation is furnished by the school, liability is a school responsibility. If a teacher takes students in his own car, responsibility for accident expenses rests with the owner of the car in nearly all cases.

Because state laws vary, the driver or owner of a vehicle carrying students should be aware of his responsibility. In some instances, if the students are transported by private cars with the consent and approval of the school administration, the school is responsible; and it usually insists upon insurance for all traveling students. Responsibility differs in various states depending upon whether the individual is riding by invitation or request, and distinctions have also been made depending upon whether or not the driver is reimbursed for the trip. Some schools require the driver to have a specified minimum insurance coverage. Teachers should investigate the restrictions of their particular situation and have their liability interpreted by a competent legal authority in case of an accident while transporting children.

LEGAL LIABILITY

Parents burdened with financial expenses of a school accident may turn to the courts for action. A liability suit may be their way of attempting to receive compensation for expenses. Liability, whether it is direct, school board, or individual, cannot be established unless negligence is proved. Negligence is measured against a standard of conduct expected of an ordinarily prudent person.

The definition of negligence indicates the importance of good practices in all aspects of administering and carrying out the recreational sports programs. Adherence to the rules of safety and observation of standards are good insurance against possible negligence by the teacher, supervisor, or administrator. The legal wrong resulting from a possibly negligent act generally involves tort law, a part of civil law which deals with legal rights and wrongs relative to noncontractual relations. Negligence, when it is involved as a basis for tort action, simply implies a failure to use due care in a particular situation not involving a contract.

Although a clear-cut statement of liability is not possible, in most states common law dominates decisions; and teachers, supervisors, and administrators generally are not protected by its immunity. The Tenth Amendment of the Constitution of the United States delegates the responsibility of education to the states; therefore, legislation and interpretation of the law differ in the various states. Furthermore, in recent years there have been attempts to modify the old common law with statutes that impose liability.

District and School Board Liability. In general, school districts, as agents of state and government, cannot be held liable for acts of negligence committed by their officers and employees nor for injuries sustained by pupils, employees, or private persons. This common-law immunity, however, is being modified, and several states have waived the immunity privilege through legislative action.

It is not uncommon for district school boards to be held responsible for negligence in performing official duties. As quasi-corporations, school boards have been held liable for the improper management and use of their property. The position of the school district's liability with respect to pupil transportation is not very clear. Some states require insurance, while in others state money cannot be used to buy insurance. In still other situations, it is a matter of local option. If public carriers are contracted for transportation, however, they, not the school, are responsible legally for negligence.

Teacher Liability. The teacher responsible for a recreational sports program has a moral obligation as a substitute parent (*in loco parentis*) to observe safety precautions and recommend professional practices. Teachers themselves are personally liable for their own negligence. In addition, a teacher is liable for any loss caused by negligence in the performance of duty.

Precautions Against Tort Liability

Recreational sports directors and supervisors who are anxious to know how to avoid tort liability will find the following to be valuable procedures:

Provide adequate supervision and proper instruction in performance of activity and include only activities within the pupils' ability.

Give good instruction, provide safety precautions, establish and enforce safety regulations.

Prohibit pupils from going on errands beyond the school grounds except in real emergencies and only as a last resort.

Assume responsibility for inspection and maintenance of facilities and equipment. Keep a record of regular inspections.

Develop adequate regulations with respect to pupil conduct, transportation of participants and spectators, medical examinations, medical care for the sick and injured.

Establish regulations for going to and from school to participate in extracurricular activities, including supervisory responsibilities which extend from when students leave home until they return.

Use common carriers for transportation.

Define and follow proper procedures which establish away-from-school functions as "school-sponsored."

In case of injury follow an established and acceptable procedure for ensuring wise action.

Make advance plans for medical and hospital care in case an accident should occur.

Whenever an accident occurs, file a detailed report of circumstances, nature of injury, first aid treatment and medical attention, and names of persons rendering service.

DISCUSSION QUESTIONS

1. Describe successful health practices that should be followed in a recreational sports program.
2. Describe the place and importance of medical examinations in the recreational sports program.
3. Is a teacher or supervisor in a recreational sports program liable for his/her negligence? Explain.
4. Can a parent sign away the legal rights of a minor? Explain.

5. If a supervisor in a recreational sports program transports participants in the program in his/her personal automobile, is he/she liable for possible negligence in case of an accident? Explain.

6. What specific information is needed on an accident form after an accident has occurred in a recreational sports program? Prepare a model accident form to illustrate your answer.

BIBLIOGRAPHY

BUTLER, GEORGE D., *Introduction to Community Recreation,* 5th ed. New York: McGraw-Hill Book Co., 1976

MEANS, LOUIS E., *Intramurals: Their Organization and Administration,* 2nd ed. Englewood Cliffs, N.J.: Prentice-Hall, Inc. 1974.

PETERSON, JAMES A., ed., *Intramural Administration: Theory and Practice.* Englewood Cliffs, N.J.: Prentice-Hall, Inc., 1976.

VAN DER SMISSEN, BETTY, *Legal Liability of Cities and Schools for Injuries in Recreation and Parks.* Cincinnati, Ohio: W. H. Anderson Co., 1968.

Participant in New Jersey A. A. U. Jr. Olympics.
(Courtesy W. David Carew, Director, Maplewood Recreation Department, Maplewood, New Jersey.)

16

Facilities, Equipment, and Supplies

Facilities are the classrooms and laboratories of a recreational sports program; they are essential in establishing a comprehensive program. In starting a new recreational sports program, usually there are some existing facilities in a school, college, or community that are already available for sports activities. Therefore, the director of a recreational sports program must move ahead to make use of available facilities, create multiple-use facilities, and work toward the acquisition of new facilities to meet the needs of those who will enter the program.

NEW FACILITIES

Those responsible for approving and designing new facilities must have an exceedingly comprehensive knowledge of the scope and content of the recreational sports program that is to be organized and maintained. Long-range planning is necessary to meet the needs of an evolving program with functional multiple-use facilities. Recreational sports programs that meet the needs and interests of the people are becoming more diversified each year.

School-community and college-community recreational sports programs are becoming the accepted norm throughout the country. To secure a functional, flexible, multiple-use facility at minimum cost, it is essential to have all units that are to be involved with the program involved in the planning stages. In many cases, schools and colleges enter into joint financing arrangements with local agencies such as recreation and park administration agencies and housing authorities to bring forward a superb facility. Increasingly, schools and colleges are the centers for late afternoon, evening, and weekend recreational sports programs.

Financing new facilities for a recreational sports program is usually extremely difficult. The acquisition of land in urban and suburban communities is almost always very costly. Because of the many serious economic obstacles facing the director, many new types of facilities are being constructed. Here are some examples. The high-rise recreational sports building is now the accepted plan of the future. It frequently has a flat roof and extends one or more levels below ground. With land for outdoor fields at a premium, the land that is acquired must become a multiple-use facility with lighting for after-dark activity. Air-supported structures for climate control over outdoor fields are proving to be superior additions throughout the country.

The acquisition and development of land and the building of structures involve a variety of local, county, state, and federal agencies. Executive and legislative approvals must be secured. And environmental safeguards and standards must be observed. Theft and vandalism have become such serious problems within the recreational sports program that preventive measures have now become a major concern receiving special attention in the construction of new facilities.

A new facility should be safe, hygienic, and very attractive architecturally. Recreational sports facilities should be an inspiration to participation. It is very important to be aware that architectural beauty and plant efficiency do not have to be in direct conflict with economizing, as any highly qualified architect will quickly point out. In the building of a new facility, it is exceedingly important to have highly qualified architects, engineers, and contractors doing the work. Legal requirements must be scrupulously observed (building codes, zoning regulations, and environmental standards). And it is absolutely essential to have a highly qualified supervisor representing the director of the recreational sports program working with the contractors from inception to completion.

Maintenance costs are becoming so expensive that a new facility should be designed to expedite repair work. For example, in constructing a swimming pool, an access area should be available around the basin of the pool so that maintenance workers will be able to reach water lines, electrical circuits, and side walls in case of needed repairs. A gymnasium should not be built without windows that can be opened for ventilation. A gymnasium without windows may not be usable in hot weather if the ventilation system breaks down and maintenance workers are not immediately available to make repairs.

At the present time in the United States, excellent facilities for a recreational sports program are available in many school, colleges, and communities. Among the many are the new recreational sports facility at the University of Illinois at Urbana, and the Flint, Michigan and Long Beach, California school-community facilities. A director of a recreational sports program should learn about the latest developments in the field and use this information to help develop a program that meets the needs and interests of the local community. An abundance of information on the construction of a new facility is available from publishing companies, sporting goods companies, construction companies, government agencies, and companies specializing in building a specific facility such as a swimming pool.

EQUIPMENT AND SUPPLIES

The success of the recreational sports program is greatly enhanced when the necessary amount, style, and design of quality sports equipment and supplies are provided. Properly chosen, quality sports equipment and supplies promote good sports competition and activity proficiency, physical fitness, spirit, and social development. It may be stated categorically that effective sports equipment and supplies contribute just as importantly to the success of the recreational sports program as does the laboratory equipment to a chemistry or physics department. This being so, the budget allocation for sports equipment and supplies should be made on the same basis as a budget for laboratory equipment for any other school, college, or community program.

The desirability of a thorough understanding of the need and place of sports equipment and supplies in recreational sports programs was dramatized at a national workshop held at the Kellogg Center for Continuing Education at Michigan State University (December 10–18, 1959). The workshop was sponsored jointly by the Athletic Institute and the American Alliance for Health, Physical Education and Recreation with the primary aim of developing a publication to facilitate the use of sports equipment and supplies. The findings were incorporated in a manual entitled *Equipment and Supplies for Athletics, Physical Education and Recreation*. It has proved to be an invaluable contribution to those concerned with the purchase and care of sports equipment and supplies. Recent national workshops in this area have used the solid guidelines established at this conference as a foundation to build upon.

Participants in the workshops distinguished sharply between the terms "equipment" and "supplies." It was the consensus that the term "equipment" referred "essentially to those items of a nonexpendable nature that are expected to be used over a period of years," including, for example, such items as nets, golf clubs, fencing masks, archery bows, and baseball gloves. Supplies, on the other hand, referred "essentially to those expendable items that might normally be replaced at frequent intervals" and included such items as balls, bats, shuttlecocks, arrows, racquets, and handball gloves.

Ideally, the institution should furnish all sports equipment and supplies used in the recreational sports program. This greatly encourages the formation of intramural teams, sports clubs, and general recreation programs. Yet realistically, current budget appropriations are seldom adequate. However, schools, colleges, and communities are moving in this direction. A large number are also providing uniforms, towels, and laundry service. The latter practice is recommended; a recreation fee, required of all participants, should be levied to cover the cost of equipment and supplies. It is the responsibility of the institution always to furnish protective equipment where an impact might result in injury to the participant. Protective equipment for tackle football, the catcher in baseball, the goalie in hockey, and the fencer are examples of items the institution should supply. On the other hand, personal sports equipment such as shoes and handball gloves are seldom furnished, though the need may be met in other ways than by the participants. Increasingly, organizations are supplying sports clothing, balls, bats, gloves, racquets, and shoes.

The allocation for sports equipment and supplies has become one of the largest items in the budget, and proper procedures in their purchase and care may well determine that these funds are wisely expended. If the director thoroughly understands the policies and procedures in their purchase and care and is aware of exact needs, it is often possible to reduce the cost of equipment and supplies without sacrificing quality or attractiveness. Within the recreational sports program the following factors will govern largely the selection and use of sports equipment and supplies: the number of participants, their age and sex, the degree of skill they possess, the facilities available, the number and type of activities in the program, and the quality of leadership and supervision.

THE PURCHASE OF EQUIPMENT AND SUPPLIES

Since the purchasing of sports equipment and supplies is business, procedures based upon sound business principles should be followed. Thus, standardization of equipment is considered good planning. This means that a specific style, color, and type of equipment should be issued over a period of years. Such equipment is usually purchased from the same merchant so that replacements may be easily made. The standardization of equipment has decided advantages. In addition to being economical, it results in a uniformity that helps to encourage a high morale among the participants. The director who is aware that styles and types of equipment change frequently will not be caught with a large amount of equipment that cannot be brought up to the amount required for the program.

It has been found that the best practice is to buy quality merchandise. This does not mean necessarily the purchase of the most expensive items. It does mean the purchase of equipment that gives longer service, provides a better fit, has a more attractive appearance, and can be repaired easily. If the budget is severely limited, it is better to continue using quality materials that have been carefully repaired and reconditioned than to purchase low-cost materials, which usually prove to be unsatisfactory.

Time to Buy

The director must be aware of the proper time to buy. Equipment and supplies needed in the fall should be ordered in the spring, and winter and spring items should be ordered early in the fall. Frequently, special designs, emblems, and colors take several months to manufacture. When the manufacturer has ample time to prepare the items ordered, the purchaser will usually get good workmanship. If the items arrive well before they are needed, there is ample time to mark and prepare them for use. Items falling below specifications can be returned and correct equipment supplied before it is scheduled to be used. There is considerable merit in purchasing for a sport at the close of that sport's season. At such a time, the director is particularly aware of his needs for equipment and supplies; moreover, he may benefit in his purchases from merchants having sales and close-outs.

The Budget

A budget system must be utilized which will give an exact record of income and expenditures for equipment and supplies. A budget correctly prepared serves as a guide for expenditures and a ready reference for keeping them in balance with allotted funds throughout the year.

In the preparation of a budget for sports equipment and supplies, the following principles should be applied. The key person in preparing the budget should be the director of the recreational sports program. It will facilitate budget preparations if he or she asks each staff member in the program to study the inventory of equipment and supplies and to present a list of items which he believes should be purchased. The budget should be realistic and in line with other segments of the program. Here again, timing is consequential. It should be prepared several weeks before being admitted for administrative approval so that last-minute errors will be kept to a minimum. Once the budget has been approved, the director should keep within its limits.

If someone other than the director of the recreational sports program does the purchasing, he should certainly consult the director, since that person knows the immediate needs better than anyone else. Encountering the daily problems, he can make valuable recommendations. In colleges and universities, the director of physical education and athletics usually makes the final recommendation on the merchandise to be purchased, even though a business officer or central purchasing agent may give final administrative approval and negotiate the purchase order. A different procedure is followed in the public schools, where a business manager, principal, or superintendent may approve the purchase. Whenever an administrative officer finds that the director of the recreation program is well qualified in the purchase and care of equipment and supplies, this person should be given a responsible role in purchasing. The director of recreation in a community recreation program should have a major responsibility in purchasing equipment and supplies.

Inventory

A good inventory is basic to the proper control and accounting of equipment and supplies used in the recreational sports program. It should describe and reveal the quantity, cost, and condition of all items. The date of purchase should be recorded for all items, as well as specific information which will show the director the state of repair of all materials at the beginning and close of a sport season. Seasonal inventory facilitates the purchase of new equipment and helps to keep the stock up to date.

Distribution and Price

It is important for the director of the recreational sports program to understand how sports equipment and supplies are distributed and priced. When the manufacturer brings a new item into production, promotional methods go into effect through dealers and salespeople, trade magazines, selected newspapers and periodicals, places where the merchandise may be used, and displays at conventions where potential customers gather.

The manufacturer establishes a market price called a list price, which is based upon the cost of production, state and federal taxes, selling expenses, and percentage of profit. The manufacturer sells to dealers at approximately 50 percent below list price. Commonly, manufacturers use a middleman, called a jobber. The jobber usually buys at 60 percent below the manufacturer's list price but must do the promotional work with the dealers. Usually the jobber sells to a dealer at 40 percent below the manufacturer's list price. In turn, the dealer in sports equipment and supplies sells to the general public at the list price or a little below. But he offers a school price, which is called a trade price. The trade price is usually 25 percent above the cost to the dealer. For example, a manufacturer sets a list price of $10 on a tennis racquet; a jobber pays $4 for it and sells it to a dealer for $6. The dealer sells the racquet to the general public for $10. The trade price will vary between $6.50 and $7.50 depending upon the quantity of the order.

Purchasing from a Reputable Dealer

It should be recognized that quality merchandise cannot be sold on a regular basis at reduced rates. Reputable sporting goods dealers who give fair rates are seldom able to lower prices. Sometimes bargains will appear in quality sports equipment and supplies sold by established firms, of which the director should take advantage. It is a waste of time and money, however, to hunt for bargains from merchants who refuse to guarantee their merchandise. A director, who is not usually well-versed in grades of materials used in the manufacture of sports equipment and supplies, must depend upon the integrity of the merchant. Experienced leaders in the field agree that purchasing sports equipment and supplies consistently from reputable dealers is the most economical and satisfactory policy that can be followed. It is, however, advisable to shop around among reputable dealers. The director and his staff must respect the rights and confidence of the representatives of sports equipment and supply houses; they should be received courteously and given ample time to display and demonstrate their products.

Generally speaking, sports equipment and supplies should be purchased from the sporting goods company whose quality products are competitively priced. However, good judgment dictates buying at least some quality items from local merchants. There will always be a few items which the local merchant can price competitively.

Local Dealers

Many directors are expected to buy from local dealers even though the price, quality, and service are not favorably competitive with national merchants. This is a serious problem since the director desires neither to make local enemies nor to sacrifice the budget and program. If there is a definite advantage in buying from a national distributor, the director should buy the bulk of the merchandise there. If a local firm can match the national merchant, then of course the local merchant should receive the order. Many schools, colleges, and communities follow the policy of buying some of their sports equipment and supplies from local dealers as long as they do not have to pay more than 10 percent above the price quoted by a national distributor; they feel that the good will created is worth the funds sacrificed. This is a delicate point which each director must evaluate very carefully.

Discounts

Occasionally it is possible to make quality purchases when a sale is on if the purchaser has a sound knowledge of sports equipment and supplies. If a sports dealer has a close-out sale, a considerable saving may be possible. A close-out of items of sports equipment and supplies means that the manufacturer is closing out a specific line, style, or design of merchandise. The purchaser must be sure that he is buying quality products and not defective equipment and supplies. Buying close-outs from a reputable firm may bring a saving of 20 to 30 percent. The dealer on occasion will offer very good buys on seconds and on reconditioned equipment and supplies. The key to successful buying at a sale or close-out is to have a thorough knowledge of sports equipment and supplies and to purchase only from a responsible dealer who guarantees the merchandise.

A director should be aware that discounts may be given if the school, college, or community pays for the goods within a stated period of time. Almost all sporting goods firms allow a 2 percent discount if the bill is settled within ten days. The merchant prefers this arrangement so that he may use the immediate payment as working capital.

Bids on Equipment and Supplies

There are considerable differences among the states with regard to legal statutes and ordinances affecting the purchasing of sports equipment and supplies. It follows that the director of the program must know the specific rules and regulations of the state as well as those of his own institution. For example, most states require a purchase exceeding $1,000 to be publicly advertised with at least three sealed bids submitted. The bids must be opened in public with the order going to the lowest bidder whose products meet specifications. In practice, however, many local and state regulations permit the local merchant to receive the order if his products meet all specifications even though his bid may be 5 to 10 percent higher than that of a national distributor. The director should urge that only bids based on guaranteed quality merchandise be considered.

There are some practices the director needs to keep in mind if he is to carry out this portion of his duties satisfactorily. He should allow the dealer at least fifteen days to prepare his bid so that he may make a thorough study of the items desired and determine with accuracy his particular bid. When the bids are examined, the unit price made by the merchant is legally binding. In many states it is illegal for the director in a state institution to accept a low bid on sports equipment and supplies that fail to meet the listed specifications after he has advertised for an item of particular specifications. A bid much lower than the others requires careful examination. Usually, either an error has occurred or else the dealer's bid is on items that fail to meet listed specifications.

A sample of the item ordered should be held until the order is delivered and carefully checked. If a sample is unobtainable, request the bidder to have the manufacturer submit a letter furnishing the exact specifications of the items. When sports equipment and supplies are delivered, the shipment should be examined before the delivery receipt is signed. Once an acceptance signature has been made, it is more difficult to correct a mistake. Errors should be called to the dealer's attention immediately. In the total process of selection the director must consider very carefully the type, style, safety factors, cost of equipment and supplies, maintenance, and availability of merchandise.

Official Specifications

Official specifications are mandatory on many items of sports equipment and supplies such as footballs, basketballs, baseballs, and track equipment. Definite weights, lengths, dimensions, and types of materials may be required. The director must have a thorough knowledge of the official specifications. Many problems will be eliminated if the director gives exact and complete specifications when requesting a bid and in the preparation of a purchase order. Any items supplied that fail to meet the specifications stated on the purchase order need not be accepted. The dealer is required to deliver the correct merchandise unless the purchaser agrees to accept substitutes.

The Purchase Order

Sound rules to follow in purchasing sports equipment and supplies are to order only in writing and to identify completely all items with exact specifications. Order blanks should be used that are specifically designed as purchase orders. An order and invoice number system should be adopted with complete and accurate records kept on all purchases. There are many purchase order, requisition, and voucher systems used in schools and colleges to order sports equipment and supplies. The systems range from the small program where the director writes out the order in longhand, to the complex school, college, and community systems where a central purchasing agent operates with an elaborate business and accounting staff. Whatever system is used, the basic principles of budgeting, purchasing, and accounting must prevail through sound business practices.

One of the most widely used plans in purchasing is the five-unit type purchase order form. When the order is made, three copies go to the business office (two copies are filed in the business office, and one copy goes to the merchant so that he may prepare and deliver the order). The third and fourth copies are held in the director's office until the purchase is delivered in correct form. Upon receiving the correct shipment, the director signs a copy of the purchase order which he has held in his files and sends it to the business office authorizing full payment to the merchant. The second copy held by the director is then placed in his permanent file as a ready reference. Regardless of the complexity of the system used, the director should thoroughly understand and follow the basic principles of business and accounting.

A standard business form for the purchasing of sports equipment and supplies should include name, address, and telephone number of the merchant; name of the department initiating the purchase; instructions for delivery; date of order and date of completed delivery; account number; description of purchase; and official approval and authorization. A purchase order that has been accepted by the merchant is a legal contract binding both parties.

Buying Sports Clothing

In selecting sports clothing, the director should strive to buy materials that are attractive, comfortable, and durable. He must be aware of colors and make selections that blend into a color pattern for the program. Sports clothing, if selected improperly, may be very difficult to launder. A careful check should be made to see how much cleaning will be necessary on a proposed item and whether it changes shape and color with the application of hot water and soap. The director must also know how to measure a participant correctly for sports clothing, and he must insist that each person wear items that fit properly. It then becomes much easier to order the correct amount and sizes in accordance with the projected needs for the program.

Buying Leather and Rubber Balls

When purchasing leather balls the director should consider several points. A cowhide leather is preferable to horsehide, since cowhide stretches less. Experienced directors of recreational sports programs believe that it is better to buy one quality leather cowhide ball than two low-grade leather balls. The price variation on cowhide balls is based upon the grade of the leather. The best leather balls have small, tight, close fibers which hold their shape. Kangaroo leather has several qualities which commend it for sports equipment. Light, soft, and very strong, it neither cracks nor scuffs easily; and it has high water-resistance. However, it is very expensive, and most directors do not have the funds to purchase items made of this leather.

Rubber balls are now used extensively in sports programs. They are less expensive than leather balls, they keep their shape, and they do not become heavy with the accumulation of moisture. If the budget is severely limited, the director may wish to order rubber balls for such activities as soccer, speedball, football, volleyball, basketball, and softball.

Tennis Racquets and Badminton Racquets

Tennis and badminton racquets constructed from second-growth ash with laminated frames and gut are very popular. They are expensive, and a director may have to choose an inexpensive frame such as steel with wire stringing. The aluminum, fiberglass, and plastic racquet frames which have recently gained a foothold in the market may prove increasingly effective as their construction is improved. It is advisable to buy from a reputable dealer who will guarantee the merchandise. In addition, the director should secure, if possible, specific information about new types of racquets from directors who have had experience with them.

Racquet strings are usually made of gut or nylon. While gut stringing is preferred, the cost is often prohibitive, so nylon is now widely used in tennis and badminton racquets. It is much less expensive than gut stringing and is not damaged easily by moisture. For long wear, tennis racquets should be strung with 15- and 16-gauge nylon string, and badminton racquets should be strung with 16- to 18-gauge nylon string.

Shuttlecocks

Shuttlecocks made from quality feathers are preferred for badminton. They are very expensive, and the cost may be prohibitive when they are used by students unskilled in the techniques of badminton play. A cheaper substitute has been found in plastic shuttlecocks, which are entirely satisfactory for recreational sports competition.

THE CARE OF EQUIPMENT AND SUPPLIES

The basic principles of maintenance include policies and procedures to prolong the life of sports equipment and supplies, to maintain them in a safe and sanitary condition, and to provide equipment, supplies, and properly fitted sports clothing attractive in color, style, and design and meeting approved specifications. The basic duties in maintenance are inspection, marking, cleaning, repairing, issuing, and storage.

Students should be taught to respect sports equipment and supplies, for considerable damage occurs whenever students fail to use them properly. This respect will develop after they learn that equipment and supplies in sound condition are essential to the success of the recreational sports program. By means of discussions in physical education classes concerning their value and care, students will gain both an understanding and appreciation of the role of sports equipment and supplies in the recreational sports program.

The Equipment Room

To ensure proper care of equipment and supplies, the equipment room should be well-ventilated, properly lighted, and protected against moths, rodents, and excessive moisture. It should be located adjacent to the locker rooms and constructed so that it can be securely locked at all times. An appropriate arrangement of steel shelves and bins will make it possible to store all equipment and supplies correctly while still ensuring adequate space. For issuing equipment and supplies, there should be a window and counter arrangement that can be securely locked when not in use and located to give the best possible view of the area for safety of people and equipment.

A drying room should be constructed in close proximity to the equipment room. Wet uniforms and all sports clothing that do not go immediately to a laundry must be dried thoroughly or they will smell and eventually rot; and, in addition, lockers will rust if wet clothing is left in them for prolonged periods. A drying room must have heat, light, and ventilation that are correctly regulated to ensure proper drying.

Equipment-Room Management

For the most efficient operation of the equipment room, a full-time manager is needed who will assume responsibility for the complete operation of the equipment room, including the safety of all equipment and supplies. Unfortunately, this is too costly for most schools, small colleges, and community units. The director, therefore, must rely on part-time assistants at selected hours such as instructors, students, custodians, and janitors. Many programs use a student manager very successfully; he usually receives a manager's award for his services. Frequently the equipment room is handled by a student who assumes the position as a part-time job and receives a small compensation. In a large operation, it is necessary to have a full-time equipment room manager and assistants; the assistants are usually student managers of teams or student aides.

Regardless of the arrangements made, one person must have the responsibility for the equipment room to ensure efficient service, to care properly for equipment and supplies, and to prevent loss. A properly managed equipment room serves as a laboratory to examine sports equipment and supplies. Comparisons can be made, statistics recorded, periodic checks undertaken for wear, damage, and shrinkage—all activities that produce a better understanding of current operations and the need for new materials.

Marking Equipment and Supplies

Sports equipment and supplies must be marked so that no question arises about identification. Identification information should encompass ownership, year of purchase, size, and sequence number. Several marking techniques used successfully include India ink for clothing and towels, and a special paint or the burning of the identification into the leather items. Sports equipment made of wood or metal may also be marked with special paint, or the identification may be burned into the material. Many items may be marked very effectively with an electric needle. For a small fee the sporting goods dealer will do the marking.

Special policies must be worked out to prevent the theft of sports equipment and supplies. In addition to a sound issue system, each school and college will need written policies. One method that is being used widely is to charge a student who lost an item a sum greater than the item costs new at a local sporting goods dealer. If the director is consistent, keeps good records, and charges each student for any item that he loses, the inventory will show very few losses in any given year. Unfortunately, theft of equipment and supplies is one of the most serious problems facing the director.

Issuing Equipment and Supplies

The director should be able to account for every item of sports equipment and supplies, and there should be no difficulty in doing so if certain basic procedures are consistently observed. When an item is issued, it should be returned to the equipment room on the day of issue. In a few cases policies may permit sports equipment and supplies to be checked out for weekend outings, picnics and parties, and special events; but this policy should be executed in a way that protects the needs of the regular program. To facilitate the issuing and safe return of equipment and supplies, the issue window should be used exclusively. If the door of the equipment room has to be used, it should be sawed in half with a counter installed on the bottom half; the bottom half of the door should be locked during operations and the entire door locked at all other times.

A very effective way to keep an accurate check on all items issued is to use physical education activity cards. This plan requires a new activity card each year with the student's picture and signature, indicating that he agrees to use facilities, equipment, and supplies according to stated regulations. The card may be laminated to ensure durability for the year. It must be presented at the issue window to check out equipment and supplies. Successful utilization of this procedure requires that all items to be checked out of the equipment room be assembled so that an activity card is visible; when the sports item is returned to its proper location, the activity card is returned to its owner.

It is recommended that a self-service basket system be installed in the wall structure of the equipment room. Each basket, when stored, locks into the support structure and fits closely on all sides to prevent loss of equipment and any supplies that may be stored there. A self-service basket and combination lock should be issued to each person registered in a recreational sports program. When the number of baskets is insufficient to handle the total number of students involved, additional banks of baskets and locks should be installed inside the equipment room. If the enrollment is small, each person who does not have a self-service basket should have his own personal basket and lock inside the equipment room. Programs with large enrollments maintain banks of inside baskets and locks to be issued on a first-call basis.

Gymnasium uniforms and towels should be furnished by the school or college. The equipment room and laundry attendants should fold the towel and gymnasium uniform into a neat roll and store them according to the waist size of the shorts. All self-service baskets in operation should always have a clean roll waiting for the participant on the next visit to the gymnasium. When a student returns a self-service basket with soiled clothing, a tag system shows the equipment room attendant that clean materials are needed. The attendant must check for the correct return of all items before issuing clean ones. Baskets located in banks inside the equipment room which are personally assigned to a student are issued when the student requests his or her basket at the issue window. The usual procedure is to have the student request his or her size in a gymnasium uniform at the same time he or she gives the attendant his or her basket number. Each standard basket issue should contain the regular gymnasium uniform and towel; this enables the equipment-room attendant to make a quick, accurate check on the articles returned in each basket. If there is an article of clothing or a towel missing, the attendant should make out a lost-item slip immediately. All other details of the basket system and the checking out of equipment and supplies can be worked out very effectively with the use of the physical education activity card.

A locker room should be located adjacent to the equipment room. The lockers should be assembled appropriately against the walls and in banks throughout the interior of the room. Valuable space is saved for activity areas if the number of lockers is held to the minimum compatible with maintaining standards of health and comfort. If a basket system is used, there is a need for only enough lockers to take care of the number of students using the facilities at the peak period of participation. This means that a student uses any available locker while he or she is engaging in physical activity and leaves it free for another participant as soon as he or she checks out of the locker room.

Many new techniques and types of carriers have been developed to transport sports equipment and supplies. Equipment carriers mounted on rollers, with a cabinet for such items as balls, racquets, archery bows, and golf clubs are very useful. A few simple procedures that will expedite their use are recommended. The cabinet should be constructed so that equipment and supplies can be locked in place until issued to participants. The rollers should be selected according to the type of surface on which the carrier will be used extensively. The most realistic way of checking on the return of all equipment and supplies is for the equipment-room attendant to keep each space in the carrier filled; the instructor will then know that he or she must return a carrier with all spaces filled. This procedure is invaluable whenever the carrier is used by several instructors before being checked back into the equipment room. Misplaced items should be located immediately. An item of sports equipment or supplies that is missing overnight is seldom found.

Laundry and Cleaning

Schools, colleges, and community programs should construct their own laundries and cleaning facilities. If the budget is severely limited, a laundry system may be started with the purchase of one quality washing machine and dryer. Part-time assistance may be secured from equipment-room personnel, team managers, students, and custodians. For the institution that develops an elaborate laundry operation, including several washers, dryers, ironers, and repair units, a full-time laundry worker is essential. This is especially true if laundry from other parts of the institution is handled as well.

The director must see that the laundry personnel understand the intricate techniques of cleaning sports clothing and equipment. In many cases this is extremely difficult; sports clothing can include several types of fabric and become stained with blood, grass, chemicals, medications, or adhesive tape. Besides learning how to cope with stains and problems of a similar nature, the laundry personnel must acquire a thorough understanding of the operation and maintenance of laundry machines.

If sports clothing and equipment are sent to a commercial laundry establishment, the director must secure the services of a reliable firm that specializes in cleaning of this type. It is recommended that samples of the sports clothing be taken to the laundry company before the beginning of the school year so that the necessary preparations may be made in advance for proper laundering.

Whenever sports clothing and equipment are moved from the equipment room to a commerical laundry, the equipment-room manager must keep an accurate record of all items and make sure that they are all returned. Otherwise, losses may occur during the interchange.

Care of Leather Goods

Leather goods require special precautions to prolong their life. A leather ball, for example, should be inflated to the pressure prescribed by the manufacturer. Overinflation or underinflation may damage both the leather and the lining. Students must be cautioned against sitting on leather balls. When inflating leather balls, the attendant should utilize a pressure gauge to determine the correct inflation. The inflating process should be gradual so that the lining will seat properly against the leather.

Weather conditions may complicate the care of leather. Stitching on a leather ball may be injured in the drying process unless it is dried very slowly at normal room temperature. A green mold allowed to accumulate on leather will cause it to rot. To stay soft and pliable even after exposure to mud and other elements, leather should be cleaned and treated with saddle soap or a cleaner approved by the manufacturer.

The storage process is also important. The best protection for the leather goods used in the recreational sports program is to keep them clean and stored in a cool, dry storage area. Before being stored, they should be cleaned, repaired, and reconditioned. Since air movement is necessary in the storage area, fans and blowers should be installed whenever needed. For questions arising from storage the director should seek the latest information available from the manufacturer.

Care of Rubber Balls

Whenever possible, rubber balls should be kept out of direct sunlight and kept free of grease and oil; these may be removed easily with warm water and soap. Ordinarily, rubber balls should be inflated to the pressure prescribed by the manufacturer; when stored for long periods of time, however, they should be only partially inflated.

Care of Archery Equipment and Supplies

Archery equipment and supplies are delicate and need careful, persistent attention. Strings should be inspected each day following extensive wear. Plastic nocks or feathers that have become damaged must be removed, and new ones cemented in. The application of an attractive, quick-drying enamel will add aesthetic appeal to otherwise dull nocks and feathers. Archery bows, when not in use, should be unstrung and hung vertically on pegs.

Good storage practices will bring rewards. Before bows are stored, they should be cleaned and a thin layer of wax applied. Leather handles should be saddlesoaped, and leather quivers and finger tabs should be treated with saddlesoap. To eliminate warping, archery arrows should be stored in racks that are constructed with three evenly spaced pressure points. If they become warped, they may be straightened by the application of steam and careful reshaping. Archery targets should be stored in a flat position in a dry, well-ventilated storage area. Powdered sulphur spread around them will prevent attacks by rodents, and their life will also be increased with a coating of paraffin.

Care of Badminton and Tennis Equipment and Supplies

Badminton and tennis equipment and supplies have a hazardous existence. The major source of racquet difficulty is broken strings, and the cause is usually too much string tension. The director should request from the manufacturer the exact string pressure that has proved satisfactory for competition in recreational sports programs. The greatest damage to shuttlecocks comes from students who still have to learn the proper skills of badminton. During the learning process they should learn their skills with fluff balls and durable plastic birds, changing to the more expensive and fragile shuttlecock after they have acquired the necessary playing skill and the sense of timing needed for correct usage. For maximum life of tennis and badminton nets, they should be loosened slightly on the standards when not in use so that tension is relieved on the fiber and canvas top and tearing and elongating prevented. Tennis-court nets should be tarred, and once every year they should be dipped in creosote.

The following storage practices are recommended. Badminton and tennis racquets constructed from wood should be placed in presses and stored in a vertical position. Additional protection is possible if the racquets are placed in a rubber covering when they are not in use. Shuttlecocks made of quality feathers should be stored in a moist environment, since their oils are lost in air that is too dry. When tennis-court nets are placed in storage, they should be put in a cool, dry area and hung horizontally on pegs. Badminton nets may be rolled or folded when they are stored.

Care of Baseball and Softball Gloves

Leather baseball and softball gloves should be cleaned with saddlesoap or a quality leather cleaner recommended by the manufacturer. When the leather becomes dry it should be treated with mineral oil or some other quality oil that is recommended by the manufacturer.

Care of Canvas Shoes

Warm water and soap give the best results in cleaning canvas basketball and tennis shoes. Many directors recommend the addition of formaldehyde to the cleaning solution to act as a deodorizer.

Care of Mats

Mats may be damaged by being bent, rolled, or dragged along the floor. When in use they should be kept flat, and they should be stored in a flat position or hung on pegs that allow even pressure points. Mat covers made of plastic or rubber should be cleaned with soap and water. Mats should be repaired as soon as a break is discovered. The manufacturers furnish excellent pamphlets on their care and maintenance.

Care of Track Equipment

Steel tapes and metal shots should be cleaned with steel wool and oiled before being placed in storage; discuses should be cleaned and shellacked; and javelins and vaulting poles should be cleaned, oiled, and stored with the points suspended downward to prevent warpage.

Care of Wood, Metal, and Plastic

Equipment and supplies made of wood should be checked for cracks, breaks, warpage, and loose screws, bolts, nails, and attachments. Sports equipment made from wood, such as pieces of apparatus, bats, hockey and lacrosse sticks, may be damaged by moisture where the finish is worn off. An application of linseed oil will protect the worn surfaces. Metal equipment should be carefully checked for rust, dents, serious bending, and loose holding parts and attachments. The metal should be kept clean, painted, and oiled to prevent rust. Since plastic may be warped and broken by heat and cold, periodic examinations are advisable to check for weaknesses. A damaged plastic is extremely hard to repair; and, in fact, the damaged item usually has to be discarded.

Repair and Reconditioning

Almost all of the repair work needed on recreational sports equipment and supplies can be done in the equipment room. The purchase of a sewing machine that is suitable for sewing sports clothing, including leather, will prove invaluable to the program. The person who uses the machine must have a thorough knowledge of its operation as well as a basic understanding of how to sew sports equipment and supplies.

A fabric cement is excellent for repairing tears in sports clothing and canvas. Inexpensive in price, it gives a solid, clean repair. The reconditioning of sports equipment requires cleaning, sterilizing, repairing, and rebuilding. Reconditioning is expensive, and good judgment must be used in determining whether to repair equipment or discard it. Frequently, it is less expensive in the long run to buy new equipment than to make costly repairs on old equipment.

Since school and college budgets do not usually provide enough money for the necessary sports equipment and supplies, it may be possible to get some items made through the carpentry shop, mechanical arts, and home economics departments. For example, the carpenters might use old lumber to make backstops, outdoor backboards, goal posts, balance beams, net posts, and track equipment such as starting blocks and jumping standards.

Improvised equipment and supplies may also be made if it is impossible to secure standard types of materials. For example, in archery, heavy cardboard and rubber bands can be used to make arm guards; bales of hay may be used for archery backstops; and finger tabs may be made from rubber inner tubes.

DISCUSSION QUESTIONS

1. Describe the significant differences between facilities, equipment, and supplies in a recreational sports program.

2. Present important ways in which multiple-use facilities are used in both indoor and outdoor recreational sports programs.

3. How do building codes and zoning regulations affect the building of a recreational sports facility?

4. What basic principles should be followed in preparing a budget for a recreational sports program?

5. Explain the use of a purchase order in ordering equipment and supplies.

6. How is office management related to the purchase and care of equipment and supplies?

7. Describe the most effective way to build an equipment room and locker and shower area in order to help prevent theft and vandalism in these areas.

8. Describe the assets and liabilities of a self-service basket system in gymnasia in urban and suburban communities.

9. How should you proceed to secure the most specific information available on facilities, equipment, and supplies for a recreational sports program?

10. Present an inventory system that will give the director of a recreational sports program an accurate accounting of all recreational sports equipment and supplies.

BIBLIOGRAPHY

BANNON, JOSEPH J., *Leisure Resources: Its Comprehensive Planning.* Englewood Cliffs, N.J.: Prentice-Hall, Inc., 1976.

BROWN, JOSEPH, *Planning for Recreation and Parks.* Englewood Cliffs, N.J.: Prentice-Hall, Inc., 1976.

"Focus on Facilities," *Journal of Physical Education and Recreation* (April, 1975), pp. 23–24.

"Focus on Facilities in Public Schools," *Journal of Physical Education and Recreation* (September, 1976), pp. 15–22.

GOLD, SEYMOUR M., *Urban Recreation Planning.* Philadelphia: Lea & Febiger, 1973.

JUBENVILLE, ALAN, *Outdoor Recreation Planning.* Philadelphia: W. B. Saunders Co., 1976.

KRAUS, RICHARD, *Recreation and Leisure in Modern Society.* Englewood Cliffs, N.J.: Prentice-Hall, Inc., 1971.

PETERSON, JAMES A., *Intramural Administration: Theory and Practice.* Englewood Cliffs, N.J.: Prentice-Hall, Inc., 1976.

WEISKOPF, DONALD C., *A Guide to Recreation and Leisure.* Boston: Allyn & Bacon, Inc., 1975.

VI

The Functioning
Program

Regulations.
(Courtesy News-Record of Maplewood and South Orange, New Jersey.)

17

Units of Competition, Regulations, and Tournament Plans

Effective formulation of units of competition and tournament plans may ultimately determine a program's success. In spite of situation differences, if units and tournaments are properly formed, well-balanced teams will compete in a comfortable environment of sportsmanship and sociability.

UNITS OF COMPETITION

Units that reflect effective grouping and also provide for various levels of skill are best developed from a situation survey. The director determines the basis for competitive units after assessing (1) the institution; (2) the environmental, geographic, and climate conditions; (3) facilities and equipment; (4) the local traditions; (5) residence distribution patterns; (6) group and age memberships; and (7) numbers of potential participants.

As members of well-developed units become acquainted, strong personalities foster team spirit in competition. Victories stir pride and enthusiasm, and participants come closer together as a result of the effort to win, the shared recognition that accrues, and the celebrating banquets at the end. There are problems here, however. The experienced program director will make every effort to lessen them by avoiding the development of long-term rivalries, encouraging the spirit of play for its own sake, and trying to bring in more participants. Team spirit and leadership are thus important, but determining the most effective units of competition is not to be minimized as a challenging task.

Grouping Guidelines

Grouping individuals—school or college students, community or industrial recreators—into successful units of competition is done in many ways. Variation is from a completely informal signup procedure to a controlled registration based upon eligibility rosters, equating formulas, fitness or health reports, and medical records. Whatever the approach used, several basic guidelines are helpful to ensure cohesive grouping.

Varied Skill Levels. It is important to provide tournament or competitive programs on a variety of skill levels. In this way all individuals interested can enjoy competing with those of comparable skills. Participation interest is often related to opportunites for stimulating well-matched competition. Therefore, it is advisable to classify units of competition in a way that equalizes ability. This is often done by using previous records, skill tests, the qualifying round, preliminary contests, heats, or handicapping.

Multi-Social Groups. Opportunities in each activity should be provided equally for the varied social groups: men, women, girls, boys, privileged, underprivileged, fraternity, and nonfraternity. Financial, space, leadership, and equipment limitations should be shared by all such groups to avoid favoritism. Representative councils can share some of the responsibilities for decision making so as to reach solutions acceptable to all.

Physical and Mental Homogeniety. To avoid having competition dominated by the physically larger and older participants, controls are often implemented by grouping according to age, grade, height and weight, physical handicap, or mental limitations. Concern with equating physical and mental capacities also tends to minimize injuries that might occur.

Interests and Sociological Development. Long-term group loyalties are more evident in the college-age student than the elementary or junior high school youngster who may not be upset by the possibility of moving from one unit to another. Adults and community members, however, may also feel strongly about playing with a friend rather than with a highly skilled team member. Signup procedures thus may be the most satisfactory.

Physical Health. Leaders in the field of recreational sports agree that special attention must be directed to growth and developmental patterns. Irreparable injury is possible when children participate in competition without due regard for factors of age, height, and weight. Physical fitness and health status of participating adults are an equally important concern of program directors. Potential participants might be classified according to physical health before developing units of competition.

Developmental Programs. It is the consensus of leaders that the recreational sports program should properly begin in the fourth grade, provided an acceptable physical education program is in operation. Rhythmic, self-testing activities and lead-up games based on units of competition may form a large part of the program on the fourth-, fifth-, and sixth-grade levels. As students move into high school and beyond, their interest shifts to team, individual, and lifetime sports.

Natural Grouping. Whenever possible, natural groupings should be maintained so that teams or units of competition evolve with potentially strong loyalties. In the case of less team-conscious and noncompetitive individuals, common loyalties and natural grouping ensure more dependable units that will continue participation throughout the sport season.

Participant Leadership. Community interest in sports programs is often given impetus by a few enthusiastic leaders. These natural "spark plugs" should be given reins of leadership long enough to facilitate organization of activities and units of competition that will most stimulate participation.

Units Classified

Units most commonly used by communities, schools, and colleges can generally be identified and classified. In some instances the suggested units summarized in Figure 17-1 can be used successfully in more than one recreational sports group.

Colleges	*Schools*	*Community*
Scheduling Units		
cities	age-height-weight	business groups
co-rec	boarding house	senior citizen units
departments	class or grade	church affiliates
dormitories	color teams	color teams
faculty	co-rec groups	handicap rating
floor, hall, wing	curriculum	leagues
foreign students	home rooms	pick-up teams
fraternity	leagues	wards
graduate students	major curriculum areas	scout troops
home states	physical education classes	skill level
independents	schools	sponsored teams

Figure 17-1   Suggested Units of Competition

REGULATIONS AND RULES

While generally accepted principles underlie the rules and regulations governing the recreational sports programs, each school, college, and community needs to make its own adaptations. This is best done by considering basic concepts, which may include some of the following.

General Principles

1. Rules and regulations are necessary for the successful management of recreational sports competition.
2. Participants and leaders should thoroughly know and understand all rules and regulations.
3. Rules and regulations should serve to ensure the educational value of the event.
4. Leadership should insist upon the best practices and highest standards in all aspects of the program.
5. Competition should be motivated by a spirit of sport for sport's sake.
6. Awards should be symbolic, and winning should be a goal for the sake of challenge and not for monetary compensation.
7. Post-season teams should be appointed objectively and judiciously by a well-supported selection committee.
8. Post-season tournament, exhibition, or playoff games should not become primarily public entertainment.
9. Championship competition should not curtail participation opportunities for those of lesser skill.
10. Women's games should not become curtain-raisers for men's games.
11. Highly skilled and highly competitive individuals should have challenging opportunities as well as the lesser-skilled.
12. Health and well-being of all participants should be of primary programming importance.
13. Safety practices should be the uppermost consideration in all planning.

Local Regulation Considerations

Limited space, facilities, time, personnel, ability, safety, and welfare of the participants often require modification of official rules for particular situations. Local regulations, therefore, should be defined and should include established procedure for the variety of situations that arise most often in the course of the year's program.

Since an extensive list of regulations is discouraging to administrators and participants, it is best to develop stated procedures for the most essential areas of control. Occasional problems should be handled informally until the situation or need for a formalized procedure becomes evident.

Controls or regulations should be developed by a representative board or committee and in final form should provide for change or revision. The following is a checklist of areas that require some local control or regulations.

Entries and Limitations	*Definitions*
Election of captains	Graduate students
Entry procedures	Amateur athletes
Number of teams permitted	Transfer students
Number of sports an individual	Independent students
may participate in at one time	Fraternity members
Number of players on a team	Dormitory
Number of substitutes	Commuters
	Freshmen, sophomores, seniors
	Adults, senior citizens

Qualifications and Eligibility	*Miscellaneous*
Team eligibility list	Forfeits, defaults
Managers	Protests, appeals
Officials	Ties
Individual eligibility	Officials
Academic qualifications	Postponements
Health qualifications	Training periods
Discipline	Disqualifications
Parental permission	Substitutes

Official Games Rules

Standardized playing rules for practically all sports have been developed and published. Over the years many schools and communities have written their own manuals of rules, which are made available for leadership reference. In addition there are publications which summarize sources for rules and regulations.

Of greatest importance to the high school programs are the rules of the National Federation of State High School Associations and the rules sanctioned by the National Association for Girls and Women in Sport (NAGWS). On the college level, the NCAA and the AIAW rules are basic to the sports programs.

Competition directed toward national or Olympic games is usually dependent upon observation of sanctioned rules of the controlling organization, such as the AAU or the particular national sports association.

In addition to organizations that develop rules or sanction existing rules, many sports activities are governed by their own national organizations, which are also a source for official rules and valuable information.

Not to be overlooked in the discussion of game rules and regulations is the experience of many directors who have found great success in modifying official rules to better serve their situation.

TOURNAMENT PLANS

Many factors influence the development of a tournament plan. Facilities, time, participants' interests and abilities, size of groups, intended purpose for the activity as well as tradition or established regulations, often dictate the kind of competition. A bowling tournament is planned quite differently than a swimming meet. Basketball and tennis are most often set up as a round robin, elimination, or ladder tournament.

The intent of a tournament may be to determine a winner, to provide competition for as many as possible, or to stimulate interest in an activity; each of these considerations has a slightly different impact on a developing plan.

The number of entries in a competitive event and the length of the season further dictate whether a more complicated league plan should be used. Flexibility in planning can be initiated with the use of the several basic forms of competition such as round robin, elimination, or challenge type tournaments. These may be combined in a variety of ways such as a round robin or challenge tournament as the preliminary to an elimination contest, many small matches before a winners' schedule in a final event, or variations on league play. All of these elements have possibilities in flexible planning.

Round Robin

In the round robin tournament each person or team plays every other person or team. In a double round robin the total schedule is repeated and each person or team plays every other person or team twice. The RR tournament plan produces a true winner, ranks the players, permits all competitiors to continue playing whether winning or losing, and lends itself to league competition.

Determining Matches. Figure 17-2 illustrates three methods of determining matches and rounds of competition: Method I, the triangular pattern, is very easy to draw up without error. Method II, the rotation pattern, can be rotated clockwise or counterclockwise. Method III, the square grid, can be used for drawing up a single RR and recording scores and court assignments in the blank squares or for drawing up double RR matches. An uneven number of teams or players should be avoided to facilitate planning matches. If there is an odd number of teams, however, a "bye" may be used as illustrated.

Letters	= Teams/Participants
Numbers	= Rounds
N	= Entrants

(R) Rounds	even no. entrants = N−1
	odd no. entrants = N
(M) Total no. matches	$= \dfrac{N(N-1)}{2}$

Method I Triangular Pattern
N = 8; R = 7; M = 28

A - B					
A - C	B - C				
A - D	B - D	C - D			
A - E	B - E	C - E	D - E		
A - F	B - F	C - F	D - F	E - F	
A - G	B - G	C - G	D - G	E - G	F - G
A - H	B - H	C - H	D - H	E - H	F - H	G - H

Method II Rotation Patterns

Even no. entrants   N=8; R=7; M=28

A - H	A - G	A - F	A - E	A - D	A - C	A - B
B - G	H - F	G - E	F - D	E - C	D - B	C - H
C - F	B - E	H - D	G - C	F - B	E - H	D - G
D - E	C - D	B - C	H - B	G - H	F - G	E - F

Odd no. entrants   N=7; R=7; M=21

BY - G	BY - F	BY - E	BY - D	BY - C	BY - B	BY - A
A - F	G - E	F - D	E - C	D - B	C - A	B - G
B - E	A - D	G - C	F - B	E - A	D - G	C - F
C - D	B - C	A - B	G - A	F - G	E - F	D - E

League ABCD vs League abcd

A - a	A - b	A - c	A - d
B - b	B - c	B - d	B - a
C - c	C - d	C - a	C - b
D - d	D - a	D - b	D - c

Method III Square Grid

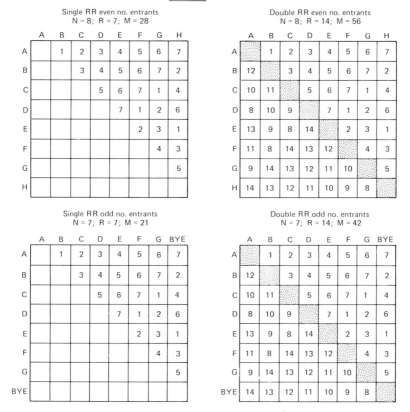

Figure 17-2. Round Robin Tournament Plans

Formulas may be helpful for quick determination of number of rounds and matches. With N representing the total number of entrants, the following are applicable except for the *two-league* round robin, which is a modified form of the basic RR.

1. Number of matches to be played $\qquad\qquad M \qquad = \dfrac{N(N-1)}{2}$

2. Number of matches to be played by
   each competitor $\qquad\qquad\qquad\qquad M \qquad = N-1$

3. Number of matches in each round;
   even number of entries $\qquad\qquad M(R-1) \quad = \dfrac{N}{2}$

   odd number of entries $\qquad\qquad M(R-1) \quad = \dfrac{N-1}{2}$

4. Number of rounds when the first round
   is represented by the first game
   by all teams or all players; the $\qquad$ even no. players $\quad R \quad = N-1$
   second game the second round, etc. $\quad$ odd no. players $\quad R \quad = N$

Scheduling Matches. After the number of matches and rounds is determined, a date and time schedule has to be developed. Facilities will determine the number of matches that can be played at any one time. The type of activity will dictate whether formal or informal scheduling is best suited for a tournament.

Formal scheduling requires a complete calendar of contests with court or field assignments. In this way all facilities will be used most efficiently, the tournament can be completed in a specified length of time, and additional time for playoffs or necessary postponements can be included in the scheduling.

Individual or dual sports are often scheduled informally by having deadline dates set for the various rounds. If there are ample facilities and time to use them, this plan may be preferable in such activities as tennis, badminton, or archery.

Recording Scores and Determining Winners. Several plans of determining winners are used.

Percentage Plan. The final standing is determined by the percentage of wins, which is obtained by dividing the number of games won by the total games played, and is usually expressed as a decimal carried to three places. Tie games are customarily counted as games not played when the percentage is computed. To determine the number of games Team A is behind B, add wins of (B minus A) to losses of (A minus B) and divide by two, as illustrated in Figure 17-3.

Point Plan. In the RR point plan, points are given for each victory and each tie. Thus, the team with the greatest number of total points is the winner.

Wins and Losses. The team with the greatest number of wins is the tournament winner. In cases of a tie, one of three procedures can be followed: a playoff is scheduled, the tie stands, or records are further analyzed. A further analysis of records in bowling, for instance, can be used as a basis for

TEAM	WON	LOST	TOTAL PLAYED	WINS LOSSES	PERCENTAGE	PLACE
A	3	4	7	3/7	.429	5
B	2	5	7	2/7	.286	7
C	5	2	7	5/7	.714	3
D	6	1	7	6/7	.857	2
E	4	3	7	4/7	.571	4
F	7	0	7	7/7	1.000	1
G	1	6	7	1/7	.143	8
H	3	4	7	3/7	.429	5
Total	31	+ 25	= 56	31/7		

Figure 17-3   Percentage Plan of Scoring

declaring the team with the greatest number of pins the winner. In team sports a tie league victory can be awarded the winner of the two-league match scheduled in a round robin. The winner can also be the high-score team as determined from the sum of its own match scores minus the sum of all opponent's match scores.

Games Won. This variation of round robin scoring requires that the winner be victorious in a defined number of games. Players draw for positions, and play proceeds as in a RR schedule until the winner is declared.

Lombard. The Lombard is a form of round robin tournament that is completed in a relatively short length of time. The teams play "limited" games, which are defined as five or ten minutes in length or as specified fractions of a regular game. For example, in basketball often the total game time is divided by the number of entered teams. This becomes total game time of each match. Each team's score is determined by adding all game scores and subtracting the total of its opponent's score. The four teams with the largest positive scores are selected to play a "full game" round robin to decide the winner. Innovative variations may better suit a particular situation. The Lombard tournament is adaptable for team games as well as individual sports, and may be played on a limited time basis, with a reduced number of games, or on a reduced number of points basis.

Elimination-Type Tournaments

Elimination-type tournaments pair off teams or individuals to play each other in a series of rounds. Losers in each round are either eliminated or rescheduled in some form of consolation play. Variations of this tournament plan serve a great many situations and should be studied to determine which best serves a particular program and provides for the greatest participation for the greatest number (see Figure 17-4).

Single Elimination. In the single-elimination tournament losers of each round are eliminated until one winner remains. A large number of

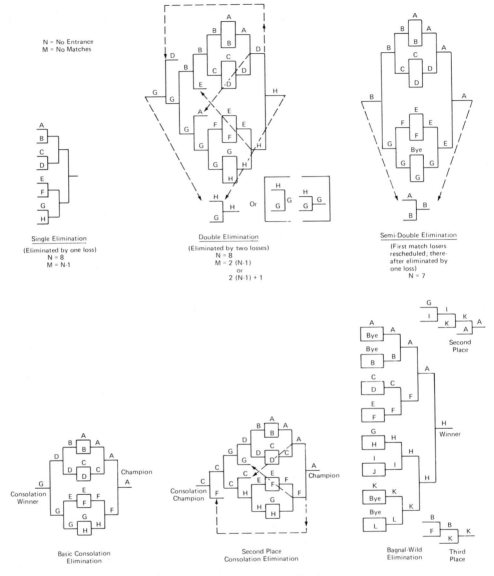

Figure 17-4 Elimination-Type Tournaments

entries is handled and the total number of matches can be run off relatively quickly. This tournament is interesting to watch, stimulates vigorous competition, and can be conducted with limited facilities. Of concern, however, are several factors: half of the participants are eliminated in the first round; a good team or player could be eliminated early in the competition; competition may become too desperate; and postponed matches can cause demoralizing delays and difficult scheduling problems.

Double Elimination. This tournament requires that a player or team be defeated twice before elimination. A player who loses the first match is rescheduled in the losers' bracket and has another chance of winning the tournament. The play continues until all but one has been defeated twice.

A double-elimination tournament of eight teams will involve either fourteen or fifteen games ($2N - 1$ or 2). The tournament requires a playoff between the finalist in the winners' bracket and the finalist in the losers' bracket. If the winner of the first elimination loses to the winner of the second elimination, he has lost only once; and the two players must play another game before an actual winner is declared.

The double-elimination system selects a more adequate winner, provides for at least twice as much play, and maintains maximum interest as compared to the single-elimination tournament.

Semi-Double Elimination. This tournament reschedules all first-round losers and second-round losers who were scheduled with byes in the first round. It provides a second chance for the players who lose their first match. Both winners' and losers' brackets continue as single eliminations, and the winners of each bracket play off for the championship.

Consolation Elimination. This tournament permits each contestant to play at least twice and declares two winners, the winner of the elimination and the winner of the consolation elimination. The number of games is equal to ($2N - 2$). All the losers in the first round, or those who lose in the second round after drawing a bye in the first round, play another single-elimination tournament. The winner of this second tournament is the consolation winner.

Second-Place Consolation. This variation of the consolation tournament gives each loser the opportunity to win the consolation championship, regardless of the round in which the loss occurred.

Bagnal-Wild Elimination. This elimination tournament selects a champion and a true second- and third-place winner. First place is determined by simple elimination play. All competitors defeated by the champion previous to the final round compete against each other in an elimination tournament. The winner of this competition plays the defeated finalist for second place. To determine third place, an elimination tournament is conducted among those defeated by the loser (A) of the finals. The winner plays the loser of the second place (K) for third place. If the defeated finalist (A) loses in the match for second place, player K becomes second-place winner and A automatically becomes the third-place winner.

Modified Double Elimination. In this elimination tournament finals of the losers' bracket determine third and fourth place (see Figure 17-5).

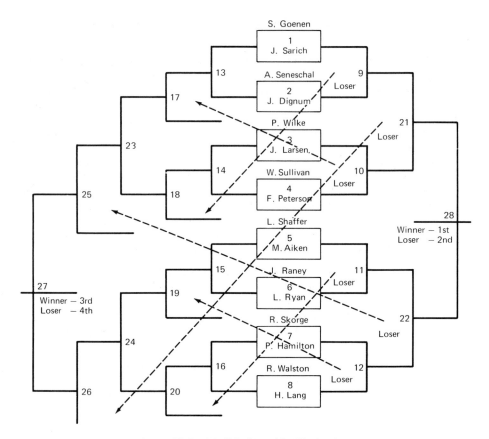

Figure 17-5   Modified Double Elimination

Planning Matches in Elimination Tournaments

Determining matches and positioning players in an elimination
tournament are dependent upon number of entries, scheduling byes,
seeding players, and a draw for position by the remaining contestants.

Number of Games. The total matches (M) or matches in first round ($MR -$
1) to be played with a given number of entrants can most easily be
determined with N = number of entries in the following formulas:

Single Elimination	*Double Elimination*
$M = N - 1$	$M = 2 (N - 1)$
$M(R-1) = N -$ $\begin{bmatrix}\text{next power of}\\ \text{2 below } N\end{bmatrix}$	or $M = 2 (N - 1) + 1$

Number of Byes. If the number of entries in an elimination tournament is not a perfect power of two, the appropriate number of byes are added. The number of byes is determined by subtracting the number of entrants (N) from the next higher power of two (next higher power of 2 minus N). This number plus the number of entrants then becomes the draw. If there are no seeded players the determined number of byes are awarded as indicated in Figure 17-6.

There are some differences in order of placement, but basically half of the byes are placed in the upper bracket and half in the lower bracket when there is an even number of byes. If there is an odd number of byes, the greatest number is placed in the lower bracket. Official rules for a specific sport should be consulted if a formal tournament is planned.

If there are seeded players in a draw requiring a certain number of byes, they usually are distributed first among the seeded entries in order of their respective ranks. If there are more byes than seeded entries, the remaining byes are awarded those nonseeded entries whose names happen to pair up with the bye lines.

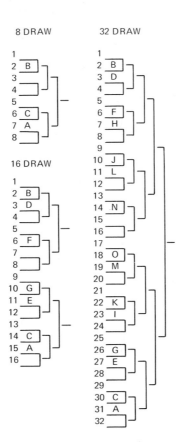

Figure 17-6 Awarding Byes in Nonseeded Tournaments

The necessity of awarding byes may be eliminated with a unique use of the qualifying round. Assuming the number of entrants to be 38 [$N - 32$], (the next lowest power of 2) indicates that there are 6 too many players. Multiplying 6 times 2 reveals that 2 potential entrants have to play qualifying rounds. A draw may be scheduled to determine who has to play in the qualifying rounds. The six winners are then qualified to participate in the tournament.

Seeding. Those teams or individuals with established reputations are seeded in accordance with one of the two systems illustrated in Figure 17-7. If planning a formal tournament, check official rules for procedure relative to a specific sport. The strongest player is seeded number 1, second strongest number 2, and so on. This distribution of players ensures that the best contestants will not meet in the first rounds.

The skill of the players is usually based upon their records in recognized tournaments or a qualifying round, or players are sometimes rated

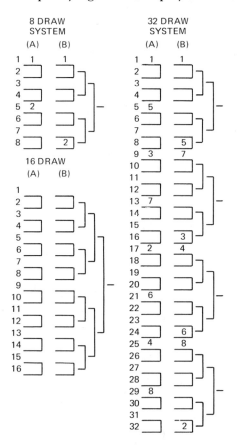

Figure 17-7 Two Systems of Seeding Players (A and B)

subjectively for intramurals. A draw is often used to determine seeded positions of equally skilled players.

Generally, one entry is seeded for every two, four, or eight entries as the tournament committee decides. In some sports, such as golf, a qualifying round is used to rank all players. Tournament position is then dependent upon rank.

After the byes, if any, are established and the seeded players, if any, are placed, the remaining players or teams draw for positions. In summary, matches are determined by the number and positions of the byes, the seeding of the reputed players, and the results of the draw for positions.

Scheduling Matches. With the number of games determined for scheduling, it is now necessary to determine the number of days available for play and the number of facilities—i.e., courts or fields that can be used for the tournaments. At this point the games can be numbered chronologically through each round and scheduled by date and time.

Scheduling must be done in such a way that no team or player will be put at a disadvantage because of having to play several games or matches consecutively.

In planning both a singles and doubles tournament in which players are permitted dual entries, it is best to complete one tournament before starting the other. If it is necessary to run both matches simultaneously, it is advisable to work out schedules around the seeded players. These matches should be played off as soon as possible, since seeded players will probably have to play the greatest number of matches. In spite of such planning, as the tournament proceeds there will be unavoidable conflicts involving the same players in both singles and doubles matches. At this time it will be necessary to hold up schedules while a player involved in both tournaments is given adequate rest time. (See Figure 17-8.)

Determining Winners. As a part of the elimination tournament regulations, potential match winners have to be defined in terms of the number of games or sets to be played and won. Place winners are most often determined by the structure of the competition as in Bagnal-Wild or the consolation tournament, where players or teams can be ranked by scheduling continuous playoffs. If modifications or special conditions for place winners are developed as part of the tournament play they should be included in the tournament regulations.

Challenge Tournaments

Challenge tournaments do not eliminate players, but rather provide the opportunity for all competitors to continue play whether they win or lose. It is an appropriate plan for informal scheduling in which most of the arrangements for play are done by the players. It is also a useful device for ranking players. The challenge tournament is particularly

TOURNAMENT SCHEDULE CALCULATOR

Teams Entered	Byes Top	Bottom	Single Elim. No. Games	Double Elim. No. Games	Round Robin No. Games
4	0	0	3	6 or 7	6
5	1	2	4	8 or 9	10
6	1	1	5	10 or 11	15
7	0	1	6	12 or 13	21
8	0	0	7	14 or 15	28
9	3	4	8	16 or 17	36
10	3	3	9	18 or 19	45
11	2	3	10	20 or 21	55
12	2	2	11	22 or 23	66
13	1	2	12	24 or 25	78
14	1	1	13	26 or 27	91
15	0	1	14	28 or 29	105
16	0	0	15	30 or 31	
17	7	8	16	32 or 33	
18	7	7	17	34 or 35	
19	6	7	18	36 or 37	
20	6	6	19	38 or 39	
21	5	6	20	40 or 41	
22	5	5	21	42 or 43	
23	4	5	22	44 or 45	
24	4	4	23	46 or 47	
25	3	4	24	48 or 49	
26	3	3	25	50 or 51	
27	2	3	26	52 or 53	
28	2	2	27	54 or 55	
29	1	2	28	56 or 57	
30	1	1	29	58 or 59	
31	0	1	30	60 or 61	
32	0	0	31	62 or 63	

Figure 17-8   Tournament Schedule Calculator

adaptable for individual and dual sports competition such as archery, badminton, golf, horseshoes, squash, and tennis.

Contestants' names and telephone numbers are placed in slots or hung so they can easily be exchanged at the end of a playoff. Positions of names can be determined by ability, with the most skilled at the bottom; order of sign-up; or by a draw for position. Local rules define game score, challenges, and playoff deadlines. Play continues until at the end of a defined period; the person at the top is declared winner, and the other players are recognized for their relative ranks (see Figure 17-9).

Ladder Tournament. In this popular tournament the contestants' names are placed one above the other. Players advance by challenging and defeating any one of a defined number of persons above their name on the ladder (usually two or three). A victorious player changes name positions with the defeated person. If a challenger loses, his place remains the same; and he may not challenge the same person for a designated period of time or number of matches. A person challenged must play within a period of three days or other defined length of time, provided he has not previously been challenged above himself. The match must be played within three days after a previously arranged match if the player is still within challenge range. At the end of play all contestants are ranked according to ability (see Figure 17-9).

Variations could permit new players to challenge the bottom of the ladder. Several ladders can be set up for the various skill levels by permitting the top person to challenge into the next higher skill group. Ladders can also be set up as divisions, with playoffs between all top-rung contestants.

Pyramid Tournament. This type of tournament involves more players than the ladder tournament, there is more flexibility in challenging, and no single person is left in the lowest position. Contestants' names are written on cards, which are placed in the shape of a pyramid (see Figure 17-9). Positions can be determined as in the ladder tournament and challenges are made to anyone in the rank above the challenger. A variation may require that a player defeat a contestant on his right, or left, or on the same row before challenging in the row above. New players may be permitted to enter the tournament by challenging and defeating someone on the last row.

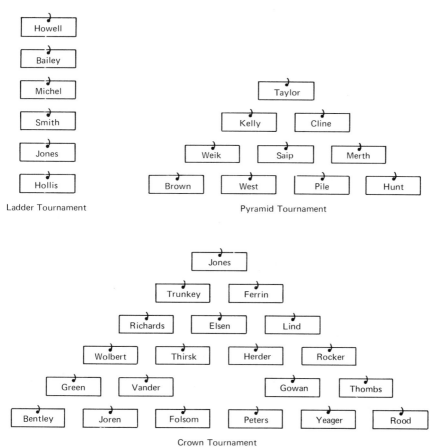

Ladder Tournament   Pyramid Tournament

Crown Tournament

Figure 17-9 Challenge Tournaments

Another plan for this tournament is that of starting with more entrants than there are places on the pyramid. A player gains a position on the bottom row by challenging and defeating another member in the tournament. The challenger advances to the next row by defeating someone on the same level when there is a vacant spot on the row above.

Several pyramids may be grouped in a large pyramid. The lower pyramids can be divisions of less-skilled players, but the players who reach the top of their division pyramid can then challenge into the bottom row of the next higher skill group. This plan is sometimes called a *crown tournament* (see Figure 17-9).

In the pyramid tournament and its variations, the winner is that person at the top of the pyramid at the end of a designated period of time.

Combination Tournaments

Some leaders have found that combination tournaments which include two or more basic tournament forms best serve the recreational sports program or a particular sport.

Single Elimination and Round Robin. In this combination a simple elimination tournament is scheduled to a designated round. Those contestants still in the tournament at the specified round are scheduled in a round robin tournament. After completion of the round robin, the champion is determined according to a percentage or point-system plan.

Double Elimination and Round Robin. In this competition two rounds of double elimination are played to classify the competitors into four leagues. Those who win twice are in the first league; those who win one and then lose one are in the second league; those who lose one and then win one are in the third league; those who lose two are in the last league. Each league is then scheduled for a round robin tournament. Winners of the leagues can terminate the competition, or one of the various elimination tournaments can be scheduled as a playoff of league winners.

Round Robin and Single Elimination. Teams are divided into leagues with four to six teams in a league. Each league plays a round robin and the teams are rated first, second, third, fourth, fifth, or sixth place or class. First-place teams are scheduled in a first-class elimination tournament; second-place teams are scheduled in a second-class tournament; and so on. A playoff between the class winners can be scheduled.

Qualifying Round and Single Elimination. When space and time are too limited for a large number of competitors to participate in a tournament, the number can be reduced by holding a qualifying round. The eight, sixteen, or designated number of players with the best qualifying scores then play a single-elimination tournament to determine the champion. Such sports as bowling, golf, swimming, and track and field are best adapted for this kind of competition.

Ladder and Pyramid. The ladder and the pyramid tournaments may be arranged in several combinations, most of which are devised by the individuals in charge. An example of this kind of combination is a pyramid tournament with a several-person ladder above the top position. In this competition, sometimes called a *funnel tournament,* the top players challenge and compete as in a ladder tournament for a designated period of time, after which the winner and places are declared. The top players may also be scheduled in an elimination or round robin playoff.

League Tournament

This tournament plan best serves a large number of team entrants. A defined number of teams are grouped together as a league, either arbitrarily, by use of signup sheets, geographic representation, or shared loyalties. A round robin tournament is drawn up scheduling each team to play every other team in its league. Games played, won, and lost are expressed in percentages (games won/games played) carried to three places to the right of the decimal. The winner of each league is that team with the highest percentage of wins. League winners can then be rescheduled in a championship playoff.

Divisions. If the number of participants in a particular league is large, it may be desirable to further separate the league into divisions. Each division would then hold a playoff to determine division championships.

Classes. Dividing participants into classes usually has reference to skill. If skill or potentials of skill as represented in classifications based on size of schools are recognized, leagues can be planned within the various classes.

Flights. This is a term usually used to refer to skill classifications in golf, tennis, badminton, etc., in much the same way as the term "class" is used.

A tournament of four leagues with two divisions in each league might be run off as illustrated in Figure 17-10 in part or whole.

Each division in Figure 17-10 involves four teams. In one plan, the teams within each division will play off to determine a winner. The division winners will play off to determine the championship within the league. This could end the competition, or the leagues can play off to determine the interleague championship. In a second plan the divisions might represent skill classes, and winners would be determined in several levels of skill represented by division 1 champion and division 2 champion.

Miscellaneous Types of Tournaments

Tombstone Tournament. This kind of competition involves the accumulation of a best score over a specified period of time or reaching an established goal in the shortest period of time. For example, golf contestants

Figure 17-10. League Competition

might submit their total score of ten rounds, or swimming contestants might indicate on a chart the distance covered each day. At the end of a certain period of time, that swimmer who has the greatest charted distance is the winner. If the distance is specified, such as ten miles, the first individual to swim that far is the winner. This tournament may be used for group or individual competition in activities such as hiking, track and field events, and basketball shooting.

Ringer Tournament. The ringer tournament permits the contestant a defined number of times to better his or her score, or contestants may submit a defined number of best scores for a total entry in the tournament. As an example, in golf, after six rounds, the player may submit the best scores for each hole and total for the tournament score.

Record Challenge. Contestants try to better existing records in particular sports.

Time-limit Tournament. Many participants can compete simultaneously in a variety of activities in this tournament plan. Activity stations are set up, such as badminton, horseshoes, tennis, and throw for distance. Groups of contestants compete at the various stations. At the end of "time" all rotate to new stations. Competition is continued until all contestants have visited all stations. Scores are totaled to determine the winner.

Flights and Qualifying Rounds. Qualifying rounds refer to preliminary competitions from which the scores are often used to divide players into various skill-level flights for further competition. Golf qualifying scores, for instance, can be used to make up several tournaments of individuals of approximately equal ability.

In some instances, qualifying rounds are used to eliminate or to reduce the number of qualified tournament entrants. This should only be resorted to if there is a limit on time or facilities.

Heats. These preliminary competitions are used when a large number of entries has to be reduced. Heats most frequently are used in track and field and swimming. As many heats are set up as are necessary to accommodate all entries. Entrants draw or are seeded for the heat numbers and best scores or best times determine winners who become entrants for the final event.

Telegraphic Meets. Tournament winners in this type of competition are determined by mail, telegraph, or telephone. In timed or scored events such as swimming, track and field, bowling, golf, and archery, contestants compete with each other at great distance and without the expense and time required to travel. Under mutually defined regulations and supervision the participants exchange scores to determine winners.

DISCUSSION QUESTIONS

1. List criteria that serve as guides in determining good units of competition. What units are commonly used?
2. The practice of equalizing competition has proponents and critics. Give reasons for supporting and opposing the practice.
3. What generally accepted principles underlie the rules and regulations governing sports programs?
4. Local regulations usually have to be developed to accommodate a variety of needs. What are some of the more common considerations?
5. Various "official rules" serve particular programs. What standardized rules are most important to schools? To communities? To colleges?
6. What are the several purposes of tournament plans? Would you offer any advice or caution?
7. What are the most common tournament plans or classifications? How are winners determined for each classification?
8. Explain the following terms: leagues, divisions, classes, and flights.
9. How does one determine in elimination tournaments the number of matches in a single elimination? A double elimination?
10. In an elimination tournament explain the procedure for determining byes and the placement of seeded players.

BIBLIOGRAPHY

BEEMAN, HARRIS F., CAROL A. HARDING, and JAMES H. HUMPHREY, *Intramural Sports: A Text and Study Guide*, 3rd ed. Dubuque, Iowa: W. C. Brown Co., 1974.

BUCHER, CHARLES A., *Administration of Health and Physical Education Programs Including Athletics*, 6th ed. Saint Louis: C. V. Mosby Co., 1975.

MEANS, LOUIS E., *Intramurals: Their Organization and Administration*, 2nd ed. Englewood Cliffs, N.J.: Prentice-Hall, Inc., 1974.

MUELLER, PAT, *Intramurals: Programming and Administration*, 4th ed. New York: The Ronald Press Co., 1971.

ROKOSZ, FRANCIS M., *Structured Intramurals*, Philadelphia, W. B. Saunders Co., 1975.

Community Pool—Championship Meet.
(Courtesy W. David Carew, Director, Maplewood Recreation Department, Maplewood, New Jersey.)

18

Planning, Time and Scheduling

It is a uniquely rewarding experience for an administrator and staff to initiate a sports program. More often responsibility for an existing program is delegated or a budding program is inherited to strengthen a leadership void. At whatever point the administrator and staff assume responsibility, planning time is best invested in the development of structured functions to support the total program design.

Planning requires decision making, program design, and the development of a management approach. A plan of unified functions stated in the form of achievable objectives gives managed direction to a designed program.

THE BEGINNING: PHILOSOPHY AND GOALS

The sports activity program is the means of putting beliefs into action. A well-framed philosophy, therefore, precedes and is fundamental to the development of a program. Effective planning should produce commonly agreed upon philosophical foundations. Identified goals and purposes are then used to facilitate the program design, which should be structured to accomplish these goals.

LEADERSHIP AND STAFF PERSONNEL

Qualified and effective leadership is of primary importance to the success of a program. However, the number of staff is always determined by budget appropriations. Program planning must function within the imposed staff limitations. The selected administration structure thus reflects the number of available professional staff.

Whether administering a recreational sports program within the framework of a college, public school, or a community or community-school situation, basic functions have to be carried out. Health, safety, and participation standards have to be enforced. Facility repairs and maintenance have to be supervised. Budget planning and purchasing has to be carried out. Obtaining volunteers and hiring staff is essential. Program planning and scheduling must be done skillfully and must be responsive to changing demands in order to maintain general support.

To carry out all the basic functions there must be a careful design of administrative time and effective use of leadership and staff personnel.

FACILITIES

Whatever the facility, careful planning should ensure its maximum use. New recreational sports-center buildings may be focal points that will serve the most fortunate students or community members. Existing facilities may be just adequate for others while some designated community schools may have unique facilities. Not all schools and communities, however, can boast of ample facilities for their desired programs.

A review of all facility needs is a primary step in planning. This should be followed by a survey of existing community and school facilities, and finally all possibilities for maximum use should be explored.

ADMINISTRATIVE STRUCTURES

Within the imposed limitations of a particular working situation, the administrative structure has to be decided upon.

Staff-Administered

This administrative structure assumes adequate professional staff to develop, direct, and supervise the program. A responsibility flow chart establishes relationships, and part-time specialists and volunteers provide supplementary leadership resources.

Special-Interest Clubs

With a minimum of administrative staff, interest groups can be given guidance to formalize to club status. A constitution and bylaws provide the means of communications, group control, and self-imposed responsibility. As the number of clubs expands, the potentials of an alliance or board can facilitate administrative needs.

Recreation Association

A recreation association functioning structure facilitates administration of a group of varied interests through its own elected board. It becomes a self-administered organization in need only of defined and agreed-upon professional guidance and direction.

Community School

This administrative approach seemingly could incorporate one or more of the above-mentioned options.

MANAGEMENT PLAN

Educators have with varying degress of success applied the business world's technique of management by objectives. Because many of the sports and recreation directors' responsibilities can be clearly identified as achievable objectives, the application has considerable merit.

As part of an initial leadership planning meeting, thinking has to be consolidated and areas of responsibility have to be defined. The execution of responsibilites should be identified in the form of achievable objectives that are consistent with the accepted program philosophy. The actual accomplishment of the objectives thus becomes an operational means of managing a program.

PROGRAM OPTIONS

The kind of program should be decided upon that can best meet the intended recreation service. Standards should be agreed upon and management objectives outlined.

Regardless of the administrative structure (professional staff, club, recreation association, or community school), the program options to be decided upon reflect the kind of activities and competitive sports to which the administration elects to become committed.

Within-House Activity Program

A "Within-House" plan provides activities and competition for and between its own membership, school, college, or identified "home base." In schools, competition is arranged between homerooms, classes, or color teams. On the college level it is scheduled between fraternities, sororities, classes, or dorms. Units of competition are discussed more fully in Chapter 17.

Communitywide Program

This program option has reference to a defined community within which scheduled activities are planned. Matches, games, or contests are planned as a day or part-day of interplay involving a minimum of expense. Developed informally or as a seasonal schedule, this program can provide excellent opportunities for those of varying skill abilities to enjoy competition and activities with a broader audience of others of like abilities and interests.

Travel Tournament

A program of activities within this classification requires substantial travel and supplementary expenses. It can be planned for the highly skilled players only or it can be offered to anyone or all of the varying skill-level participants. The program limitations are dictated by budget.

ACTIVITIES

Evaluation of program activities should be an ongoing procedure. Various barometers should be implemented occasionally to measure the reception of the offered sports, and participation records should be kept up to date to provide a continuous profile of program support.

Since there are "in" activities, "has-been" sports, and fad favorites, periodic interest surveys will help keep program offerings attuned to current interests and needs. Visitations to other community programs will reveal program overlap and stimulate leadership with new ideas.

The balance of activity offerings included in a program design should reflect the several kinds of potential participants: (1) the fitness-oriented, (2) the recreational and socially oriented, and (3) the highly skilled competitor.

Competitive and Noncompetitive Activities

Program balance requires attention to equating offerings of competitive and noncompetitive sports activities. Traditional team, individual, and dual sports are supported by a basic group of enthusiasts. A team captain is usually responsible for the team's appearance at scheduled games and one or two planned practice sessions each week. Attendance at a designated number of practices should be required to encourage participation, develop individual and team skills, perfect offense and defense technique, improve strategy of play, enable rules interpretation of the game, and physically condition the players.

On occasion folk, square, and modern dance contests have been planned in such areas as: technical skill, choreography, composition, creativeness, costumes, and accompaniments. Swimming is a popular activity which usually includes competition in form, speed, medleys, diving, aquatic art, and synchronized swim.

In April of 1975, 5,000 students of the Renton, Washington schools were surveyed as to their interest in participation in competitive sports. Results of the survey's general findings indicated the "durability" of the traditional activities in their popular appeal.

Student Interest Survey[1]
Renton School District #403
1975

Student Interest Ranked by the Top Ten Sports

High School Rankings		Middle School Rankings	
Girls	*Boys*	*Girls*	*Boys*
Volleyball	Tackle football	Tennis	Tackle football
Tennis	Basketball	Volleyball	Basketball
Softball	Baseball	Swimming	Baseball
Badminton	Soccer	Softball	Swimming
Baseball	Bowling	Badminton	Tennis
Swimming	Tennis	Bowling	Bowling
Basketball	Softball	Baseball	Soccer
Bowling	Swimming	Basketball	Flag football
Track and field	Flag football	Gymnastics	Volleyball
Flag football	Track and field	Soccer	Track and field

In addition to using the traditional format of structured competition in programming sports, noncompetitive activities should be an important part of the program design. Dance, swimming, boating, conditioning, hiking, jogging, and climbing are just some of the vigorous activities that should be included.

If the program is serving a broad age group, the following list of activities selected from Lincoln Community Education Program's "Interest and Talent Survey" suggests many less vigorous program potentials:

---

[1]"Activities Report to the Board of Directors," Renton School District No. 403, Activities Department (Renton, Washington: 1975), p. 2.

Interest and Talent Survey[2]

Recreation and Hobbies

Archery	Dance: folk	Family recreation	Shuffleboard
Badminton	Dance: square	Judo	Table tennis
Bird watching	Dance: modern	Karate	Tennis
Bridge	Fishing skills	Model building	Volleyball
Camping skills	Fly tying	Physical fitness	Weight lifting
Canoeing	Golf	Pinochle	Wilderness survival
Checkers and chess	Hiking club	Roller skating	Yoga
Dance, ballet	Jogging class	Sailing	

Open Activities

The opportunity to "drop in" for a game or a workout should be included in program planning, and there are a variety of ways in which this is done. One plan is that of making facilities and equipment available whenever they are not in use for classes or scheduled activity. Other organizations set aside a certain evening or day of the week when the facilities may be used informally. A third plan is that of scheduling time for unorganized play in certain activities.

Regularly scheduled evenings and days such as Friday afternoons and evenings and all day Saturday and Sunday are most satisfactory. By setting aside regular times for unorganized activity, participants establish recreation habits and are able to plan to play on certain days or evenings.

Activities enjoyed by interest groups and outing clubs are often publicized in a calendar of activities. These include such things as canoeing expeditions, cave exploring ventures, bird walks, hikes, and camping trips. Those interested appear at the acknowledged time and place.

Drop-in programs offered by college and university student unions are aimed at the busy activity-oriented student. A very successful program is illustrated by the Washington State University's weekly co-recreation program in Figure 18-1.

Variety

A variety of activities should characterize the program offerings. There are individuals who are interested in playing for the sake of activity. There are others who are highly competitive and gain their greatest satisfactions in strenuous competition. There are some who are primarily interested in recreation for exercise, to keep trim, and to main-

[2]Recreation and Hobbies section of "Lincoln Community Education Program—Interest and Talent Survey," Lincoln High School (PTSA), Seattle, Washington.

A S W S U   C O - R E C R E A T I O N   P R O G R A M

The indoor recreation facilities of the New Gym, Smith Gym, Bohler Gym and the fieldhouse are open to students in the evening and all day on weekends for "free time" recreation. Following is a schedule of the various activities offered. For further information, call ASWSU Recreation, CUB B-27, 335-2651.

Badminton	Co-Ed, Friday, Saturday and Monday, 7:00 - 10:00 pm Sunday, 2:00 - 5:00 pm, Smith Gym
Basketball	Co-Ed, Monday - Friday, 5:00 - 10:00 pm, Saturday and Sunday 10:00 am - 10:00 pm
Co-Ed Gymnastics	Friday 7:00 - 10:00 pm, Saturday and Sunday 2:00 - 5:00 pm Bohler Gynmastic Room
Women's Gymnastics	Tuesday and Thursday, 7:00 - 9:00 pm, Bohler Gymnastic Room
Handball/Racquetball	Monday - Friday 12 noon - 1:00 pm and 5:00 - 10:00 pm, Saturday and Sunday 10:00 am - 10:00 pm, New Gym and Bohler Courts
Co-Ed Swimming	Monday - Friday, 12 noon - 1:00 pm and 7:00 - 10:00 pm, Saturday and Sunday 2:00 - 5:00 pm and 7:00 - 10:00 pm, New Gym Pool
Family Swimming	Friday 7:00 - 10:00 pm, Saturday 2:00 - 5:00 pm and 7:00 - 10:00 pm, and Sunday 2:00 - 5:00 pm, Smith Gym Pool
Women's Weight Training	Every evening 7:00 - 10:00 pm, Smith 124
Men's Weight Training	Monday - Friday 5:00 - 10:00 pm, Saturday and Sunday 10:00 am - 10:00 pm, New Gym
Olympic Weight Training	Monday - Friday 7:00 - 9:00 pm, Bohler Olympic Room
Sauna	Monday - Friday 5:00 - 10:00 pm, Saturday and Sunday 10:00 am - 10:00 pm, New Gym Locker Rooms
Tennis (Indoor)	Monday, Wednesday, Friday 7:00 - 10:00 pm, Saturday and Sunday 2:00 - 10:00 pm, Fieldhouse
Volleyball	Monday, Thursday, Friday 7:00 - 10:00 pm, Saturday and Sunday 10:00 am - 10:00 pm, New Gym 144

<u>Recreation Equipment Check-out</u> - New Gym Locker Rooms

1.	Swim Suits	6.	Basketballs
2.	Towels	7.	Soccer Balls
3.	Badminton Rackets	8.	Softballs and bats
4.	Tennis Rackets	9.	Racquetball Rackets (25¢ hour)
5.	Volleyballs	10.	Racquetballs - Handballs (For Sale)

Figure 18-1. Associated Students Washington State University Co-Recreation Program

tain their good physical health and appearance. There are others who are interested in recreation because of its importance to their social life. A good program contributes to the satisfaction of all of these individuals.

Co-Recreation

The challenge of providing equal opportunities for boys and girls in
sports has stimulated many more programs that include mixed competition for those of appropriate and compatible skill abilities. Boy-girl,
men-women mixed activities have an educationally and socially valuable
role in program planning. For the young-co-recreation is an excellent
opportunity to educate for social maturity. For adults, co-recreation provides enjoyable social experience. With health and physical safeguards
enforced, co-recreation and sports competition for the equally skilled is an
important part of program planning.

Flexibility

Effective and appropriate planning of recreational sports programs
requires attention to a constant awareness of changing needs and interests. It requires leadership that provides the kind of opportune experiences that will enable all ages to enjoy a variety of skills and activities
when they are most meaningful. Important to good program planning is
built-in flexibility that will allow response to surges of interest such as
that recently evidenced in hiking, canoeing, parachuting, gliding, skydiv-
ing, spelunking, rock climbing, and sports activities in which both sexes
are able to enjoy participation together.

Voluntary

Voluntary participation insures greater chances of success. A program sensitized by support of those who elect to participate will succeed
to the degree that the program meets the needs and interests of the
greatest number.

Sports Skills and Knowledge

Developmental opportunities should be planned for the nonskilled
as well as for the highly skilled. Because an activity is more enjoyable if
the participants know the fundamental skills and rules of the game,
some plans should be made available for those interested in self-
improvement. Bulletin boards, practice sessions, drills, achievement,
skill tests, and planned courses of instruction have all been used to provide such opportunities.

EVALUATION AND REPORTS

An evaluation and reports procedure is an important aspect of planning that should be built into the overall program design. It is the means of producing resources that can give justifiable support for the decisions of director and staff.

Program support and promotion is revealed in participation data.

Needs and interests can be determined from interest surveys of participants.

Staff effectiveness is determined by mutually developed evaluation tools.

Financial accountability can be interpreted in light of participant cost analysis for the various phases of the program.

ACTIVITY PERIODS

Busy schedules include varied pieces of free time. Most often no one period of free time is common to all potential participants. Multi-scheduled informal programs function effectively in spite of this planning limitation, but for those programs dependent on date, time, and place tournament schedules, the planning problems become very complex. All possibilities for time slots and facilities must be explored and sometimes directors must lobby and convince others of the need. Computerized scheduling can be used by some to facilitate the matching process.

The discussion that follows considers the school-age recreator as well as the post-school participant.

Early Morning

The early program provides an opportunity to engage in programs for those many who could not during the day, after school, or after work. The pre-work scheduling provides for early activity in the daily schedule. Although not extensively used by the schools, the early-morning time can also serve students who arrive early and have no constructive use for their time. Advanced planning and arrangements for equipment should maximize playing time, which must end promptly when daily classes begin. The activities that meet with greatest success in this time include jogging, volleyball, table tennis, shuffleboard, horseshoes, archery, basketball, golf putting and driving contests, and bowling.

Noon Hour

The demands of transportation and work compel a great number of participants to consider the noon hour as the only possible time for recreation and intramural activities. This is particularly applicable for students in the consolidated school systems, the working persons in large cities, and college personnel who are overscheduled with committee and class commitments.

To ensure an unhurried lunch for students, directors most often either plan activities only after a lunch period of at least twenty minutes, or start activities immediately after the last morning period and then allow adequate time for a shower and twenty-minute lunch period before afternoon classes. Both plans, whether supervised by a director or rotating faculty member, require strict enforcement of the activity and lunchtime periods.

As greater flexibility is introduced into the lives of students and working persons, support for the noon-hour program grows. The benefits from a varied program including competitive team and individual sports as well as noncompetitive recreation activities become evident. In the schools, student and teacher participation promotes good rapport. Good use of students' formerly idle time has in some schools improved social conditions and reduced discipline problems connected with gambling, drinking, drugs, and undesirable sex behavior.

Among faculty, teachers, and businesspeople there has been an increased interest in noon-hour fitness programs, informal recreation, and "pick-up" team games. Improved on-the-job efficiency seems evident from favorable reports of noon-hour programs from such corporations as United States Steel, Radio Corporation of America, International Business Machines, American Telephone & Telegraph, and others.[3]

Early Afternoon

The daytime recreational sports program serves the student, housewife, and retiree or the businessperson who can schedule his or her own kind of free time. Because many students arrive just before classes begin and leave immediately at their finish, scheduling intramural and recreation programs at unusual periods during the day is possible. To serve full-time students, programs often must be scheduled for recess free periods, club periods, special extracurricular periods, and special day periods. Sometimes physical education periods or parts of

[3]Charles A. Bucher and Stanley L. Englebardt, "Exercise is 'Plain Good Business,'" *The Reader's Digest* (February 1976), pp. 127-130.

class hours are devoted to intramural and recreation competition, but this move can weaken the basic instructional program. If activities are scheduled during free periods at the end of either the morning or after-noon classes, the time is sufficient for participation and for showering. Teachers may also be available to help assist in supervising the program. When special periods of the school day are set aside for activities, the intramural and recreation program will be well attended, but pressures of the short time limitation will soon become apparent.

Late Afternoon

Late-afternoon programs are most popular for the school and community programs geared for the school-aged youngster. While the adults have less free time between 3 to 6 P.M., most students are free and ready for activity. The college class schedules, however, continue to offer conflicts—except for the smaller colleges, which make a particular effort to protect this time block for recreational activity. Some of them have developed unique and extensive indoor and outdoor courts, fields, gymnasia, and pools. Well-planned late-afternoon programs avoid con-flict with varsity teams, and make more play time available for all par-ticipants. Increasingly school and community are cooperating in use and administration of facilities during complementing peak and off-peak hours of use.

Evening

As more individuals have turned to recreational sports in school, colleges, and the community, the evening programs have grown in popularity. In schools and colleges, such programs are on the increase because of heavy daytime academic commitments; unavailability of staff, facilities, and equipment; programming conflicts; and increasing con-struction of new buildings on playing fields necessitating more intensive use of the remaining facilities. With the growth of the evening programs come possible conflicts with varsity schedules, alumni and community groups who wish to use the same facilities, and unforeseen changes of events. Though students currently enrolled should unquestionably have priority with regard to facilities and equipment, long-range planning is imperative for a smoothly functioning program.

A most important part of the community recreation program is the evening program, often heavily designed to serve adult working people. Here as well as in the schools, schedules should be formulated as early as possible. It is also helpful to set aside hours of the week for special groups so that facilities and equipment are not arbitrarily taken from a program already planned.

Saturday and Sunday

Intramural directors as a group have not made use of Saturday and Sunday for scheduling team events in recreational sports because of a variety of commitments on the part of the students, staffing, and administering facilities. The greatest success has been with unscheduled recreational activities over the weekend made possible by providing facilities, equipment, and supervision through a signup and signout service usually administered by qualified part-time help.

The community or community-school programs thrive on weekend schedules of activities planned for all age groups. The biggest challenge to these directors is that of working out scheduled use of facilities such as the swimming pool, gym, bowling alleys, exercise rooms, and so forth.

Vacation and Summer Programs

Recreational sports and competition attracts many students during vacation periods and the summer months and during the academic year. Municipal and community-school recreation programs are expanding summer programs, and the schools and colleges continue to broaden their recreation services during the vacation periods of the academic year. The vacation recreation responsibilities are often reflected in the role of the school in a particular town or city.

SCHEDULING

To schedule effectively the units of competition in the community and school recreational sports program, the director and staff must skillfully match the available time of participants in the program with the available equipment and staff.

Limitations

Scheduling limitations that most commonly must be considered include inadequate facilities, double-session school programs, priority use of facilities by other groups, job and working-time demands made upon participants, available transportation, and the number and experience of leaders.

In addition to facility, time, and personnel limitations that affect scheduling, careful attention must be given to a whole series of other factors. These include the number of entries in a given activity; the skill level of the various participants; the type of competition and thus the number of practices, and games to be played; conflicts; and possible postponements because of unforeseen conditions.

Signup Procedures

Entry. To sign up officially as participants in a program, *team managers* should ensure completion of entry blanks which contain date; name; alphabetical list of team members, and eligibility verification; team managers' name, address, and phone number; a list of event entries; a list of days and hours when individuals or teams will be available for participation. Space should be provided for departmental information such as code or name to signify that the entry has been processed. If an organization enters more than one team, a separate entry sheet should be completed for each entrant in order to maintain proper records and scheduling. Figure 18-2 illustrates the use of a team membership entry form.

VOLLEYBALL

Co-Ed Sign-Up

Team Name ______

Manager ______ Address ______ Phone ______

Men	Eligibility	Women	Eligibility
1.		1.	
2.		2.	
3.		3.	
4.		4.	
5.		5.	
6.		6.	

Check Schedule Time Available

PM	M	T	W	T	F
3					
4					
5					
6					
7					
8					
9					

Approval	
Schedule	

Figure 18-2. Team Signup Form

Deadlines. Deadlines are the responsibility of the director as well as the participants. The participants must meet the deadline of registering and the director must administer the program so as to keep participants informed well in advance about the activities, including all deadlines for registration.

Signup procedures are either set up with registration deadlines for all participants or deadlines for team registration, with the team retaining the flexibility of filling its roster following last-minute dropouts. Success for the team registration procedure rests upon the strength of the team captain or manager. Figure 18-3 illustrates the use of a team roster form.

Forfeits and Postponements. Both forfeits and postponements damage a program. In the case of forfeits, which occur when a team fails to appear but makes no arrangement for a postponement, the team that does arrive ready for play is disappointed. Even though it is declared the winner through forfeit, its members tend to lose interest.

Postponements have a comparable effect and usually arise from conflicting demands on time and facilities or inclement weather. In the case of requests for postponement, the director, after careful evaluation, should grant them only for urgent reasons. A strict, though equitable policy should be enforced because postponements, too easily secured, may lead to total disintegration of the program.

Inclement weather creates special problems that sometimes necessitates decisions being made only at game time. A plan that has been adopted with some success has the teams appear on schedule ready to play unless the team managers receive postponement notification at least an hour before game time. A last-minute cancellation is the product of a joint decision made by an intramural staff member, the officials, and the team managers. If serious disagreement arises, the intramural staff member usually has the authority to cancel a contest if it is deemed that cancellation is in the best interests of the participants and the program.

Rules and Regulations. Sometimes included in entry forms are supplemental printout sheets of rules that allow understanding and acceptance of the terms under which participants will compete. This practice enhances mutual understanding and good relationships.

Schedule Calendar

Immediately after all entries are in, schedules should be developed and participants informed as soon as possible.

Date, Time, Place. After deadline dates have passed, the director knows the number of participants involved in an activity. Assuming the tour-

Department of Physical Education: Recreation Sports Division

....
Name of Organization

Date: ....

Rules of Eligibility:

1. Clubs in "open" division are limited to 15 members, no more than three of whom may be physical Education "Majors".
2. Any student in good standing may compete for only 1 organization. Pledgees are ineligible.
3. No man who has earned a varsity (major or minor) letter may compete in his sport.
4. No member of a varsity or frosh squad may compete in intramurals during the season in which he is active.
5. No man who has been assigned to Modified Physical Education or who has been exempted from the required courses for medical reasons shall be eligible unless he has been cleared by the College Physician.

| PRINT ALPHABETICALLY | | STUDENT NO. | CURR. NO. | VARSITY OR FROSH. (INDICATE SPORT) | MOD. P. E. | SIGNATURE |
LAST NAME	FIRST					

The above members of the .... are to my knowledge members in good standing in
(Name of Organization)
Brooklyn College. I further certify that their signatures are valid.

Athletic Chairman: ....

ROSTER FORM

Form 52 ◄━━► 61

Figure 18-3. Intramural Team Roster at Brooklyn College of the City University of New York

nament plan had been established before registration (round robin, elimination, etc.), the number of matches necessary to schedule can then be determined. With the available time and dates of the participants and facilities in mind, the director develops a schedule of matches.

Whenever possible, the director should honor the stated preferences of the participants for playing time. Sometimes scheduling teams to play the same time slot each week works well. When inevitable conflicts arise, the staff and team managers should work out solutions satisfactory to the interested parties that are also in accordance with the welfare of the program.

Duplication and Distribution. Schedules, once completed, should be entered on schedule calendars and mailed to team managers, participants, and the editors or sports writers of the school, college, and/or community newspaper. Copies should also be posted on the appropriate bulletin boards. It is customary to assemble all available information on daily, weekly, monthly, or seasonal and yearly calendars. The yearly calendar provides a broad view of the events scheduled in the program: the entry dates; the dates of the beginning of competition; and the traditional events that take place each year, such as the spring track meet or the intramural picnic. The seasonal or monthly calendars contain the more detailed pertinent information such as sport, teams, date, time of contests, and location of facility. As supplementary information is acquired, it should be distributed as quickly as possible on daily or weekly calendars.

In addition to using the calendar as a notification and promotional technique, many directors call or write participating organizations to insure that all details are in order or that a group has not accidentally overlooked a notification. This last-minute checking, however, should be used with care lest it encourage too much reliance on professional staff. Such an outcome defeats the goals of the program.

Rescheduling Postponements

When postponements have made it almost impossible to reschedule full games, some have found it satisfactory to shorten the time of rescheduled matches, either at the end of season during allotted time or during an open date in the schedule. Elimination-type competition requires that all games be postponed because future games are dependent on the outcome of postponed games.

Forms

The kind and number of forms developed for scheduling reflects the size of the total program. A relatively small program may be able to operate satisfactorily from an original work schedule for the year indicating a relatively few sport seasons and activities overlapping. More highly developed programs having many things going on at once can develop daily schedules for office use, with mimeographed duplicates for staff, participants, and publicity. Sheets should include sport, competitors, date, time, place, officials, and contact person notified. Some forms are designed with a place for scores and participants' standing in the competition.

Some programs include a notification form whereby competitors are reminded a couple of days ahead of time of their upcoming match.

DISCUSSION QUESTIONS

1. What is a fundamental starting base for the development of a recreational sports program? How would you develop this base?

2. How would you develop personnel needs? What part of the budget monies would personnel represent?

3. An inventory of facility resources is essential to program design. How may this be done?

4. What is a management plan? Outline one for a proposed program. Justify your choices.

5. Participation interests should be reflected in program offerings. How would you propose to keep up with changing interests?

6. What is program balance? How would you propose maintaining it?

7. Outline an evaluation and reports procedure that strengthens future planning and portrays the present program.

8. What periods of scheduling time are most successful for the school program? College program? Community program?

9. What are the scheduling limitations that most commonly must be considered?

10. How would you minimize the problems encountered in signup procedures with regard to entries, deadlines, forfeits, postponements, etc.?

BIBLIOGRAPHY

BEEMAN, HARRIS F., CAROL A. HARDING, and JAMES H. HUMPHREY, *Intramural Sports: A Text and Study Guide*, 3rd ed. Dubuque, Iowa: W. C. Brown Co., Publishers, 1974.

MEANS, LOUIS E., *Intramurals: Their Organization and Administration*, 2nd ed. Englewood Cliffs, N.J.: Prentice-Hall, Inc., 1974.

MUELLER, PAT, *Intramurals: Programming and Administration*, 4th ed. New York: Ronald Press Co., 1971.

ROKOSZ, FRANCIS M., *Structured Intramurals*. Philadelphia: W. B. Saunders Co., 1975.

Lacrosse.
(Courtesy News-Record of Maplewood and South Orange, New Jersey.)

19

National Organizations
and Sports
Information Sources

A great number of different sports characterize school, college, and community recreational sports programs. Whether a director, a participants' committee, or a representative board recommends activities, those selected will differ from program to program and will change year to year to reflect changing interests. This chapter therefore evolves as an extensive but by no means complete summary of amateur sports and recreational sports associations and organizations that will serve as resources for specific information, official rules, and regulations.

NATIONAL ORGANIZATIONS FOR AMATEURS

National organizations have been developed for a number of very valid reasons: (1) to better regulate amateur sports through enforced standards that safeguard players' welfare; (2) to serve individuals, schools, and communities by enabling them to share solutions to common problems; (3) to effect changes for mutual good through united action; and (4) to develop rules and regulations consistent with best practices in sports participation for the amateur.

Organizations are of two kinds. The first may be described as an umbrella-type association concerned with several activities. The first half of this chapter describes these associations. The second classification is concerned only with a specific sport. The second half of this chapter describes these organizations in chart form.

THE AMERICAN ALLIANCE FOR HEALTH, PHYSICAL EDUCATION AND RECREATION (AAHPER)
(1201 16th Street, N.W., Washington, D.C. 20036)

A long and honorably serving AAHPER can be traced back to 1885, when it came into being as the Association for the Advancement of Physical Education. With a name change to American Physical Education Association and eventual additions of "health" and "recreation," its expansion in title stabilized as American Association for Health, Physical Education and Recreation. Related and allied interest groups, however, have continued to affiliate and grow within the structure until reorganization and interest-group self-autonomy has become the most practical direction for continued growth and survival.

In 1974 the American Association for Health, Physical Education and Recreation underwent reorganization to become the American Alliance for Health, Physical Education and Recreation. Seven allied independent associations representing specialized interests include

American Association for Leisure and Recreation

American School and Community Safety

Association for the Advancement of Health Education

Association for Research, Administration, Professional Councils and Societies

National Association for Girls and Women in Sport

National Association for Sport and Physical Education

National Dance Association

The alliance functions to serve and promote the interests of its member associations. Its publications include the *Journal of Physical Education and Recreation, Research Quarterly*, and many special materials and books.

THE NATIONAL ASSOCIATION FOR GIRLS AND WOMEN IN SPORT (NAGWS)
(1201 16th Street, N.W., Washington, D.C. 20036)

An alliance member of AAHPER, this group is primarily concerned with the development of "quality sports programs for girls and women both inside and outside the school environment." It establishes standards of women's sports in all grades, colleges, and various after-school recreation programs and supports both intramural and interscholastic programs to serve those of varied skill abilities.

The Association sponsors women's (1) national and regional coaches seminars, (2) athletic trainers' workshops, (3) officials' update clinics, and (4) a variety of in-service leadership training programs that reflect the expressed needs of its membership.

Where women conduct programs similar to those of other national organizations, the Association acts as an interest group whose purpose it is to uphold the standards for women's participation as well as to safeguard the health and welfare of the players.

Through liaison representation, the NAGWS maintains contact with allied organizations and associations of related interests such as the National Federation of State High School Associations, the National Collegiate Athletic Association, the United States Olympic Games Commitee, and the Amateur Athletic Union. Through established channels of communications, such matters in common as philosophies, standards, new interests, and decisions are shared via exchanges and reports.

The NAGWS is responsible for many publications, including teaching materials, technique articles, resource books, and official rules for women. These rules, developed in light of current sound practices for girls and women, are continually updated and printed in respective sports guidebooks.

THE NATIONAL ASSOCIATION OF SPORTS AND PHYSICAL EDUCATION (NASPE)

(1201 16th Street, N.E., Washington, D.C. 20036)

The reorganization of the American Association for Health, Physical Education and Recreation to become the American Alliance for Health, Physical Education and Recreation evolved with the creation of a new venture known as NASPE. This alliance member became fully operational in 1977 and identifies three organizationally structured areas: (1) Physical Education Instructional Programs, (2) Physical Education and Sports Administration, and (3) Sports Development.

Councils function within each area to serve specific interests. The Administration of Physical Education and Sport and the Sport Development components of the association serve those interest groups concerned with sport and recreation programs on the elementary, high school, and college levels.

Councils involved with various aspects of the sports programs include (1) National Officials Council (2) National Trainers Council (3) National Coaches Council (4) National Sports Clubs Council (5) National Council of Secondary School Athletic Directors (6) National Intramural Sports Council.

NATIONAL INTRAMURAL SPORTS COUNCIL (NISC)
(1201 16th Street, N.W., Washington, D.C. 20036)

The NISC was cooperatively sponsored by the Division of Girls' and Women's Sports and the Division of Men's Athletics in May 1965 for the purpose of serving as a coordinating structure for men's and women's intramurals. The objective of the council is to provide leadership to initiate and improve intramural programs at all educational levels.

In January 1966 a National Intramural Sports Council Committee of six met in Washington, D.C., to develop an operating code and to initiate its first projects. Granted permanent status in 1968 by the board of the AAHPER, the Council continues its affiliation under the co-sponsorship of NASPE and NAGWS.

The NISC schedules an annual executive committee meeting, has state representatives, and develops regional conferences. The publication *Intramural Messenger* aims to keep members informed of related activities, new programs, changing philosophies, practices, and new publications.

NATIONAL COUNCIL OF SECONDARY SCHOOL ATHLETIC DIRECTORS (NCSSAD)
(1201 16th Street, N.W., Washington, D.C. 20036)

Formed in 1969, the NCSSAD, a structure of the NASPE, aims to increase services to secondary-school athletic directors. Membership is open to all AAHPER-NASPE associates having "primary responsibility for directing, administering or coordinating the interscholastic athletic programs at the junior and senior high school levels." The Council is open to both women and men of responsibility and interest, and is actively exploring ways to involve women in the council membership and activities.

The Council publishes a newsletter, *The Athletic Director,* six times a year. In 1972, together with AAHPER and Schering Corporation, the Council initiated the "Athletic Director of the Year Award" to give recognition to that person who exemplifies the highest standards of the profession and has had outstanding positive impact on children, school, and community. In 1973 the recognition program was extended to include state awards; and regionals were identified in 1975.

The executive board and advisory board meet annually, and others in attendance include presidents of state athletic directors' associations and representatives of those states not so organized, female directors and administrators in all states, the National Federation of State High School Athletic Associations, and the National Association of Secondary Schools.

NATIONAL FEDERATION OF STATE HIGH SCHOOL ASSOCIATIONS (NFSHA)
(400 Leslie Street, P.O. Box 98, Elgin, Illinois 60120)

Formerly (1970) the National Federation of High School Athletic Associations, and founded in 1920, this organization is a federation of fifty independent state high school athletic (activities) associations and nine Canadian affiliates. It is the coordinating agency for high school extracurricular activities including sports. It protects and supervises interstate interests and the activities of the state associations and establishes and annually publishes rules and official training material for a variety of sports.

State High School Athletic and Activity Association affiliates of the NFSHA are the regulatory bodies for its state member schools. State Association concerns include athletic insurance, officials, awards, equipment, meets and tournaments, and classification of schools. Activity concerns usually include boys' and girls' athletics, and forensic and music activities. Rules, regulations, and standards are spelled out in an annually published state handbook.

An increasing number of state associations are devoting more attention to girls' activities, affording to them the same athletic opportunities that have been available to boys for many years. Associations are expanding to include female representation and executive secretaries and are supporting rules and regulations based upon NAGWS guidelines and standards.

The NFSHA unites the thinking and practices of its membership. A full-time executive staff, a legislative body known as the National Council, and an executive body known as the Executive Committee coordinate efforts which give direction to the association's interest.

THE NATIONAL COMMUNITY EDUCATION ASSOCIATION (NCEA)
(1017 Avon Street, Flint, Michigan 48503)

Founded in 1966, NCEA grew out of the community education movement in Flint, Michigan and the efforts of a group of community school directors to share experience and problems. Incorporated in Michigan with nineteen charter members, the organization serves people interested in the development of community education.

The NCEA is dedicated to the advancement and expansion of

community education, and acts as a clearinghouse and active liaison agency. It alerts members to important legislation, awards, outstanding leadership, and service in the field of community education. Publications include *NCEA News, Community Education Journal,* and the annual *Who's Who in Community Education.*

The Association's membership provides program evaluations and consultant services and sponsors regional and national conferences. An executive secretary coordinates and carries out the business of the Association.

Increasingly, community education associations are organizing on the state level and affiliating with the national group. Leadership in this direction has been initiated by Oregon, Missouri, Ohio, Alabama, Colorado, Michigan, Florida, Texas, Arizona, and Washington.

ASSOCIATION FOR INTERCOLLEGIATE ATHLETICS FOR WOMEN (AIAW)
(1201 16th Street, N.W., Washington, D.C. 20036)

A resource for leadership, guidelines, and standards in women's collegiate sports, the AIAW has evolved from the long history of women's increasing interest in skilled competition that dates back to the formalization, in June 1956, of the Tripartite Committee on Golf, which in turn sponsored a precedent-establishing golf championship.

Evolving from Tripartite Committee leadership, in 1958 the National Joint Committee on Extramural Sports for college women was formed, including representatives from AAHPER and women's allied professional associations. It served to develop and extend extramural sports for women. In 1965 the Conference on Competition developed *Guidelines for Intercollegiate Athletic Programs for Women.* The Joint Committee was dissolved and was soon followed by the Commission on Intercollegiate Athletics for Women (CIAW) in 1967. The thrust of the Commission, to encourage and support women's leadership in intercollegiate local, state, regional, and national championships, produced regional and state governing groups and seven national championships.

In 1971–72 the AIAW was formally organized and replaced CIAW. The AIAW sponsors national championships for women in basketball, golf, gymnastics, track and field, badminton, swimming and diving, and volleyball. An executive director was hired in 1974. The structure of the Association includes officers and the following committees: nominating, ethics and eligibility, constitution and bylaws, handbook, sports archivist, research, and delegate assembly. Nine regional organizations with representation on the executive board are recognized as governance units: Eastern, Southern, Southeastern, Southwest, Midwest, Region 6, Intermountain, Western, and Northwest. AIAW membership requires regional affiliation.[1]

The publication *AIAW Handbook-Directory* includes the group's organizational structure and purpose, position statements, policies and procedures for championships, code of ethics, eligibility rules, tournament schedules, and a directory of AIAW member institutions. A newsletter three times a year keeps membership up to date, as does its semiannual convention.

NATIONAL COLLEGIATE ATHLETIC ASSOCIATION (NCAA)
(U.S. Highway 50 and Hall Ave., P.O. Box 1906, Shawnee Mission, Kansas 66222)

The National Collegiate Athletic Association was originally formed in 1906 to assist in the development of sound regulations and foundations for intercollegiate athletics for men and to promote the concept of amateurism.

An association of universities, colleges, and allied education associations, the NCAA is governed by a policy-making council. Through geographic districts it continues its original task of promoting uniform and high standards of intercollegiate sports. It preserves records, and sponsors and supervises regional and national meets and tournaments for member institutions. It serves as a headquarters for collegiate athletic matters of national importance.

In addition to numerous rule books, handbooks, and special reports, the National Collegiate Athletic Association publishes official guides in football, basketball, swimming, track and field, soccer, lacrosse, boxing, ice hockey, and wrestling. It also compiles statistics and offers the services of a film library.

NATIONAL ASSOCIATION OF INTERCOLLEGIATE ATHLETICS (NAIA)
(1205 Baltimore, Kansas City, Missouri 64105)

This is an association of four-year colleges of small and moderate enrollments interested in sharing problems and promoting educationally sound intercollegiate programs. It sponsors national sports championships, compiles statistics, and conducts coaches' workshops and clinics. Its stated purpose is to "develop intercollegiate athletic programs as an

---

[1]National Association for Girls and Women in Sport, *AIAW Handbook Directory* (Washington, D.C.: American Alliance for Health, Physical Education and Recreation, 1975–76).

integral part of the total educational program of the college rather than as a separate commercial or promotional adjunct."

NATIONAL JUNIOR COLLEGE ATHLETIC ASSOCIATION (NJCAA)
(P.O. Box 1586, Hutchinson, Kansas 67501)

The NJCAA promotes junior college athletics on international and national levels. It functions through regional offices, elected directors, and services of special committees. The Association is affiliated with many national sports organizations, maintains a Hall of Fame, and compiles statistics on sport rankings.

AMATEUR ATHLETIC UNION OF THE UNITED STATES (AAU)
(3400 W. 86 Street, Indianapolis, Indiana 46268)

Formed in 1888 to end abuses, corruption, and gambling with which sport was becoming associated, the Union was organized as a federation of athletic clubs, educational institutions, and bona fide amateur athletic associations. There was, at the time, a felt need to control the evils of professionalism in men's sports, promote legitimate sports, standardize rules, and conduct orderly, respectable, and fair competition.

The Union was successful in its efforts and grew in strength—today this voluntary service organization is made up of fifty-seven district associations that operate under a constitution laid down by the national organization.

The officers and committees of these geographical groups promote and develop district and local athletic programs as well as stimulate participation in the various championships sponsored by the national organization. Each member club is represented in the territory association and each association (geographical group) is represented in the national organization.

The AAU recognizes all amateur sports, supports the Olympic games program, and claims jurisdiction over track and field, basketball, boxing, gymnastics, handball, swimming, water polo, tug-of-war, wrestling, weightlifting, volleyball, codeball, field ball, bobsledding, ice hockey, indoor horseshoe pitching, skindiving, and baton twirling. This jurisdiction includes the development of official rules of the sports and regulations for national competition.

For boys and girls up to 17 years of age the Union conducts and sanctions local, state, regional, national, and international competition. It also conducts Junior Olympics in basketball, boxing, gymnastics, judo, swimming, track and field, water polo, weightlifting, and wrestling.

NATIONAL RECREATION AND PARK ASSOCIATION (NRPA)
(1601 N. Kent Street, Arlington, Virginia 22209)

This group, founded in 1965, represents a merger of the American Institute of Park Executives, the American Recreation Society, National Conference of State Parks, and the National Recreation Association. The membership and staff aim to improve the human environment through improved park recreation and leisure opportunities. Through regional service centers the Association provides programs to upgrade leadership, disseminates innovative ideas and research, and provides technical assistance to member groups. In addition to special publications, the association makes available *Parks and Recreation Magazine, Recreation and Park Yearbook, Journal of Leisure Research,* and *Therapeutic Recreation Journal.*

THE ATHLETIC INSTITUTE
(805 Merchandise Mart, Chicago, Illinois 606504)

This institute is a manufacturer of athletic equipment, trophies, and visual aids. As a service organization the institute has sponsored workshops and organized national conferences on areas of concern in health, recreation, and physical education. It publishes *Sportscope,* handbooks, and pamphlets.

NATIONAL WHEELCHAIR ATHLETIC ASSOCIATION (NWAA)
(40-24 62nd Street, Woodside, N.J. 11377)

Administered by the National Wheelchair Athletic Committee, this group is concerned with promoting regional and national sports activities and competition for men and women wheelchair athletes. Programs are planned in track and field, swimming, archery, table tennis, bowling, and weightlifting. National champions are eligible for selection on the United States wheelchair "Paralympic Team" to compete internationally.

ATHLETICS FOR THE BLIND
(152 West 42nd Street, New York, N.Y. 10036)

Athletics for the Blind concerns itself with developing innovative ways of enabling the blind to enjoy athletic experiences. The members develop methods of teaching and disseminate printed and Braille material and athletic equipment to organizations for the blind. Activities in which the Association has been involved include bowling, roller skating, wrestling, dancing, weightlifting, photography, chess, checkers, dominoes, and cards.

NATIONAL THERAPEUTIC RECREATION SOCIETY (NTRS)
(1700 Pennsylvania Avenue, N.W., Washington, D.C. 20006)

Founded by a merger of the National Association of Recreation Therapists and the American Park and Recreation Society Hospital Section, this group of professional persons is concerned with the therapeutic use of recreation for the ill and handicapped. The Society promotes professional growth through in-service training. It publishes *Therapeutic Recreation Journal* and *Therapeutic Recreation Annual*.

NATIONAL SPORTS AND RECREATION ASSOCIATIONS

The promotion of a particular sport and the concerns of its leadership often join forces in a national organization of that activity. A resource chart is included on the following pages.

Archery

American Archery Council 618 Chalmers Street Flint, Mich. 48503	Representative of national archery organizations. Promotes, develops, and promulgates archery.	*AAC Newsletter* *ABC's of Archery*
National Archery Association of the United States (NAA) 1951 Geraldson Drive Lancaster, Pa. 17601	Individual and club memberships for bow hunting, field, recreation, and target archery. The Association standardizes rules, procedures, maintains official records, and sponsors national championships and matches.	*Archery World* Pamphlets Handbooks

Archery (cont.)

National Field Archery Association (NFAA) Route 2, Box 514 Redlands, Calif. 92373	Membership of field archers and bow-hunters that sponsor national and sectional tournaments and national mail tournaments, establishes standard rules, promotes the sport and game conservation through field archery schools.	*Archery Official Handbook of Field Archery*

Badminton

American Badminton Association (ABA) 1330 Alexandria Drive San Diego, Calif. 92107	The governing body in the United States upholds rules and sponsors tournaments.	*Badminton U.S.A. ABA Bulletin Annual Report*

Baseball

American Amateur Baseball Congress (AABC) 212 Plaza Bldg., 2855 W. Market St., P.O. Box 5332 Akron, Ohio 44313	An association of state and regional baseball affiliates in the U.S.A. and Canada. Sponsors national tournaments in five age divisions. Provides standardized rules of play and eligibility.	*Amateur Baseball News* Handbooks on rules, tournament play, clinics, scoring
Little League Baseball P.O. Box 925 Williamsport, Pa. 17701	Concerned with organized baseball programs for children 9 through 18 years of age.	*Handbook Rule Book* Manuals

Bicycling

Amateur Bicycling League of America (ABLA) P.O. Box 699, Wall St. Stn. New York, N.Y. 10005	Serves as the governing body of amateur cycling in the United States. Concerned with competition, recreational touring, and safety education.	*Cycling Newsletter National Championships*

Billiards

Billiard Congress of American (BCA) 717 N. Michigan Ave. Chicago, Ill. 60611	Develops and interprets rules. Acts as clearinghouse for billiard's affairs.	*BCA Break* (Mo) *Official Rule Book* Pamphlets

Boating

American Canoe Association (ACA) 4260 E. Evans Ave. Denver, Colo. 80222	Governing body of canoe activity in U.S. Concerned with saving streams and rivers.	*American Canoeist Yearbook*
American White- water Affiliation (AWWA) P.O. Box 1584 San Bruno, Calif. 94066	Individuals, families, organizations interested in all forms of river travel and competition. Disseminates information, encourages seminars on safety, techniques, conservation, boat design, etc.	*American Whitewater Quarterly*
United States Power Squadron (USPS) 50 Craig Road Montvale, N.J. 07645	Information and education service to all pleasure-boat owners. Offers free courses in safe boating, seamanship, navigation, etc.	*The Ensign Monthly*
North American Yacht Racing Union (NAYRU) 37 West 44th Street New York, N.Y. 10036	A membership of clubs, associations, and individuals that coordinates sailboat racing in the U.S.	*NAYRU Yearbook*

Bowling

American Bowling Congress (ABC) 5301 S. 76th Street Greendale, Wis. 53129	Has state and local associations. Sanctions teams and competition. Provides standard rules and tests.	*ABC Newsletter* *Bowling Magazine* Various literature
American Junior Bowling Congress (AJBC) 5301 S. 76th Street Greendale, Wis. 53129	Sanctions activities and tournaments for boys and girls 21 years and under. Sponsored by ABC and WIBC.	*Junior Bowling* Instructional aids
National Duck Pin Bowling 711 14th Street, N.W. Washington, D.C. 20005	Develops rules and governs duck pin bowling activities.	*Duck Pin World*
Women's Inter- national Bowling Congress (WIBC) 5301 S. 76th Street Greendale, Wis. 53129	Sanctions bowling for women's leagues through local associations. Sponsors championship tournaments, provides field service, maintains news service and statistics files.	*The Woman Bowler* *News Bulletin* *Tournament and Record Guide*

Casting

American Casting Association (ACA) P.O. Box 51 Nashville, Tenn. 37202

Control organization for fly and bait casters' competition. Promotes casting and angling as a recreational activity. Coordinates, regulates, and establishes rules for tournaments.

Creel (bi-monthly)

Fencing

Amateur Fencers League of America (AFLA) 249 Eton Place Westfield, N.J. 07090

Functions as offical organization for a membership of amateur and professional fencers. Governs national championships, sponsors educational activities.

American Fencing Official Rules Manual

Field Hockey

Field Hockey Association of America (FHAA) 1160 Third Ave. New York, N.Y. 10021

A membership of individuals and clubs that serves as the governing body of men's amateur field hockey. Sponsors national and international competition.

FHAA Bulletin Roster of Officers Officials

United States Field Hockey Association (USFHA) 107 School House Lane Philadelphia, Pa. 19144

Individuals, local and sectional groups, clubs, schools and colleges interested in women's field hockey. Sponsors competition and educational programs.

The Eagle

Golf

United States Golf Association (USGA) Golf House Far Hills, N.J. 07931

An organization of golf clubs and golf courses that serves as a governing body on golf in the U.S. Sponsors annual championships for men, women, and junior age groups, provides data on amateur status, tournament procedure, rules, etc.

USGA Golf Journal USGA Green Section Record Rules of Golf Decisions on the Rules of Golf

Handball

United States Handball Association (USHA) 4101 Dempster Street Skokie, Ill. 60076

A membership of handball players and coaches that supports games and tournaments for adults and youngsters. Establishes rules and promotes activity.

Handball (bi-monthly) *Annual Guide and Directory*

Hiking

Appalachian Mountain Club (AMC) Five Joy Street Boston, Mass. 02108

Promotes recreation and scientific interest in the White Mountains area of New Hampshire. Club members also assume responsibility for the area trails and shelters.

Appalachian (monthly) Guides Maps

Florida Trail Association 33 Southwest 18th Terrace Miami, Fla. 33129

An association of conservationists and recreationalists interested in preserving and enjoying the Florida wilderness and scenic areas.

International Federation of Orienteering Tegnergatan 36 C 752 27 Uppsala, Sweden

A federation of national associations interested in promoting orienteering. Provides technical help, issues maps and instructional courses, sponsors championships and develops rules.

1OF *Mitteilungsblatt* (annual)

Intercollegiate Outing Club Association (IOCA) 3410 - G Paul Ave. Bronx, N.Y. 10468

Collegiates and graduates from college outing clubs represent a membership that aims to encourage safe enjoyment of the wilderness.

News Bulletin

United States Orienteering Federation (USOF) P.O. Box 1081 Athens, Ohio 45701

An organization of individuals interested in the sport of finding one's way in the out-of-doors using map and compass

The Mountaineers 719 Pike Street Seattle, Wash. 98111

Members interested in exploring, conserving, and studying the mountains, forests, and waterways of the Northwest. Conducts hiking, skiing, camping, and climbing expeditions.

The Mountaineer Books

Potomac Appalachian Trail 1718 N. Street N.W. Washington, D.C. 20036

Maintains Pennsylvania, Maryland, West Virginia, and Virginia Appalachian Trail. Also maintains

Potomac Appalachian Maps Guides Pamphlets

Hiking (cont.)

shelters, tests
mountaineering equip-
ment, and provides moun-
taineering library.

*Trail Riders of
the Wilderness*
American
Forestry
Association
1319 18th Street, N.W.
Washington, D.C.
20036

Sponsored by the American
Forestry Association,
this organization pro-
vides trips so the
American public can
enjoy the wilderness
areas via canoe,
horseback, or foot trail.

*National Campers
and Hikers
Association
(NCHA)*
7172 Transit Road
Buffalo, N.Y.
14221

Family and individuals
interested in outdoor
activities and conserva-
tion. Exchanges of in-
formation on routes,
campsites, equipment, etc.,
through regional, state,
and local chapters.

*Tent and Trail
Bulletin
NCHA News*

Ice Skating

*Amateur Hockey
Association of
the United States
(AHAUS)*
7901 Cedar Avenue
Bloomington, Minn.
55420

Promotes amateur hockey
in the United States. Provides services in
organizing leagues
and arranging tourna-
ments. Awards national,
sectional, and local
tournament trophies.

Bulletin
(monthly official
guide)
Referee's Manual

*Amateur Skating
Union of the
United States*
Route 2, Box 464
Kenoska, Wis. 63126

Promotes and controls
amateur speed skating in
the United States.

*United States
Figure Skating
Association
(USFSA)*
178 Fremont Street
Boston, Mass.
02111

The association and
its committees estab-
lish rules, appoint
officials for competi-
tion, sponsor tests,
carnivals, and exhibi-
tions. Also determine the
amateur status of
figure skaters.

*Skating
Evaluation of
Errors in
Figures
How to Organize
and Conduct
Competition
Ice Dances
Annual Rulebook*

Jogging

*National Jogging
Association (NJA)*
1910 K. Street, N.W.

An association of individuals and
groups interested in healthful
jogging. Sets performance

The Jogger
(monthly
bibliography on

Jogging (cont.)

Washington, D.C. standards and guidelines in   jogging)
                  participation at various levels   *Guidelines for*
                  of fitness and sponsors awards   *Successful Jogging*
                  and annual achievement
                  programs.

Judo/Karate

United States Judo Formerly the Amateur Judo   *Judo Illustrated*
Association   Association and the Black Belt   *Handbook*
4367 Bishop Road   Federation of the U.S.A., the   *Rule Book*
Detroit, Mich.   Federation supervises all   *Procedure Book*
48224   technical aspects of the sport.

United Karate   This membership of recognized   *U.K.F. Newsletter*
Federation   karate schools is concerned
c/o Karate Institute, with setting the standards for
315 7th Street   American karate, establishing
New York, N.Y.   rules and regulations, and
10011   governing championship
                     matches.

Lacrosse

United States   The college and university   *LaCrosse Newsletter*
Intercollegiate   membership concerns itself   *LaCrosse Guide*
LaCrosse Association with promoting and develop-
(USILA)   ing interest in the sports,
Washington College   pursuing equipment research,
Chestertown, Md.   championship awards and
21620   communicating through its
                      various publications.

United States   Interest in women's LaCrosse is *Cross Checks*
Women's LaCrosse   stimulated and served by this   Rules and coaching
Association   association. USWLA establish-   booklets
20 East Sunset Ave.   es rules for competition and
Philadelphia, Pa.   sponsors a national
19118   tournament.

Riding

American Horse   Membership of individuals or   *Horse Show*
Shows Association   groups wishing to operate   *Annual Revised*
(AHSA)   recognized shows. An associa-   *Rules*
527 Madison Avenue   tion interested in promoting
New York, N.Y.   recognized shows, licensing
10022   judges and stewards, etc.

National Inter-   A membership of college and   *NIRA Newsletter*
collegiate Rodeo   university rodeo clubs and   (monthly)
Association (NIRA)   individuals who participate in
P.O. Box 2088   college rodeos. Clubs sponsor
S.H.S.V.   local competition and the
Huntsville, Texas   association sponsors National
77340   Finals Rodeo.

Riding (cont.)

United States Combined Training Association (USCTA) 50 Congress Street Boston, Mass. 02109

Horsemen and others interested in promoting instruction, standards, rules, and regulations for combined training instruction and events. Disseminates manuals and maintains training centers, clinics, classes, and conferences. Supports the Olympic games, approves competitions, compiles records and statistics.

Newsletter

United States Pony Club (USPC) Pleasant Street Dover, Mass. 02030

An association of individuals and groups interested in promoting riding and mounted sports and care of horses and ponies for those under 21 years of age. Sponsors local, regional, and national events. Maintains library and resource center.

USPC Annual The Pony Club Handbook

Roller Skating

United States of America Confederation (USAC) 7700 A Street Lincoln, Nebraska 68510

Founded in 1971 by merger of U.S. Federation of Amateur Roller Skaters and the U.S. Amateur Roller Skating Association. Sponsors competitive roller skating, proficiency testing program, annual convention.

Shooting

National Rifle Association (NRA) 1600 Rhode Island Ave., N.W. Washington, D.C. 20036

Individual memberships organized on state and local levels. Promotes proper and safe handling of firearms. Provides assistance in basic shooting instruction, hunting technique, accident prevention, and target shooting. Sponsors competition, awards program, and instructor certification.

The American Rifleman Tournament News Uniform Hunter Casualty Report

National Skeet Shooting Association (NSSA) 2608 Inwood Rd., Suite 212 Dallas, Texas 75235

Membership of amateur skeet shooters. Registers and supervises competitive shoots. Enforces rules.

Skeet Shooting Review

Shuffleboard

National Shuffle-board Association (NSA) 10418 N.E. 2nd Ave. Miami, Fla. 33138

A federation of state associations that promotes and supervises tournaments and national championship. Establishes official rules.

Review (annual)
National Rules

Skiing

American Water Ski Association (AWSA) Seventh Street and G Ave., S.W. Winter Haven, Fla. 33880

Dedicated to promoting competitive and noncompetitive water skiing activities. Establishes rules, certifies performance records.

American Water Skier (bi-monthly)

National Ski Patrol System (NSPS) 2901 Sheridon Blvd. Denver, Colo. 80214

Promotes ski safety and handling of injuries at areas; assists municipal and federal agencies in cold-weather disasters and rescue operations. Serves in consultant capacity.

Ski Patrol Manual
Ski Patrol Mountaineering
Ski Safety Training and Testing
Avalanche Handbook

Ski Touring Council c/o Rudolf F. Mattesich West Hill Road Troy, Vt. 05868

A group interested in promoting noncompetitive cross-country skiing. Arranges free ski-touring trips and sponsors workshops.

Ski Touring Guide (annual)
Schedule of Events (annual)

United States Ski Association (USSA) 1726 Champa St., Suite 300 Denver, Colo. 80202

Promotes amateur competitive skiing in the U.S. Sanctions ski-hill engineering, sponsors testing and awards programs.

Ski America

Soaring and Parachuting

United States Parachute Association (USPA) P.O. Box 109 Monterey, Calif. 93940

As association of persons interested in sport parachuting. Sanctions competition, national, and collegiate championships. Sponsors safety education and instructor certification programs.

Parachutist (monthly)
Directory
Reference sources
Films

Soaring Society of America (SSA) P.O. Box 66071

For persons interested in soaring and gliding. Promotes the sports, sanctions contests,

Motorgliding (monthly)
Technical Soaring

Los Angeles, Calif. 90066

administers awards, tests sail-planes, sponsors flight instruction, maintains a library.

(quarterly)
SSA Soaring Directory

Softball

Amateur Softball Association of America (ASA)
P.O. Box 11437
Oklahoma City, Okla. 73111

The governing body for amateur softball in the U.S. Develops standard rules, sponsors competitions, clinics, and special awards.

Newsletter
(semi-monthly)
Balls and Strikes
(monthly)
ASA Football
(bi-monthly)
Official Guide and Rulebook

Squash

United States Women's Squash Racquets Association (USWSRA)
P.O. Box 962
Bryn Mawr, Pa. 19010

Sponsors local, regional collegiate, national, and international competition.

National Tourna-ment Schedule
USWSRA Handbook

United States Squash Racquets Association (USSRA)
211 Ford Rd.
Bala-Cynwyd, Pa. 19004

Aims to establish and enforce uniformity in rules and court specifications of the game. Schedules and sponsors tournaments.

USSRA Official Yearbook

Tennis

United States Table Tennis Association (USTTA)
c/o Jack Carr
5 Roberta Dr.
Hampton, Va. 23366

Sanctions tournaments, develops and modifies rules, gives instructional exhibitions. Sponsors U.S. players to Canadian and world championships.

Table Tennis Topics
Instructional book-lets
Motion picture films

United States Lawn Tennis Association (USLTA)
51 E. 42nd Street
New York, N.Y. 10017

An association of individual and club memberships interested in the promotion of tennis. Sponsors junior and senior tournaments and national championships. Supports international competition.

Tennis U.S.A.
(monthly)
USLTA Champion-ships (magazine)
USLTA Yearbook
Tennis Guide
Instructional materials

Swimming

Underwater Society of American (USA)

An association of individuals interested in supporting and

Underwater Report-er (quarterly)

Ambler, Pa.
19002

participating in skindiving,
spearfishing, and lung diving.
Sponsors exploration, science
research, skin and scuba
competition.

*Underwater Society
Yearbook*

Volleyball

*United States Volley-
ball Association
(USVBA)*
P.O. Box 554
Encino, Calif.
91316

Membership promotes tournaments, establishes rules,
certifies officials, and grants
awards.

*Official Guide and
Rulebook
International Volleyball
Review* (quarterly)

DISCUSSION QUESTIONS

1. What is an umbrella-type sports organization for amateurs? Describe several.
2. Give a condensed history of the AAHPER and its service role to recreational sports leaders.
3. What are the relationships between NAGWS, NASPE, and AAHPER?
4. What is the NISC? Does it serve men and women leadership? How?
5. Whom does the National Council of Secondary School Athletic Directors represent? What are the services? Who are the representative members?
6. Explain the relationship of the state high school athletic associations and the National Federation of High School Athletics.
7. How might the National Community Education Association be of interest to the administrator of a recreational sports program?
8. Review the past and present role of the AIAW in women's sports.
9. For what age group is the AAU program planned? How is the Union organized to serve the country?
10. Give examples of national sports and recreation associations and their services.

BIBLIOGRAPHY

Association for Intercollegiate Athletics for Women, *AIAW Handbook-Directory 1975–76*. Washington, D.C.: National Association for Girls and Women in Sport, 1975.

BURTON, GILL, *The Sportsman's Encyclopedia*. New York: Grosset & Dunlap, 1971.

FISK, MARGARET, ed., *National Organizations of the United States, Vol. 1*. Detroit Mich.: Gale Research Co., 1975.

National Association for Girls and Women in Sport, *Official Sports Guides*.

Washington, D.C.: American Alliance for Health, Physical Education and Recreation, 1975–76.

National Collegiate Athletic Association, *The Story of NCAA.* Kansas City, Mo.: The Association, 1975.

Ski Meet.
(Courtesy Allsop Inc., Bellingham, Washington,)

20

Sports Tournaments, Meets, and Matches

This chapter includes outlines of meets and matches that are appropriate for recreational sports programs. They are patterned after official procedures but are simplified to facilitate administration. In some instances it may be desirable to further simplify events and combine duties of the officials. For those who want to develop official procedures, details for formal events can be found in the official publications for each sport.

ARCHERY TOURNAMENTS

Competitive archery is enjoyed by all ages in several areas of specialization: (1) individual or team target archery, (2) the clout shoot, (3) the wand shoot, (4) flight shooting, (5) archery golf, and (6) field archery. Tournaments are usually planned as an American Round or Columbia Round for individuals or team target archery. Although these rounds are most popular, the clout shoot is very adapatable, as is flight shooting, archery golf, and field archery, if there is adequate space.

Officials and Committees

Tournament Chairperson or Manager oversees the organization of the tournament; is in charge of appointing all tournament officials, assigning duties, and is responsible for ultimate decisions during the competition.

Lady Paramount (women) or Field Captain (men) appoints any necessary assistants; organizes, supervises, and regulates the practice sessions and the meet; enforces rules; makes final decisions in cases of protest; makes and checks target assignments, and gives instructions to target captains and scorers; also signals the beginning and end of shooting; signs scorecards, and announces first, second, and third places at the conclusion of the tournament.

Target Captains are appointed for each target and preside over the archers and that target. This official, often a member of the shooting group and selected by its members, ensures that archers shoot in proper order; settles local questions; draws the arrows from the target, and calls the values to the scorers.

Scorers are the second and third contestants assigned to each target and appointed by the tournament chairperson to serve as scorers. They report and record the score of each arrow on an official scorecard and complete totals of hits and scores. The fourth contestant acts as a checker of the target captain.

Regulations

Decisions and regulations must be made with respect to some or all of the following local considerations:

1. Procedures, qualifications, and deadline dates for participant signup
2. Definition of the kind of tournament and any local ground rules
3. Safety rules and regulations (it may be wise to define age and skill classifications or divisions)
4. Definition of official target faces to be used and rules that will be observed

Kinds of Tournaments

Target Tournament. Contestants shoot at standard targets for high score, use any kind of conventional bow without mechanical assistance or support, and any type of sight or aiming device may be attached to the bow. Archery teams are made up of four archers of the same classified division. Target assignments of four competitors to a target initially are made by any objective and fair system designed by the tournament officials to ensure equated use of facilities for each contestant. Archers can be reassigned targets after each round.

Championship rounds most commonly used include the following:*

	Arrows	*Distance*
The York Round (1)	72, 48, 24	at 100, 80 and 60 yards respectively
The American Round (1,2,3,4)	30	at 60, 50, and 40 yards respectively

Junior American Round			
(5,6)	30	at 50, 40,	and 30 yards respectively
The National Round (2,4)	48, 24	at 60	and 50 yards respectively
The Columbia Round			
(2,4,6)	24	at 50, 40,	and 30 yards respectively
Junior Columbia Round			
(7)	24	at 40, 30,	and 20 yards respectively
Team Round (1,3)	96	at 60	yards respectively
Team Round (2,4)	96	at 50	yards respectively
Team Round (5,6)	96	at 40	yards respectively
Scholastic Round (5,6,7)	24	at 40	and 30 yards respectively
Junior Scholastic (5,6,7)	24	at 30	and 20 yards respectively
Range Round (adapt)	60 from a single distance of either 50, 40, 30, or		
			20 yards respectively

*1—men; 2—women; 3—intermediate boys; 4—intermediate girls; 5—Jr. boys; 6—Jr. girls; 7—beginners

FITA (Federation International de Tir a l'Arc) International Round

The International Round is shot on the FITA target face, which is a standard 48-inch (122cm) target face except that each color is divided precisely in half by a fine line. The value of the rings from the center out is 10, 9, 8, 7, 6, 5, 4, 3, 2, 1. At 50 and 30 meters an 80-centimeter face is used; it is divided into rings as explained for the 48-inch face.

Ladies

36 arrows at 70 meters		
(76.6 yards),	122 cm 10 rings target	(score after each 6 arrows)
36 arrows at 60 meters		
(65.6 yards),	122 cm 10 rings target	
36 arrows at 50 meters		
(54.7 yards),	80 cm 10 rings target	(score after each 3 arrows)
36 arrows at 30 meters		
(32.8 yards),	80 cm 10 rings target	

Men

36 arrows at 90 meters		
(98.4 yards),	122 cm 10 rings target	
36 arrows at 70 meters		
(76.6 yards),	122 cm 10 rings target	
36 arrows at 50 meters		
(54.7 yards),	80 cm 10 rings target	(score after each 3 arrows)
36 arrows at 30 meters		
(32.8 yards),	80 cm 10 rings target	

Clout Shoot. In the clout shoot the contestants shoot 36 arrows into the air from designated distances (180 yards, men; 140 yards, women; 120

yards, intermediates) and score on a 48-foot target laid out on the ground. A simplified target is made possible by having contestants shoot at a flag. At the completion of an end of shooting, a wire, steel tape, or small link chain, accurately marked for the appropriate rings of the clout, is rotated around the stake or flag. For each ring of the clout, the lady paramount or field captain appoints one archer, who follows behind the chain, pulls out and sorts the arrows. (The rules and scoring are the same as in target archery.) When all arrows are pulled, sorted, and laid in the clout ring from which they were pulled, a scorer is appointed for each ten archers. The archers then enter the clout target, and, beginning with golds, call the value of their arrows out to their respective scorers.

Wand Shoot. The wand shoot is six ends (36 arrows) of competitive shooting at a stake of soft wood or other suitable material that holds arrows. The wand is 2 inches wide and projects 6 feet above the ground. The distance may be established as 100, 80, 60, 50, 40, or 30 yards. The rules of target shooting apply to this shoot and only those arrows count that are embedded in the wand or that are witnessed rebounds.

Flight Shooting. Flight shooting is competitive distance shooting from a base line, down an established fairway, to a defined landing area. Either flight bows, hand-drawn, or foot bows (drawn using the feet) may be used. Weight classes for men usually include 50 pounds, 65 pounds, 80 pounds, unlimited, and foot bows; for women, weight classes usually include 35 pounds, 50 pounds, unlimited, and foot bows (which are also the same classes for juniors).

Archery Golf. The object of this game is to put an arrow through each of a defined number of 4-inch ball targets made of cotton batting and string in the least possible number of shots. The course can be set on a golf course with the targets mounted on the green. The game and etiquette are similar to golf, and play may be either metal or match, or both.

Field Archery. Field archery includes hunting with bow, roving (shooting at various inanimate objects while strolling through the woods), shooting a field round roving, or shooting a field archery course. A course is made up of fourteen target layouts which may be cardboard animals with indicated bull's-eyes. A round is defined as twice around the course or twenty-eight target layouts. Each archer shoots four arrows at each of the layouts. The scoring is 5 points for a bull's-eye and 3 for the outer circle. Details of the competition, classification, handicapping, and scoring are available in the National Field Archery Association literature or in the NAGWS Archery Guide.

Scheduling

Scheduling problems for target, clout, wand, and flight shooting tournaments can be reduced if there are enough targets to minimize the number of relays that have to be scheduled. Usually best scores determine winners; therefore, scheduling is a simple method of assigning each competitor a turn to shoot.

Scoring Target Shooting

Scoring: In target and clout, points are awarded as follows:

gold—9 pts.
red—7 pts.
blue—5 pts.
black—3 pts.
white—1 pt.

Arrows hitting outside of the white do not count for score or hit.

An arrow cutting two colors is scored for the higher value.

An arrow shot from 60 yards or less and rebounding or passing through the

						Hits	Score
Name							
Rounds							
Date							
At 50 Yards						Hits	Score
9	7	7	7	5		5	35
9	7	7	7	7	5	6	42
9	7	7	7	7		5	37
9	9	7	7	5	5	6	42
						22	156
At 40 Yards							
9	7	7	7	7	5	6	42
7	7	7	7	7	5	6	40
9	9	9	9	5	1	6	42
7	7	7	7	5	3	6	36
						24	160
At 30 Yards							
9	9	7	7	3	1	6	36
9	9	7	7	5	3	6	40
9	9	7	7	3	1	6	36
9	9	7	7	5	1	6	38
						24	150
				Total Score		70	466

Figure 20-1   Archery Scorecard

scoring face counts for 1 hit, 7 points. Other rebounds or pass-throughs score 5 points.

As each distance is completed, the scorer totals the number of hits and the score of all ends from that distance. At the end of the round all hits and scores are totaled for the final score. Team score is the total hits and scores of all team members. In less formal competition team averages are used to determine winners or the scores of a predetermined number of high-score contestants. Figure 20-1 illustrates a typical scorecard.

BADMINTON TOURNAMENTS

Badminton is a year-round activity enjoyed by participants of all ages and of varying degrees of skill. In good weather adults and children alike enjoy it as an outdoor game. During the winter months, clubs, church groups, and recreation associations offer tournaments and informal badminton competition indoors.

This sport is a popular intramural recreation activity. A great many students of a variety of skill abilities can enjoy participation; yet badminton is a sport that provides much post-school recreation enjoyment. Intramurals are usually planned as part of a tournament either scheduled over a season, or if the number of entries is small, as a weekend of concentrated competition.

Officials and Committees

Chairperson or Manager supervises and coordinates all operations of the tournament, appoints officials and committees, assigns responsibilities, and provides necessary instructions, forms, and equipment.

Entry Committee is responsible for handling the entries and conducting the seeding, drawing, and scheduling of the tournament.

Publicity Committee handles advance notices, news coverage, and all forms of appropriate publicity before, during, and after the tournament.

Referee is in charge of match play, inspects equipment, enforces the rules, has available the official rulebook, makes final decisions with respect to questions of regulations and their interpretation, and is on hand for all matches.

Umpire is in charge of the match from an elevated vantage point outside the sidelines at the net, enters the names of the players in the scorebook, and arranges for the toss for service or court. The umpire then introduces the players to the audience, starts play, scores the match, announces the score after each play, and calls the lets, carriers, faults, and calls of other officials.

The option of "setting" is supervised, as is the contestants' obligation to remain on the court except when given permission to leave. At the end of the game the umpire announces the winning score and at the end of the match announces the winner and the game scores.

Lines Officials are responsible for judging shots as being good or out on designated positions and lines. The call is "out" or "outside" along with a raised hand. There is no call for "in" or good shots.

Service Court Judge primarily calls service faults, server and receiver foot faults, and illegal rushing of the service.

Regulations

Badminton, like similar court games, has a code of etiquette that should be observed.

1. Participants should be required to observe proper etiquette and court dress.

2. The number and kind of entries must be defined.

3. Local rules must be developed for special situations such as low ceilings, obstructions, and similar limitations.

Kinds of Tournaments

Singles and Doubles. These are the most popular tournaments, and often in co-recreation activities a mixed doubles tournament is planned.

Team Tournaments. In this kind of tournament a house or group enters a combination of singles and doubles players—for instance, a team of one doubles and two singles players. The total points won by a team determine the tournament winner.

Scheduling Matches

Seeding, draw, and scheduling matches is done in accordance with accepted procedure in drawing up elimination or round robin tournaments.

Planning for court use is conveniently done by allowing approximately a half-hour for each two out of three game matches. A half-hour rest should be planned for players between matches. Figure 20-2 illustrates a chart that can be drawn up to assign courts and playing time. The numbers from this chart are then assigned to the matches on the draw sheet starting at the top of the draw and numbering down.

If facilities and time permit, the matches should start at least an hour apart, allowing players at least a half-hour rest between matches.

TIME		COURTS					
		A	B	C	D	E	F
9:00 a.m.	Match No.	1	2	3	4	5	6
9:30	" "	7	8	9	10	11	12
10:00	" "	13	14	15	16	17	18
10:30	" "	19	20	21	22	23	24
11:00	" "	25	26	27	28	29	30

Figure 20-2   Scheduling Chart

Scoring

The women's singles game is 11 points, and doubles is 15 points. Men's singles is 15 or 21 points for doubles. A match is the best 3, 5, or 7 sets. Scorecards can be drawn up to include the name of the tournament event, names of contestants, court assignments, and a convenient form for recording scores.

A vertical line through both scoring columns indicates "side out." "Set 2, 3, or 5" or "No Set" above the server's current score indicates the setting decision. "   " over a score indicates the point number on which the "hand out" occurred. Figure 20-3 illustrates scoring procedure.

BOWLING TOURNAMENTS

In school and out of school, there is increased participation in bowling leagues. With a growing number of facilities, bowling is a popular activity for people of all ages.

Ladies' Singles (11 Pts)			Set 3		
Brown/	012345	56789			9
Decker/		01234		456789	123	12

Men's Doubles (21 Pts)			Set 5		
Green Brown	17		18,19	12345	24
Davies Decker		16, 17, 18, 19			19

Figure 20-3   Badminton Scorecards

Bowling tournaments are often planned as a part of intramural, community, co-recreation, or interschool competition. Matches are usually scheduled for individual competitors as well as for teams. Eligibility is often defined by age, business, living units, class, skill, social club, or sex.

Officials

Tournament President or Manager supervises the organization of the tournament and appoints necessary committees and officials. The tournament president conducts a pre-tournament meeting with officials and representatives of the teams to develop and adopt tournament rules. This official enforces all rules and regulations of the tournament and makes final decisions with respect to protests and interpretations of the rules. This official may also assume the duties of secretary.

Tournament Committee, with the help of appointed assistants, organizes, manages, conducts, and controls the tournament; recommends entry procedures to the secretary; decides upon the tournament events; works out a schedule; and arranges the details of carrying out these responsibilities.

Secretary adopts the recommended system of handling entries and observing entry deadline dates; distributes to contestants copies of the regulations and schedule including order of events, name, time, and alley for each competitor and posts them; keeps an up-to-date record of individual and team standings; and at the end of the tournament makes official copies of the participants' names, number of games bowled, averages, and scores.

Captains assume the responsibility of properly entering their teams and substitutes with established averages; during competition the captain is responsible for calling fouls of the opposing team in case of mechanical failure of foul detecting device.

Scorers are appointed by the tournament committee to keep the official score during the competition. At the end of the game the opposing captains sign the score sheets. The official scorer also signs it, and this becomes the official score. Each team or individual entrant appoints his own scorer, who may also keep score and has the right to check with the official scorer. Any discrepancies are settled immediately by the secretary.

Regulations

Before a tournament, regulations will have to be decided upon with respect to several aspects of the competition:

1. Regulations should be established to determine the number of contestants there will be on a team and the substitution rules that are to be observed.

2. Definition of a forfeit and the procedure to be followed by the other team must be established.

3. It is necessary to determine the method and number of games required to establish averages. A defined number of games bowled just before the tour-

nament, or 12, 15, 18, 21, or more games during a specified period, may be required to determine averages.

    4. It must be decided whether teams will draw for or be assigned to lanes for the first game.

    5. Regulations should be established to determine if games are to count as won and lost or if pins are to be totaled.

    6. The number of pins to be scored for a blind score must be decided upon, as well as the maximum number of blind scores that may be used by a team.

Kinds of Tournaments

    A bowling tournament has been defined as a prearranged contest involving teams, individuals, or a combination of individual and team competition. Bowling is organized as handicap tournaments in which skill is equated by giving the less skilled bowler a calculated number of pins advantage or as a scratch tournament in which no handicaps are given.

Open Competition. In open competition all individuals or teams compete against all entrants.

Class or Division Tournaments. This kind of tournament invites contestants to compete within one of several divisions or averages. Individuals or teams having averages within designated limits may enter and compete in that division of players having approximately the same average. In this way individuals or teams compete in groups of approximately equal ability. Division classification is usually not necessary in small tournaments. Handicaps, however, ensure that the competition is fair.

    Using either of the above organizational plans, the following kinds of tournaments may be scheduled:

League Competition. Four or more teams meet regularly in scheduled competition similar to a round robin.

Elimination Tournament. This is planned as any one of the forms of elimination tournaments.

Individual or Doubles Classic. Only individuals or doubles compete in this competition, usually planned as an elimination or round robin tournament.

Combination of Events. Contestants compete in several events and the winner is determined by the combined results of all of these events. A series of such events might include a combination of any of the following: (1) five-member team event, (2) four-member team event, (3) three-member team event, (4) two-member doubles event, (5) one-member singles event.

Scheduling

Scheduling procedures vary depending upon the kind of tournament planned and the number of alleys available.

Planning tournaments for individual competition is a comparatively easy matter. Contestants draw for or are assigned alleys and then bowl for individual high score. Combination events present more of a problem. It is usually most advantageous to complete one event before proceeding to the next, and doubles or team events are usually scheduled first. The ease with which this can be done depends, of course, upon the number of alleys available for scheduling.

Scoring

Averages. Everyone is very much interested in bowling averages, and of course, in improving his or her own average. It is necessary information if a tournament is to be made interesting for all skill groups. Furthermore, an average is a challenge for the individuals and teams to try to improve their game. The individual average is computed using the following formula:

$$\text{Individual Average} = \frac{\text{Total pin fall}}{\text{Total no. games}}$$

Team average is determined in the same manner, except that the total pin fall of the team is substituted for the individuals' total pin fall and the formula becomes:

$$\text{Team Average} = \frac{\text{Total team pin fall}}{\text{Total no. team games}}$$

Handicaps. Individual and team handicaps are effective techniques used to add interest and stimulate greater participation in all bowling competition. Awarding handicaps gives the less-skilled individual an equal chance of winning.

Handicaps are usually awarded on a 60, 66 2/3, 70 or 75 percent basis, which is decided upon before an event. In mixed bowling men are often awarded a 66 2/3 percent handicap and women a 75 percent handicap.

The formulas used are as follows:

Individual Handicap	*Team Handicap*
(200 scratch-Indiv. Aver.) × % Handicap	(1,000 scratch-Team Aver.) × % Handicap
(210, 200, 190, or 180 scratch are used by ABC)	(1050, 1000, 950, 900 scratch are used by ABC)

In intramural competition it is also a common practice to award individual or team handicaps on the basis of a certain percentage of the difference between averages, with a maximum handicap defined. For example, if team A had a 750 average and team B had 690, the handicap for team B would be 75 percent of 60 (750 − 690) or 45 pins (unless the maximum handicap had to be defined as some lesser number of pins).

Scoring. Tournament scoring requires a scorer to keep the official record of each team. In addition to completing the official score sheet indicating strikes (x), spare (/), blows (−), splits (0), and score, a running total of team marks is often indicated for the benefit of the team members. This is done by totaling one mark for each spare, two marks when a bowler gets two strikes in a row. If a bowler fails to bowl down less than five pins the frame after he has spared, one mark is subtracted. The total marks for the first frame in Figure 20-4 is 2, the second frame is 4, the third is 6, and so on.

Regardless of the kind of tournament, winners are determined either by the number of pins scored or by the number of games won.

Name	1	2	3	4	5	6	7	8	9	10	Total
Jean	X / 17	6 1 / 24	8 1 / 33	X / 48	3 2 / 53	X / 70	3 4 / 77	7 2 / 86	X / 116	X X 2 / 138	138
John	2 0 / 2	3 1 / 6	X / 23	2 5 / 30	8 1 / 39	7 2 / 48	X / 64	5 9/ / 70	X / 100	X X 1 / 121	121
Helen	X / 27	⌃ / 46	7 2 / 55	6 1 / 62	X / 80	6 2 / 88	7 1 / 96	X / 118	X / 132	2 2 0 / 136	136
Mary	8 1 / 9	9 - / 18	X / 48	X / 76	X / 96	8 / / 113	7 2 / 122	8 / / 138	6 3 / 147	X 6 / / 167	167
Marks	2	4	6	9	12	15	16	18	22	33	

Figure 20-4   Official Bowling Score Sheet

FENCING COMPETITION

Fencing has usual reference to competition using the foil, the sabre, and the épée as weapons. The foil, lightest of the three, is most commonly used in intramural or informal recreation competition. Not as well-known as other sports, fencing is increasingly being offered by private schools, camps, colleges, and communities.

Officials and Committees

Director or Manager is responsible for the overall supervision of the competition; appoints the necessary officials and committees, assigns responsibilities, and obtains necessary administrative authorization for the use of buildings and facilities.

Bout Committee or Organizing Committee is responsible for organizing the sign-up and qualification procedure, definitions of the competition, arrangements for necessary equipment; appointment of special representative to check the contestants' weapons, equipment, and clothing; enforcing the rules of competition; and rendering interpretations unless there is a jury of appeal specifically responsible for handling cases of appeal.

Team Captain may or may not fence but is responsible for the team's observation of all regulations and procedures, including proper registration.

Bout Jury consists of a president and four judges who watch and verify touches.

President directs the bout, calls upon the judges for decisions, announces rulings and score; stands about thirteen feet out from the center of the fencing strip, starts the contest with the command, "Play," and stops it with "Halt."

Judges, two or four for each bout, watch and call touches on the two contestants; stand outside the strip, two on a side, each approximately three feet behind an assigned contestant, and move up and down with the action of the contest. Decisions called include "Yes" "No" for a successful or unsuccessful touch, "Foul" and "Abstain" denoting uncertainty.

Scorer keeps the score sheets on which the touch by touch of each bout is entered, advises change of ends after two touches, announces the touches reported by the president, reports them on the scoreboard, and also announces the conclusion of the bout.

Timekeeper clocks the duration of each bout (8 minutes for women, 10 minutes for men) with a stopwatch and gives two-minute and one-minute warnings before the expiration of time.

Apparatus Manager handles the electrical equipment (if it is used), resetting it after each touch has been awarded.

Regulations

Regulations must be developed for the following considerations, which may vary in different situations.

1. Kind of competition, number of entrants permitted, qualifications, and signup procedure.
2. Size and material of playing strip (advise contestants)
3. Weapons, equipment, clothing, and practices that ensure safety
4. Proper etiquette and sportsmanlike conduct

Kinds of Contests

Loose Play. A friendly combat between two fencers.

Bouts. When a score is kept between two fencers in loose play.

Match. The total of the bouts fenced between members of two teams.

Competition. The aggregate of bouts or matches necessary to determine the winner of an event.

Team Competition. Team competition is basically organized as a round robin in which each team competes as a unit. Each fencer on a team meets all fencers on the opposing team, and each team eventually meets all teams. In those instances where there are a great many teams competing, they may be divided into groups which play in an organizational plan similar to that used in league play, called *pools* in fencing. In team competition it would be pools of teams.

Individual Competition. This kind of competition is organized in one of two ways: (1.) pool, or (2.) direct elimination.

1.(a) *Pools.* In this organizational plan each pool is an elimination tournament with seeded contestants. The winners of the first pools participate in another pool referred to as the second round. This is followed by another round until a final "fence-off" round.

2. (b) *Direct Elimination.* In this elimination tournament competition is based upon winning the best two out of three standard bouts or modified standard bouts. If planned for singles, it is similar to other elimination tournaments. If this plan is used for team elimination, each team member meets an opposing team member once during the match, and teams win or lose depending on their total wins. Losers drop out.

Scheduling

Team competition usually precedes the individual events, and the one kind of competition is completed before the other is started. Other scheduling considerations are dependent upon the number of available fencing strips and time planned for the competition.

Round Robin. In a four-person team competition between team A and team B, the order of bouts would be as follows (the first contestant called would stand at the right of the president or director):

A1 vs B1	A1 vs B2	B3 vs A1	B4 vs A1
B2 vs A2	B3 vs A2	A2 vs B4	A2 vs B1
A3 vs B3	A3 vs B4	B1 vs A3	B2 vs A3
B4 vs A4	B1 vs A4	A4 vs B2	A4 vs B3

Direct Elimination. Scheduling this tournament involves awarding byes and seeding on the basis of the rank of the players. Matches are then scheduled as follows:

8 Fencers		*16 Fencers*		*32 Fencers*	
Upper Bracket	*Lower Bracket*	*Upper Bracket*	*Lower Bracket*	*Upper Bracket*	*Lower Bracket*
1 vs 8	3 vs 6	1 vs 16	3 vs 14	1 vs 32	3 vs 30
5 vs 4	7 vs 2	9 vs 8	11 vs 6	17 vs 16	19 vs 14
		5 vs 12	7 vs 10	9 vs 24	11 vs 22
		13 vs 4	15 vs 2	25 vs 8	27 vs 6
				5 vs 28	7 vs 26
				21 vs 12	23 vs 10
				13 vs 20	15 vs 18
				29 vs 4	31 vs 2

Combined Round Robin and Direct Elimination. One or more rounds of elimination pools are scheduled until there remain 2, 4, or 8 pools from which the top four players can be scheduled in a direct elimination of 8, 16, or 32 competitors.

Scoring

Bout winners must score four (women) or five (men) valid touches. Simultaneous touches are frequently awarded on the basis of the principle of the "right of way." The one who initiates the offense has the right of way until parried by his opponent, who then gains the right of way. If at the end of the time limit neither opponent has scored a winning number of touches, enough touches are awarded both contestants so that one may be declared a winner.

The scorer records touches against the fencer who has been touched and announces the score aloud. If no timekeeper is available the scorer also acts as a timer, starting time "In" from the command, "Play," until "Halt," with the time "Out" for jury deliberations and other interruptions.

The winning team or contestant is the one with the greatest number of individual victories. If tied, decision is based on the least number of touches received. If this is a tie, it is awarded to the one with the greatest number of touches scored. If victories and touches are tied, the match is declared a draw.

Match points are usually awarded as follows:.

Team victory	2 match points
Drawn match	2 match points
Defeat	0 match points

Marks above the horizontal line indicate touches which the contestant received in each of the diagrammed bouts. Marks below the line indicate "won" or "lost," as illustrated in Figure 20-5.

Name	No.	1	2	3	4	5	Bouts Won	Bouts Lost	Touches Rec'd	Touches Scored	Place
Cain	1		1/W	0/W	1111/L	0/W	3	1	5	13	1
Green	2	1111/L		1111/L	11/W	1111/L	1	3	14	6	5
Cox	3	1111/L	1/W		1111/L	0/W	2	2	9	9	3
Brown	4	1/W	1111/L	1/W		1111/L	2	2	10	12	2
Doe	5	1111/L	0/W	1111/L	11/W		2	2	10	8	4

Figure 20-5   Fencing Scorecard

FIGURE SKATING

The addition of ice skating rinks to campus and city recreation facilities has attracted many participants to this activity and figure-skating competition lends itself very well to recreation and intramural programs.

Officials and Committees

Chairperson or Manager is responsible for overall organization of the event; appoints the necessary officials and committee chairpersons, and ensures that there is adequate publicity with respect to date, time, place, schedule of events, and deadlines.

Program Committee is responsible for developing a list of events, arranging for entries, and ensuring that facilities are adequate and available.

Publicity Committee prepares notices, posters, and news stories; contacts newspapers, radio and TV personnel; arranges for publicity pictures; and ensures news coverage for advanced, current, and past stories.

Referee is responsible for conduct of the competition, final decisions on protests, interpretations of the regulations, and questions not covered by the official rules. This official acts as chairperson of the judges, collects scorecards, determines awarding of places based on summary sheets, has the accountant record results, and supervises all aspects of the competition.

Accountant tabulates and records scores on an official score sheet; posts a master record sheet as the judges award points and turn in the personal record sheets, and keeps the official records of the event.

Announcer keeps the audience informed of events; alerts contestants when necessary, and interprets various aspects of the sport to the audience.

Judges, not less than three nor more than seven, judge and award points for each event.

In Open Judging the judges are responsible for awarding points so that the audience can witness each judgment.

In Modified Open Judging each judge records scores on a personal record sheet for each compulsory figure or dance. The sheet for each figure or dance includes the item to be performed, with its degree of difficulty, and the names of the contestants. For the final rounds of the freestyle and dance, or in the case of pair or group skating, the judges record scores on a separate personal record sheet. Traditionally, at the conclusion of these events the judges line up and as each contestant's name is read each judge flashes a card indicating the score awarded the contestant.

In Closed Judging each judge awards points by a secret written ballot.

Clerk summons skaters for their various events.

Timers (one or more official timers) time the free skating, dance, and pairs events; stand up as a warning that time is almost up, and then blow the whistle to end the event.

Regulations

Regulations will have to be determined with respect to local situations and should include consideration of some or all of the following:

1. Procedure and etiquette to be observed by all contestants

2. Definition of events defined including a statement of the required elective skills

3. Number of acceptable entries

4. Starting time of each event, and skaters' responsibility for appearing within two minutes of starting time or accepting a "not skated" mark for the event

Kinds of Competition

Competition in figure skating includes compulsory figures, prescribed dance, and free skating. Events may include individual, pair, or group figure skating.

Figure Skating. This event is divided into free skating—which incorporates unspecified dance steps, jumps, spins, and turns executed to music of a defined time and chosen by the contestant—and compulsory figures. Compulsory figures are prescribed movements, either announced in advance or determined by draw fifteen minutes before events. They are derived from the basic figures (circles, three turns, serpentines, brackets, counters, rockers) and are selected from a defined list such as:

Circle eight	Rocker	Change bracket
Serpentine	Counter	Paragraph three
Three	One foot eight	Paragraph double
Double threes	Change three	Paragraph loop
Loop	Change double three	Paragraph bracket
Bracket	Change loop	Others

Dance Skating. Dance competition is divided into free dance and compulsory dance forms and steps. Free dance is a timed event which requires the competitor to present a dance composition to music chosen by the skater. Prescribed or compulsory dance requires the skating of selected dance forms from a list similar to the following:

Dances	*Turns*	*Steps*
Foxtrot, Argentine, Viennese, Paso Doble	Three turn	Open stroke
European Waltz, Argentine,	Dropped three	Cross stroke
Westminster, Kilian	Mohawk	Cross step forward
Tango, Blues, Viennese,	Closed Mohawk	Cross step behind
Quickstep	Open Mohawk	Chasse
American Waltz, Argentine,	Swing Mohawk	Slide chasse
Viennese, Kilian	Choctaw	Cross chasse
Kilian	Choctaw	Cross Chasse
Rockers Foxtrot, Blues,	Closed Choctaw	Progressive or run
Westminster, Paso Doble	Open Choctaw	Swing roll
Fourteenstep, Blues,	Swing Choctaw	Cross roll
Westminster, Quickstep	Swing Rocker and Swing Counter	
	Twizzle	

Individual Skating. Events include competition in compulsory figure and free skating.

Pair and Group Skating. Pair and group skating consist only of free skating. Only pairs and groups of the same composition (i.e., two men, lady and man, two ladies) may compete against each other.

Scheduling

Contestants may be divided into different classes or skill-level groups. The order in which contestants skate in the various events is determined by a draw executed by the referee, the chairperson, or the competitors, in the presence of at least two judges or other officials.

The compulsory figures to be a part of the competition are decided upon in one of two ways: (1) several weeks before the event the figures are arbitrarily decided upon and announced to the contestants; (2) figures or dances are drawn by lot and announced just fifteen minutes before the time of the event.

In competition, compulsory figures are skated in order of their in-

EVENTS	POINTS	FACTOR	COMPUTATION	TOTAL POINTS	ORDINAL
Individual Compulsory Figures (style technique)	0-6	Reference rule book	Pts X Factor		
Individual Free Style		(computed by Referee or criteria developed by school)	Sum Pts. X Factor		
Content of Program	0-6				
Manner of Performance	0-6	Sum of factors for compulsory figures ———— 3			
Individual Dance			Pts X Factor		
Compulsory Initial round for all competitors Final round for four or eight finalists Music Interp. Style		Reference rule book			
Technique	0-6				
Free Dance Contents of Program	0-6				
Manner of Perform	0-6				
Pairs and Groups		(computed by Referee or criteria developed by school)			
Free Skating only					
Content of Program	0-6				
Manner of Perform	0-6				

Dance score equals total points of Initial Round and Final Round

Figure 20-6   Figure Skating Scoring Chart

creasing difficulty. In dance competition there is usually an initial round and a final round, and the events may include either or both compulsory dances and free dancing.

Scoring

USFSA scoring procedure may be found described in the official rulebook. Charts indicating factor or degree of difficulty are included in the rulebook. Ordinal or rank order numbers are assigned to competitors after compulsory figures, and after free skating. The winner is that individual who is awarded the first place ordinal number by a majority of the judges. A modified scoring procedure may be used as is shown in Figure 20-6.

GOLF TOURNAMENT

Almost every community has a golf course open to the public, as well as several private or semi-private courses. Such facilities provide a great many opportunities for golf competition on a variety of skill levels, and it is not presumptuous to assume that many golfers take part in a variety of golf tournaments. Golf matches usually include individual or team competition or a combination of these. The competition is either organized as an intramural activity, in which units compete, or as a championship tournament.

Officials and Committees

Chairperson or Manager is responsible for the overall supervision of the tournament; appoints all necessary officials and personnel, and acts as chairperson of the tournament committee.

Tournament committee organizes the details of the tournament; arranges for entry procedures, tournament scheduling, and appointment of any additional, necessary officials or assistants; and also makes final decisions with respect to questions that arise during the competition.

Referee for each match is appointed by the committee to accompany match play, and decide questions of fact and of golf rules. In some instances referees are not assigned until the final matches of the tournament and often are not used in local tournaments.

Marker is assigned to each match by the committee to keep the official score on the scorecard. Markers are sometimes assigned only for the final matches. In those cases where markers are not assigned, competitors keep each others' score, and sign and approve the scorecard at the end of the round to make it official.

Regulations

All players must be informed of posted local rules before they begin their matches. Golf courses often have local rules printed on scorecards and include some or all of the following concerns:

1. Nonplayed matches including definitions of when a game becomes a forfeit as well as under what conditions a match is postponed.

2. Avoiding interference by requiring that each match start off by itself; three to seven minutes between starting times has been found to work satisfactorily.

3. Procedure in case a match ends "all even." This can be handled by playing a defined number of holes for the playoff. Another method is that of a sudden-death playoff. Starting at the first hole, contestants play until one or the other wins a hole.

Kinds of Tournaments

Medal Play–Stroke Play. The winner in medal or stroke play is that person who plays the stipulated round (usually eighteen holes) in the fewest strokes. This kind of tournament must be run off so that all competitors play on the same course, on the same day, and under similar conditions.

Match Play. In match play, each hole of the golf course is a stroke contest that is either won, lost, or halved (tied). In most tournaments competition is between two players; however, there may be one, two, or more players on a side. The winner is the player who has won the most holes by the end of the round. The match play can be planned formally by scheduling matches for a specific date and time or informally by only indicating deadline dates for the completion of each round.

Open Tournament. This kind of tournament accepts entries from both professional and amateur players. It may be planned as medal or match play.

Amateur Tournament. In contrast to the open tournament, an amateur tournament is only open to contestants of amateur standing.

Handicap Tournament. Handicap tournaments are planned for individuals of varying ability. The inequality of ability, however, is equated by awarding a calculated advantage.

Qualifying Round. Often in golf competition qualifying rounds are required. All players are requested to play a medal round of a defined number of holes. The qualifying scores are then used in one of several ways: (1) those individuals with a certain score or better qualify to play in the tournament; (2) the ranked qualifying scores are used to place the contestants in a numerical draw; (3) players are placed in tournament flights according to skill.

In addition to these general types of tournaments there are numerous novelty tournaments such as four-ball foursome, fewest putts, challenge tournaments, round robin, best ball, and many others. (See "Golf Events" by the National Golf Foundation for additional variations.)

Scheduling

Flights. Scheduling flights is a means of planning several small tournaments when there are a great many contestants. Contestants may be divided in tournament skill groups by scheduling a qualifying round or by using established handicaps to group competitors; or players may draw for flight and position. The tournament may end with the winners of each flight, or it may be carried to a playoff tournament between the winners of each flight.

Partners and Positions for Medal Play. Medal play, intramural-planned programs often allow contestants to elect their own partners, and draw, assign, or pair players off as they arrive at the golf course. The order for teeing off can be determined formally by draw or informally by the order in which the players and their partners arrive ready to start play. Winners are determined by final scores turned in by all contestants.

Partners and Positions for Match Play. In match play, if there are no seeded players an elimination chart is drawn up and contestants can "blind draw" for position and opponents. If there are seeded players and byes to be awarded this is done as described in Chapter 17.

Another method, "numerical draw," is based upon the rank of the competitors as established in a qualifying round. A defined number of players—64, 32, 16, or 8—are qualified by play and also ranked. The players are then scheduled as illustrated in Figure 20-7.

Handicaps

Intramural handicaps are frequently established on the average of a minimum of five rounds of medal play. The following formula can be used in determining stroke handicap: 5 rds/5 – course rating (found on scorecard).

Handicaps in medley play are subtracted from the gross score to determine the net score. In match play handicaps are figured the same

GOLF MATCH PLAY DRAW							
64 QUALIFIERS				**32 QUALIFIERS**			
UPPER HALF		LOWER HALF		UPPER HALF		LOWER HALF	
MATCH	RANK	MATCH	RANK	MATCH	RANK	MATCH	RANK
1	(1-33)	17	(2-34)	1	(1-17)	9	(2-18)
2	(17-49)	18	(18-50)	2	(9-25)	10	(10-26)
3	(9-41)	19	(10-42)	3	(5-21)	11	(6-22)
4	(25-57)	20	(26-58)	4	(13-29)	12	(14-30)
5	(5-37)	21	(6-38)	5	(3-19)	13	(4-20)
6	(21-53)	22	(22-54)	6	(11-27)	14	(12-28)
7	(13-45)	23	(14-46)	7	(7-23)	15	(8-24)
8	(29-61)	24	(30-62)	8	(15-31)	16	(16-32)
9	(3-35)	25	(4-36)	**16 QUALIFIERS**			
10	(19-51)	26	(20-52)				
11	(11-43)	27	(12-44)	1	(1-9)	5	(2-10)
12	(27-59)	28	(28-60)	2	(5-13)	6	(6-14)
13	(7-39)	29	(8-40)	3	(3-11)	7	(4-12)
14	(23-55)	30	(24-56)	4	(7-15)	8	(8-16)
15	(15-47)	31	(16-48)	**8 QUALIFIERS**			
16	(31-63)	32	(32-64)				
				1	(1-5)	3	(2-6)
				2	(3-7)	4	(4-8)

Figure 20-7   Numerical Draw in Match Play

way to determine the number of strokes handicap; however, the strokes can only be awarded as indicated on the official scorecard of the course.

There are several systems for determining handicaps, and the USGA describes its system in the booklet, *The Conduct of Women's Golf.* Others popularly used include "five-best-to-par," "Callaway," and "Peoria" systems.

In five-best-to-par handicapping if the difference of the total five best scores and the total of the five pars is 0–3, there is no handicap. A difference of 4–9 receives a handicap of 1; for 10–15, the handicap is 2; for 16–21, it is 3, and so forth (see Figure 20-8).

The Callaway system determines the handicap after play of one round and is computed from gross score, poorest holes, and the table given in Figure 20-8.

In the Peoria system, before play and unknown to the players, six holes are selected (suggest 2 par 3 holes, 2 par 4, and 2 par 5 holes) and the following formula is applied: total score of 6 selected holes times 3 minus par of the course.

Scoring

After each hole, the marker checks the score with the competitors and records it on the scorecard. If there are no markers, opponents check each other's cards. After the match, the scorecard is signed by both players attesting to its accuracy, and is turned in to the committee as an

CALLAWAY GOLF

CLASS A		CLASS B	
GROSS SCORE	HANDICAP	GROSS SCORE	HANDICAP
Less than Par —	Scratch	101 — 105	Three worst holes plus ½
One Over Par — 75	½ worst hole	106 — 110	next worst
76 — 80	Worst hole	106 — 110	Four worst holes
81 — 85	Worst hole plus ½	111 — 115	Four worst holes plus ½
	next worst	121 — 125	next worst
86 — 90	Two worst holes	116 — 120	Five worst holes
91 — 95	Two worst holes plus	121 — 125	Five worst holes plus ½
	½ next worst		next worst
96 — 100	Three worst holes		

CLASS C

GROSS SCORE	HANDICAP
126 — 130	Six worst holes
131 — 135	Six worst holes plus ½ next worst
136 — 140	Seven worst holes
141 — 145	Seven worst holes plus ½ next worst
146 — 150	Eight worst holes

Callaway System of Handicapping — Courtesy
The National Golf Foundation.

FIVE BEST TO PAR HANDICAP

A popular approved system of handicapping is based upon the five best-to-par scores. When the difference between the total of the five best scores and the total of the five pars is 0 through 3, either above or below, the handicap is SCRATCH.

When the difference is:

4 thru 9 hdcp. is 1	35 thru 40 hdcp. is 6	66 thru 71 hdcp. is 51
10 " 15 " " 2	41 " 46 " " 7	72 " 78 " " 12
16 " 21 " " 3	47 " 53 " " 8	79 " 84 " " 13
22 " 28 " " 4	54 " 59 " " 9	85 " 90 " " 14
29 " 34 " " 5	60 " 65 " " 10	91 " 96 " " 15
		etc.	

The above handicaps were figured by the Short Formula; taking 4/5 of 1/5 of the difference between the total of par for the five rounds played and the total of the five best-to-par scores, one-half or over to count as a stroke.

Courtesy Wilson Sporting Goods Co

ADJUSTING STROKES IN HANDICAP MATCHES

Although the U.S. Golf Assn. recommends 7/8 of the difference between handicaps in match play (play by holes) as in the table below, some clubs allow the full difference between handicaps and others, the player with the lesser stroke-play handicap allows the player with the greater handicap 3/4 of the difference, a fraction of one-half or over counting as one stroke. The strokes allowed are used on certain holes as designated on the club score card.

When the difference between handicaps is:

1 give 1 stroke	11 give 10 strokes	21 give 18 strokes
2 " 2 stroke	12 " 11 "	22 " 19 "
3 " 3 "	13 " 11 "	23 " 20 "
4 " 4 "	14 " 12 "	24 " 21 "
5 " 4 "	15 " 13 "	25 " 22 "
6 " 5 "	16 " 14 "	26 " 23 "
7 " 6 "	17 " 15 "	27 " 24 "
8 " 7 "	18 " 16 "	28 " 25 "
9 " 8 "	19 " 17 "	29 " 25 "
10 " 9 "	20 " 18 "	30 " 26 "

Figure 20-8   Computing Golf Handicaps, Courtesy: The National Golf Foundation

official record. The winner of the match is responsible for posting results on the draw sheet for the next round of play. A golf scorecard is illustrated in Figure 20-9.

GYMNASTIC MEETS

A national enthusiasm for gymnastics has stimulated a great deal of participation in this sport during the last several years. Competition on a variety of skill levels has created a demand for leadership qualified to plan and conduct gymnastics meets.

| Holes | Yards | Handicap | PAR | | Jim | Ann | Dave | Donna | Holes | Yards | Handicap | PAR | | Jim | Ann | Dave | Donna |
			Men	Women								Men	Women				
1	438	2	4	5					10	142	9	3	3				
2	142	9	3	3					11	302	8	4	4				
3	347	5	4	4					12	515	3	5	6				
4	302	8	4	4					13	359	4	4	4				
5	321	7	4	4					14	438	2	4	5				
6	515	3	5	6					15	347	5	4	4				
7	225	6	3	4					16	321	7	4	4				
8	359	4	4	4					17	225	6	3	4				
9	510	2	1	6					18	510	1	5	6				
Tot.	3159		36	40					Tot.	3159		36	40				
DATE			SCORER						DATE			SCORER					

Figure 20-9   Golf scorecard

Officials and Committees

Meet Manager can serve as a one-person meet official or, together with several officials, can form a committee to assume responsibility for date of the meet; appointment of all officials and committees, obtaining approval for use of facilities and equipment; program of events and time schedule; development of registration and entry procedures; and overall supervision of the various events.

Referee has full jurisdiction over the meet, giving it direction; enforcing rules and regulations; and deciding upon disqualifications, protests, and matters not covered by the rules. This official assigns judges to the events and designates the head judge; appoints assistants as needed and gives the list of entries for each event to the scorer, chief clerk, and to the announcer.

Superior or Head Judge of each event directs the *Acting Judges* to their places on all sides or head of the demonstration area, signals the contestants to begin the exercise. Upon a given signal the acting judges send scores to superior or head judge, who looks them over for correctness in scoring and then sends the scores to the scoring table. The scoring table then flashes the score.

Runners take positions next to each judge to "run" scores to head judge.

Chief Clerk, with a list of entrants that has been provided, checks in contestants and alerts them for each event.

Chief Scorer appoints two acting scorers, supervises all scoring and recording of scorers, provides the referee with a statement of final results of each event, and reviews and checks the score sheet before turning it over to the referee.

Announcer advises the order of contestants, alerts entrants for their turns, and announces the results of each event. If time permits, the announcer can add interest in the meet by describing some of the equipment, giving the competition record of the outstanding contestants, and/or reporting the nationwide increase in gymnastics participation.

Timers report lapsed time to the chief judge in all timed events.

Regulations

1. Regulations covering the dimensions of the apparatus and areas must be determined by mutual agreement.

2. A description of the events to be included in the meet should ensure common understanding.

3. The size of a team needs to be predetermined and defined; order of taking turns in each event must be established; when and where spotters should be used must be mutually understood; repeat performances in order to improve score and false starts must be defined.

4. The procedures for participants or team members who become injured in the meet; the number of events an individual may enter; procedure for classifying skill levels of the contestants all have to be decided.

Kinds of Meets

Gymnastic meets can be planned as dual meets or tournament-type meets to include those events most appropriate for the age and skill level of the participants. Possible events include the following:

# *	Floor exercise (both boys and girls)	*	Side horse vault (girls only)
*	Uneven paralle bars (girls only)	#	Still rings (boys only)
#	Parallel bars (boys only)	# *	Tumbling (both)
*	Balance beam (girls only)	#	Side horse
#	Long horse vault (boys only)	#	Horizontal bar

An *All-Around Event* is often included. This consists of the total points earned in: (girls) four individual events (*); (boys) six individual events (#).

A *Team Event* may be included in an intramural or informal meet. This event consists of an exercise using small hand equipment such as ball, wands, ropes, etc., and usually set to music.

For each event two categories of exercise are included: (1) compulsory exercises, in which each move is described in detail and sequence of movement; and (2) optional exercises, which are unique compositions of each contestant.

Scheduling

The order of events in a meet is determined by the meet committee. The order in which the competitors perform is usually determined by drawing names out of a hat. No contestant will be first or last in more than one event.

In meets which include both compulsory and optional exercises, each contestant completes the compulsory exercises and then all, in turn, complete their optionals.

Competitors are usually divided into novice, junior, or senior skill classifications for purposes of scheduling. Once an individual has won a first, second, or third in any of these divisions he or she moves up to the next classificiation for competitive events.

Scoring

Scoring may be done in several ways:

Compulsory and Optional Exercises		All-Around Events	Special Events Requiring Only Optionals
Completely failed	0–0.9	1st place–7	1st–3.5
Unsatisfactory	1–2.9	2nd place–5	2nd–2.5
Deficient	3–4.9	3rd place–4	3rd–2
Satisfactory	5–6.9	4th place–3	4th–1.5
Good	7–8	5th place–2	5th–1
Very good	8.1–9	6th place–1	6th–0.5
Excellent	9.1–10		

The scores of the five judges are recorded on the official score sheet; the highest and lowest scores are crossed out. The middle marks are totaled and averaged to obtain the score for the exercise.

The winner in each event is determined by totaling the scores in compulsory and optional exercises. In special events, if they are a part of the meet, the winner is determined by the highest score. A girl may not enter more than four events. Team scores are usually determined by totaling the five highest team member scores in each event.

HORSE SHOW

Increasingly, opportunities for riding are becoming more available, and children are benefiting the most. Riding is a popular activity at private schools, colleges, camps, Western communities, and as a highlight of special occasions.

Officials, Committees, and Key Personnel

Chairperson or Manager is responsible for supervising the overall organization of the show, makes arrangements for facilities and equipment; makes sure that there is adequate insurance coverage including liability, property damage, accident, and medical reimbursement.

Show or Program Committee appoints and procures all necessary personnel with the approval of the chairperson; plans the kind of show, events, and eligibility requirements; devises a system of registration for the contestants; alphabetizes and assigns numbers to the riders, and usually has programs printed. Programs should include the following: (1) time, date, and place of show including directions of how to get there; (2) names and addresses of important show personnel—secretary, judges, stewards; (3) trophy donors, class sponsors, and/or other individuals and persons cooperating with the show committee; (4) statement of fees, number of ribbons, prizes, and trophies offered in each class; (5) statement on post entries and illustrations or clear description of all hunter and jumper courses.

Ticket Sales Committee takes charge of advanced and regular ticket sales if there are any; takes care of sale of programs, and arranges for parking space.

Ring, Grounds, and Stable Committee plans the saddle horse, hunter, and jumper courses; sees that all necessary equipment is available and in good condition; sets up necessary judges' stands with chairs and tables. It starts to function well in advance of the show to ensure that grounds are well planned, clean, and in good condition; prepares the stables and necessary temporary stalls; and has the ring graded and watered before the show.

First Aid Committee ensures that first-aid materials, an ambulance, and hospital services are available if needed. (Appoint an interested doctor to be in charge of this committee.)

Trophies Committee solicits or orders trophies, takes care of engraving, and plans for their presentation at the show.

Concessions or Refreshment Committee can set up its own booths and arrange for supplies and selling, or arrange for concessions which are sometimes permitted to handle the sale of food.

Clean-Up Committee is on hand after the show to sweep out all rooms and clean up all buildings and grounds.

Secretary orders ribbons and badges for judges, stewards, and committee members and distributes the exhibitors' numbers. The secretary keeps an official entry catalogue; arranges for all necessary printing and, after the show, prepares summaries for the press and manager. At the show, the secretary should have a place on the judges' stand to be able to keep records efficiently.

Treasurer collects all money and pays all the bills.

Judges are selected after the type of show has been decided upon. The roster of recognized judges in the AHSA rulebook can serve as a source for names. In less formal shows a guest judge may be asked to participate, or experienced persons often serve as judges.

Stewards for those formal shows desiring recognition are AHSA stewards obtained to act as consultants and arbiters for each performance in each ring.

Announcer calls up the horses, and, with the in-gate man's help, gets them into the ring; keeps the audience informed of program corrections; gives the results of each class; describes the various events when appropriate.

Ringmaster is the judge's aide; he helps to keep the events moving, and works to prevent accidents; and works with the jump crew.

Jump Crew checks the course to avoid any delays (if hunter or jumper classes are included).

In- and Out-Gate Person opens and closes the gate during the show, and keeps the ring clear of spectators; checks riders for correct numbers, and makes sure the entries for the next class are ready.

Paddock Person checks on bitting, ensures the use of proper equipment, and keeps track of ring appointments.

Veterinarian and Blacksmith should be available at all times for well-run shows.

Regulations

Local rules and regulations covering policy with respect to the following will have to be decided upon:

1. Refund of entries if there are fees
2. Method of distributing exhibitors' exhibits, events, and number of class entries
3. Instructions concerning arrival and removal of horses, availability of stabling, and fees
4. Contestant reminders that they are responsible for the neatness of their equipment and the grooming of their horses
5. Appropriate apparel for the various classes

Programs

A typical program might include any one or all of the following:

Exhibition drill	Pair class	Bareback
Equitation class	Jumping	Games

Other possibilities might include gymkana events, parade, foxtrot classes, and pleasure walking horse events.

A schedule of events for an informal show is illustrated by the following list of classes and class requirements:

Class 1.—SADDLEBRED PLEASURE

Walk, trot, and canter both ways of the ring. Ride on a loose rein on command. Stop on rail, back, drop reins. Pick up mail and deliver it to assigned point. Dismount and mount from mounting block. Horsemanship only to count.

Class 2.—COMBINATION SADDLE AND HUNT

Enter the ring saddle seat. Walk, trot, canter, slow gait, and rack one way. Figure eight once at a trot or canter. Two pole jumps not over 2 1/2 feet. Trot into jump, stop, walk off, then trot into the other jump. To be judged on versatility of the rider and ability.

Class 3.—LADIES' WESTERN PLEASURE

To be shown at a walk, jog, lope, both ways of the ring on reasonably loose reins. Horsemanship only to count.

Class 4.—BEGINNING THREE-GAITED

To be shown at a walk, trot, and canter. Trot one figure eight, address reins from saddle. Horsemanship only to count.

Class 5.—BEGINNING FIVE-GAITED

To be shown at a walk, trot, canter, slow gait, and rack. Horsemanship only to count.

Class 6.—WESTERN TRAIL

To be shown at a walk, jog, and lope both ways of the ring. Individual workouts to be performed as shown in the diagram (see Figure 20-10). This is to be performed at a flat-footed walk or slow jog and breaking gait will be penalized. Horsemanship only to be judged.

Class 7.—FIVE-GAITED COMBINATION

Horses to enter in harness and show at a walk and trot both ways of the ring. They will be lined up, harness taken off, and the saddle and bridle put on. Horses will be shown at a walk, trot, canter, slow gait,

HORSE SHOW SCHEDULE OF EVENTS

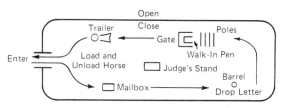

Figure 20-10   Western Trail

and rack. The best combination will be the winner. Horsemanship only to count.

Class 8.—PROGRAM RIDE

(1) Enter ring, salute judge; (2) back 4 to 6 strides; (3) figure eight—1/2 at trot, 1/2 at canter; (4) circle right (as in a regular jumping class), pick up a canter, and go down over the brush jump; (5) pull to sitting trot and do designated amount of serpentines; (6) approach jump (sitting trot), halt, back 4 (approximately) steps, jump fence at a trot; (7) slow trot-extended trot, down jumpless side, pull to walk, reverse collected canter, extended canter, halt at corner; (8) posting trot over "road closed," jump, sitting trot for a few strides; (9) pick up canter-jump brush; (10) trot by end gate— make circle exit at a walk. Horsemanship only to be judged (see Figure 20-11).

HORSE SHOW

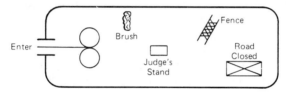

Figure 20-11   Program Ride

Class 9.—STUDENT COACH

In this event a student selects a pupil who has had no previous experience and teaches him or her to ride.

Students to ride at a walk and trot both ways of the ring. Diagonals and control of horse to count. Back and address reins. Horsemanship only to count.

Class 10.—LADIES' THREE-GAITED

To be shown at a walk, trot, and canter both ways of the ring. Horsemanship only to count.

Scheduling

Schedules of events vary depending on local situations, age, and the skill participants. For informal shows contestants often draw for horses and/or positions. In this procedure a drawing is held for each class before the meet.

RIFLE MATCH

With the expansion of game conservation programs, controlled hunting is becoming available for a greater number of sports-minded people and riflery, for many, proves to be an introduction to the safe use of firearms. Rifle matches are well adapted to intramural competition as part of a rifle club program or ROTC units.

Officials and Committees

Executive Officer or Manager is responsible for the efficient conduct of the entire tournament including publicity, registration of contestants, and official records; appoints necessary committees and officials and renders any necessary final decisions.

Official Referee (if the tournament is an official NRA match) is responsible for the correct interpretation of the NRA rules.

Supervisor is also responsible for correct interpretation of the NRA rules and shall rule on all field challenges and protests.

Chief Range Officer has full charge of the range; conducts the matches on a schedule approved by the executive officer; is responsible for range safety; and enforces all match rules.

Range Officer (competitors may be assigned this duty) is an assistant to the chief range officer and is responsible for the safety and discipline of the range personnel, competitors, and spectators in the section of the range assigned.

Statistical Officer is in charge of all statistical work in connection with the match.

Target Officers are responsible for the safety and discipline of personnel engaged in the handling of targets; and ensure the proper condition, correct mounting, and dismounting of the targets.

Regulations

The following considerations should be included in the regulations and literature sent to the competing teams:

1. Competitors should be familiar with the program; cooperate with tournament officials in conducting a safe, efficient tournament; enter only those events and classifications for which they are eligible; assume responsibility for securing their squad tickets for each match and for reporting at the proper time and place for each match.

2. The rifle to be used in competition should be defined. For small-bore

matches it is the .22 caliber rimfire rifle champered for ".22 Short," ".22 Long Rifle" cartridges. Sights permitted should be specified as metallic, telescopic, or any kind. Use of the following should be defined: ground clothes, gloves, padding, slings, palm rest, kneeling pads, butt plates, compensators, or muzzle brakes.

3. Complete instruction on range safety should be included in the match regulations. The following should be stressed: (1) rifles pointed down range at all times, (2) single shot leading, (3) all competitors must be put to but not across the safety line, and (4) if any competitor witnesses an unsafe act, he should immediately call "cease fire."

4. Time allowed to complete various stages is computed as follows:

Individual time—50–75 feet		one minute per shot
50 yds.–100 yds.		prone—one minute per shot
		kneeling—1 1/2 minutes per shot

Team time—the same as above or can be multiplied by the number of shots and the number of team members to determine the total team time when the team members fire consecutively.

5. The following etiquette should be enforced at the range: (1) no loud language, (2) no delay of matches due to individual tardiness, (3) after each stage the competitors should police the range. The following firing line commands should be used:

"Relay No. 1, match no. _____ on the firing line."

"Ready on the right—ready on the left" (an individual shall raise an arm and call "Not ready on target"—after correction or delay).

"Ready on target," "Load," "Ready on firing line."

"Commence firing," "Cease firing—bolts open."

6. Official NRA regulations and targets should be observed and used in the conduct of all matches. Targets should be changed after each 20 shots. Most commonly used is one or a combination of:

50 ft. target (5, 10, 11, bull)	50 yd target	(single bull)
75 ft. target (5, 10, bull)	100 yd target	(single bull)
	200 yd target	(single bull)

Kinds of Matches

Matches usually consist of short range, 50 or 75 feet; medium range, 50 or 100 yards; or long range, over 100 yards. However, 50-foot indoor gallery-type matches are most common since only this type of range is normally available for use.

Re-entry Match. The competitor is permitted to fire more than one score for the record and the highest scores are used to determine the winners. The number of re-entries permitted must be specified in the program.

Aggregate Match. An aggregate of the scores from two or more matches or of match stages are used to determine winners. There may be individual matches and team matches that make up the aggregate match score.

Telegraphic Match. Teams compete on their own ranges and exchange scores via mail, telephone, or telegraph to determine winners.

The positions used in match competition include the following:

Prone—Body extended on the ground with the head toward the target.

Sitting—Weight of the body supported on the buttocks and the feet or ankles and no other portion of the body touching the ground.

Kneeling—Buttocks clear of the ground but may rest on one foot.

Standing—Erect on both feet with no other portion of the body touching the ground or any supporting surface.

Course of Fire—Refers to the number and kind of shots required in a given match. Although there are numerous other courses of firing, the following are typical matches fired at 50 feet indoors.

A. *300-pt. match*

(30 minutes or 10 minutes for each stage)
10 shots prone
10 shots kneeling
10 shots standing

B. *400-pt. match*

(40 minutes or 10 minutes for each stage)
10 shots prone
10 shots sitting
10 shots kneeling
10 shots standing

C. *200-pt. match*—5 bull targets

5 minutes per stage (prone, sitting, kneeling, standing)

D. *200-pt. match*—10 bull targets

(10 minutes per target) fire 2 prone targets of 10 bulls each

Matches C and D are the most convenient type to be fired by beginning teams. For the first year or so the telegraphic (postal) meet is very popular. (A list of teams is available through NRA.)

Scheduling Matches

Competition can be scheduled in many ways. The following are suggested as possibilities.

League Competition. Teams compete against each other in a round robin type of tournament. Final standings are determined by the percentrage of matches won.

Squadded Individual or Team Match. Each competitor or team is assigned a definite relay and target. Failure to report on the proper relay or firing point causes competitor to forfeit the right to fire and winners are determined by total number of points won.

Unsquadded Individual or Team Match. Competitors or teams report to the range officer within time limits specified in the program and are then assigned target and a relay in which to fire.

Scoring

The targets are the scorecards and competitors can act as scorers when requested to do so. The targets are usually scored after each ten or twenty shots by the scorer, who adds the value of the shots, places the total on the scorecard, and signs it. The competitor checks the score and also signs the card. Team captains also verify and sign the cards. Any protest should be lodged at this time.

SKI MEETS

Many developed ski areas, ski clubs, and city recreation programs climax the winter season with a ski meet. This kind of competition has to be organized to provide opportunities for the many different age and skill groups enjoying the sport.

Skiing intramurals for those schools and communities fortunate enough to be located in the right part of the country are popular. They are usually well-supported by boys and girls, men and women alike and planning the competition is often a co-recreational undertaking.

Officials and Committees

Manager or Tournament Director carries out the organization of the ski meet, often with the help of the school ski team or local ski patrol; delegates specified responsibilities to a meet committee, a games committee, and a race committee. Before the meet an open meeting is planned for representatives of all competing houses; the manager supervises a draw to determine the order in which the houses will compete in each event, and collects lists of the teams' starting order.

Meet Committee appoints necessary assistants to (1) develop and distribute preliminary notices, deadline dates, signup sheets, entry forms, team starting orders, and a summary of rules to be observed by the contestants; (2) develop and distribute printed programs which include events, their time and location, a list of starting orders, contestants, their dorms, houses, or addresses, and the names of the officials; (3) organize registration procedure and obtain personnel to check in contestants as they arrive, issue numbers, and give out instructions.

Awards Committee is responsible for securing trophies for the winners; these which usually include place, team and/or traveling trophies and/or medals.

Race Committee is made up of the manager or tournament director and at least two other members who are responsible for all technical aspects of the competition. The committee selects and prepares the courses; judges grievances of contestants; rules on all protests, and makes decisions with respect to the continuance or postponement of a race; appoints the director of officials, and votes on matters that arise from events with which they are officially connected.

Director of Officials appoints and secures all officials for the race committee and provides them with the necessary instructions, information, facilities, and equipment.

Referee alerts the contestants to any special conditions and makes the final decisions in situations not covered by the adopted rules of the meet.

Clerk of Office provides secretarial and general office help; puts out notices of the meet, the program, entry blanks, and adequate pencils and clipboards; gets forms ready for starters, timekeepers, scorers, and checkers; posts final results after each event; and sends the results to campus and local newspapers.

Chief of Course, one for each event, reports to the tournament director and is responsible for the success of an assigned event. Each chief of course appoints a subcommittee to carry out the specific jobs of setting the course, preparing and maintaining it, and taking care of equipment.

Chief Gatekeeper appoints gatekeepers who know the rules and procedures for reporting disqualifications; is responsible for giving adequate instructions to these individuals; and at the end of the event collects the gatekeepers' report cards and turns them in to the referee.

Chief Timer procures all the necessary equipment such as watches, radio or telephone instruments, calculators, electrical timers, and forms; appoints additional personnel to operate the equipment and time events; gives them proper instructions; and ensures that times are properly taken and recorded. Assistant timekeepers, at least three for every event, inform their recorders of the starting number of each contestant and the time when the contestant passes the finish line.

Recorders, one for each timer, records the finishing time of each racer as given by the timer.

Starter and Assistant Starter summon contestants in the proper order, supervise them, issue their numbers, and check them in. The starter sees that the numbers correspond to the individual starting positions and are reissued for each event; establishes the racing order of events; and is responsible for the warning and starting signals. The races are started by the starter's watch in accordance with the time shown on the starting list. Contestants are timed at the finish line and the differences of these two times to the tenth of a second is the record time. Starting intervals are 60–120 seconds for the downhill, 30–60 seconds for the cross-country. In the slalom the next contestant does not start until the previous one has completed the course.

Director of Equipment is responsible for distributing racing numbers and stop watches, and collecting equipment necessary to the various chiefs of courses.

Medical Director is responsible for organizing and equipping a first-aid unit capable of servicing any possible injury or sickness that might occur. The services of a doctor should be secured.

Director of Transportation arranges for all necessary transportation.

Forerunners and Postrunners run the course before the start of the first contestant in the downhill and slalom (at least one or two) and in cross-country (three forerunners); clear the course of spectators; check upon and alert course officials, and determine that all direction and control flags are in position. At least one postrunner closes the course of the cross-country.

Regulations

Local regulations must be defined with respect to several aspects of the ski meet.

1. The number of contestants on a team and the number of teams and individuals each house shall be allowed to enter in the meet must be decided.

2. Participants must be informed of deadline dates for entries and the starting order of contestants in each event.

3. A representative of each team should attend an opening meeting and draw to determine which should be scheduled in the program.

4. The courses should be set and open on the day preceding the race and closed on the day of the race.

5. It is practical to have number-one racers from each school reverse their order for the second run while all other racers run in their original order.

6. Starting signals should be described and may include 1-minute warning, 30-second warning, 15-second warning and 10, 5, 3, 2, 1, "Go."

7. Substitution regulations should be understood. Some meets stipulate that a contestant not present at the time scheduled in the starting list cannot be replaced by another contestants.

8. False starts should be defined and the results explained.

Kinds of Meets

Ski competition usually includes five events: the slalom, giant slalom, downhill, cross-country, and jumping. All of these events are seldom included in one meet. The number and kind of events that can be included will depend upon skill level.

Downhill. The downhill race is one in which the skier selects a line of quickest descent in order to negotiate a long, rugged terrain in the best possible time.

Slalom. This race is shorter than the downhill but the contestant has to pass through a pattern of "open gates" (set across the fall line) and "closed gates" (set parallel to the fall line).

Giant Slalom. This race is shorter than the downhill but has fewer gates than the slalom.

Cross-Country. The cross-country race is an endurance contest over a well-marked, lengthy course which includes equal distances of uphill, downhill, and flat terrain.

Jumping. This event is a jumping contest judged on form and distance.

Classification Races. Ski meets do not have to be planned just for the expert. Classification races enable competitors to compete in a class of equal ability. Every skier enters a classification run and the contestant's class is determined by time and the rating of the judges. Classes included are usually Class III Novice, Class II Intermediate, and Class I Advanced.

Scheduling Meets

The greatest scheduling difficulty with respect to this sport involves the weather and adequate snow conditions. Alternate plans should be developed and understood by all contestants in case the meet has to be changed.

The order of events can be planned to best fit the local situation and conditions. Downhill can be run off more quickly than slalom and slalom usually goes faster than jumping.

Scoring

Determining points won in the various events can be done in the following manner:

Slalom, Downhill, and Cross-Country	*Jumping*
Individual points (to tenths) $$\frac{200 - (\text{Individual time} \times 100)}{\text{best individual time}}$$	Each contestant is judged on the basis of style points and distance points. Final points of each contestant shall be total points of best two jumps.

$$\frac{\text{Team score}}{\text{sum of best 3 team members' pts.}}$$
3

A more simple way of scoring is to use 100 points to represent the winning time. Every contestant is awarded points proportionate to the ratio of his time to the winner's time. As an example: if a contestant's time was 175 seconds and the winner's was 150 seconds, the loss was 25 seconds or $25/150 \times 100/1 = 16.6$ points. The point score is 83.4 (100 − 16.6).

SPEED SKATING

Speed skating, while little publicized, attracts a growing number of boys and girls, young men and women. The increased participation in winter sports has given further impetus to an already growing interest in speed skating.

Officials

Manager is responsible for the overall organization of the event and for appointing the necessary committees and officials. The manager also has to secure permission to use the facilities and necessary equipment.

Referee is responsible for the proper conduct of the meet; he approves or rejects the list of officials; enforces the official rules; decides upon disputes and protests; and renders final decisions in all matters concerned with the meet, including decisions as to whether conditions of weather and ice warrant the running of the event.

Assistant Referees perform all duties assigned to them by the referee. They are usually stationed at the corners of the course, watch the competitors, and report any observed foul in irregularity to the referee immediately after the event or race.

Judges, one for each of the first four "places," are responsible for determining the winner of a particular place, recording on cards provided the number only of the skater finishing in the "place" assigned (1st, 2nd, 3rd, etc.), and turning cards over to a chief judge who computes final standings and times.

Timekeepers, including the chief timer, two assistants, and one substitute timer, time each event starting with the flash of a pistol. The substitute timer's time is used only when one of the three regular timers fails to record the time of an event. After the finish of each event, timers show their watches to the chief timer, who records the results. If three watches agree, that time shall be considered official.

Scorers include a chief scorer who appoints assistant scorers and assigns race responsibilities to them. A lap scorer keeps record of laps made by each competitor; notifies the skaters by card or voice as to the number of laps remaining and with a pistol or bell announces when the leading skater enters the last lap. Each assistant scorer records the time of the competitor in assigned race and the chief scorer records the order in which the first four competitors finished each event.

Clerk of the Course verifies and records the names of the competitors, and gives them a number of each race in which they are entered, fairly arranges and equitably distributes the competitors in the heats, and verifies each competitor's number at the starting line before every event.

Starter has jurisdiction over the competitors at the starting line after the duties of the clerk of the course have been completed. The starter makes sure all persons are excluded from the course except the officials; briefly calls the contestants' attention to any rules deemed appropriate or necessary; and when the chief judge signals that the judges and timers are ready, this official starts the race with the sound of a pistol.

Track Surveyor or Measurer is responsible for properly laying out and marking the track for the speed events.

Announcer receives the race results from the scorer and keeps the audience informed of each event and its results verbally and also may use a bulletin board or scoreboard to provide a continuous report of results.

Regulations

Speed racing competition may be organized on a variety of levels of formality; the following points, however, should be decided upon and stated in adopted regulations.

1. A signup procedure for contestants and deadline dates should be established. Check-in or registration procedures should be explained to all contestants.

2. Requirements and procedure with respect to positions, events, assignments, and the wearing of distinguishing numbers should be included in the literature or regulations.

3. A statement should be made to the effect that racers are responsible for reporting promptly and on time for their events without further notice.

Suggested Classes of Races

Women–Indoor

Seniors	Past 18th birthday	440, 880 yds, 3/4 mile, 1 mile
Intermediates	Past 16th birthday	440, 880 yds, 3/4 mile
Juniors	Past 14th birthday	1/6 mile, 440 yds, 880 yds
Juvenile	Past 12th birthday	1/6 mile, 440 yds, 1/3 mile
Midget	Has not reached 12th birthday	220 yds, 1/6 mile, 440 yds

Men—Indoor

Seniors	Past 18th birthday	440, 880 yds, 3/4 mile, 1 mile, 2 mile
Intermediates	Past 16th birthday	440, 880 yds, 3/4 mile, 1 mile
Juniors	Past 14th birthday	440, 880 yds, 3/4 mile
Juvenile	Past 12th birthday	220, 440, 880 yds
Midget	Has not reached 12th birthday	220, 330, 440 yds

Handicap. As in golf or bowling, speed skating can be made interesting and challenging for the highly and the not so highly skilled by planning handicap events. In this instance slower skaters are given a time advantage that is determined before the event.

Qualifying Heats

In those instances where there are a great number of entrants, a number of preliminary runoffs are scheduled. In these qualifying heats usually the highly skilled are seeded or scheduled in different heats.

Before the start of each heat, the starter announces the number of competitors who may qualify for the final heat. These individuals are usually determined by best time or as winners of the various heats.

Scheduling

Competitors shall draw lots from the clerk of the course before going to the starting line to determine respective places in the starting line.

Scoring

First place — 5 points
Second place — 3 points
Third place — 2 points
Fourth place — 1 point

$$\text{Tie} = \frac{5 + 3}{2} = 4$$

SWIMMING MEETS

Swimming competition is as much a part of summer recreation and camp programs as it is a part of school recreation programs. A swim meet is a popular event in all aquatic programs.

Officials and Committees

Swim Manager, in cooperation with the referee, appoints all necessary committees and officials, informs them of their duties and responsibilities, and engages the use of the pool and building for practice sessions as well as for the meet itself. The manager also enlists the services of individuals willing to help with coaching the teams or individuals desiring help. A meeting with elected or appointed team captains to outline their responsibilities, review procedure of the meet and hand out instruction sheets and signup forms makes a meet run smoothly. On practice nights this official keeps a record of qualifying swims if contestants are to be seeded in the heats. On night of competition, the manager is free to oversee the meet but makes sure that the following equipment is on hand for the event:

Clipboards—One for each official
Flash cards—One set for each judge of form or diving
Gun or whistle—Advisable to have both should gun prove inoperable
Instructions—Sheets for each official
PA system—Should be checked before meet to ensure its proper function
Scoreboard—Located so audience can keep ahead of next event
Score table—Placed away from center of activity for scorer and assistants
Stop watches—One or two for each lane or place
Towels—Available for swimmers
Forms—Scorer—master score sheet and order of events (if diving is included, a degree of difficulty table): clerk of course—entry forms for each event, order of events; runners—report cards for the various events.

Swim Captains are responsible for having their house, dorm, class, or group represented in the meet. They submit completed entry forms by the deadline date. They are responsible for their team's observation of meet instructions and practice session requirements.

Referee has full jurisdiction over the meet, and with the manager appoints officials, assigns duties, and gives necessary instructions. The referee knows the responsibilities of the officials, is familiar with the official rules and regulations, answers any questions that arise, and is responsible for making official decisions. The referee also acts as chief judge and assists in naming the first-place winner in each race.

Clerk of Course receives a copy of the order of events from the referee and a copy of all entry lists, verifies correct entry listings in each event with the competitors at least five minutes before each event, has contestants draw by lot for starting positions, and then sends the contestants "on deck" to a specified place to wait for the announcer to "call" their event.

Announcer effectively keeps the meet moving, makes it interesting and sometimes entertaining. This official has a schedule of the order of events, names of contestants, officials, and meet assistants. At the beginning of the meet the announcer informs the audience of (1) the names of competing teams, (2) the meet manager, (3) officials (and briefly some of their duties), (4) names of individuals who have assisted with the meet, (5) any appropriate words of appreciation, and (6) the order of events and procedures.

At the start of each event the announcer states (1) the name and number of the event, (2) the number of the heat, and (3) the name and team affiliation of each contestant.

As the contestants assemble, the announcer "calls" the next event and advises the contestants to be "on deck." After the finish of each event the results are announced, stating the winner of place, team affiliation, and points as delivered to the announcer by the runner from the scorekeeper. After the last event this official announces the final total score and winners.

Starter has control of the contestants after they have been assigned their proper positions by the referee. This official wears an appropriate outfit, has gun, cartridges, and whistle ready, and stands in a position that can easily be seen by the contestants and timers. Starting signals are preceded with: "Judges and timers, ready? Swimmers ready' There is a pause for acknowledgement or objection; then the next command is, "Swimmers, take your marks"; and the next signal is a pistol shot or whistle to start the race. On a false start a recall signal is indicated with a second pistol shot or whistle.

Relay Starter, one for each lane, who as the swimmer touches the end of the pool, tags the next swimmer on the leg as the starting signal.

Inspector of Turns and Lanes reports any turn or lane rule infractions to the referee.

Timekeepers, at least one timer for each lane, preferably two plus a chief official timekeeper who organizes the timekeepers of each event, makes lane or place assignments, and sees that the final report is given to the runner for the scorekeeper.

Timekeepers should check the units of division of their watch, see that it is wound and in proper working order, and practice starting and stopping it by pushing the stem with the first joint of the thumb. They should stand at the finish line, be able to see down the length of the edge of the pool; should signal "Ready" when asked by the starter before each race; watch the starter; start the watch instantly on the flash of the starter's pistol and stop it when the contestant touches the wall. The time should be recorded immediately and the watch should not be reset until the chief timekeeper has checked the reading.

Judges, usually three kinds: finish judges, form judges, diving judges.

Finish Judges, stationed at the finish line, determine the order in which the contestants finish, and report the results to the referee.

Form Judges (three) award scores for each entrant in the form events. Flash cards are used to flash the score to the scorekeeper or chief judge, who may be used to help report results and help with the scorekeeper's computations.

Form strokes must be executed and judged on the following principles:

Rhythm. The rhythm but not the speed of the stroke is evaluated and includes a consideration of the arms and legs.

Relaxation. The degree of relaxation of the stroke as a whole is evaluated and should include relaxation of the body, head, arms, and legs.

Power. The power but not speed of the stroke is evaluated and includes the power of the arm stroke and the leg stroke.

Form. The form of the stroke is evaluated and this includes the way in which the body is carried in the water, the position of the head, and the movements of the arms and legs. The style of the stroke should be consistent for the length of the pool.

Diving Judges award scores for each entrant for each of the dives performed. Flash cards are again used. A *Diving Referee* may be used to supervise these events.

Diving must be executed and judged on the following principles:

Approach. The approach from the starting position should be smooth, straight, and forceful. The diver's position must be straight, head erect, hands at the sides.

Takeoff. The takeoff should be bold, confident, and in running dives must be from both feet simultaneously.

Height. The diver should obtain the maximum amount of height.

Execution. The execution of the dive must be done in correct form and style.

Entry. Entry must be vertical or nearly so with the body straight and the toes pointed.

Form and diving judges award scores from 0 – 10 points in accordance with the following criteria:

Completely failed (or wrong stroke or dive)	0 through	1/2 point
Unsatisfactory	1 through	21/2 points
Deficient	3 through	41/2 points
Satisfactory	5 through	61/2 points
Good	7 through	81/2 points
Very good	9 through	10 points

Scorekeeper has a minimum of one, preferably two, assistants to help keep a running score of the meet and make possible prompt announcement of results at the end of each event. Before the meet, the scorekeeper should make a chart of events including space to record place, time, and score. This official assigns responsibilities to the assistants—one assistant should check the recording and addition of the scorekeeper. If diving is included an assistant should compute degree of difficulty at the same time that the points are awarded. This person advises the runners of the procedures to be followed with respect to turning results in to the scorekeeper and having results taken to the announcer. At the end of the meet the scorekeeper has the score ready to announce to the audience and the contestants.

Runners get the necessary information from one place to another. It is suggested that form report cards including event, houses, contestant, time, score, and place be used for relaying information from one official to another. A runner is assigned to assist officials in each event.

Runner for Timers brings the names of the 1st, 2nd, 3rd, 4th, and other place winners to the scorekeeper.

Runner for Chief Judge brings the names and scores of the 1st, 2nd, 3rd, 4th, and other place winners to the scorekeeper.

Regulations

Regulations that have to be determined for each situation should be concerned with the following:

    1. The events that are to be included in the meet and the number of entries that are to be permitted for each event and for each theme.
    2. An agreed-upon defined amount of conditioning and practice
    3. Establishment of deadline dates for signup and/or changes in the entries

Kinds of Meets

Racing Meets. These meets are planned to include only the individual and team speed events.

Speed and Form. In order to include more contestants as participants, particularly those with other than speed ability, form events for strokes and diving are often included in this combination-type meet. The following are possible program events that may be selected and combined for a particular situation:

Speed	*Form*	*Demonstration*	*Relays*
Front crawl	Front crawl	Lifesaving	Medley relay
Back crawl	Back crawl	Diving	Freestyle relay
Breast stroke	Breast stroke	Synchronized swim	Obstacle or comic
Freestyle	Elementary back	Water safety	Butterfly
	Side stroke	Scuba diving	Freestyle relay
	Trudgeon	Comedy routine	
	Diving	Aquatic art	

Synchronized Swim or Aquatic Art Meet. Competitive synchronized swimming or aquatic art can be included as a part of another meet or can be planned as an entire meet. Information is given in the Official Aquatics Guide Book.

Scheduling

Although the schedule of events varies with different schools and the ability of the particular participant, the number of events one individual may enter should be limited, and a schedule so developed as to minimize demands of strenuous events.

Before an actual meet, practice sessions should be scheduled (1) to ensure contestants' good condition, (2) so that accurate records of the various preliminary races can be kept, and (3) to increase participation.

After entries and practice sessions are complete, seeded heats must be scheduled if winners of heat are going to compete in the final race. If "best time" determines contestants for the final heat there is no need for seeding.

Scoring

Scoring requires the services of a chief scorer and one or two assistants; and, if diving is included, there should be another assistant to do the computations. Points are usually awarded as follows:

Dual Meets

	Freestyle	*Medley*	*Other Events*
1st place	8 pts.	8 pts. 6 pts.	5 pts.
2nd place	4 pts.	4 pts. 3 pts.	3 pts.
3rd place			1 pt.

Group Meets

	Freestyle and Medley	*Other Events*
4 lanes	10, 6, 4, 2	5, 3, 2, 1
5 lanes	12, 8, 6, 4, 2	6, 4, 3, 2, 1
6 lanes	14, 10, 8, 6, 2	7, 5, 4, 3, 1

Places for speed events are determined by the fastest time. In form events the individual's score is the average of the total points awarded by the judges for each event. Place winners are determined by the total number of points awarded for each form event.

Diving scores are determined by multiplying the average of the judges' awarded score for each dive by the degree of difficulty of the dive. Place winners are determined by the total calculated scores for all dives executed.

If there is a tie for first place, the first- and second-place points are added and divided by two. Each contestant is awarded the points thus determined and there is no second place. The same procedure is used to determine the awarding of points in cases of ties for any other place.

TENNIS TOURNAMENT

Tennis is one of the most popular social recreation sports offered by public parks, private clubs, summer camps, and schools. The typical summer recreation program almost always includes tennis tournaments and school recreation programs usually include tennis competition in the fall or spring or both. These tournaments vary in the degree of formality with which they are managed. However, the higher the skill level of the competitors, usually, the more formal the tournament.

Officials and Committees

Chairperson or Manager supervises the overall organization and management of the tournament, appoints the necessary committees and officials and assigns duties, makes official arrangements for the use of facilities and equipment, and in some instances also serves as referee.

Tournament Committee decides upon the conditions of the competition and develops a procedure for handling entries; it also carries out the seeding of players, supervises the draw and arranges the scheduling of the matches, secures necessary equipment, and decides upon any questions referred to it except those concerned with points of law.

Publicity Committee is responsible for publicizing the tournament and informing the potential competitors of the conditions of the competition; it is also responsible for publicity before, during, and after the tournament.

Referee, as an ex-officio member of the tournament committee, assigns courts to all competitors, starts all matches, enforces tournament regulations, and makes final decisions on all points of law including postponement of matches. He also instructs umpires, is present during all tournament play or appoints a substitute, and keeps an official record of the results of the matches.

Umpire obtains necessary balls, rulebooks, scorecards, and pencils and is on time and in position as soon as the referee announces the match. He checks the height of the net, adjusts it if necessary, verifies the pronunciation of the players' names, and supervises the toss for choice of sides and the right to be server or receiver. After a warmup period, he introduces the players, enters their names in the score book, and starts the match. During the game the umpire has complete jurisdiction of the match and its proper conduct, enforces all rules, and calls all plays that are not the responsibility of the officiating lines officials. The umpire instructs players to start service in the right-hand court, announces the server's name before service for the first time, marks all points as they are made, calls the score after marking, directs players to change positions on the odd games, and sees that play is promptly resumed at the end of resting time. After the game the umpire announces the winner, signs the scorecard, and turns it and the balls in to the referee.

Lines Officials are responsible for being prepared and on time as soon as the referee announces the match. They sit in assigned chairs, concentrate on the boundary lines, not the ball, call "outs" or "faults," but only call balls "good" if asked by the umpire. In addition the base lines officials call the foot faults and no lines official talks or distracts the players or leaves the court except during resting time or when the umpire grants permission and a substitute is obtained.

Net Umpire sits near the net post and calls "Let" on serves that touch the net, and "Fault" or "Through" on balls that go through the net; he also keeps a duplicate score to check the umpire's score.

Ball Chasers, usually used in final matches, assume stations that do not distract the players. After the umpire's decision they retrieve balls and keep contestants supplied.

Regulations

Regulations and procedures must be decided upon and developed with respect to the following considerations:

1. The requirements of court and tournament dress
2. Definition of defaults and maximum waiting periods before a forfeit
3. The number of sets in a match and the procedure of play
4. Instructions with respect to reporting for a match, assignment of court and officials, recording of final score, and assignment for next match

For informal tournaments in which matches are scheduled by the players and rounds are completed by deadline dates, the contestants will need instructions for arranging their own matches, keeping score, reporting score, means of settling questions, and the source of official rules.

Kinds of Tournament

Tennis tournaments traditionally are organized as elimination tournaments or round robins (see Chapter 17). Singles and doubles for men, women or mixed doubles for men and women are scheduled as separate tournaments or as team efforts in which the tournament committee states in the regulations the number of participants a particular group may enter in each match.

Scheduling Matches

In some instances the seeding, draw, and scheduling is done by the tournament committee and is completed before the tournament. Some committees, however, prefer to do this at a meeting with the contestants. At this time seeding is announced and the contestants draw for positions.

Tennis tournaments are either planned formally, in which case each match is scheduled as to time and date, or informally, when a deadline date is set for the completion of a round.

In the formally planned tournaments the tournament committee works out a time schedule for each match observing adequate rest periods between matches and a limited number of matches per day for each contestant. The tournament is completed in a relatively short period of time.

For the informally planned tournament the contestants arrange their own matches until the quarter, or semi-finals, at which time the matches are formally scheduled and officials are provided. Dates for these matches should be set early enough in the season so that the playoff may be rescheduled in case of rain. An up-to-date tournament chart showing time and deadlines for the matches should be posted. In this way, time conflicts can be avoided and participants can be kept alert to the tournament schedule.

Scoring

Correct scoring terminology includes the following point score: 15, 30, 40, game; 30–30 is 30 all, and 40–40 is deuce. An advantage is announced, "Advantage, Miss Jones." Nothing is said when a ball is good. In other instances, "Out," "Fault," "Let," or "Net" should be called promptly, clearly, and sufficiently loud. The lines officials call "Out" but this should be repeated by the umpire for the benefit of the players and the spectators.

Score announcements include the following:

Point score—"15–love, Miss Jones." (Give server's score first.)

Game score—"Game, Miss Jones; games are two to one; Miss Jones leads first set."

Set score—"Game and second set, Miss Jones, 6–4; sets are one all."

Match score—"Game, set, and match, Miss Jones. Games score 3–6, 6–4, 6–3."

All points are recorded as they are made. Large tournaments require players to win three out of five sets in the final rounds. Small tournaments require a match of two out of three sets. Variations may require one-set matches in the first two rounds and two out of three set matches for the semi-finals and finals (see Figure 20-12 for tennis scorecard).

TRACK AND FIELD MEETS

Indoor and outdoor track and field has become a popular activity for all young people in the last several years.

Officials and Committees

Meet Director or Manager supervises the organization of the meet, appoints necessary committees and officials, assigns responsibilities to the officials, and provides them with necessary instructions, forms, and equipment. The

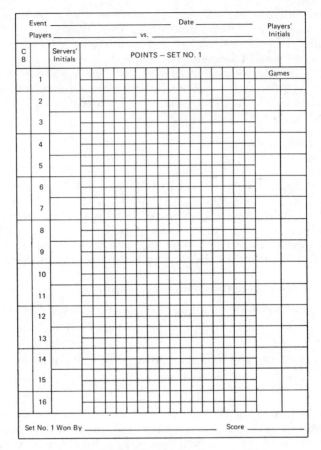

Figure 20-12   Tennis Scorecard

director develops a procedure for entries and registration, approves the
program of events and time schedule developed by the games committee,
secures permission for the use of the grounds and equipment, and handles
all other necessary administrative responsibilities including a filing of necessary reports.

Games Committee determines the events and the time schedules. With the help
of the referee and clerk of course it conducts drawings for heats and lanes,
determines the number to qualify in each heat, distributes instructions to the
contestants, and assigns them numbers. This committee also ensures that
the grounds are properly prepared, that arrangements have been made for
checking equipment in and out, and that the PA system is hooked up.

Track Referee–Starter is in charge of all the meet activities. He checks the list
of entries and the arrangement of the heats, ensures that all officials are on
hand and informed of their duties, settles questions relative to rules and
their interpretation, makes final decisions in cases of protest, ensures that

laps are called for runners, and acts as a starter if no official is appointed by the meet director.

As a starter, this official has jurisdiction over competitors at the starting line and judges whether or not competitors go over the line too soon. In this capacity the official gives necessary instructions, keeps events moving, signals the beginning of the race, and signals the beginning of the last lap in each distance race.

Inspectors and/or Custodians usually number four or six. They are appointed to inspect and assume responsibility for the equipment and at points designated by the referee watch for competition irregularities such as crowding, knocking down hurdles, or violating rules.

Surveyor is responsible for plotting and marking the areas and courses necessary for the meet.

Clerk of Course arranges heats so that the best performers will not be in the same heat, secures the name and number of each competitor, is at the starting mark before each race, holds each competitor responsible for reporting early, records lane assignments, and assigns proper heats and starting positions.

Announcer has to keep the audience and the participants informed of the events on the program and the results of the various events. He also has a list of current records and thus is able to announce any new records that may be broken in the meet; he periodically announces the running score, and at the end of the meet announces the final results.

Head Judge of the Finish and Assistants are responsible for determining the order in which competitors finish a race. At least two judges are assigned to pick each place. Immediately after the race each judge records the number of the winner selected on a card and gives the report to the head finish judge.

Head Timer and Assistants are responsible for timing each track event. The head timer checks all watches, and, only after the results are confirmed, orders the watches to be cleared.

Field Referee–Chief Field Judge is in charge of all field events; he obtains assistant judges, checks and approves all implements and equipment, and measures, judges, and records results of all field trials.

Scorer keeps the official record of the results of each event; he records the order of the finishes and the time, height, or distance of each contestant. The scorer also ensures that the information is sent to the announcer.

Regulations

Local regulations must be established; these will probably differ slightly with each meet.

1. The events to be included in the meet, their order, and time schedule must be decided upon. A fast-moving meet is dependent upon a good schedule.

2. The procedure for signup, the entries for each event, and the number of events in which each individual is permitted to participate must be included in the instructions distributed to potential participants.

3. Physical checks, conditioning, and practice requirements should be a part of the regulations. Where and when to report, how to obtain participants' identification numbers, and information relative to locker and dressing room provisions should also be a part of the regulations.

Kinds of Meets

A meet consists of a variety of races called track events and contests of jumping and throwing called field events. Each meet is likely to be different from the previous one because the events included in the program differ, depending on the skill of the contestants. The following are suggested for track and field events:

High School Boys	*High School Girls*

Indoor

24-yard dash	25-yard dash
100-yard shuttle relay	100-yard shuttle relay
Special obstacle relay	Special obstacle relay
Standing broad jump	Standing broad jump
Medicine ball far throw	Softball pitching for accuracy
Swinging rope vault	Modified pull-up
30–35-yard low hurdles	Other improvised events
Pull-up and/or jump reach	
Other improvised events	

Outdoor

75-yard dash	50-yard dash
100-yard dash	75-yard dash
220-yard dash	100-yard dash
440-yard run	300-yard relay
880-yard run	440-yard relay
One-mile run	Sprint medley relay
300-yard relay	(100-75-75-50)
440-yard relay	50-yard low hurdles
880-yard relay	70-yard low hurdles
Sprint medley relay	Softball throw for distance
(440-110-110-220)	Co-ed relay (boy—440; girl—110;
Medley relay	girl—110; boy—220)
(440-220-220-880)	
180-yard low hurdles	
120-yard low hurdles	
120-yard high hurdles	
Running hop, step, and jump	
Pole vault	

High School Boys   High School Girls

Outdoor

High jump
Running broad jump
Shot put—12 lbs
Discus throw (optional)
Javelin throw (optional)
Co-ed relay (boy—440; girl—110;
   girl—110; boy—220)

College Men   College Women

Outdoor

College Men	College Women
75-yard dash (optional)	50-yard dash
100-yard dash	75-yard dash
220-yard dash	100-yard dash
440-yard dash	220-yard dash
880-yard run	440-yard run
One-mile run	880-yard run
220-yard low hurdles	70-yard low hurdles
120-yard high hurdles	440-yard relay
440-yard relay	880-yard relay
880-yard relay	High jump
Sprint medley relay	Running broad jump
(440-100-110-220)	Shot put—8 lbs
Special sprint medley relay	Softball throw-distance
(440-110-110-220)	Standing broad jump
High jump	Co-ed relay
Running broad jump	(440—M; 110—W; 110—W;
	220—M)
Pole Vault	Javelin throw, optional
Shot put—16 pounds	Discus throw,
	optional
Running hop, step, and jump	
Co-ed relay (440—M;	
110—W; 110—W; 220—M)	

Scheduling

Scheduling track meets so that there is a minimum of delays requires a lot of planning and good coordination between officials and committees. If trial heats are used they must be scheduled with adequate rest before the finals; field events and running events must be scheduled to allow for those who may be in both events, and all events must be run off promptly and on time. The number of entries will be the chief determinant of the time necessary to run off the meet. The kind of facilities, number of judging pits, and amount of equipment that has to be moved will also determine the length of a meet.

The scheduling problems are primarily those of getting the events run off promptly; time must be saved for the trial heats as well as the finals. The final events, which take longer, should start before the track events. The high jump and pole vault have to be started as early as possible.

Ideally, entrants should submit entry forms listing names of all competitors for the various events. Even if this plan is used, last-minute "scratches" make it difficult to arrange heats from these lists.

Small entry cards can be requested from the contestants just before the event. Competition can then be arranged from these entries.

Another method to determine heats for large numbers of entries is to simply divide the contestants into groups by some objective method.

Scoring

The scorer keeps a record of the starters, the point winners in each race, their respective courses, and complete scores. This official also delivers his records to the game committee at the end of the meet.

Points are usually awarded on the basis of 5, 3, 2, and 1 for the four places, and 10, 8, 6, 4, 2, and 1 for six places. In case of ties, the points of the tied places are divided equally between the tied individuals and one place award is eliminated.

DISCUSSION QUESTIONS

1. Assuming you have the administrative responsibility for conducting a variety of meets and matches, how would you train leaders and officials to assume the necessary responsibilities?

2. Outline a program of events for competition in one of the following sports: figure skating, horse show, rifle match, ski meet, swim meet, or track and field meet.

3. Specify a particular tournament and whether it is for men, women, or both; what rules would you use? Where would you obtain resource literature? What standards of competition would you use?

4. Select a particular sport and draw up samples of all the necessary forms for conducting a tournament.

5. How would available facilities influence the tournament plan?

6. At the tournament planning stage would potential participants have input or serve on a planning committee? Explain.

7. In any planned tournament how would you provide for individuals with a variety of skill abilities?

8. Would the tournaments be sanctioned? What would influence your decision? How would you proceed to meet requirements?

9. What would be the respective roles of volunteers, students, and staff in the tournament organization and administration?

10. How should the safety and health of competitors be ensured through the organization and regulation of the competition?

BIBLIOGRAPHY

BANNON, JOSEPH J., *Leisure Resources: Its Comprehensive Planning.* Englewood Cliffs, New Jersey: Prentice-Hall, Inc., 1976.

BUTLER, GEORGE D., *Introduction to Community Recreation.* 5th ed., New York: McGraw-Hill Book Company, 1976.

HYATT, RONALD W., *Intramural Sports Programs: Their Organization and Administration:* St. Louis: C. V. Mosby Co., 1976.

MEANS, LOUIS E., *Intramurals: Their Organization and Administration* (2nd ed.), Englewood Cliffs, New Jersey: Prentice-Hall, Inc., 1974.

PETERSON, JAMES A., editor, *Intramural Administration: Theory and Practice.* Englewood Cliffs, New Jersey: Prentice-Hall, Inc., 1976.

ROKOSZ, FRANCIS M., *Structured Intramurals*, Philadelphia: W. B. Saunders Company, 1975.

Distance Relay, Wheelchair Olympics.
(Courtesy National Wheelchair Athletic Association, Woodside, New York.)

21

Special Recreation
and Recreational
Sports Programs

Recreation and recreational sports programs are designed to serve the needs and interests of the participants. Grouped in this chapter under "special programs" are a great many innovative activity ideas. Although too numerous to be offered in any single program, some of them may serve the director who is aware of expressed needs, alert to new waves of interest, and willing to introduce change.

The special programs are classified as follows: (1) co-recreation, (2) free-time recreation, (3) extramural events, (4) variety and traditional, (5) instructional, (6) noncompetitive, (7) outdoor education and camping, (8) trends and ideas for the handicapped.

CO-RECREATION

Equal sports opportunities for many persons have been made possible through co-recreation programs. Co-recreation, as used here, has reference both to those activities in which boys and girls, or men and women are paired or equated to ensure that the same number are on the competing teams, and to those noncontact "open events" in which girls and women match their sport skills against those of the boys and men.

Co-Recreation Tournaments. Open to both sexes on an equal basis are the popularly scheduled tournaments in noncontact sports such as archery, badminton, bowling, golf, riding, and tennis.

Co-Recreation Challenge Games. Women's or girls' groups or individuals challenge the men's or boys' groups or individuals in noncontact sports.

Challenge games often follow or come at the end of a particular sport season.

Co-Recreation Teams. Volleyball, bowling, softball, skiing, skating, swimming, and similar noncontact sports tournaments, meets, and matches are scheduled over a specified period of time. Each team is composed of an equal number of boys and girls or men and women. Winners and runners-up receive a trophy. For young participants recreational games such as tug-of-war, dodgeball, foot races, and musical chairs can be used.

Co-Recreation Modified Games. Many recreation directors and participants use modified games, rules, and equipment as means of introducing co-education fun activity in such traditional sports as basketball, softball, volleyball, and ice hockey. Ice broomball, broom hockey, flag football, inner-tube water polo, balloon volleyball, and left-handed basketball are just a few kinds of modifications that have been successful.

Co-Recreation Lake, River, and Salt-Water Races. Racing on the rivers in a variety of crafts is a popular warm-weather co-ed activity. Rubber rafts, canoes, kayaks, inner tubes, and bathtubs have all been tried in competition, and in some instances the events have become a tradition.

Dances. Traditional and seasonal social dances, square dances, and hoedowns all prove to be popular when well planned.

Equitation. Riding shows are comparatively easy to sponsor on a co-recreation basis. Races, relays, and fun competition numbers can be in the program with the serious events.

Open Houses. Basketball, swimming, table tennis, volleyball, and a great variety of sports are offered at sports open houses. These are usually scheduled from 8 to 10 P.M. on predetermined popular nights. Everyone is welcome.

Skating Parties. The skating rink is engaged for an evening of skating to music. The program includes a certain amount of planned skating numbers such as couples, trios, waltz numbers, grand march, and elimination games. A figure-skating demonstration might be included and refreshments are essential. A bonfire and frankfurter roast could also be a part of this kind of party.

Splash Parties. The swimming pool is opened for co-ed swim. There is very little organized or planned activity and the party may or may not be limited to specific age groups.

Sports Date Nites. Members and their dates participate in mixers, play volleyball, cage ball, badminton, table tennis, shuffleboard, bowling, and similar games.

Sports Carnival. Activities for this program can include badminton, table tennis, shuffleboard, box hockey, tetherball, volleyball, and archery. Partners compete in the sports as well as in carnival adaptations of games such as bouncing basketballs into trash cans, bowling with a softball, spinning tops, blowing out candles, ring toss, baseball throw at dolls or bowling pins.

FREE-TIME RECREATION

Popular in school communities and college recreation programs are the "open hours" for informally organized sports activities. Without structured teams or games the opportunity to "drop in" for a game or a workout is valued by many sportspersons.

Free-time recreation facilities are most popularly open in the early mornings, evenings, and weekends. A schedule of the available activities is publicized and usually includes some of the following:

Badminton	Men's weight training
Basketball	Squash
Co-ed gymnastics	Tennis
Co-ed swimming	Volleyball
Family swimming	Women's gymnastics
Handball/racketball	Women's weight training

EXTRAMURAL EVENTS

An extramural event is a tournament organized in observation of mutually understood plans, standards, and rules. In contrast to the tournament or championship schedule of competition, extramural events usually are planned for completion in one day or part of a day. The length of these programs is an important feature as well as the social aspect. Usually a luncheon, snacks, or supper is planned by the host school. Informal talks, dancing, singing, and skits as program activities provide opportunities for all participants to get acquainted and enjoy each other socially.

The host community or school announces an area, district, intercollegiate, or interschool competitive event for one or more levels of skill ability. The host follows through with all necessary arrangements for registration, housing, and procedures for organizational sanctioning, if that is desired.

Organization and Management

Responsibility for a playday, sports day, or invitation day is facilitated if the host group appoints some or all of the following committees to carry out the described responsibilities:

Chairperson	Decorations
Invitation and correspondance	Equipment

Registration and guides   Entertainment
Program   Food and Cleanup
Officials and awards   Evaluation

Chairperson. The chairperson appoints committee members and assigns duties, calls necessary meetings, confirms dates, establishes budget allocations, decides upon groups to be invited and theme. This person obtains official permission to hold the function and to use the building, facilities, and equipment; supervises and lends advice and help to functioning committees; ensures that eligibility is checked (meets established rules, approved medical examinations, parental and/or administrative permission to play).

Invitation and Correspondence. This committee develops and has approved a mailing list and letter of invitation; sends a first letter out stating time, place, date, registration, and the specific activities at least six weeks in advance; and requests a return within two weeks indicating interest and approximate number planning to attend. When replies are in, the committee sends a follow-up letter including specific instructions about time and place of registration, fees, permits to play; any request for: (1) talks, (2) skits and special talents, (3) stunts and demonstrations, information about clothes, equipment, arrangements for lunch, others attending, and officials that will be needed. Finally a letter of invitiation is sent to staff members of the host organization and other interested personnel.

Registration and Guides. This committee arranges for an adequately managed registration desk with sufficient change on hand; collects fees for lunch, bowling, swimming, and other necessary charges; registers each person by name and affiliation (places person on a team if a playday); assigns a locker, gives a name tag, a program of general instructions, including methods of team rotation, a schedule of activities; registers sponsors and gives them a list of officiating responsibilities, a program, and the times of any special meeting arranged for them; sets up a lost-and-found desk and a first-aid station; and provides a centrally located scoring device to indicate the progress and running scores. A half hour before the guests arrive this committee has identifiable guides on hand and ready to give out information at the registration desk, provide checking accommodations, show visitors around the building, and arrange conducted tours.

Program. This committee signs up players for the host group, gets a report of the number of expected visitors from the invitation committee, and plans a program of activities in light of equipment and facilities available for one of several plans: (1) a whole day, (2) a schedule of games for the morning and informal or free-choice activities for the afternoon, or (3) if the participants are close enough, for an afternoon of activity. If the program is outdoors, the committee plans a rainy-day program and mimeographs a program booklet that includes information about the planned entertainment, songs, lists of groups and sponsors, and an autograph or notes pages.

Officials and Awards. This committee works out the schedule of officials for each event and has this explained in the letter sent out by the invitation committee; at registration it hands out officials' schedules with duties, positions of courts, fields, teams' schedules, time of events, length of playing time, starting and stopping signals; has all scores and/or points reported to the head scorekeeper of the day; provides appropriate awards such as ribbons for the winning color team of a playday and a small cup for winners of intercollegiate skill competition; works with the entertainment committee in planning a time for recognition of the award winners.

Decorations. This committee carries out the theme of the playday with decorations in the reception hall and the room and tables where the luncheon is planned; makes plans for taking down and storing the decorations for use at another time.

Equipment. This committee takes charge of issuing and checking in all balls, racquets, whistles, and equipment necessary for the day's activities which may be issued to responsible captains for players or the officials of the various activities.

Entertainment. This committee plans some kind of program during the lunch hour or before going home which may include skits, group singing, mixers, films, demonstrations, workshops, or clinics; arranges for pianos, microphones, and necessary equipment for this entertainment; works with the award committee in planning time for the granting of awards.

Food and Cleanup. This committee decides upon food and/or refreshments, makes necessary procurement arrangements, and assumes responsibility for cleanup.

Evaluation. Following the day of activity, this committee plans an evaluation of the program; makes notes and suggestions for the next year using suggestion boxes, discussions immediately after the event, or similar techniques.

Playdays

A playday is defined as a day or part of a day when individuals from several schools, colleges, classes, or communities meet to play with, rather than against, each other. The host invites groups to participate in a day of sports activity for fun. Each group invited sends a designated number of players for one or more activities. However, the players do not participate as a team. Upon arrival at the host site or school, teams are made up of players from different schools or communities including the host group and are designated by colors, numbers, or names. Events are organized so that representative groups lose their identity in competition. This is usually done at the registration desk when the participants arrive.

The activities are many and varied, and may include team and individual sports, noncompetitive activities, demonstrations, and clinics. The organization of a playday is such that all players have many opportunities to get acquainted and to play with and against each other. Usually the number attending is limited only by the facilities and interests of the potential participants.

Sports Days

In this type of competition a host school or community invites several schools or communities to meet for a day of competition in which one or more representative teams play against each other in one or more activities. In contrast with the playday, each team is identified with the school or community it represents. The number of activities may be one or many, though generally there are fewer kinds of activities than are included in a playday. Awards are significant, but the emphasis on winning is minimized.

Invitation Days

An invitation day involves a limited number of representative teams or groups with common interets in one or two activities. A host invites one or more groups over for competition, symposium, or demonstration in, for example, badminton, riding, skating, skiing, dance, or swimming. Activities other than the traditional team and dual sports can also be highlighted in a successful yet different kind of invitation day.

Telegraphic or Postal Meets

Results of this competition are compared by wire, mail, or phone. Pre-tournament rules are agreed upon and competitions are not limited by travel distances.

NONCOMPETITIVE ACTIVITIES

Participating in sports for the fun of doing and the fun of learning and improving skills, as contrasted to the satisfactions of competing, is a growing aspect of all recreational sports.

The varied sports activities suggested here have been offered by city and county parks departments, community school programs, and school district winter and summer recreation directors. The programs, however, are not aligned with any one administrative plan, as the footnoted sources verify.

Canoeing, Boating, and Aquatics[1]

Skagit River Canoe Camping.[1] The beautiful Skagit offers some white water but this trip should be considered a run to lay back and enjoy the river, mountain peaks, and camp on one of the many sand bars. Limited to eleven (11) per two-day trip. Fee ———.

Lake Canoe Touring. A basic lake canoeing course which covers all of the paddle strokes, boat-handling technique, and safety precautions but also offers the chance to tour Whatcom, Silver, Samish and Padden Lakes. Four sessions. Fee includes all equipment.

San Juan Island Canoe Tours. Portage the canoes via Washington State Ferries to Orcas Island and canoe explore for several days among the Wasp Island group. Limited to eleven (11) per three-day trip. Fee ———.

Piloting and Coastline Navigation Course. A comprehensive course designed for the beginning and experienced boatman and sailor. Navigation skills will be taught using chart, compass, and workbook. Meetings are once a week October to December 3. Fee ———.

Beginning/Intermediate Sailing. These comprehensive courses cover nomenclature, theory of sail, points of sailing, tacking, jibing, sail trim, and small-boat safety. The boats will be El Toros with graduation into International 420. Limited to nine (9) per class. Fee ———.

Sailing Cruise with Instruction in Sailing and Seamanship. A three-day cruise on an ocean sailing vessel combined with instruction that will cover theory of sailing, tacking, running and reaching, sail trim, general boat handling, navigation problems, marline spike anchoring, weather predictions, storm precautions, marine natural history and edibles, diving with snorkel and wet suit. Fee includes meals, equipment, and breakfast buffet.

Diving for Fun and Marine Edibles. This is a course designed to teach snorkeling skills as well as foraging and preparation of marine edibles. There will be four lectures on diving techniques and edibles, a preparation dive and a weekend overnight of dives. Fee ———.

Scuba Diving. For fun and adventure there's nothing like sport diving! Learn through classroom, pool, and open-water experience. Certification available. Minimum age 16. Fee ———.[2]

Cycling, Fitness, and Self-Defense

Bike Marathon. A fifty-mile bike marathon consists of riders who obtain

---

[1]The first seven activities are quoted from a booklet entitled *Whatcom County Parks Outdoor Environmental Program* (Washington: Whatcom County Parks, Autumn 1975), pp. 2A, 3A.

[2]*Gladstone Community School Winter 1976* (Gladstone, Oregon: Gladstone School District #115 and Clackamas Community College, 1976), p. 5.

pledges for a per-mile donation. The pledges will go only for a proposed bike trail.[3]

Family Bike Rides. An opportunity for cycling families to get together, enjoy some of the community sights, and exercise. An escorted route will be taken, stopping for a break at about three miles. A second three-mile route will be possible for those interested, and those not interested may stay at break until others return. The group then returns to starting point together.[4]

Men's Keep Fit. Ten weekly sessions. Basketball, volleyball, and floor hockey played each week. Adults. Fee ———.[5]

Ladies' Slim and Trim. Ten weekly sessions. Instructions in a series of exercises accompanied usually by music. Volleyball or badminton included. Teens and adults. Fee ———.[6]

Yoga. Qualified instruction in nutrition, breathing exercises, and various postures to promote proper blood circulation and gland function. Age 16 and over. Ten weekly sessions. Fee ———.[7]

Beginners and Intermediate Belly Dancing. The art of Middle Eastern dancing and a sacred dance developed by ancient Mediterranean civilizations for religious ritual dating back to 6,000 years ago. Instruction includes history, basic exercises, dance steps, and costume design. Belly dancing is excellent for muscle tone and weight control.[8]

Karate–Korean "Tackwon-Do." Course covers basic Korean Karate forms, natural weapons, and vital spots. Tackwon-Do is a Korean ancient martial art as well as a fighting art which has orginally come from Buddhist monks to develop mental and physical discipline by using empty hands and bare feet. Fee ———.[9]

Hiking and Mountaineering

Basic Mountaineering and Winter Travel. A course designed to teach techniques that will extend the climbing season into the fall and spring months. A basic mountaineering section includes equipment selection, rock climbing, navigation, knots and rope handling, mountain hazards, snow climbing, rescue techniques, survival, trip planning, and outdoor photography. Winter travel sections will cover cross-country skiing, snowshoeing,

[3]*Super Summer '75* (Des Moines, Iowa: Recreation Department, 1975), pp. 4, 5.

[4]Ibid.

[5]*Surrey Community and Recreation Programs Winter 1976* (Surrey, B.C., Canada: Surrey Parks and Recreation Commission, Douglas College, and Community Education Department School District 36, 1976), pp. 19. 23.

[6]Ibid.

[7]Ibid.

[8]Estacada Community School, *Estacada Community School Winter 1976* (Estacada, Oregon: Clackamas Community College and Estacada School District 108, 1976), pp. 4, 6.

[9]Ibid.

Alpine ski touring, snow camping, and avalanche hazards and rescue. The course consists of ten classroom sessions, two evening practices, and twelve days in the field. Field sessions include rock climbing, cravasse rescue practice, a fall climb of Mt. Baker, ski practice sessions, and a winter attempt of Mt. Shuksan on skis or snowshoes. Fee includes instruction, text materials, group equipment, and technical climbing equipment.[10]

Backpacking Clinic. Basic backpacking techniques and usage ethics. Bring your own pack for loading demonstration.[11]

Backpacking Class. Serves as a beginning point for those wanting to get into the outdoors. Five classes. Fee ————.[12]

Survival Course. November to January once a week plus field trip. Fee ————.[13]

Fall Climbing Series. An opportunity to climb three prominent peaks in local area. No previous experience is required although a basic mountaineering course is recommended. Fee includes the use of group equipment, transportation, and guide. Limited to eleven participants.[14]

Orienteering and Map Reading. Two sessions 9:00 A.M.–4:00 P.M. Saturday and Sunday for teens and adults. One theory session and a practical at Chilliwack River Valley. Fee ————.[15]

Rock Climbing. Two sessions 9:00 A.M.—4:00 P.M. Saturday and Sunday for teens and adults. Fee ————.[16]

Skiing, Touring and Winter Sports

Winter Sports Seminar. Prepare your skis and winter equipment for winter activities. Bring your own equipment. Free.[17]

Ski Lessons. Ski lessons will be given at Mt. Hood Ski Bowl. Five-week programs will be offered during January, February, and March. Lessons fee plus lift ticket. Register and payment of fees must be made before January 5.[18]

Community Ski Bus. The community school will be running a bus to the mountain on Saturdays provided there are twenty-five riders.[19]

[10]*Whatcom County Parks Outdoor Environmental Program,* pp. 6A, 7A.

[11]Associated Students Washington State University, *Activities and Special Events Fall 1975* (Pullman, Washington: Outdoors Activity Program—a branch of the Campus Recreation Department), 1975).

[12]Ibid.

[13]Ibid.

[14]*Whatcom County Parks Outdoor Environmental Program.*

[15]*Surrey Community and Recreation Programs Winter 1976,* p. 4.

[16]Ibid.

[17]Associated Students Washington State University.

[18]Estacada Community School.

[19]Ibid.

Cross-Country Ski Touring. This course covers all phases of cross-country skiing. Classroom sessions cover equipment selection, waxing, map and compass, avalanches, the cold environment, and snow camping. The tours and one overnight will emphasize technique and will cover many routes and varying terrain. There will be three classroom sessions and five field sessions. Limited to twelve. Fee ———.[20]

INSTRUCTIONAL PROGRAMS

A multitude of instructional programs can be uniquely effective for increasing participants' skills, knowledge, and interest in specific sports. Planned as program features, each instructional activity differs in purpose and therefore should be carefully considered and developed.

Clinics

Deriving its connotation from medical terminology, a clinic usually represents an opportunity for interested individuals to bring their problems for solution. Consultants are available to offer advice through talks, demonstrations, and exhibitions. Often clinics are set up to serve a particular area and are organized within a framework of anticipated or known problems.

Clinics are commonly planned for team and individual sports. Generally, there is a nationally known guest (or guests) who acts as a resource person. Specialists may put on an exhibition, give an informative and instructional talk, demonstrate, and interpret sport skills, techniques, and strategies. If time permits, or if the clinic is planed for several sessions, one of the sessions may be devoted to instruction, analysis, and practice of skills by the participants. In any event, those in attendance are given opportunities to discuss their particular problems.

Local, state, or district amateur and professional sports associations are often able and anxious to assist in establishing clinics. Equipment and sports purveyors also often prove to be very helpful in such an undertaking.

In addition to sports clinics, many associations sponsor clinics in officiating, leadership, ski patrol, water safety, and first aid.

Demonstrations

Demonstrations refer to one or more performances in which someone who is sufficiently skilled demonstrates to spectators. There are, in

[20]*Whatcom Parks Outdoor Environmental Program.*

other words, demonstrators and spectators. To facilitate communication a demonstration should include appropriate equipment and visual aids.

A demonstration can be planned for teaching ideas, skills, attitudes, and processes. However, most commonly it is used to teach skills. Many times, groups of skilled individuals give demonstrations of techniques used in specific sports such as tennis, badminton, hockey, or soccer. In other instances, one or two individuals give skill demonstrations in such things as synchronized swimming, archery, or dance.

Demonstrations are quite frequently combined with master lessons, clinics, and other structured programs. It is a popular practice to have skilled players and instructors as well as experts from outside the local situation give demonstrations.

Master Lessons

A master lesson has reference to a program in which an outstanding teacher presents a lesson for all interested. This is usually done by an expert or professional artist in a particular activity.

Master lessons are generally associated with dance—i.e., master lessons in modern, social, folk, or square dancing. The master teacher is usually from the academic world or is a professional dancer. Frequently, a master lesson is arranged as a part of a dance troupe's engagement agreement. For instance, if a cultural series board or modern dance club engages a modern dance troupe for one or two evening performances the troupe is often asked to sponsor a one- or two-hour afternoon master lesson for interested participants. The lesson usually includes introductory, philosophical, and interpretive comments, techniques, demonstrations, and possibly a small composition or dance presentation. The activity is led by the master teacher with those in attendance participating.

Mini-Courses

Mini-courses representating eight to twelve lessons in sport skills have been a most popular innovation in school curricula. Structuring several courses in a semester or quarter enables students to develop skills in a great variety of sports. Apart from the formal education curriculum, sport clubs and recreation associations also have successfully offered mini-courses.

In the community, Y's, public recreation departments, and community education programs have attracted a great deal of interest in short courses to improve sport skills. The individual and dual recreational sports of golf, swimming, tennis, and badminton are equally popular as the team sports. Mini-courses are a growing and important part of a sports recreation program.

Practicums

Practicums have traditionally been comparable to "in-service training" or short-term apprenticeships under expert supervision. The experiences most often have involved teaching in an internship role. The concept, however, can be applied to the acquisition of sports skills.

At different stages of sports skill development it is valuable to play with, against, or "under the eye" of, an expert. This opportunity, provided as a part of recreation programs, can be offered as skills practicums. The perfecting of coaching and officiating skills is often an important and popular part of a recreation program. Abilities can be enhanced by practicum experiences organized as part of the recreational sports program.

Symposia

These programs offer the opportunity to bring together the best thinking of experts in a particular field. Each of the leaders discusses or writes about a previously selected question relative to his own area of authority. The speakers are given a definite time limit in which to present their similar or opposing points of view. Usually the results of the discussion or writings are summarized verbally or in written form by the chairperson and made available to all participating members. The symposium may take the form of a discussion in which the audience listens. However, the audience may have an opportunity to participate and this involvement usually stimulates audience interest.

Symposia are often used to discuss problems, ideas, formulation of standards, regulations, establishment of purposes, direction, or philosophy for an association. This is a very appropriate way to treat problems. Symposia are also arranged in such a way as to cover problems in many other areas such as dance, aquatics, and sports.

Workshops

Workshops are planned to involve all participants in a working, contributing situation. One or more leaders may structure the workshop around a variety of interests or problem areas. The problems may be of a discussion or action type. Usually the workshop is dominated by other than experts, although there may be consultants available. Workshops, like clinics or master lessons, are an effective means of improving skills and learning new ideas under able leadership. The leaders and participants work out problems together in a short period of time or over several days.

VARIETY AND TRADITIONAL

A recreational sports program often includes a variety of meetings, traditional events, money-raising projects, and special occasion programs.

General Meeting Program Ideas

Planning "raps," business sessions, or orientation meetings are enhanced with the following:

Talks—Interesting and stimulating guest speakers who talk on some phase of recreation, fitness, or ecological concerns are very popular and may be available from local colleges, agriculture extension departments, community authorities, various branches of federal or state government.

Discussions—People of all ages are interested in health, fitness, and personal health problems. These can be discussed as they relate to recreation participation, and local doctors or public health department personnel may be available as resource speakers.

Demonstrations—Improved skills and know-how increase participation. Demonstrations are one effective means of increasing the sports skills and knowledge.

Movies—Movies on sports, sports events, Olympics, skills, and health have educational value and can be of interest to all participants.

Pep Rallies—Sports managers can increase participation in their activities through clever skits and short pep meetings.

Social Games—Ten or fifteen minutes of fun and social games can end a meeting on a good note.

Traditional Programs

The fall, winter, and spring sports seasons seem to dictate the need for a traditional program at the end of each of these seasons. In some cases there is an awards party at the end of the sports season. In other cases "change-of-pace" activities are planned to conclude each season.

Award Parties

Field Week—This type of traditional program represents a final chapter of each of the fall, winter, and spring seasons. There is a week of keen competition and spirited rivalry. At the end of each field week, a cup is presented to a representative from the winning group; all-star teams are announced, awards are granted, and new participants are welcomed.

Just Desserts Awards Party—Instead of an elaborate banquet, some programs include seasonal sports get-togethers call "just desserts" parties with planned award programs.

Sports Banquet—Many recreation programs include sports banquets one or more times a year. Awards, recognition of honor teams, and results of the various sports competitions are typical parts of the program. Sports managers for the coming season may give pep talks about their sports, their plans for the season, and the fun they have in their activities. Speakers can be included along with skits, singing, and music.

Sports Day—Some sport seasons are ended with a class or group rivalry type of program. One or more activities are planned, after which an awards and recognition ceremony marks the end of the season.

Fall Seasonal Parties

A Coke Party—During the fall promotion or orientation period a Coke party is planned for all potential participants. Recreational games are planned as well as sports activities, and the new programs and personnel are introduced.

A Series of Events—Two, three, or more events are scheduled during the promotion or orientation period that are open to all interested sports participants. Such a series might include: (1) a sports mixer, (2) a bonfire with a skit and introduction of managers and captains, or (3) an original presentation of the different sport activities.

All-Sports Jamboree—A jamboree is planned around a theme and a program featuring demonstrations in volleyball, softball, tennis, golf, and many other sports. Participation in several activities is planned after the demonstrations.

Buddy Picnics—Every old participant is a "buddy" to one or more prospective newcomers. This is a good means to promote the program.

Camping Cabin Trip—Some organizations are fortunate enough to have a camp cabin. A traditional fall party at the cabin starts the year and provides a wonderful opportunity to explain the program.

Carnival—The carnival theme has been carried out as a successful fall party. Barkers, booths, games, and sideshows all provide opportunities to present sports activities to potential new participants.

Fall Bonfire-Party—This bonfire party is complete with skits and traditional songs. It serves as a means of introducing program activities and personnel.

Fall Hayride—As many wagons as needed are hired complete with hay and horses. There is an open invitation for a moonlight ride through the country with lots of singing and perhaps refreshments around a campfire or back at the gym.

Fall Picnic—A fall picnic is planned during which time the various program activities are introduced.

Fall TV Program—All are invited to visit the "gym TV studio." Upon arrival, the MC invites everyone to become a TV star. The presentations teach something about the sports program and its purpose. After the program there is a tour of the "studio," with various booths depicting the sports clubs.

Fall Dessert Party—The season of activities is started by having a dessert party for all interested participants. After refreshments, short talks are given by the various sport managers to promote and interpret the various planned programs.

Fall Dinner—A dinner is open to all participants, but the new members or participants are guests of honor and the program is planned around their introduction to the program of the organization or club.

General Association Meeting—Many organizations introduce their activities to new participants at a general meeting. Everyone is invited to a mass meeting. The purpose of the programs, leaders, and plans for the year are presented to those in attendance.

Gym Jam—Many new faces appear in the fall and a jammed gym together with mixers and party games is a good way to get acquainted. Introduction of officers, sports managers, and club presidents allows each to describe activities and acquaint the new participants with the sports program.

Open House—The gym becomes an open house. The purpose, of course, is to introduce the sports program. There are refreshments and entertainment. Display booths of each of the sports and clubs explain the activities and provide opportunities to sign up for participation.

Pancake Breakfast—For this introductory activity, there is a hike to a nearby park for a cookout breakfast. A short program is planned, but the purpose is primarily to get acquainted and have fun.

Winter Seasonal Parties

Christmas Dinner Party—This is a party with a planned program of singing, skits, and monologues appropriate to the time of the year. Each person is asked to bring some Christmas dinner canned food. Baskets are then made up, and the group goes out caroling and delivering the food to needy people.

Christmas Party—Admission to this party is a sock filled with goodies and toys. The socks are later distributed to the underprivileged. Holiday games and relays open the program, but the highlight of the party is the breaking of the piñata, a large sack of sweets suspended from the ceiling.

Christmas in a Foreign Land—This is a traditional party with the same general organization of songs, skits, and monologues except that each year the party takes place in a different country, observing its customs and traditions.

Old English Christmas Party—Old English costumes and traditions are the theme of this banquet. With everyone dressed in the traditional English manner, a sports procession is led into the banquet hall. The yule is burned and Wassail songs are sung, each symbolizing ancient custom and tradition. The evening's program of speeches and reports is planned around the basic theme evident in costumes, decorations, and program.

Party for the Handicapped or Underprivileged—Some sports organizations have a traditional party at a local hospital, orphanage, or home for the crippled children. Someone plays Santa Claus with his bag full of gifts. Entertainment usually includes songs, skits, stories, or talent presentations.

Santa Party—This is a traditional Christmas party with carols, appropriate skits, poems, choral reading, and climaxed with a visit from Saint Nick with a bag full of awards and gifts.

Santa Workshop Party—A short program and refreshments are planned for this party, but the main purpose is to make and repair toys that are given to the underprivileged at Christmastime. Each person planning to attend is asked to bring toys.

Skating Party—A bonfire, hot dogs, hot chocolate, skating music, planned numbers such as couples only, women only, men only, trios only, form a wonderful traditional party. Sometimes this is continued with a Christmas theme and carolers come by to sing. In other situations, a skating party can be based on an Alpine theme and setting or can follow an ice show with a skating review and figure-skating demonstration.

Ski Lodge Party—In those areas where skiing is a popular and available sport, a ski lodge weekend is a popular party for those who like to get out on the slopes and for the non-skiers who enjoy the lodge recreation, tobogganing, sledding, and hiking.

Sleighride Party—Two or three hired sleighs, horses, and a crystal-clear winter night provide the beginning of a winter party. A ride through the country ending with hot cider and a fire is popular with many as a traditional party.

Spring Seasonal Parties

Camping and Outing—An evening campfire program or overnight with campfire skits, songs, and games all enhance sports programs, business meetings, award ceremonies, or pep rallies.

Fitness Day—The gym is converted into a series of booths and fitness demonstration centers and is open to all. The importance of sports activity and its relationship to fitness is stressed.

Fashions for Spring—A spring sports fashion show, as a separate function or as a part of the traditional spring party, is a most successful program event for boys and girls, men and women. Those interested in modeling and clothing design often will sponsor such a show. Frequently local stores have a modeling department.

Field Day—Field day is a day of sports-centered contests. Teams are usually color teams, class teams, or house teams. Each team has members participating in a number of activities, similar to a playday. At the end of the day awards are given out, refreshments served, and a short program planned.

May Day—This is often a traditional program. In some instances a morning of May Day dances are scheduled along with a traditional May drama and a crowing of the May Day Queen.

Olympic Day—This is a traditional spring program during which teams represent various countries. They participate in Olympic-type contests, relays, jumping, throwing, fencing, gymnastics, swimming, hockey, boating, and similar sports. Refreshments are usually served informally. Awards, short talks, and traditional ceremonies end the day's activities.

Steak Fry—A spring steak fry, fish fry, or chicken roast may become a gala affair. If the party is properly planned and organized, hundreds of participants can be served a main entry, tossed salad, hard roll, milk, and ice cream. The program may be combined with an awards program and or outdoor sports such as softball and volleyball.

Woodsman's Frolic—A woodsman's frolic features various teams that compete in camping skills such as boiling water, building fires, chopping wood, splitting wood, putting up tents, frying eggs on a buddy burner, lashing, survival cooking, safety practices in the woods, square dancing, and outdoor contests.

Initiation Parties

Board Initiation Dinner—Rather than having a large dinner for all interested participants, many organizations have a dinner for the old and new officers, administrators, captains, and managers. Guests are invited, and a guest speaker and a message from the old and new presidents usually make up the evening program.

Camping and Initiation Weekend—A most successful initiation program is that of having a camping weekend. All interested individuals sign up for a weekend of camping, cooking out, fishing, and sports. A part of the weekend program consists of the initiation ceremonies and training sessions.

Initiation Banquet—In some situations the initiation banquet is the function of the year. It is a fairly formal affair and quite the highlight of the year's activities. The old officers leave a last will and testament; the outgoing and new officials give short talks; sometimes there is a guest speaker; and the new leaders take their oaths of responsibility.

Officers' Training Social—Initiation and the taking of the officers' oath is sometimes done at an old and new officers' social. Like the board dinner, a few words are usually said by the old and new president, and then each old officer goes over job details with the new officer.

Initiation Sports Night—In lieu of dinners or socials, an equally effective job can be done with an initiation sports night. Planning requires minimum time. Whatever formal initiation ceremonies and training sessions that are necessary can be carried out before or after informal games and refreshments.

SPECIAL-OCCASION ACTIVITIES

In addition to the general meeting and traditional programs, there are a number of different special events often included in the sports program. These events include activities that are in keeping with the accepted objectives and nature of the programs, but more likely reflect new interests and ideas that have not yet become traditions. Parents, friends, faculty, and members of the community or student body are often invited to take part in some of these events.

All-Star versus Supervisors—A volleyball, basketball, or softball team of all-star players challenges the supervisory personnel, faculty, or administration.

Basketball Kickoff Dinner—Board members of the recreation council have a kickoff dinner. The board starts the season by having a dinner together before going to the kickoff game.

Buddy Picnic—This is an enjoyable party that helps everyone get acquainted. Two weeks before the picnic, old participants draw the name of a newcomer for whom they secretly do nice things. The night of the picnic the identities are revealed, resulting in pleasure to all.

Casino Party–Annual Open House—Decorations of dice and cards, hall games, exhibitions of various sports with names based on gambling terms, and food "on the house," provide the setting and theme for a sports casino. Games can include shaving a balloon, throwing darts at cards, and playing sports such as basketball, squash, and volleyball.

Float Nite—Float Nite is often a part of an all-out effort to publicize and present all sport programs to potential participants.

Father's/Mother's Day—This is a day or weekend during which all activities are devoted to participation by the honored parents of activities members.

Homecoming Games with Alumni—Students challenge the alums to morning team sport games. After the games, refreshments are served to everyone.

Mock Track Meet—This is an event open to all students and includes relay races and various obstacle races.

Olympic Day—Olympic Day is a day of track and field events similar to those of the Olympic games. Hurdle races, the javelin, shot-put throws, and relays are some of the events of the program.

Parents' Tea—This is a party which provides an opportunity to meet all the parents; they, in turn, meet the sponsors and managers.

Party for the Underprivileged—Parties for the underprivileged, handicapped, or orphans are some of the potential service projects that can be included in the annual calendar.

Rally Day or Field Day—This is similar to a sports day, but the participants are all from within the school or community. Competition is between classes, houses, or color teams.

Seasonal Parties—Skating, bicycling, and swimming parties are often planned seasonally. A bonfire, skating party with hot dogs, a bicycling trip to nearby places of interest, or an evening splash party all prove very popular.

Skit Night—This is a competition of sports or campus-related skits. It is often combined with a game night at the gym, and the evening activities are climaxed by a program of informally developed skits.

Splash Party—This is scheduled as an open house at the swimming pool. Music and games may be provided but generally the event is comparatively unorganized.

Sports Movie Night—Two or three times a year an outstanding sports film is shown. Such films as the *Olympics, Fitness Research, Ski* films, *Mountain Climbing, White Water Canoeing, Running the Rapids, Cave Exploring,* or *Sky Diving* are popular.

Sports Open House—On a Friday, Saturday, or Sunday night, or sometimes all day, the gym is opened for a sports open house. Equipment is made available and there is opportunity to participate in unorganized activity.

Sports Period—One afternoon each week participants may play in any one of several activities such as badminton, fencing, shuffleboard, table tennis, or similar sports.

Youngster–Oldster Day—This is an event which provides an opportunity for the oldsters to limber up and play with the young people. Games and social activities are commonly planned.

Vaudeville—Each organized group presents a ten-minute skit on a theme devised by the recreation association such as "A Day in History," "College Capers," or "Our Heritage."

Winter Weekend—This is a weekend in the mountains to enjoy skating, skiing, and tobogganing. In the event there is no snow, such activities as horseback riding and the indoor sports of bowling, table tennis, and dancing may be substituted.

MONEY-RAISING PROJECTS

Recreation associations are financed in a number of ways, and, in some instances, income earned by the memberhsip is the primary source for the operating budget. Besides money needed to operate the program, some recreation associations raise money for special projects such as scholarships, conventions, and playdays. In such instances special money-raising programs may be undertaken. The following are suggestions that have proven successful.

Annual Coffee and Doughnut Sale—Coffee and doughnuts are sold at registration to provide money for the RA budget.

Balloon Sale—A good money-making project is that of selling balloons at homecoming or regular football games. The balloons are filled with helium, and are sold before the game. There are prizes for the high sales of the day plus a free ticket to that day's game. Proceeds, of course, go into the association treasury.

Box Supper—Half the members make a box supper for two and they are auctioned off at a co-recreation picnic.

Car Wash—Recreation association members volunteer to wash cars of faculty and students for an appropriate charge. Income goes into the RA treasury.

Carnival or Circus—Booths which offer such activities as shooting out a candle, bowling, hitting a badminton bird through loops, pitching pennies, and throwing washer rings at pegs are appropriate and a good means of income when a slight fee is charged. Free doughnuts and cider may be included in the program.

Club Programs—Dance clubs, swim clubs, gymnastic clubs, and riding clubs often sponsor traditional programs or shows which are very well attended and bring in needed money. Some RAs receive the profits from these programs; others share the profits with the clubs, which often have financial obligations of their own.

Cosmetic Sales—School girls are always interested in cosmetics. Some associations capitalize on this interest and sell lines of popular cosmetics and sundries such as powder, lipstick, creams, nail polish, and toiletry articles.

Dances—Sock hops, hoedowns, square dances, and similar parties usually a part of the co-rec program also represent money-making possibilities for the RA. A small charge helps the treasury.

Demonstrations—Experts in any one of a variety of sports activities can ensure the success of demonstrations as an income venture.

Equipment Sales—Various sports equipment such as tennis and badminton racquets, golf clubs, bowling balls, etc., are sold by some associations for profits that can be added to the treasury.

Food Sales—Cakes, cookies, and pies made by volunteers in their homes are sold by the members of the recreation association. This has proved to be a popular source of income.

Football Programs—RA members often sell football programs at the home games and the proceeds go into the association treasury.

Movies—Special-interest movies at popular prices provide profits for the association.

Mum Sale—A mum sale at the homecoming football game is a traditional activity and money-raising project on many campuses.

Rummage Sale—All RA members donate cleaned and pressed discarded clothes to this project. A store or room is engaged and board members with the help of several committees manage the sale.

Sales—RA dormitory representatives sell many articles in the dormitories under the direction of the board members in charge of the concessions. Bulletin boards, calendars, candy, laundry racks, pencils, rain hats, sandwiches, slickers, T-shirts, and sweatshirts are some of the articles that can be sold successfully.

Shaker Parties—This is a simple party at which members make shakers (school color crepe paper streamers on a stick) to be sold at homecoming or any football game.

Student-Faculty Directories—Printing and selling of directories is done by association members at several schools. These directories include the addresses of both the students and the faculty and are sold in the dormitories.

Vending Machines—A successful business venture is that of handling soda, milk, apple, candy, or popcorn vending machines owned or rented by RA.

OUTDOOR EDUCATION AND CAMPING

Special recreation programs set in the out-of-doors are important to recreation leadership both for self-improvement and creative recreation programming.

Outdoor Education—Curriculum Oriented

A growing public interest in outdoor activities and a mounting anxiety to preserve our lands and their recreation environment has placed increased responsibilities on leadership for outdoor education. Recreation and education in the out-of-doors is attracting the interest of an expanding age group.

In the recent past, public schools have dominated interpretation of outdoor education, its concept and implementation. Elementary classroom teachers provided experienced leadership and reported rewarding results using the out-of-doors classroom to facilitate the teaching process.

Extending the classroom outside the four walls of the school evolved into the development of outdoor classroom resource centers for curriculum-related learning opportunities. Teachers in training or retraining, as well as school youngsters, have been benefactors in science, social studies, art, conservation, and ecology education.

Today, included under the descriptive umbrella of outdoor education, are field trips, expeditions, digs, outdoor laboratories on government land, experimental learning projects on purchased or leased acreage, school forests, school farms, and school camps.

Outdoor Education—Skills Oriented

As the demand has increased for high levels of technological skills in climbing, mountaineering, boating, scuba diving, sailing, soaring, and similar sports requiring unique expertise, communities, colleges, and schools have expanded opportunities for perfecting the specialized skills in doing-learning experiences also under the broad classification of outdoor education. Illustrating some of the activities are the following:

Survival Skills. Through lecture and structured field experiences survival skills are learned and put to practice.

Pack Trips. Horseback trips to high country or wilderness areas provide skill development experiences in packing, riding, horse care, camping, and outdoor cooking. The terrain, wild life, and area balance of nature provide innumerable natural science revelations.

Mountaineering Skills. Through trip preparation, actual climbs, and follow-up evaluations, the would-be mountaineer learns by accepting the challenge to climb.

Wilderness Camping. One- or two-week wilderness trips provide meaningful opportunities to learn by doing in the out-of-doors.

Aquatic Skills. Scuba diving expeditions, sailing and boating cruises, white-water canoe runs, raft and float trips each offered as week or two-week outdoor experiences provide skill learning and developmental opportunities.

Cycling and Social Studies. Conditioning, cycling skills, social studies, and history can all be combined as vital learning experiences during a two-week trip through historic areas of the country.

Eco-Education. Often combined with camping experiences, ecology education makes real the problems of pollution in the air, water, and land and dramatizes the delicate balance of nature. Planned experiences at college and university summer camps, Audubon camps, public school and community camps serve the popular demands for environmental and conservation education.

Camping

Camping has many ramifications for the recreation leader. In one respect camping is purely a recreational experience. In others it is a supportive necessity for planned activities or required learning experiences.

Camp Living and Recreational Camping. The supportive role of camping is evidenced in those experiences planned for skill development or challenge that can best be carried out in an outdoor living situation. Survival, mountaineering, wilderness living skills, and eco-education are best learned and subjected to challenge in a camping situation. In contrast to these extended goals, camping in the out-of-doors is an end in itself and a satisfying experience for many, as verified by the great numbers of individuals and families who visit state and national parks.

The School Camp. As a part of public education, this facility provides children with the opportunity to participate in academic and recreational activities in a camping environment. The program of the school camp can be briefly described.

On the elementary-school level educators place stress on the exploratory trips throughout the area. Enjoyed and included in programming are cookouts, tree planting, use of the compass, shelter construction, and trail building. Camping experiences are usually scheduled for the spring, summer, and fall, although some schools extend the programs through the winter. To some degree, therefore, the activities will vary with the seasons.

Secondary students enjoy a more challenging program of work learning experiences and a higher degree of adventure in outdoor activities. Student leadership assumes an important role. Conservation activities, such as fish and game management, are special projects. Hiking, exploring and archaeological digs add adventure. Natural arts and crafts together with making and using camp equipment bring alive forest skills. Some of the popular camp recreational sports include casting and angling, shooting and hunting, boating, sailing, canoeing, and other water activities. Winter programs often include skating, skiing, toboganning, and snowshoeing.

Teacher in Training Camps. Colleges and universities offering teacher education curricula include outdoor education and camping experiences as a vital part of the teacher training curriculum. Typical is the Ithaca College two-week camp experience. The curriculum includes fishing, field archery, hunter safety, canoeing, orienteering, camp administration, nature arts and crafts, man and nature, camping and survival crafts. The program goal is to develop teachers competent in outdoor education skills and programming.

Developmental objectives of the camp experience include:

Knowledge and appreciation of school camping programs

Knowledge and skills in outdoor recreation and outdoor sports

Outdoor living and survival skills

Understanding the relationship of man and environment as applicable to outdoor education programs[21]

PROGRAM TRENDS AND IDEAS FOR THE HANDICAPPED

As support grows for education to assume responsibilities for teaching lifetime skills and leisure activities, attention is focused on benefactors other than the traditionally envisioned student. Julien Stein has suggested that "the differences of impaired, disabled and handicapped

[21]Hugh Hurst, "Outdoor Education at Ithaca College," *Journal of Physical Education and Recreation* (January 1976), p. 55.

people and the *specialness* of programs and activities designed to meet their needs have been over-emphasized."[22]

The foundations of education's efforts to mainstream handicapped children in regular classes have comparable implications in recreation. Increased attention is being given to accommodating the handicapped in recreation education and leisure-time recreation opportunities. Implementing the concept of *recreation for all*, Nesbitt and Neal define the scope of the challenge:

> The issue of special/segregated versus integrated programming is one which we will be confronting increasingly in the next ten years. . . . Ultimately and ideally total integration is our goal. However, every person, group, and situation must be taken on its own merit.[23]

Identifying the Handicapped

The word "handicapped" covers a broad area; it includes those individuals unable to participate in life's activities in a normal manner.

The Physically Handicapped are those people disabled due to injury, chronic illness, or birth defects. Often they are the individuals most eager for the normal rewards of recreation participation. With the use of modified equipment and game rules, many physically handicapped people can enjoy the rigorous challenges of competition and the personal satisfactions of improving their sports skills.

The Emotionally Disturbed present many variations and degrees in withdrawal, distorted self- and body images, short attention spans, uncontrolled emotions, and impeded understanding of space and time. Characteristics and needs of the emotionally disturbed are individualistic, and recreational sports experiences, therefore, need individual prescriptions and supervision.

The Hard-of-Hearing and Blind are usually mentally alert and the benefactors of overdeveloped compensating senses. They are easily accepted socially. With adequate leadership direction they have the potentials of developing excellent coordination and enjoying sports activities and rewards in ways comparable to the nonhandicapped.

The Mentally Retarded function with short interest spans and a slower approach to learning and doing. Recreation sports participation is rewarding and satisfying. The mentally retarded person is capable of developing high-level skill abilities through repetitive practice which in itself is challenging and satisfying.

---

[22]"Sense and Nonsense About Mainstreaming," *Journal of Physical Education and Recreation* (January 1976), p. 43.

[23]John A. Nesbitt and Larry L. Neal, *Therapeutic Recreation Service: State of the Art 1971* (Arlington, Va.: National Recreation and Park Association, 1972), p. 3.

Removing Barriers

To facilitate mainstreaming the handicapped into established recreation education and sports programs several kinds of barriers must be removed.

Physical Barriers. Accommodations that must be made in buildings and participation areas include steps, curbs, narrow walkways, doors, toilet seats, stalls, drinking fountains, light switches, and playground designs.

Equipment Modifications. One of the burdens to be endured by the physically handicapped, but one that can be easily overcome, is the lack of compensating devices or adaptations of sports equipment.

Transportation Mobility. An important requirement for recreation mainstreaming is enabling the handicapped to comfortably move from place to place.

Social Acceptance. The public, contemporaries, and leadership must give impetus to participation by replacing barriers of rejection with social acceptance.

Modified Games and Programs

To facilitate involving and integrating handicapped individuals in sports activities, creative leaders have modified game rules and adapted sports equipment. Wheelchair basketball and volleyball, paraplegic track and field, archery and bowling for the blind enable participants to develop positive self-images and pursue the opportunities of becoming winners.

With innovative teaching aids, recreation directors and therapists have used the potentials of aquatics in particular to develop sociability, physical strength, and coordination. Modified swimming styles have been developed to provide rehabilitation exercise necessary to restore use of disabled or limited parts of the body. Recreation water activities have been used to combine instruction play and socializing.

In October 1975 Northwest Outward Bound School in Eugene, Oregon sponsored a pilot course that successfully demonstrated the feasibility of involving the handicapped in regular or modifed courses.[24]

Services, Research, and Resources

As a means of developing teacher abilities to serve the handicapped, education institutions are placing students in clinical programs. Prac-

---

[24]Larry Jessen, "Outward Bound for the Handicapped," *Journal of Physical Education and Recreation* (May 1976), p. 54.

ticum experiences are providing needed skills and stimulating new interests. Results of these efforts to prepare teachers better have added
program vitality and visibility to the needs of the handicapped.[25]

Professional organizations are also trying in their several ways to
serve better the handicapped by collecting and disseminating information. Thus the AAHPER has IRUC (Information and Research Utilization Center), a demonstration project of the Unit on Programs for the
Handicapped, funded by the Division of Research, Bureau of Education
for the Handicapped, U.S. Office of Education.[26]

Schools and communities as the recreation service centers are modifying facilities and programs to accommodate the handicapped. Commercial and industrial providers of recreation services are being encouraged to become more involved in services to the disadvantaged.

A needs assessment conference of 1974 sponsored by the National
Recreation and Park Association through a contract with the Bureau of
Education for the Handicapped (hosted by the Department of Recreation and Park Administration, University of Missouri) identified the
questions and concerns facing the leadership of leisure-time activity for
the handicapped as follows:

Activity and mainstreaming

Leisure activities and socialization

Leisure participation and self-image

Equipment adaptations to allow participation entrance

Games adaptations to meet special needs

Community involvement and services

Study of the effects of analyzing and counseling

Study of the attitudes of leadership and fellow participants and peer
groups[27]

DISCUSSION QUESTIONS

1. What co-recreation activities are most popular? Are there equal opportunities for participation by both sexes?
2. Should more time be given for free-time recreation in most programs?
Should participants be more involved in program planning? Why?
3. What are extramural events? Their distinctive characteristics?
4. How should noncompetitive activities be administered as a part of the
recreation sports program? What leadership resources are available?

[25]Jerry Freischlag and Rick McCarthy, "Community-University Cooperative Physical
Education Programming for the Retarded," The Physical Educator, 32, No. 1 (March 1975),
11–13.

[26]Dan W. Kennedy, "Evaluation and Research in Therapeutic Recreation," Journal of
Physical Education and Recreation (May 1976), p. 52.

[27]Ibid., p. 54.

5. Describe the various instructional approaches that may be incorporated in a sports program.

6. What traditional sports programs have you most enjoyed? Why?

7. How would you plan for an awards recognition program? Is the proposed program consistent with what you believe is the role of awards in a sports program?

8. Should sports recreation programs be dependent upon money-raising projects? Why?

9. Discuss the changes that have had the greatest impact on outdoor education.

10. What new challenges face recreation leadership trying to serve all potential participants?

BIBLIOGRAPHY

ADAMS, RONALD C., ALFRED N. DAMEL, and LEE RULLMAN, *Games, Sports and Exercises for the Physically Handicapped,* 2nd ed. Philadelphia: Lea & Febiger, 1975.

AMARY, ISSAM B., *Creative Recreation for the Mentally Retarded.* Springfield, Ill.: Charles C. Thomas, 1975.

BUELL, CHARLES E., *Physical Education for Blind Children,* 2nd ed. Springfield, Ill.: Charles C. Thomas, 1974.

HAMMERMAN, DONALD R., and WILLIAM M. HAMMERMAN, *Outdoor Education.* Minneapolis, Minn.: Burgess Publishing Co., 1973.

JENSEN, CLAYNE R., with the National Recreation and Park Association, *Outdoor Recreation in America: Trends, Problems, and Opportunities,* 2nd ed. Minneapolis, Minn.: Burgess Publishing Co., 1973.

KRAUS, RICHARD G., and BARBARA J. BATES, *Recreation Leadership and Supervision: Guidelines for Professional Development.* Philadelphia: W. B. Saunders Co., 1975.

KUJOTH, JEAN SPEALMAN, *The Recreation Program Guide: Organizing Activities for School, Camp, Park Playground or Children's Club.* Metuchen, N.J.: Scarecrow Press, 1972.

MURPHY, JAMES FREDERICK, *Recreation and Leisure Services.* Dubuque, Iowa: W. C. Brown, Co., Publishers, 1975.

WHEELER, RUTH HOOK, and AGNES M. HOOLEY, *Physical Education for the Handicapped.* Philadelphia: Lea & Febiger, 1976.

Appendix

A specific school, college or community recreational sports program comprises a selected number of the following recreational sports based upon the age, needs and interests of the participants, geographic region of the country and the facilities and equipment available.

aerial darts
aerial tennis
archery
archery golf
badminton
bait and fly casting
baseball
basketball
basketball golf
bat ball
bicycling
billiards
blitzball
board track relays
bombardment
bowling
bowling on the green
box hockey

boxing
canoeing
clock golf
codeball
corkball
crew
cricket
croquet
cross country
curling
decathlon
deck tennis
dodge ball
fencing
field floor hockey
field hockey
figure skating
flag football

flicker ball
football
golf
gymnastics
handball
hexathlon
hockey
horseshoes
ice hockey
ice skating
indoor baseball
judo
junior olympics
kickball
kite flying
lacrosse
paddleball
paddle tennis

pass ball
pistol shooting
polo
pushball
riding
rifle shooting
rodeo events
roller hockey
roller skating
sailing

shuffleboard
skeet shooting
skiing
soccer
softball
speedball
speed skating
squash
swimming
table tennis

tennis
tether ball
touch football
track and field
tumbling
volleyball
volleywallball
water basketball
water polo
wrestling

Index

487